the Unofficial Guide® to

Microsoft® Office

Access™ 2007

Jim Keogh

BICENTENNIAL
1807
WILEY
2007
BICENTENNIAL

Wiley Publishing, Inc.

The Unofficial Guide® to Microsoft® Office Access™ 2007

Published by
Wiley Publishing, Inc.
111 River Street
Hoboken, NJ 07030-5774
www.wiley.com

Copyright © 2007 by Wiley Publishing, Inc., Indianapolis, Indiana

Published simultaneously in Canada

For general information on our other products and services or to obtain technical support please contact our Customer Care Department within the U.S. at (800) 762-2974, outside the U.S. at (317) 572-3993 or fax (317) 572-4002.

Wiley also publishes its books in a variety of electronic formats. Some content that appears in print may not be available in electronic books. For more information about Wiley products, please visit our web site at www.wiley.com.

Library of Congress Control Number: 2006939465

ISBN: 978-0-470-04597-8

Manufactured in the United States of America

10 9 8 7 6 5 4 3 2 1

Page creation by Wiley Publishing, Inc. Composition Services

This book is dedicated to Anne, Sandy, Joanne, and Amber-Leigh Christine, without whose help and support this book couldn't have been written.

Acknowledgements

I especially want to acknowledge the fine contributions of Beth Taylor, Jody Lefevere, and Ken Davidson to this book. Their efforts are much appreciated.

Credits

Acquisitions Editor
Jody Lefevere

Project Editor
Beth Taylor

Technical Editor
Ken Davidson

Copy Editor
Beth Taylor

Editorial Manager
Robyn Siesky

Vice President & Group Executive Publisher
Richard Swadley

Vice President & Publisher
Barry Pruett

Project Coordinator
Adrienne Martinez

Graphics & Production Specialists
Carrie A. Foster
Brooke Graczyk
Jennifer Mayberry

Quality Control Technicians
Cynthia Fields
John Greenough
Charles Spencer

Proofreading
Melissa Buddendeck

Indexing
Potomac Indexing, LLC

Book Interior Design
Lissa Auciello-Brogan
Elizabeth Brooks

About the Author

Jim Keogh is on the faculty of New York University and Saint Peter's College in Jersey City, New Jersey where he teaches Microsoft Access and other computer courses. He was a member of the faculty at Columbia University where he developed the e-commerce tract. Keogh has spent decades developing applications for major Wall Street corporations and is the author of more than 70 books including *Java Database Programming for Dummies*, *Unix Programming For Dummies*, and *Linux Programming For Dummies*.

Contents

Chances are you are reading this book because you have a copy of Access 2007 on your computer as part of an upgrade and want to quickly get up to speed using it or because you want to enhance your Microsoft Office skills by learning how to use Access 2007.

Chances are also good that other books on Access 2007 either tell you more than you ever wanted to know about Access 2007 or not enough for you to get your job done efficiently.

I write the kind of books that I like to use. A book that gives a brief but to-the-point explanation of what needs to be done to achieve my desired result and then immediately jumps to the steps I need to perform to complete my task.

Judging by the size of the book you probably realize this isn't a compendium of all the features in Access 2007. There are many more features in Access 2007 than what I cover in this book. These you'll rarely use and are specifically designed for high power Access 2007 developers. And there are plenty of books on the market that show how to use these features. Pick up one of them if you find a need to span your horizons beyond features that I show you in this book.

When you're at work and need a quick reminder on how to do something in Access 2007 more easily and faster, grab hold of this book. I do when something puzzles me when building an Access 2007 application.

Getting in and out

Microsoft Access has undergone a complete makeover. With a new look and feel – the Ribbon replaces menus. Take a moment for a look-see, kick the tires, and take Access 2007 for a spin. Access 2007 is new so don't skip a chapter even if you currently use a previous version of Microsoft Access. If you do, you'll be lost and miss out on many timesaving new features.

All about data and designing a database

Begin your transformation from a mere mortal database user to a database application developer by learning how to organize data into so your database application can find that one piece of data you want from amongst millions in a split second. Chapters in this part show how to get your data into topnotch shape.

Tables are at the heart of your database design because this is where information is stored, organized, and retrieved. Sure I'll show you how to create a table. That takes about five minutes to do and you didn't need to buy a book to learn this because you can find out how to do it   yourself by poking around Access 2007 or surfing the Web.

The big deal is that I show you the smart way to create and use tables. These are the tips and tricks that I picked up from using Access 2007. I also show you how to filter unwanted records and sort records trapped by a filter. Then you find out how to trade data electronically with practically any application. Your colleagues will look to you as the whiz of tables after you read the tables chapters.

Creating Queries

You have a Jeanie who answers all questions. Well, kind of a Jeanie. It is called Access 2007. Access 2007 can tell you the product that will make you the most money — assuming the right data is in the database. Picking a winning lottery number? Access 2007 leaves that up to a real Jeanie.

Ask Access 2007 your question correctly in a form of a query. And like a real Jeanine Access 2007 answers it in seconds — minus the blink-of-the-eye and a puff of smoke. I'll show you how to write questions and ask Access 2007 to answer them in the query chapters.

Designing and using forms

A form is the face of your Access 2007 database application. It is where data is entered and displayed. It is used to interact with your application much like the form you use to complete a transaction at the ATM machine.

Creating a form is easy to do. However, creating a form that makes your database application easy to use and that gets a *wow* from the person using it requires a little know-how and a few tricks to dress-up your database application. I call this dressing for success. I'll show you how to design and create forms and add bells and whistles that you expect in a professional database application in the forms chapters.

Designing and using reports

The paperless office that so many of us expected hasn't materialized. Although e-mails dramatically reduce demand for paper, I'm forever going to meetings and being handed a hard copy of a report and then told the report is also being e-mailed to me.

Paper reports will be around for a while, but that shouldn't be your concern because Access 2007 can generate practically any report that you can imagine — even reports that can be viewed on the screen. Rest assured that I'm not going to show you how to create the blah, dull, and unimpressive reports that you probably receive all the time from your colleagues. I show you ways to insert pizzazz into your report — pizzazz that you won't find on the Access 2007 Ribbon. These are reports that include charts, graphs, crosstabs, and pictures, too! I share with you these techniques in the report chapters.

Automate your database application

You probably used an application where you pressed one button and the application performed a bunch of tasks automatically. I show you how to create an Access 2007 database application that does this.

You come up with the tasks to automate, and I show you how to write a macro that automates those tasks in the macro chapter. A macro is like a computer program, but it's much easier to write than a computer program.

Managing and maintaining your database

Garbage in...garbage out. A poorly managed and maintained database generates garbage, unreliable information that gives the appearance of respectability but is really junk information. You cannot prevent garbage information from finding its way into a database, but there are steps that can be taken to minimize it. I show you these steps in the managing and maintaining your database chapter so you can implement them in your Access 2007 database application.

Securing your database

The question you're probably asking yourself is how secure is the data in my Access 2007 database application? The answer depends on whether or not you implemented security features that are available in Access 2007. Nothing guarantees that your database won't be hacked. However, you can place obstacles in the database that a hacker must overcome to gain access to the information. I'll show you how to use the Access 2007 security features to secure your Access 2007 database application in the security chapter.

Developing your database application with your colleagues

Developing an application collaboratively with colleagues invites the risk that two of you work on the same component simultaneously. There's a good chance that the last person to save his or her changes overwrites changes made by the other, since only one copy of the component is saved.

Not a problem if you use SharePoint because an electronic librarian tracks changes for you. You'll learn how to use SharePointwith you Access 2007 database application projects in the SharePoint chapter.

Making the most of this book

Every book in the Unofficial Guide series offers sidebars that are devised to help you get things done cheaply, efficiently, and smartly. Each takes a different approach to providing you with useful information about the material in the chapters. Use them to educate, inform, and guide your

way through the sometimes conflicting or confusing information provided by Microsoft.

1. **Hacks:** If you are comfortable with advanced techniques, the Hacks
   sidebars will show you ways to get things done using more efficient
   techniques or by using techniques that take you into the expert's
   realm.

2. **Watch Out!:** There are times when the route to success is flanked
   with traps for the unwary. The Watch Out! Sidebars warn you when
   you need to be open-eyed and sure-footed and provide you with
   guidance so you avoid potential harmful results.

3. **Bright Idea:** If Watch Out! Sidebars point you away from danger,
   Bright Idea sides bars point you towards time, effort-, or money-
   saving techniques. You don't have to use these tips but they will
   reward you if you do.

4. **Inside Scoop:** These sidebars give you real-world perspective and lift
   the material from the theoretical to the practical. Use them to guide
   your own approach and choose which path is best for you.

Getting Started

GET THE SCOOP ON...
The Access 2007 environment ▪ Getting started with
Access 2007 ▪ Templates ▪ Building a database from a
template ▪ Building a database from scratch

Getting In and Out

Microsoft Access 2003 has undergone a complete makeover. It has a new name, Microsoft Office Access 2007 to complement its new look and feel. The most noticeable change is that Ribbons now replace menus. Under the hood is the power to manage any data that you can throw at it.

Before you learn how to harness this power to create database applications that the pros in IT will envy, take a moment for a look-see — kick the tires and take Access 2007 for a spin.

Access 2007 is new, so don't skip this chapter even if you currently use a previous version of Microsoft Access; otherwise you'll be lost and miss out on many time-saving new features.

Starting Access 2007

Starting Access 2007 is the same as starting other programs. Click the Windows Start button, then All Programs, and find the Microsoft Office entry. Access 2007 is listed among the other products that comprise Microsoft Office.

A faster, more efficient way to start the program is to add the Access 2007 icon to your desktop, so you need only to double-click the icon to open Access 2007, or place Access 2007 on the Quick Launch toolbar.

Start from the desktop

Some programs automatically place an icon on the desktop for you when you install the program, whether or not you want to launch the program from your desktop.

To place Access 2007 on your desktop, follow these steps:

1. Create a shortcut in the Microsoft Office section of the All Programs window.

2. Highlight the Microsoft Office Access 2007 entry and right-click the mouse button.

3. Click the Create Shortcut entry on the pop-up menu, and another entry of Microsoft Office Access 2007 appears in the Microsoft Office section. A 2 next to the name indicates that this is a shortcut entry.

4. Drag and drop it to your desktop.

To remove Access 2007 from your desktop, right-click the icon and select Delete. Although the icon is gone from the desktop, the entry is still in the Microsoft Office section of the All Programs window.

Start from the Quick Launch toolbar

The Quick Launch toolbar (see Figure 1.1) is to the right of the Start button and is a great time-saver when you have multiple programs open at the same time that obscure the desktop. Simply kick off Access 2007 from the Quick Launch toolbar instead of digging through open screens to find Access 2007 on your desktop.

To place Access 2007 on the Quick Launch toolbar:

1. Create a shortcut for Access 2007 (see "Start from the desktop").

2. Drag and drop the shortcut onto the Quick Launch toolbar.

You can remove Access 2007 from the Quick Launch toolbar by right-clicking the icon on the Quick Launch toolbar and then clicking Delete.

Inside Scoop

Can't see the Quick Launch toolbar? Right-click the taskbar and then click Quick Launch from the Toolbars menu item.

Office Access 2007

Figure 1.1. The Quick Launch toolbar on my taskbar.

The Access 2007 environment

You'll find a lot of unfamiliar terms and objects in the Access 2007 land-scape if you're new to Microsoft Access. If you currently use Microsoft Access, you notice that the new landscape is much different than previous versions.

The first thing you notice is that there are no menus or toolbars. These items are a thing of the past and are replaced by tabs that contain many features that use to be found on menus. This is a good thing because many time-saving features were overlooked, buried beneath layers of menus.

The Ribbon

The Ribbon (see Figure 1.2) is the area on top of the program window where you choose commands. Commands are grouped in a logical way.

Related commands are grouped into a tab. For example, you'll find all commands needed to design a page layout in the Page Layout tab.

Many tabs are hidden until you need them to work on a task. These are called contextual tabs. So you won't see the Page Layout command tab if you are not designing a page layout.

Command tabs

Active command tab   Name of current database   Ribbon

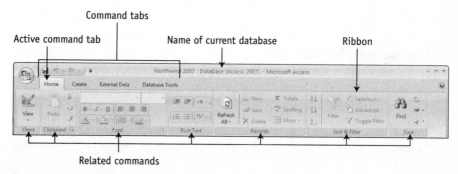

Related commands

Figure 1.2. The Ribbon contains tabs that group together related commands.

Inside Scoop

You might find that the Ribbon takes up too much screen space. You can mini-mize a Ribbon by double-clicking the name of a tab on the Ribbon. Double-click the tab name again to maximize the Ribbon.

Galleries

A gallery (see Figure 1.3) is a control that shows what the command can do and the results of using the command. For example, the Margin gallery control displays options for standard margins, such as Normal, Narrow, and Wide. Each option displays measurements for the top, bottom, right, and left margins and shows a thumbnail image of the margin.

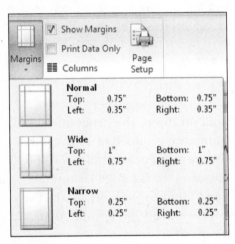

Figure 1.3. A gallery control for setting margins.

Quick Access toolbar

Some commands need to be handy. You find these commands on the Quick Access toolbar (see Figure 1.4) in the upper-left corner of the win-dow next to the Office Button.

Save, Print, and Undo are the default commands on the Quick Access toolbar. They appear as small icons. Simply click the icon to use the command.

Office Button

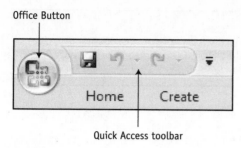

Quick Access toolbar

Figure 1.4. The Quick Access toolbar contains the most frequently used commands.

Customizing the Quick Access toolbar

Microsoft's engineers knew that you and I want to add commands we use all the time to the Quick Access toolbar, so they gave us a way to do it. Follow these steps:

1. Right-click the Quick Access toolbar.

2. Click Customize Quick Action Toolbar from the pop-up menu.

3. Select Choose from drop-down list box (see Figure 1.5).

4. Pick the tab containing the command that you want to drop onto the Quick Access toolbar.

The Popular commands are displayed by default.

To add a command to the Quick Access toolbar, do the following:

1. Highlight the command in the left column.

2. Click the Add button, and the command pops onto the Quick Access toolbar.

To remove a command from the Quick Access toolbar, follow these steps:

1. Highlight the command in the right column.

2. Click the Remove button and the command pops off the Quick Access toolbar.

3. Click OK to activate your selection.

Inside Scoop

Change the order that commands appear on the Quick Access toolbar by highlighting the command in the right column of the Access Options window and then clicking the up and down position buttons.

Bright Idea

If the Quick Access toolbar becomes too cluttered with commands, then move the Quick Access toolbar below the Ribbon. To do this, click the Customize Quick Access toolbar and select the Show Quick Access Toolbar Below the Ribbon.

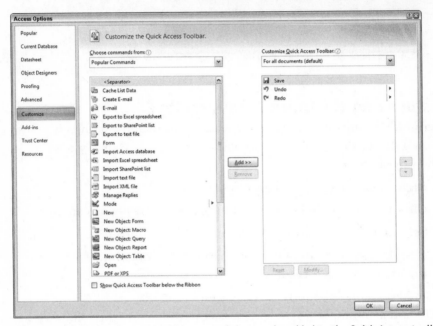

Figure 1.5. The left column contains command that can be added to the Quick Access toolbar.

The Office Button

The Microsoft Office logo (see Figure 1.6) in the upper-left corner of the window is more than a pretty picture, it is a button. Click it and you'll find useful commands to help manage the objects of your database and set options for Access 2007.

You use the Office Button to create new objects, open existing objects, and save current objects. Think of an object as a component of a database.

Access options are settings that let you customize how Office Access 2007 works. Options include choosing the default folder for your database, default file format for the database, database sort order, personalizing your copy of Access 2007, and setting the appearance of parts of Access 2007.

Figure 1.6. The Office Button displays commands that help you manage Office Access 2007.

Getting Started with Access

When Access 2007 starts, you see the Getting Started with Microsoft Office Access screen first (see Figure 1.7). From here, you can create a new blank database or open an existing database. The screen is divided into three panes:

■ The left pane contains categories of templates for creating different kinds of databases. Click a category to see a list of templates that appears in the center pane and then click the template you want to use for your database.

■ The center pane also contains an icon for creating a new blank database. Click this to create a database from scratch.

■ The right pane lists the most recent databases that you've used. Click the database name to open it. And if you can't find your database listed, then click More to display the Open window where you can pick the database from your disk drive as you do with other Windows programs.

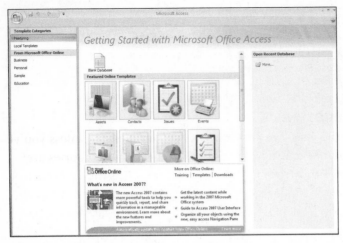

Figure 1.7. The left pane contains template categories. The center pane lists templates in the selected category. The right pane lists recently opened databases.

Using templates

Rather than creating a database from scratch, you can use one of several database templates that come with Office Access 2007 or download others from Microsoft Office Online.

A *template* is a prebuilt database that you can use to manage data for a particular type of business operation, such as managing customers and tracking expenses. It contains all elements of a database that you need — except the data.

When you select a template, Access 2007 automatically builds tables, queries, forms, reports, and other components that you would have to build yourself. All you need to do is enter data.

Using a template is the best way to build a database for a business operation. Even if your business operation isn't quite the same as the one that the template designer had in mind, you can easily create, remove, or modify any part of the database to meet your requirements.

> ### Watch Out!
> You already have a version of the Northwind database installed if you are running a previous version of Access. It is best to use the Northwind version that comes with Access 2007, otherwise the older version might have to be converted to be used by Access 2007. Although this is done automatically when you open it, errors can result.

Inside Scoop

Make sure that you're connected to the Internet before clicking any of the sub-categories under From Microsoft Office Online, otherwise Access 2007 won't be able to access the Microsoft Web site.

Template Categories

Template Categories lists two subcategories of templates (unless you've added more) available to use in Access 2007. These subcategories are:

- **Featuring.** This subcategory is the default, and it lists the Customer Service Database and Marketing Projects Database in the center pane.
- **Local Templates.** You can use eight templates for databases common to most users.

From Microsoft Office Online

The From Microsoft Office Online section of the left pane lists sub-categories of templates that are available free of charge from Microsoft's Web site. Clicking a subcategory takes you to the section of the Microsoft Web site that has these templates. A list appears on the center pane.

Building a database from a template

You're probably anxious to put Access 2007 through its paces, so start building a database from a template. Then I can continue your tour of Access 2007. Follow these steps:

1. Under the Template Categories in the left pane, select Local Templates. Several templates for databases that were part of the installation are displayed in the center pane (see Figure 1.8).

2. Click the Assets template and then enter a filename for your database (see Figure 1.9). The default filename is Assets followed by a number.

Inside Scoop

Microsoft validates your copy of Microsoft Office when downloading templates.

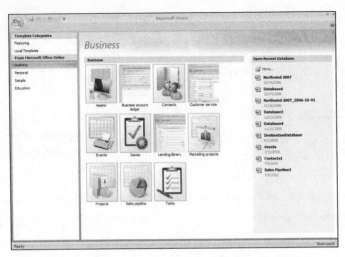

Figure 1.8. The center pane contains several Business templates.

3. Highlight the default filename and enter a new name.

By default, the database is created in my C:\Documents and Settings\Owner\My Documents folder. You might have a different default folder, but this is the one that appears in my copy of Access 2007.

4. Click the open folder icon and then enter the name of a different folder if you want to store your database in a folder other than the default folder.

Figure 1.9. Name the database.

5. Click Create and Access 2007 builds the database using the Assets template.

When the database is built, you see the Asset List form (see Figure 1.10), ready for you to enter information about your luxury car, your get-away hideaway on Maui, and your 145-foot yacht.

Click the Shutter Bar to open the Navigation Pane where you see all the components of the database, including tables, forms, reports, and charts. I show you how to use these and how to create your own throughout this book. For now feel free to double-click these components and see what happens.

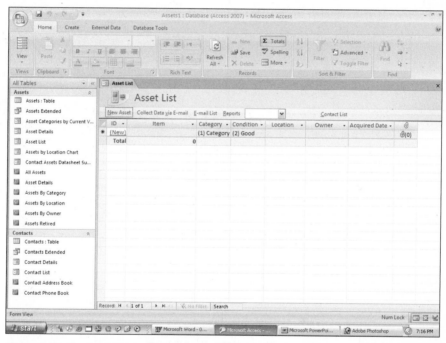

Figure 1.10. The Asset List is displayed once the database is created.

Return to the Getting Started with Microsoft Office Access screen.

Click the Office Button and then click Close Database (see Figure 1.11) to close the Assets database and return to the Getting Started with Microsoft Office Access screen.

Bright Idea

Press the Alt key once, and shortcut keys appear (see Figure 1.12). Press the shortcut key for the feature you want to use.

Figure 1.11. Close the Assets database.

Shortcut keys

Figure 1.12. Press Alt to see shortcut keys that you can use to access some of the Access 2007 features.

Building a database from scratch

Templates give you a leg up when building a database application, but you may find yourself spending a lot of time trying to locate a template that fits your needs. In this situation, building a database from scratch may be the better choice.

To build a blank database, follow these steps:

1. Click the Blank Database icon (see Figure 1.13) from the Getting Started with Microsoft Office Access screen that appears when you start Access 2007.

Inside Scoop

It is always best to overwrite the default filename with a name that describes the kind of information that will be stored in the database and change the default folder to a folder that you create for your database application.

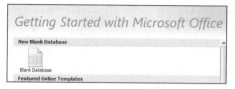

Figure 1.13. Create a new blank database.

2. Enter the filename for the database (see Figure 1.14).

Figure 1.14. Enter a filename that describes the kind of information that will be stored in the database.

3. Click the folder icon to select a folder other than the default folder to store the database. You select the folder the same way as you do with other Windows applications.

4. Click the Create button to create the database. Access 2007 automatically creates a table for the database and opens, prompting you to add a new field.

In Chapter 4, you find out how to transform a blank database into a powerful Access 2007 database application.

Inside Scoop

Access 2007 creates a default filename using the word Database followed by a digit. The digit represents the next available number for the database.

Opening the Northwind 2007 database

Access 2007 has a complete database — including data — called the Northwind 2007 database that you use to see how a database works. You can use this database to explore Access 2007.

The Northwind 2007 database is in the form of a database template. You use this template to create the actual Northwind 2007 database. Here's how to use the Northwind 2007 template to create the Northwind 2007 database.

1. Click Local Templates under the Template Categories. The Northwind 2007 database icon appears in the center pane.

2. Click the icon and enter a filename for the database. (You also see this prompt when you create a database from a template.)

3. Click the Create button.

4. Close the Startup screen.

5. Click the Shutter Bar to open the Navigation Pane where you can see categories of objects (Reports, for example) for the database (see Figure 1.15).

6. Click the down arrow next to the category name to see the objects.

Working with form views

A form is used to display, enter, or modify information on the screen much like the screens that you use at your ATM machine or for a database application in your office.

In the following sections, I detail the three types of views you use when working with forms.

Figure 1.15. Categories of objects for the Northwind 2007 database.

Form view

People who use your Access 2007 database application typically see data in a form much like an order form you fill out when buying something online.

The form seen by users of your Access 2007 database application is called the Form view. To explore the Form view open the Customer List form and then do the following:

1. Click the down arrow alongside the Customers & Orders category to see all the objects in this category.

2. Double-click the Customer List form, and the Customer List form displays (see Figure 1.16). This is one way the person who uses the database application sees and interacts with information in the database.

The Customer List form displays customer information in columns and rows much like you see in a spreadsheet. Columns are referred to as fields, and rows are called records.

The terms *fields* and *records* might be new to you and a little confusing. We use Access 2007 to manage our information. Information is a collection of data. Data is a fact that has no meaning, such as a person's first name. A field (column of a spreadsheet) stores a piece of data — first name. A record stores information — all the data related to a particular customer. I tell you all you need to know about fields and records in the next chapter.

Vertical and horizontal scroll bars are automatically displayed whenever all the information cannot fit on the screen just like they are on most Windows applications.

At the bottom of the screen is a control bar used to move through the information. This too is standard on many Windows applications. It lists the number of the current record and the total number of records on the form. Click the control buttons to move through the form.

Place the cursor in each field on the form if you want to enter or modify data in the field. However, you are unable to change the form itself in the Form view.

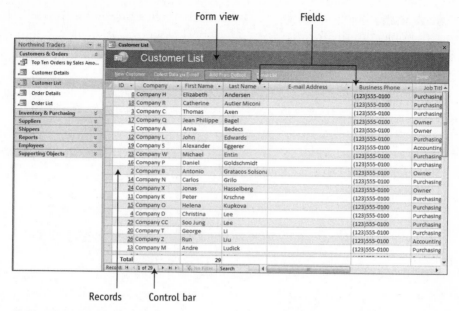

Figure 1.16. Here is the Customer List for containing information about customers.

Design view

The Design view is used to design a form by dragging and dropping images, fields, menus, and a whole bunch of other things onto the form that make your form useful and easy to use.

Right-click the Customer List tab and click Design view to see the pieces of the form.

The form is divided the following three sections:

- **Form Header.** Contains objects that appear on all pages of the form.
- **Detail.** Contains objects such as records that are the body of the form.
- **Form Footer.** Contains objects that appear at the bottom of every page such as a page number. (See Figure 1.17.)

The Design tab contains tools you need to insert objects onto the form. I explain in Chapter 12 that these objects include radio buttons, combo boxes, list boxes, check boxes, and others that give your form intelligence.

1. Click an object on the Design tab and then click on the form to add the object to the form.

2. Drag the object into position using grid lines as a guide for lining up objects.

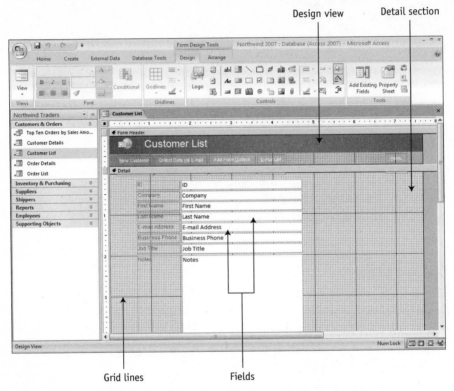

Figure 1.17. The Design view is used to place objects on a form.

Layout view

The Layout view is a combination of the Form view and Design view — well almost. The Layout view contains information just like the Form view, plus you can add, edit, and remove database objects as you do in the Design view. However, the Layout view doesn't have form sections, the grid, and other helpful tools found in the Design view.

1. Right-click the Customer List tab and click Layout view to display the same form in the Layout view (see Figure 1.18). At the top of the screen, you find two tabs.

2. Click the Format tab to see the tools to change the font, size, and all kinds of other things you expect to find when formatting a document.

3. Click the Arrange tab for tools that let you create nearly any layout you can imagine (see Figure 1.19).

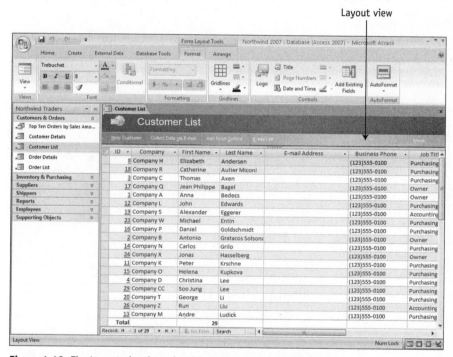

Figure 1.18. The Layout view is an intuitive tool to use to build a form.

Figure 1.19. The Form Layout Tools tab contains all the tools you need to lay out a form.

Working with data views

Access 2007 has its own way to display information without you having to build a form. These are referred to as data views. Think of these as built-in forms. These data views are the Datasheet view, the Design view, PivotTable view, and PivotChart view.

Let's take a look at data views for the Northwind 2007 database.

1. Click the Supporting Objects category in the left pane to see all the supporting objects. A supporting object is part of the database that is not normally seen by the person who uses your database because he uses forms instead.

2. Double-click Sales Analysis (see Figure 1.20). You'll probably have to scroll the vertical scroll bar to find it.

Datasheet view

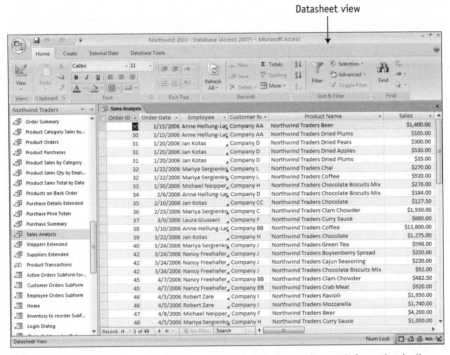

Figure 1.20. The Datasheet view displays information similar to the way information is displayed in a spreadsheet.

Datasheet view

The Datasheet view is one that you use a lot when developing your Access 2007 database applications.

The Datasheet view has columns and rows similar to a spreadsheet. You use the Datasheet view to display, add, modify, and remove information.

Click the cursor in a field to change the value of the field just like you do in a spreadsheet.

Right-click the left-most column to display a pop-up menu where you can choose options to insert a new record, delete the record, and copy and paste the record.

Design view

The Design view is used to select the type of records that will appear in the Datasheet view. I go over this in Chapter 6. For now, open the Design view.

1. Right-click the Sales Analysis tab.

2. Click Design view from the pop-up menu to display the Design view (see Figure 1.21).

Wow! This looks very confusing, but it will be old hat to you by the time you finish reading this book. The diagram shows boxes connected together with lines. Each box is a table in the database. Inside the box are names of fields of that table.

At the bottom of the screen is the query tool. A query is a request you make to Access 2007 for information. The query tool is used to create the request. I'll show you how to do this in Chapter 8.

Many times we want to see information contained in two or more tables. In this example, we're seeing the Order ID and Order Date from the Orders table and the Customer Name from the Customer Extended table. We're also picking up information from other tables in the Northwind 2007 database. These are listed in the Field and Table rows of the query tool. Check marks tell Access 2007 that we want those fields to appear in the Datasheet view.

Hack

Access 2007 is a relational database management system (DBMS). Relational means to relate together information in two or more tables. Tables are joined together using a value that is common to a field in both tables.

The lines show the fields used to link together two tables. I'll stop here because I think you have an idea what's going on in the Design view. I'll go into the nitty-gritty of designing a Datasheet view throughout this book.

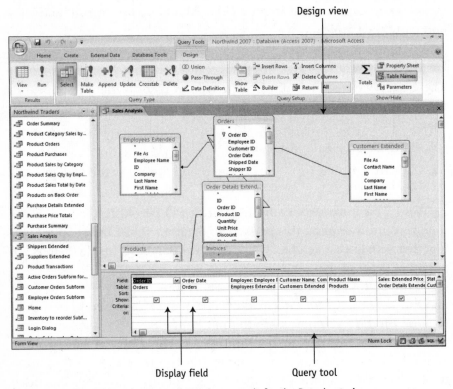

Figure 1.21. The Design view is used to select records for the Datasheet view.

PivotTable view and PivotChart view

PivotTable and PivotChart are no doubt something you don't hear spoken about every day. They are used to arrange data in a way that makes it easy to perform data analysis interactively.

The PivotTable view is used to arrange data and the PivotChart view is used to create a graphic representation of the data in the PivotTable.

As information changes in the database, corresponding changes are made to the PivotTable and PivotChart enabling you to immediately see the impact of the change on your analysis.

You'll learn how to create and use PivotTables and PivotCharts in Chapter 11.

Working with report views

A report is used to display information on a printed page or on the screen. There are four views used with a report. These are the Report view, Layout view, Design view, and Print view.

Take a look at report views for the Northwind 2007 database. Follow these steps:

1. Click the Reports category in the left pane to see available reports.

2. Double-click the Customer Address Book (see Figure 1.22). You'll probably have to scroll the vertical scroll bar to find it.

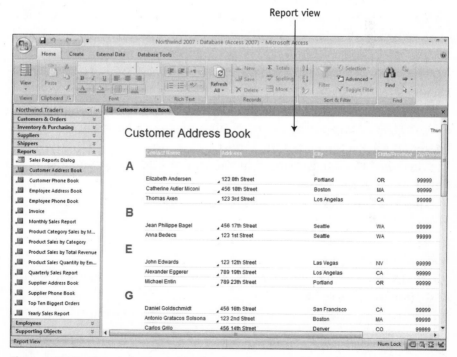

Figure 1.22. The Report view is used to show how data appears in print.

Inside Scoop

Access 2007 displays a message whenever there isn't data to display in the Report view. Click OK if you see this message so that you can see the Report view without the data.

Report view

The Report view shows customer names and addresses in a tabular report. Kind of strange that all the customers live at the same address, but remember this is only sample information.

The report has a title, column headings, and a page number (you have to scroll down to see it).

Notice that the names are underlined and there is an arrowhead at the beginning of each address. Click these to see a form that contains detailed information about the customer and address.

Layout view and Design view

The *report* Layout view and the Design view are nearly the same as the *form* Layout view and Design view, and they are used to create a report.

Right-click the Customer Address Book tab and select the Layout view or Design view.

In the Design view the report is divided into sections.

The report Design view sections the report as Report Header, Page Header, File As Header, Detail, Page Footer, and Report Footer.

Objects in the Report Header and Report Footer appear just once. The Report Header appears at the beginning of the report, and the Report Footer appears at the end of the report.

The Page Header is printed at the top of every page and the page footer prints at the end of every page.

File As Header is used to group information that is identified as a group.

The Detail section appears once for each record. This is the main body of the report.

At the top of the screen is the Design tab that contains tools for designing the report.

Print Preview

Right-click the Customer Address Book tab and click Print Preview from the pop-up menu to see how the report will look when printed by your printer. The Print Preview tab (see Figure 1.23) at the top of the screen provides tools to modify how the report is printed.

These tools should be very familiar because they combine the Page Setup, Print Preview, and Print options that you find in the File menu of most Windows applications.

Figure 1.23. The Print Preview tab has all the tools you need to decide how your report is printed on paper.

Navigating the Ribbon

The Ribbon replaces menus and contains all the tools you need to complete any job. The contents of the tab change depending on what you're doing.

Some tools are grayed, indicating that they're only available if you do something else. For example, sorting is grayed until records are entered into a table. This is standard operating procedure for most Windows applications.

There are five tabs that are available when you create a blank database. These are Home, Create, External Data, Database Tools, and the Datasheet tab.

The Home tab is available all the time (see Figure 1.24) and contains many of the tools you use all the time.

Inside Scoop

The mouse cursor changes to a plus or minus when you move it onto the report. The plus indicates you can enlarge the image of the report, and the minus reduces the image of the report when you click the mouse button.

Figure 1.24. The Home tab appears all the time.

The Create tab (see Figure 1.25) has tools you need to create tables, forms, reports, queries, and macros. *Macro* is probably one of those new terms you rarely heard before. Think of a macro as instructions for Access 2007 to do something, such as when the user clicks a button on a form.

Figure 1.25. The Create tab is used to create tables, forms, reports, queries, and macros.

The External Data tab (see Figure 1-26) has tools to import data from other sources such as Excel and export data so it can be used with other applications. There are also tools to create and reply to e-mails and share your database to a SharePoint Web site.

Figure 1.26. The External Data tab is used to import and export data enabling interaction with other applications.

The Database Tools tab (see Figure 1-27) is used to interact with the database such as running a macro, show or hide, move data, or analyze data. There are also tools to secure the database.

Figure 1.27. The Database Tools tab is used to interact with the database.

The Datasheet tab (see Figure 1.28) has tools used to modify the table, such as inserting new fields and adding a lookup column. You also find tools to associate tables, which I discuss further in the next chapter.

Figure 1.28. The Datasheet tab is used to modify the table.

Just the facts

- Place Access 2007 on the Quick Launch toolbar for a quick start
- Create a shortcut for Access 2007 and place it on the desktop.
- Tabs on the Ribbon replace menus and contain groups of commands used to interact with Access 2007.
- A gallery is a control that shows what the command can do and the results of using the command.
- The Quick Access toolbar is in the upper-left corner of the window next to the Office Button.
- There are three types of views for working with forms: Form view, Layout view, and Design view.
- Data views are used to display data without building a form. Data views are: Datasheet view, Design view, PivotTable view, and PivotChart view.
- A report is used to display information on a printed page. There are four views used with a report — Report view, Layout view, Design view, and Print view.

GET THE SCOOP ON...
Information versus data ▪ Database and tables ▪
Sharing data ▪ Data security

Chapter 2

All About Data

You use databases all the time, probably without realizing it. When you do everyday things such as order an item online, withdraw money from an ATM machine, and even log into the computer network at work, you are using a database.

Any time you search for information using a computer chances are good that somewhere behind the scenes you are really looking through a database for data. The database is obscured because you interact with a database application, which is a computer program that makes it easy for you and me to search a database and manage data.

This chapter begins your transformation from a mere mortal database user to a database application developer. This might sound challenging, but I can assure that the transition will be a smooth and exciting one.

Going over basic concepts

Access 2007 is a database management system (DBMS) because it has a generic user interface that you use to manage information stored in the Access 2007 database.

However, Access 2007 also has the tools you need to build a database application that looks like — and works like — database applications built by the IT department at work.

Many terms and concepts that you'll be reading are likely new to you, but don't be concerned, because by the end of this chapter they'll be as familiar to you as terms and concepts that you use at work.

Your transition from database user to database developer begins with an introduction of some concepts that you'll use to learn how to build a database application using Access 2007.

A database

A *database* is a collection of information that is stored usually on the hard drive of a computer in a way that the information can be quickly retrieved. (Think of a database as a well-organized filing cabinet.)

You use a database to

- Insert new information into the database.
- Update information already in the database.
- Retrieve information.
- Delete information.

A database management system

To retrieve the information that is stored in a computer, you use computer software called a *database management system,* or DBMS for short. Think of a DBMS as an assistant who maintains all information in the filing cabinet and who can retrieve any information at a moment's notice.

You make requests to the DBMS by using a set of computer screens called a user interface much like you use screens in Microsoft Word to write, save, edit, and delete a word-processing document.

A database application

A database application is a computer program used to make requests to the DBMS. Déjà vu? Sure sounds like a database application is the same as the DBMS user interface. In fact, they are very similar.

Inside Scoop

The terms computer software and computer program are used interchangeably. Both are instructions written by a programmer to tell a computer how to perform a task.

Inside Scoop

The database that you create using Access 2007 can be used by database applications built using most programming languages such as Java and C++.

Both have screens that we use to interact with information stored in the database. However, the DBMS user interface is generic. Every user sees the same interface regardless of his or her needs. A database application is customized for a particular need.

For example, you use a database application when ordering a book online. However, the folks who developed the database application probably use the DBMS user interface whenever they need to interact with the database.

Differentiating between information and data

No doubt you heard the terms *data* and *information* long before you picked up this book. Most of us use these terms interchangeably because they seem to mean the same thing.

Actually, data and information are markedly different. Data is a fact that on its own has no meaning. Information is a collection of data that has meaning.

For example, Jim is data and not information. Although you know Jim is a person's name, you don't know which Jim I'm talking about unless you see more facts.

Suppose that I gave you the following facts: Jim Keogh, Apartment 6801, Trump Tower 725 Fifth Avenue, New York City, NY, 10022. It becomes meaningful to you after assembling these facts — it is information because collectively these facts refer to a particular person. Unfortunately, it isn't me.

From information to data

Why is it important to know the difference between data and information? Because you need to know the difference between information and data in order to build a database with Access 2007. It is your job to break down information into data before storing it into the database. You learn how to do this in the next chapter.

Let's say you are creating a database of the rich and famous and you come across Jim Keogh, Apartment 6801, Trump Tower 725 Fifth Avenue, New York City, NY, 10022. Remember we're just pretending.

You separate this information into the following data: first name, last name, street 1, street 2, city, state, and postal code.

From data to information

Why not simply store the entire information in the database? Intuitively, it makes sense to store it as one chunk.

However, data is frequently used to create different kinds of information. Suppose that you want to see the names of your friends who live in the area covered by postal code 10022. Access 2007 displays the postal code, first name, and last name. You couldn't do this unless the information was broken into its data because postal code, first name, and last name are each chunks of information.

Organizing data

After you understand the difference between information and data, you can plunge deeper into other aspects of the database and see how data is stored. Earlier in this chapter, I said that a database is a collection of information. Expounding on that definition, in addition a database is a collection of data that can be assembled into information.

Data is organized within the database into one or more tables, just like a spreadsheet. A table has columns and rows. In Access 2007, columns and rows are called fields and records (see Figure 2.1).

Each field is assigned a datum, which is one piece of data; first name, for example. A field contains the same kind of data. That is, all first names appear in the same field.

Each record is a collection of related data, such as Mr. Trump's name and address. In many instances, a record is information.

Inside Scoop

Some DBMS refer to columns and rows simply as — columns and rows. A column is always a field and a field is always a column; the same is true with rows and records.

Fields

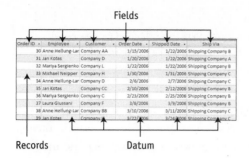

Records   Datum

Figure 2.1. A table consists of fields and records.

Name fields

You name each field, using a descriptive term about the data to appear in the field. You can call a field practically anything you want as long as you keep within the naming rules for Access 2007, which you'll learn about in Chapter 4.

For example, if the first field in the table contains the first names of your rich and famous friends, nothing stops you from naming this field field1; however, First Name is a much better name because it describes the kind of data stored in the field.

Name tables

You give every table in a database a unique name that should describe the kind of information stored in the table. Notice I used the word *information* and not *data* because most of us think of a table as a collection of records, and a record as a collection of fields. A record usually contains information.

Typically tables contain particular kinds of information that require you to be specific in naming the table. Take your table of rich and famous friends, for example. You could name it My Rich and Famous Friends, but that really doesn't describe the information contained in the table. The table contains the names and addresses of your rich and famous friends.

Inside Scoop

You'll see field names written a lot of different ways, such as fName, FName, fname, FirstName, and First Name. Each way is referred to as a naming convention. You should pick one convention and use it throughout all your databases.

Inside Scoop

Field names must be unique within the table, so Access 2007 doesn't become confused. However, the same field name can be used in different tables because the field name is associated with the table name.

You might think that I'm being picky; however, in the Chapters you see that related information is stored in other tables — you'll have a table of names and addresses, another table of your friends' telephone numbers, and so on.

A closer look at a field

A field is the place within a database where data is stored. However, you must tell Access 2007 something about the data before storing it. This information is referred to as meta data. Meta data is information that describes other data.

Access 2007 wants to know the field's data type, its size, and other pieces of information about the data (see Figure 2.2). You find out about how meta data is used to describe fields in Access 2007 in the next chapter.

Figure 2.2. Meta data is used to describe a field.

Inside Scoop

Think of a database as a collection of tables and a table as a collection of records and a record as a collection of fields.

Data type

Access 2007 must know which type of data you are placing into the field. *Type* is the data type of a field. A data type is a characteristic of data that tells Access 2007 what data values can be stored in a field. Common data types include the following:

- **Text data type.** Use for a field that contains plain text.
- **Numeric data type.** Use for a field that contains only numbers.
- **Date/time data type.** Use for fields that contain only dates or time values.
- **Boolean data type.** Use for fields holding true or false values.

Access 2007 is careful not to allow the wrong type of data to be stored in a field. For example, all sorts of bells and whistles sound if someone tries to place a person's name in a field that is a numeric data type. Numeric data type fields only accept numbers. (I discuss other data types in Chapter 3.)

Data size

Access 2007 also needs to know the size of the data you want to store in the field. Think of a field as a box that Access 2007 is going to build for the data you want to store in the database. How big should that box be? That's the question you must answer for Access 2007.

Access 2007 knows the size for many data types because it is implied when you pick the data type such as a date/time and Boolean. The size of a date and time are fixed. Boolean data is fixed at one character because its value can only be either true or false.

Other data types such as text are different because the size of the data can vary based on the kind of data that is stored in the field. Notice that I said "kind of data" because I mean first name, state, and other kinds of data. This is different than data type.

You determine the data size based on the number of characters in the data. For example, the size of a state is two because two characters are used to store the state's abbreviation in a field. Pick the size carefully; otherwise an error message is displayed when Access 2007 saves the data to the field.

The primary key

Access 2007 must be able to distinguish data such as two people with the same first and last names, otherwise Access 2007 won't know which one to display when it is asked to display one of them.

Avoid this confusion by creating a primary key for a table. A *primary key* is a unique value that identifies each record in a table (see Figure 2.3).

Primary key

Order ID ▾	Employee ▾	Customer ▾	Order Date ▾
30	Anne Hellung-Lar	Company AA	1/15/2006
31	Jan Kotas	Company D	1/20/2006
32	Mariya Sergienko	Company L	1/22/2006
33	Michael Neipper	Company H	1/30/2006
34	Anne Hellung-Lar	Company D	2/6/2006
35	Jan Kotas	Company CC	2/10/2006

Figure 2.3. A primary key uniquely identifies each record in a table.

One way to create a primary key is by combining multiple columns that contain names and addresses. Although there might be two people with the exact same name living in the same house, chances of this happening are rare. So combining these columns could uniquely identify them.

Often, you assign a unique value to each record. This value can be a person's Social Security number, customer number, and the like.

I cover primary keys in detail in Chapter 3.

Data entry

After you build the database and all its tables, you can enter data into the database. (You can find out how to do this in the next chapter.) Data entry is the process of entering data into one or more tables of the database.

It goes without saying that you know how to enter data. You've done it many times by placing an order online and entering information into an ATM machine.

However, you need to look at data entry in a new perspective now that you are learning to create your own database application using Access 2007.

The extra u

A simple, everyday typo can have long-term repercussions. My daughter can attest to this. Someone at her college entered her name in their database as Keough instead of Keogh.

At the end of the first term when she received her grades, she submitted a form asking for the college to correct her name. You would think this is an easy fix. In fact, after reading this book, you'll know how to fix it yourself in less than 10 seconds.

Due to the crackdown on identity theft, having a name changed on a permanent record has become a very big deal. My daughter had to provide the college with government-issued documents showing her correct name before school officials would even consider changing their records.

Three years have passed. And as you probably guessed, her records haven't been changed. The college claims that information in their database is correct.

It seems that college officials — and probably most of us — believe information generated by a database application to be more reliable than that of a human.

Garbage in, garbage out

You probably heard the expression "garbage in, garbage out" used to explain why it is important to be careful when doing anything. The same saying is true with Access 2007. Information generated by Access 2007 is only as good as the data entered into it.

You can reduce the likelihood of garbage data entering your database by building in traps that catch data errors before garbage data reaches the database.

Access 2007 has built-in error-trapping features that you can use when you define fields. You learn how to use them in Chapter 3.

Datasheets

Access 2007 has a number of ways to enter data into a table. One of these ways is by using the Datasheet view. The Datasheet view looks like a spreadsheet (see Chapter 1). Across the top are fields showing the name that you assigned to each field. Records go down the Datasheet view.

You enter data nearly the same way as data is entered into a spreadsheet — with two restrictions:

- You must start a new record before entering data (see Figure 2.4).

- Don't format data. You might be inclined to insert blank rows to make your spreadsheet look pretty or place formatting characters such as hyphens and currency symbols in the cell with the data. In Access 2007, formatting is handled using forms, reports, and field properties.

Order ID ▾	Employee ▾	Customer ▾	Order Date ▾	Shipped Date ▾	Ship Via ▾
30	Anne Hellung-Lar	Company AA	1/15/2006	1/22/2006	Shipping Company B
31	Jan Kotas	Company D	1/20/2006	1/22/2006	Shipping Company A
32	Mariya Sergienko	Company L	1/22/2006	1/22/2006	Shipping Company B

Figure 2.4. Data must be entered contiguously.

Data entry form

The Datasheet view is perfect when you are working with data behind the scenes; however, a data entry form **is** preferred when others are entering data. A data entry form is what you use at the ATM machine to enter information about your account.

A data entry form makes it efficient for the person who uses your database application to enter data because you place fields in the most advantageous position on the form rather than in a spreadsheet layout.

Furthermore, you can make a form look like a paper form that your colleagues use at work. Doing this eases the transition from a manual process of entering data on a paper form to using an electronic one because the paper form looks like the Access 2007 form. Your colleagues see the electronic form and say to themselves, "This is identical to our old form." You learn how to do this in Chapter 12.

Data validation

Data validation is the process of assuring that only correct data enters the database. This is easier said than done. Access 2007 prevents storing a first name in a date field because a first name isn't a date. Access 2007 knows this by looking at the data type of the field. However, Access 2007 has no way of knowing if the first name is the correct first name.

Luckily, there are various ways (other than data types) to validate data. To validate data, you can do the following:

- Pick data from a list of valid data (see Figure 2.5), which is what you do when picking a state from a list of states.

- Compare data that is entered to valid data contained in a table of the database. This happens when you log on using your user ID and password.

- Create a reasonableness test. A reasonableness test tells Access 2007 to determine if the data entered makes sense.

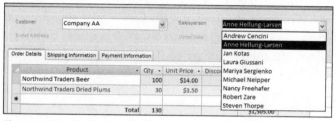

Figure 2.5. Provide a list of valid entries.

Let's say a person is filling out an employment application. She writes that she started with her current employer in 2006 and started with her previous employer in 2007. That doesn't make sense. It isn't reasonable. Access 2007 should give a warning asking her to check her dates before her employment application is saved to the database.

You set the rules for determining if data makes sense. I show you how to do this in Chapter 3.

Querying the database

The power of Access 2007 is its capability to manipulate and present data any way you need it. All you need to do is tell Access 2007 what to do by writing a query.

A *query* is a request for information that you send to Access 2007. This process is referred as *querying the database*. In the query, you specify the fields and records that you want to see, and Access 2007 sifts through the database and returns them to you.

Writing a query

You can write a query a number of ways — use the query design tool, Structured Query Language (SQL), or the Simple Query wizard.

The query design tool lets you create a query by picking and choosing query components, such as tables and fields, from a list of possible components. You learn to use this in Chapter 8.

SQL is a special language for writing a query that Access 2007 and other DBMS understand. Think of this as writing a query in longhand. You probably won't need to do this step after you get the hang of using the query design tool.

The Simple Query wizard (see Figure 2.6) is similar to wizards that you've used in other Windows applications that walk you step by step through writing the query. This is a great way to write a query until you feel comfortable using the query design tool — then you'll find the Simple Query wizard slow to use.

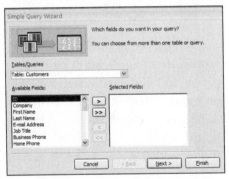

Figure 2.6. The Simple Query Wizard makes it easy to query a database.

Return data

A query returns fields and records that you requested in a dynamic subset called a *dynaset*. Think of this as a subset of data in the database. The dynaset appears as a spreadsheet. In the spreadsheet, the fields that you selected in the query appear across the top and the records go down the spreadsheet.

Inside Scoop

A query is great because it can be used again without having to write it from scratch. A query can be saved and reused by simply calling the query.

The dynaset may not contain the data that you had in mind, so you need to keep refining and rerunning your query until you get the dynaset you need. After you do, save the dynaset so that you can display the data in forms and reports. (I discuss how to refine your query in detail in Chapter 8.)

Query expressions

You can have Access 2007 select a subset of records from the database by using a query expression. A query expression specifies the rules for including a record in a dynaset.

The word *expression* gives some people the chills and not-so-fond memories of high school math class. Set your fears to rest if you are one of them because query expressions are very straightforward.

Here's a query expression: first name = "Bob." If Bob is the value of the first name field, then include the record in the dynaset.

Multiple tables

Your databases will likely have several tables. You can write a query that selects data from multiple tables and then has Access 2007 return the data from multiple tables in one dynaset.

For example, you might have a table of customer names and addresses and another table of customer orders. A query can return a dynaset that contains a customer name, address, and order.

Inside Scoop

Tables are linked together by a value that is common to both tables such as a customer number. The customer number is assigned to a customer name and address in one table and assigned to a customer order in another table.

Data display

Information stored in a database can be retrieved using a query and displayed in practically any way you can imagine. You design how the information is displayed by using the Access 2007 Form Designer and the Report Designer.

These designers are straightforward and easy to use, as you discover when you learn how to build forms in Chapter 12 and reports in Chapter 16. You simply drag and drop fields from the dynaset returned by your query onto the form or report, and then type text directly on it.

You can also spiff up the form or report with images by dragging and dropping them anywhere on the form or report. This feature enables you to generate customized invoices, mailing lists, inventory lists, and practically any other type of online or printed document needed by your organization.

What's a form?

A form is used to display information on the screen. It is also used for data entry and to modify information currently stored in the database. The screen that appears on an ATM machine is a form, and so is the screen you use to enter an online order.

For all practical purposes, a form isn't used to print information on paper although nothing stops you from doing so. A form is designed for the computer screen and not for paper.

Certain features are missing from the Form Designer that prevents you from creating a classy, professional-looking printed document. However, I show all the techniques you need to create a top-notch form using the Form Designer in Chapter 12.

What's a report?

You probably surmised that a report is used to display information on paper. The Report Designer lets you include features that are only found in printed documents.

Typically, a report has multiple pages with each page having the same kind of information at the top (called a header) and bottom (called a footer) of every page, such as the title and page number.

The Report Designer lets you create a header and footer simply by typing the information that you want to appear on every page into the Report Designer. You can find out how to use features of the Report Designer in Chapter 16.

Calculating data

A form and report can contain calculated data besides the dynaset fields returned by your query. Calculated data is data that is the result of a calculation that is performed right before a form is displayed on the screen and before a report is printed on paper.

Suppose that you want to see a customer's current balance. To do this, you need the original amount owed and the amount paid. Then, you subtract the amount paid from the amount owed to find the current balance.

One way to do this is to retrieve the amount owed and the amount paid from the database by using a query; then subtract these numbers in a form or report to display the current balance.

Practically any calculation you require can be performed within a form or report and can also be performed in a query.

Sharing data

Access 2007 enables you to share some or all the information in your database by making the database available over a computer network.

A computer network is like a town where computers are houses and cables are streets. An electronic message is sent using a computer to ask a neighbor to share information. The neighbor using the computer returns the information in another electronic message if he wants to be neighborly and share the information.

Sharing over a local network

You can share information within your organization's local network by granting access rights to your database. I discuss this in detail in Chapter 22.

Inside Scoop

Save space in a database by not storing the result of a calculation in the database. Instead perform calculations in queries or in reports.

Inside Scoop

Where possible, I prefer to use forms and reports to share my information because then I can decide what information is shared and how that information is displayed.

You could give them direct access and let them use the Access 2007 interface to interact with your information. Alternatively, you can give them indirect access requiring that they use your forms and reports, which directly interact with your database.

Sharing over the Internet

It goes without saying that you know enough about the Internet to surf the Web efficiently. Now you can share information stored in your database with the world because Access 2007 gives you the ability to include data in your Web page.

To do this, create a Web form in your Web page that is used to request your information similar to Web forms you used when placing an online order. When the Submit button is clicked, the request travels over the Internet to your Web server. A Web server is a computer connected to the Internet that serves up Web pages to anyone requesting them.

A computer program on the Web server called a CGI program, such as Microsoft's ASP.NET, runs a query and then places the dynaset inside another Web page and sends it back to the computer that made the request. You find out how to do this in Chapter 24.

Local network versus the Internet

You might be wondering what the difference is between the local network in your organization and the Internet. Surprisingly, there isn't much of a difference.

Think of the local network as your town and the Internet as the whole world. Both have computers (houses) and cables (streets), and share information using electronic messages.

Inside Scoop

Sharing information over the Internet is more involved than sharing information with your colleagues at work. You'll probably require help from the IT folks who host your Web site to get your database connected to the Web server.

However, you probably are willing to give some colleagues on your local network more access to your information than you would strangers on the Internet.

Exchanging information

Another way to share information is to exchange data with another DBMS. This might sound a little strange; however, many organizations exchange data electronically rather than re-enter data into their database.

Imagine an online retailer collecting thousands of credit card orders each day and having to submit them to the credit card company for processing. No way could this exchange be handled manually.

The online retailer exports credit card order information from its database into a file that the credit card company imports into its database. The credit card company can use the information immediately after the transfer is completed.

Access 2007 data can be exported into various popular data formats so the data can be directly used with applications such as Excel, Word, and popular DBMS. Likewise, Access 2007 can import data that was entered using popular applications and DBMS so you don't have to enter data yourself. I discuss how to import and export data in Chapter 7.

Data security

Data security is one of the most pressing concerns about building a database application. You probably know that data security protects your database from unauthorized access, but you might not realize that data security also provides a way to restore the database if the computer containing the database is destroyed.

Access 2007 has data security features that enable you to protect information in your database from various threats that include unauthorized access and outright corruption of the database.

Inside Scoop

Exchanging data electronically eliminates the risk of introducing typographical errors into the data by re-entering the data manually.

Unauthorized access

Access 2007 enables you to set up a user ID and password for each person who wants to access the database (see Figure 2.7). A user ID is assigned access rights to the database. An access right grants permission to use all or a portion of the database.

You can grant permission to access all tables, selected tables, or selected fields of tables. Permission can be granted to insert, update, display, and delete records — or only some of those tasks.

Furthermore, Access 2007 enables you to encrypt the database. Encryption is the process of encoding data so that it can't be read without a cipher — an electronic magic decoder ring. See Chapter 23 for more information on how to encrypt a database.

Figure 2.7. Each authorized user can be assigned an ID and password.

Data backup

Access 2007 is installed on a hard drive, which you already know. If the hard drive crashes, you can install Access 2007 on a new hard drive because you have the original CDs. On the other hand, the database — and all its data — is gone forever.

No one can assure that your hard drive won't crash, but you can restore the database that was on the hard drive if you back up the database regularly. Backing up is nothing more than copying the entire database to another hard drive, CD, or tape and then placing it in a secure location outside the building that houses your database.

Some organizations back up their databases once or twice a day and ship the copy off to a storage facility inside a mountain. You don't have to go to this extreme, but it is wise to back up the database on days when the database is updated. More on backing up and restoring your database in Chapter 21.

Watch Out!

Often, unauthorized access to a database is made by using an authorized person's user ID and password, which are easy to guess or are written down and stored in an obvious location.

Watch Out!

Expect to lose some data if the drive crashes, even if you back up the database regularly. Changes made to the database since the last backup will be lost.

Corrupt data

Access 2007 performs a lot of behind-the-scenes work to make sure that your information is stored in the most efficient way. Occasionally, something happens to corrupt the data, and the entire database or a portion of it falls into disrepair — as a result information cannot be accessed.

Don't panic. Access 2007 has its own onboard service department — actually just another feature of Access 2007 — that you can use to repair the database. See Chapter 21 for more details on this tool.

Data compacting

Information seems to grow exponentially. You may reach a point when your hard drive is full, and this often happens at the worst possible time.

Don't sweat the little things. Access 2007 has a tool to compact the database into a smaller space without losing any information. In Chapter 21, I cover how to use this tool.

Understanding indexes

You might be as amazed as I am at how quickly Access 2007 can find one record from a million stored in the database. Access 2007's secret has less to do with the speed of the computer than it does how information is organized in the database.

Access 2007 uses an index to quickly find information in a database. An index is very similar in concept to an index of a book in that both are references to key words.

In a book's index, key words are listed alphabetically alongside the page that contains the word. In an index of a database, key words are listed alphabetically alongside the record number that contains the key word. A record number is the location of a record in a table. The key word in an index is referred to simply as the key of the index.

How does Access 2007 know which are key words? You provide the key words when you design a table.

Picking the key

A key is the value of one or more fields in a table such as a customer's last name or a combination of last name and first name such as Keogh Jim.

Pick values that you frequently use as search criteria when looking for information in the database. For example, you'll probably look up a customer using the customer's full name.

You don't have to pick a value that is the primary key for a table because Access 2007 automatically indexes the primary key. So you won't select a customer number as a value to index since customer number is likely the primary key.

Duplicate values

You have a choice to create a unique index or allow duplicate key values (see Figure 2.8). A unique index requires that the key contain only unique values. This is fine for keys that are Social Security numbers or customer numbers because you don't want duplicates.

Sometimes duplicates are wanted as in the case of using customer name as the key because there could be two or more customers with the same name.

Duplicate values won't bother Access 2007. If you search for information by customer name and Access 2007 uses this index, all records containing this customer name are returned to you. You can then pick through them to find the correct customer.

Figure 2.8. You decide if an index is allowed to have duplicated values.

 Inside Scoop

Access 2007 has its own way of finding information. Many times Access 2007 uses an index that you created for a table and other times it might use an alternative method known only to the folks who built Access 2007.

Locating the index

Each index is part of the database. Think of it as another table because conceptually an index resembles a table in that it has fields and records. There are two fields in an index, one for the record number and the other for the key. Each row has the key for an entry.

An index is unlike a table because you can't see or directly use it. Only Access 2007 can do that. You really don't care how Access 2007 finds the information as long as it does it quickly and accurately.

Knowing when to create an index

The purpose of creating an index is to increase speed of searching for information in the database.

Instead of searching all the information in a table, Access 2007 searches the index. It compares the search criteria to the value in the key field. If there is a match, Access 2007 uses the value in the record number field of the index to find the record that contains the search criteria in the table.

You should ask Access 2007 to create an index for fields that are frequently searched. It makes sense to have an index for customer name since you'll search for a customer name if you don't have the customer number handy. It doesn't make sense to create an index for street name because rarely do you search for a customer's street address. I show you how to ask Access 2007 to create an index in Chapter 4.

Too many indexes

You're probably thinking that indexes are a good thing because they speed up searching for information. However, too much of any good thing can be bad — and so it is the case with too many indexes.

Access 2007 updates each index every time its table is modified. That's not a problem unless too many indexes are created for the same table, then you begin to notice that Access 2007 isn't responding in its usual way.

How many is too many indexes? The best rule is to create an index only if Access 2007 isn't responding quickly to your queries.

Just the facts

- Data is a fact that has no meaning.

- Information is a collection of data that has meaning.

- A database is a collection of tables.

- A table is a collection of records that contains information.

- A record is a collection of fields with each field containing data.

- Access 2007 is a Database Management System (DBMS) that manages information.

- Meta data is information that describes data, such as a field name.

- A data type is a characteristic of data that tells Access 2007 what data values can be stored in a field.

- Access 2007 can attempt to repair corrupt data in a database.

- An index is like a book index where key values are associated with the location of the key value in the database.

Data Design and the Database

GET THE SCOOP ON...
Decomposing an entity into kinds of information ■
Decomposing information into data ■ Transforming
information into a table ■ Describing data ■
Relating tables

PART II

Designing a Database

You have several questions to answer before you create a database. What information do you want stored in the database? What data is necessary to create this information? How many tables are needed? What data goes into which tables?

After you answer these questions, you can concentrate on designing a top-notch Access 2007 database. A design is a blueprint that identifies database components and how those components go together to form a database.

Aside from using Access 2007 templates, there is no easy way to automatically design a database. Search Access 2007 all you want; you won't find a button to click that generates a database design tailored specifically to your database — although sometimes Access 2007 templates come close. This isn't unusual because no other DBMS has such a button either.

Designing a database requires a little more thinking and figuring than it does to build the database, which you learned to do in the first chapter. Professional database designers have a bag of tricks that keep head scratching to a minimum and let them focus on coming up with a design in no time. (You learn these tricks later in this chapter as I show you how to design your database.)

Identifying entities

A system is a way of doing something. It can be a system for beating the house in Las Vegas (dream on) or a system for placing a customer's order. Bet you think I'm talking about a computer system, one that uses the computer to do something. I'm not, because a system can be either a manual system (without computers), a computer system (only computers), or a combination.

Practically every database application that you build either converts a manual system to a computerized system or upgrades an existing computerized system.

This is good. The system already exists, so much of the figuring has been done for you.

Your job is to identify pieces of the system and transform them into components of an Access 2007 database application. These pieces are referred to as entities.

Entity is a term you know. It is an object, a thing — a very important thing when it comes to designing a database because an entity contains all the information you need for the database.

An entity is something used to make the system work. An order form, invoice, product, and even a customer are entities. The list is endless. Fortunately, you don't have to memorize them, but you do have to identify them so that you can transform entities into information to store in your database.

After you finish reading this book, you will become the expert who is building the Access 2007 version of the database application. Another person, the user, is the expert in the existing system because he uses the system daily. Remembering this is important because the user can help you identify entities.

Start your search for entities by asking the user to walk you through the system. Ask to find out how the system works and then sit back and take good notes.

Hack

Reports and forms that display information are also entities.

Entities and procedures

The user will show you how his job is done by using entities and procedures. A procedure is how to do something with an entity, such as how to place an order form.

For now, concentrate on identifying entities. You need a thorough understanding of entities before any procedure makes sense.

Access 2007 is capable of managing a database and running procedures to process the data. I show you how to identify procedures and rewrite them for Access 2007 to process in Chapter 19.

Take samples

Ask for a sample of each entity so that you can analyze it back at your desk. The user should be able to give you a blank form, such as an order form or a print-out of a computer screen if the system is already computerized.

Also ask for samples that have representative information such as the customer's first name and last name on an order form.

A form containing representative information is better to analyze than one that has gobbledy-gook where you have to guess at what the information looks like.

Hack

The confidentiality policy of the organization might prevent you from seeing actual information.

Deconstructing an entity

Deconstructing is the process of identifying the kind of information that is in an entity. You'll find this easy to do because it almost jumps out at you.

Take a customer information form as an example. You'll find customer name, customer address, customer office phone, customer cell phone — you get the point.

Don't confuse the kind of information with actual information because we're not interested in Bob Smith, 555 Any Street, Any Town, NJ 07665, 201-555-1212, 201-555-1234, at least not yet.

You need to deconstruct the information into data. This can at times seem insurmountable but it isn't. In the next sections, I go over the technique that I use to deconstruct information into data.

Make a list

To begin the process of decomposing an entity, you must first create a list of the kind of information extracted from the entity (see Figure 3.1). Jot it down with paper and pencil or do what I do — use a word processor. I find it easier to work with an electronic version than with paper and pencil.

Take your time compiling this list. Making sure that the list is complete is very important. Overlooking even a small piece of information isn't a good thing because the information won't appear in your database.

Compare the list to the entity before moving on to the next entity.

Find duplicates

You'll have a list of information for each entity. Compare these lists and you're bound to find the same kind of information appearing on more than one list (see Figure 3.2). For example, the customer name appears on the customer information form, an order form, and an invoice.

Duplicates are not a good thing. Having duplicates wastes storage space, and updating each copy wastes time. Having duplicates also risks data errors because you might miss finding a copy of the information when trying to update it.

Customer Information

Customer Number: _____

                    First Name   Middle Name   Last Name
Customer Name: _____ _____ _____

Company: _____

                    Address
Street 1:_____

Street 2:_____

City: _____ State: _____ Postal Code: _____

Office Telephone: _____ Cell Telephone: _____

Fax Number: _____ E-mail Address: _____

List of Customer Information
        Customer Number
        Customer Name
        Company
        Customer Address
        Office Telephone
        Cell Phone
        Fax Number
        E-mail Address

Figure 3.1. List information contained in an entity.

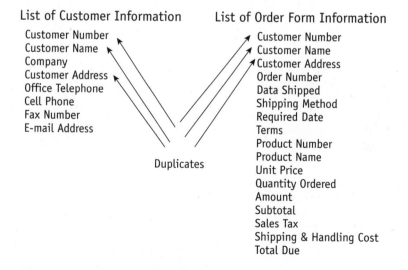

List of Customer Information
        Customer Number
        Customer Name
        Company
        Customer Address
        Office Telephone
        Cell Phone
        Fax Number
        E-mail Address

List of Order Form Information
        Customer Number
        Customer Name
        Customer Address
        Order Number
        Data Shipped
        Shipping Method
        Required Date
        Terms
        Product Number
        Product Name
        Unit Price
        Quantity Ordered
        Amount
        Subtotal
        Sales Tax
        Shipping & Handling Cost
        Total Due

Duplicates

Figure 3.2. Remove duplicate information.

Hack

The process of eliminating redundancy in a database structure is called normalization.

Remove duplicates by combining lists into one big list, and then sort the list and delete duplicates. This process is a breeze to do if you use a word processor.

Group information

The original list shrinks after the duplicates are removed. Divide the list into groups of related information (see Figure 3.3). Each group becomes a separate list.

For example, place all customer information into one group, product information into another group, invoice information into a third group, and so on.

Seems simple to do, but it is tricky because you tend to associate information with its entity and not with related information.

Take customer name, for example. Do you put it in the customer information group or in the invoice group?

Customer name is related to other customer information and belongs in the customer information group. When you create an invoice, you copy the customer name from the customer information group and place it in the invoice, which is an entity.

Customer Information	Order Information	Product Information
Customer Number	Order Number	Product Number
Customer Name	Data Shipped	Product Name
Company	Shipping Method	Product Unit Price
Customer Address	Required Date	
Office Telephone	Terms	
Cell Phone	Product Number	
Fax Number	Quantity Ordered	
E-mail Address	Order Unit Price	
	Amount	
	Subtotal	
	Sales Tax	
	Shipping & Handling Cost	
	Total Due	

Figure 3.3. Arrange related information into groups.

Hack

Each group of information is the beginning of a table of the database.

Decomposing information into data

After you complete the initial steps of database design, you can separate information into data (see Figure 3.4). Data is the smallest useful part of information. (Refer to Chapter 2.) Review each piece of information in your groups and ask yourself, "Is this the smallest useful part of the information?"

Take a look at customer name. Is this the smallest useful part? No—customer name can be separated into first name, middle name, last name. In this case, we also must include the prefix, such as Mr. and Dr. and suffix, such as M.D. and PhD.

List each of these beneath the information in the group. I like to indent this list of data to show its relationship to the information.

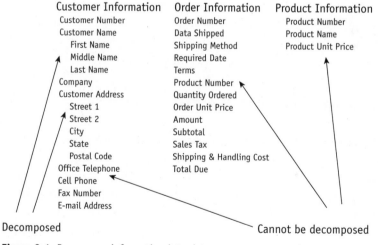

Decomposed   Cannot be decomposed

Figure 3.4. Decompose information into data.

Information and data, same thing

Not all information can be separated because it is already the smallest useful part. For example, a product's unit price doesn't have any useful parts. Neither does an invoice date.

Information that is already the smallest useful part is also data. In these situations, I usually place a copy of the information on the next line and indent it as if it were data.

Calculated data

As you decompose information into data, you will come across calculated data. *Calculated data* is data generated from other data such as the purchase price of an item on an invoice. The purchase price is calculated by multiplying the quantity purchased by the unit price.

As you decompose information into data, you are bound to find that some data is the result of a calculation. That is, calculated data. Write down the name of the calculated data. Beneath the name write down the formula used to calculate the data. You'll use this formula to calculate the data whenever the data is needed on a form or in a report.

Calculated data isn't stored in the database because that would be a waste of space. Instead, calculated data is calculated whenever it is needed by Access 2007.

The only exception is if the calculation is too time-consuming for Access 2007 to perform the affects response time. Response time is the amount of time Access 2007 requires to respond to a user's request.

In these cases, the calculation is usually performed whenever data in the calculation changes and is stored in the database, similar to other data.

Transforming information into a table

Each group of related information is a preliminary table. I call it *preliminary* because a little tweaking is usually necessary before the table is finalized.

Give each group a name. This name becomes the name of the table. Make sure that the name reflects the kind of information that will be stored in the table as a reminder to you whenever you look at the table.

For example, customer information is a good name for the group that has all the information about customers.

Hack

Each data element becomes a field of the table.

Organize each group into a preliminary table. Some Access 2007 developers like to create a mockup table using Word and use data from the group as column headings in the table. This might look pretty, but it isn't very functional when designing the database.

I prefer to list data under the table name (see Figure 3.5). This gives me room to describe the data.

Customer Information Table	Order Table	Product Table
Customer Number	Order Number	Product Number
First Name	Data Shipped	Product Name
Middle Name	Shipping Method	Product Unit Price
Last Name	Required Date	
Company	Terms	
Street 1	Product Number	
Street 2	Quantity Ordered	
City	Order Unit Price	
State	Amount	
Postal Code	Subtotal	
Office Telephone	Sales Tax	
Cell Phone	Shipping & Handling Cost	
Fax Number	Total Due	
E-mail Address		

Figure 3.5. Organize data into tables.

Describing data

Access 2007 needs to know how to store the data that you identified. You may recall from Chapter 2 that data is described by data type, data size, and other ways that help Access 2007 store and manipulate the data.

Review each data element on your list and write down a description for it (see Figure 3.6). Use terms that Access 2007 understands when writing the description. Doing this makes transforming your table design into an actual table much easier. (I go over creating the table in Chapter 4.)

Data types

A data type is a characteristic of data that tells Access 2007 what data values can be stored in a field. You can choose from ten data types. Each data type has a definition. Your job is to match characteristics of data on your list with the definition of a data type to describe the data type for the data.

Description of the Customer Information Table

Customer Number	Street 1	Office Telephone
Number	Text	Text
Size: Integer	Size: 50	Size: 10
Required	Required	Required
Primary Key	Caption: Street 1	Format/Mask: (xxx) xxx-xxxx
Auto Generate by System	Street 2	Caption: Office Phone
Caption: Customer Number	Text	Cell Phone
First Name	Size: 50	Text
Text	Caption: Street 2	Size: 10
Size: 30	City	Format/Mask: (xxx) xxx-xxxx
Required	Text	Caption: Cell Phone
Caption: Customer First Name	Size: 50	Fax Number
Middle Name	Required	Text
Text	Caption: City	Size: 10
Size: 30	State	Format/Mask: (xxx) xxx-xxxx
Caption: Customer Middle Name	Text	Caption: Fax
Last Name	Size: 2	Email Address
Text	Required	Text
Size: 50	Caption: State	Size: 30
Required	Postal Code	Format/Mask: xxx@xxxxxx.xxx
Caption: Customer Last Name	Text	Caption: E-mail
Company	Size: 15	
Text	Required	
Size: 30	Validate: Using State	
Caption: Company	Caption: Postal Code	

Figure 3.6. Place the description below the data.

Text data type

Text data type is used to store text, punctuation, and numbers that are not used in calculations. A limit of 255 characters can be stored in a field designated as text data type. You cannot apply RichText formatting (RTF) to a text field. Rich-Text formatting is a special code that tells a word processor and other computer programs how to display the text (i.e. bold, italic). Use the Text data type for names, addresses, product IDs, and other short text.

Memo data type

A memo data type is similar to the text data type, except that a memo field can store up to 2 gigabytes of data. With two bytes per character, this means that 1 gigabyte of characters and Rich-Text formatting, you can display 65,535 characters at one time. (You can find out more about this data type when you learn about forms in Chapter 12.) Use the memo data type for product descriptions, comments, and text that have bold, underline, and other formatting characters. Also use it when you need more than 255 characters.

Number data type

The number data type is used strictly for numbers, which you probably gathered from its name. A number field holds integers or fractional values used in calculations. You have to describe the size of the number that you want stored in the number field. Access 2007 has predefined sizes (see Table 3.1). You must match the data on your list to the appropriate size.

Table 3.1. Predefined sizes for the number data type

Predefined Size	Value Range
Byte	0 to 255
Integer	-32,768 to + 32,767
Long Integer	-2,147,483,648 to + 2,147,483,647
Single	-3.4×10^{38} to $+3.4 \times 10^{38}$. Seven significant digits.
Double	-1.787×10^{308} to $+1.797 \times 10^{308}$. Up to 15 significant digits.
Replication ID	A number randomly generated by Access 2007 used as a globally unique identifier (GUID).
Decimal	-1028 to +1038. By default 18 decimal places can be displayed but you can change this to 28 decimal places.

Date/Time data type

You can use the Date/Time data type for dates or times or both. Access 2007 can perform date and time calculations using values stored in a Date/Time field. Combine to get rid of redundant information.

Currency data type

You can use the Currency data type for any monetary value. Use this for prices, salaries, and similar data.

AutoNumber data type

Use the AutoNumber data type to have Access 2007 generate a value each time a record is inserted into the table. The value can be incremented sequentially, incremented by a value of your choosing, or by a random number. Use the AutoNumber data type to have Access 2007 automatically create a Primary Key (see the "Identifying a primary key" section later in this chapter).

Yes/No data type

Use the Yes/No data type for Boolean values. A Boolean value is a value that can be either true or false, on or off, yes or no, 1 or 0. Use this for storing decisions.

OLE Object data type

The OLE object data type is used to store large binary objects up to 2 gigabytes in size. A binary object is a spreadsheet, presentation, or similar object created by other Windows applications. Reference to the object is stored in the field. The object itself is stored as a file on the disk drive. Use this data type for data that was created by another program.

Attachment data type

Use the Attachment data type to store images, audio, video, and binary files generated by other Office programs (Word, Excel, and PowerPoint, for example). Use this instead of the OLE Object data type because it provides more flexibility because it doesn't require an OLE server. The Attachment data type can hold 700 Kbytes if the file is not compressed and 2 gigabytes for a compressed file.

Hyperlink data type

Use the Hyperlink data type to store hyperlinks to Web pages using the Uniform Resource Locator (URL) or files using the Universal Naming Convention (UNC).

Mask and format

Note any specialty formatting used for the data, such as the hyphens used in a Social Security number and the parentheses and hyphens in a telephone number.

Access 2007 enables you to store formatting characters separately from the data to save storage room in the database. Access 2007 then automatically applies formatting to the data during data entry and data display.

The formatting applied during data entry is called a *mask,* and it is called *format* when the data is displayed. I discuss how to specify the mask and format in Chapter 4.

Validation rules

Only good data should be stored in the database. One way to ensure that this happens is to have Access 2007 validate the data before placing it into the database.

Analyze each data element on your list and determine if there is a way the data element can be validated. If so, then note the rules you want Access 2007 to follow to validate the data. For example, the customer phone number must be numeric.

Jot down the rules so that you can understand them. In Chapter 4, I show you how to translate them into words that Access 2007 understands.

Caption

Create a default caption for each data element on the list. A default caption is text that Access 2007 displays whenever the field is displayed on a form or in a report. Think of this as a label on a form.

Keep the caption short and to the point, yet long enough to describe the data to the person using your Access 2007 database application. You can always override the default caption when you create a form or report.

Default value

Access 2007 enables you to store a default value for each data element. A default value is the most common value assigned to the data element such as US for country or today's date for the order date.

Access 2007 automatically enters the default value in the field each time a new record is inserted into the table. The user has the option to overwrite the default value.

It doesn't make sense to set a default value for some fields such as first name, yet for others it saves time during data entry and reduces the risk of erroneous data from entering the database.

Decimal places

Earlier in this chapter, I mention that you can set the size of a number data type to decimal to allow both integer and decimal values to be stored in the field.

Access 2007 uses eight decimal places by default. However, many database applications require three or fewer decimal places.

Jot down the number of decimal places required for each data element on your list. Access 2007 enables you to adjust the number of decimal places when you create the field.

Text alignment

On rare occasions, you come across data that must be aligned differently than the default alignment. Standard alignment is text flushed and numbers and dates are flush right when they are displayed.

Note any exception to this alignment alongside the data element on your list. You can overwrite the default alignment when you create the field in the table.

Smart Tags

Time to put on your Sherlock Holmes hat and do a little investigating. Find out what the user does with the data after it is entered into the database.

For example, he might copy the customer's name, company name, and e-mail address into a e-mail address list each time a new customer is entered into the database or when information about an existing customer changes.

You can automate this and similar processes in your Access 2007 database application by using Smart Tags. I show you how to do this in Chapter 4. For now, make note of any candidates.

Required and Allow Zero Length

Note if a data element on your list is required for every record. You can ask Access 2007 to reject any incoming record that doesn't have a value for a required field. You do this by making the field required. Fields that are not required can be set to Allow Zero Length, which tells Access 2007 that the field can be left empty.

For example, first and last name fields are usually required, but the middle name field can be set at Allow Zero Length.

Lookup wizard

As you analyze the list of data elements, ask yourself if the value can be copied from another field or table in the database. If so, then Access

2007 can display a Lookup wizard that enables the user to pick a value from a list of valid values shown in a combo box. You've seen this done in a lot of Windows applications.

Customer number in the Orders table is a good candidate for the Lookup wizard because the list contains only valid customer numbers and customer names from the Customers Information table.

Identifying a primary key

Pick a primary key for each preliminary table. A primary key is a value that uniquely identifies each row in the table, which you learned about in Chapter 2. The value you choose must appear in every row and must be unique. This makes picking a primary key tricky.

Some values seem to be unique, but upon closer examination they aren't. This is the case of a customer name. You could have more than one customer with the same name.

Some values are unique values, but not required for each record such as a cell phone number. Not every customer has a cell phone.

And sometimes there isn't a unique value in the record as is the situation with a customer address book. More than one person with the same name can live at the same address. Although rare, you must address this possibility in the design of your database.

Single field

Often, one field meets the criteria for becoming the primary key. This is especially true if the system already exists. Customer number, product number, invoice number, order number are all good candidates for the primary key of their respective table.

Compound primary key

A primary key can consist of values from two or more fields. A compound primary key is handy to use if none of the fields has unique values.

Inside Scoop

Make note which field is going to be used as the primary key. I simply write (primary key) next to the data in the preliminary table.

Hack

The ID field created by Access 2007 is an AUTO-GEN data type. Any field can be designed an AUTO-GEN type even if it isn't designated the primary key.

I had a situation like this. A company encoded order numbers with country, sales region, sales year, sales month, and order sequence. Anyone reading the order number knew where the order was placed, what month and year it was placed, and the sequence of the order.

The order number 01340802123 signifies the United States (01), sales region 34, 2008 sales year (08), February (02), and it is the 123 order in that region for February 2008.

Each part of the order number is in its own field and none has a unique value. However, combining them creates a unique value that is perfect as the primary key.

Auto-generated primary key

Access 2007 can create a primary key for you. It does so by inserting a field called ID when you create the table. Access 2007 automatically assigns a unique, sequential value to this field when a record is inserted into the table.

This is a quick-and-dirty way to create a primary key for a table. The downside — you have little control over the value used as the primary key.

Relating tables

At this point in your database design, you decomposed information contained in entities into preliminary tables where each row in the table is uniquely identified by a primary key.

Now you must figure out how to generate a course roster when information about the course is contained in two tables — courses and students.

The solution is to link together records of these tables to create information needed for the course roster. This step is referred to as *relating tables*.

Access 2007 is a relational DBMS, which means it enables you to relate tables together to form one virtual table. The virtual table doesn't really exist. Instead Access 2007 temporarily combines them behind the scenes to fulfill your request for information.

Foreign keys

The primary key is used to link together two tables by placing the value of the primary key of one table into a field in the other table. This field is referred to as a *foreign key*.

Here's how this works. The student number is the primary key of the students table. Link the students table to the dorm assignment table by placing the student number into a field in the dorm assignment table.

How linking works

Here's an example: Say you want to display the roster for Course 1234. The roster contains information about the course and names of students who are registered for the course.

You send a query containing the course number to Access 2007 asking it to display the roster. Access 2007 searches the courses table for the course number. Once found, Access 2007 searches for the course number in the students table for students who are registered for the course. Access 2007 returns the names of students registered for the course and the course name, course number, and other information about the course.

The course number probably is in multiple records of the students table because more than one student has registered for the course. This isn't a problem because the course number isn't the primary key of the students table. Access 2007 simply continues searching the students table until there are no more records that contain the course number.

Creating relationships

You bring information together by creating relationships among tables of your database. There are three kinds of relationships that you can create: one-to-many relationship, many-to-many relationship, and a one-to-one relationship.

The type of relationship you choose depends a lot on how entities are related to each other.

Take a sales representative and customers as an example. One sales representative has many customers. This is a one-to-many relationship.

Now consider an order and a product. An order can have many products and a product can appear on many orders. This referred to as a many-to-many relationship.

Think about an employee and a salary. One employee receives one salary. This is a one-to-one relationship.

Identifying Instances

Identifying the relationships among tables can be tricky at times because the relationship isn't always obvious. Professional database designers focus on instances of an entity to help determine relationships.

An instance is an occurrence of an entity. It is simply an entity with data associated with it. That is, order 1234 placed by customer 9876, where the numbers are the order number and customer number.

Sometimes identifying a relationship becomes baffling. Here's how I tackle this problem:

1. Draw boxes to represent instances of entities.

2. Walk through a real-life scenario such as customer 9876 placing an order today and another order tomorrow.

3. Customers-to-orders is at least a one-to-many relationship because one customer can place many orders.

4. Reverse the process to determine if there can be a many-to-many relationship, such as how many customers can place order 1234. The answer is one customer.

5. An order-to-customer is a one-to-one relationship.

One-to-many relationship

A one-to-many relationship is created by placing the value primary key of one table into the other table as a foreign key. For example, the customer number, which is the primary key of the customers table, becomes the foreign key in the orders table.

Create another field in your preliminary table for the foreign key. Name the foreign key field the same as the primary key field in the other table. In our example, I'd insert the customer number field into the orders table.

Hack

Tables are linked by a common value — not by a common field. The foreign key field can be named differently than the primary key field in the other table as long as the values are the same.

Many-to-many relationship

A many-to-many relationship is tricky to create because many records of one table can relate to many records of the other table. The relationship between orders and products is a common example of a many-to-many relationship. One order can have many products. One product can appear in many orders.

Creating this relationship seems straightforward. Place the order number, which is the primary key of the orders table, as a foreign key in the products table and then place the product number, the primary key of the products table, as a foreign key in the orders table.

However, this design is poor because data is repeated. The same order number appears in the products table multiple times — once for each product ordered. Likewise, the same product number appears multiple times in the orders table — once for each order that ordered the product.

Remember that repeating data isn't a good thing. It makes for inefficient storage.

The solution is to create another table called the detail table (see Figure 3.7). The detail table has a one-to-many relationship with the other tables. It contains data associated with primary keys of both tables in the many-to-many relationship.

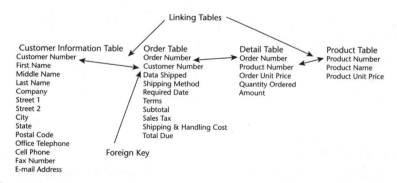

Figure 3.7. Create a detail table to transform a many-to-many relationship into a one-to-many relationship.

Two of the fields in the detail table are the primary keys of the other tables. This would be the order number and the product number if the orders table and products table are being related. Both these fields are foreign keys in the detail table.

The detail table's primary key is the combined value of the two foreign keys — the combination of order number and product number.

Remember that a primary key is a value that uniquely identifies a record. This value doesn't have to be from a single field.

Other fields in the detail table contain data relating to that product for that order such as quantity ordered and price per item.

Modify your database design to include detail tables for each many-to-many relationship that you created between tables.

One-to-one relationship

A one-to-one relationship is the easiest to create because you can use the same primary key for both tables. There isn't a need for a foreign key. For example, an employee table and a salary table both can use the employee's Social Security number as their primary key.

However, nothing stops you from using a foreign key if these tables have different primary keys.

Normalizing the database design

The database design is almost completed. There is one more step to do — determine if your database design is normalized. Earlier in this chapter I said that normalization is the process of removing redundancy in the database. It is a little more involved than that.

A normalized database design is where information from entities is stored efficiently in the database.

To determine this, you must apply the normalization rules, known as normal forms. There are five normal forms in all; however, practically every database that you design should conform to the first three normal forms.

First normal form

The first normal form requires that a single value is at the intersection of every record and field. This simply means that a field in a record can have only one value such as product 1234 (record) has a price (field) of

$40. In other words, you can't have multiple values such as a list of prices for product 1234 in its price field.

Nearly all your tables conform to the first normal form.

Second normal form

The second normal form is a little tricky to understand because it applies only when a primary key is composed of multiple values. The second normal form states that each nonkey field be fully dependent on the entire primary key.

This means that fields that are not part of the primary key must have a relationship with all fields that comprise the primary key.

The best way to understand this is to revisit the detail table created in the many-to-many relationship (see "Many-to-many felationship"). The detail table has four fields. These are the order ID, product ID, unit price, and quantity ordered. Order ID and product ID are combined to form the primary key.

Unit price and quantity ordered directly relate to both the order ID and product ID. That is, on order 1234 the customer bought 10 (quantity) of product 5678 for a unit price of $5. Keep in mind that the unit price for the same product could increase on succeeding orders.

If a vendor ID field is included in the detail table, the table would violate the second normal form because vendor ID is related to one — not both — of the values that make up the primary key. It is related to product ID and not to order ID. The vendor has nothing to do with the order.

Third normal form

The third normal form requires that each nonkey field be independent of each other and dependent only on the primary key. Refer back to the detail table to see how to apply the third normal form.

Assume for a moment that the unit price for the product depends on the quantity that the customer ordered. The more the customer orders, the lower the unit price.

This makes good business sense, but it is the third normal form because the unit price is dependent on the quantity order fields, both of which are nonkey fields in the table.

In this case, you'd have to come up with a different database design.

Designing forms and reports

Your database design is completed except for designing forms and reports that people use to interact with your Access 2007 database application.

Designing these should be straightforward. Many forms and reports replicate entities from the original system. You can use the original form or report as a model for those you build for your Access 2007 database application.

Here's how I decide forms and reports that I'll need for my Access 2007 database application.

1. List each form and report.

2. Below each, list data elements that appear on them.

3. Alongside each data element list the table/field name where the data element is stored.

4. If the data element is derived using a calculation, then alongside the data element list the calculation, being sure to include the table and field name of data used in the calculation.

One form that you probably won't find in the original system unless you are upgrading an existing database application is the data entry form. The data entry form is specially designed to assure that quality data is entered into the database.

You'll probably have several different data entry forms, practically one for each entity (order form or customer information form, for example).

Use the blank form as a model for the data entry form. You get this when you identify entities of the existing system.

List data elements that need to be entered into the form. Alongside each indicate if the data element:

■ Can be generated by Access 2007, such as an order number. If so, describe how Access 2007 will do this.

■ Can be picked from a combo box (i.e. Access 2007 generated list). If so, write the table/field whose values are displayed in the combo box.

■ Is a Smart Tag. If so, describe the process that occurs when the data is entered into the form.

■ Is validated. If so, define the validation rules.

■ Requires formatting. If so, define the format.

What queries do you need?

You'll remember from Chapter 2 that a query is a request you make to Access 2007 for information contained in the database. An advantage of using Access 2007 is that you can query the database at any time by using the Query Tool (see Chapter 8).

Another advantage is you can store frequently used queries in the database and have them executed automatically in a number of ways such as at the click of a button on a form or in response to an event, which is something that happens while the database is running.

Try to think ahead a little and anticipate queries that will be made frequently. The users of the existing system can probably tell you what information they retrieve often and how they retrieve it.

For example they might recall information about a customer by using the customer number, customer first and last name, or company name. Each is a separate query.

Likewise, an order might be retrieved using order number, order date, customer number, customer first and last name, or company. Again, each is a separate query.

Here's how I decide on the queries that I'll need for my Access 2007 database application.

1. List each query. Give it a name that describes it such as Retrieve Orders By Order Number.

2. List the table/field(s) you want Access 2007 to retrieve. Include calculations if Access 2007 needs to calculate the data element.

3. List the table/field(s) used as the selection criteria.

What's next?

Get ready to see your design come alive. Starting with the next chapter, I show you how to transform your database design into a full-fledged working Access 2007 database application.

Pardon me for a moment if I sound like your teacher, but spending time checking your work in the design phase of the project could save you days of work later on.

Take a few moments before moving ahead and double-check your design. Make sure you identified and described all components needed to build your database.

Just the facts

- Decompose entities into information.
- Remove duplication information.
- Decompose information into data.
- Describe data in a table.
- Identify the primary key.
- Relate tables using primary keys and foreign keys.

Working with Tables

Chapter 4

The database design created in Chapter 3 is a blue print for building a robust Access 2007 database application that can handle data management needs for practically any organization.

You'll begin transforming your database design into a working Access 2007 database in this chapter by creating tables. Tables are at the heart of your database design because it is here where information is stored, organized, and retrieved.

Creating a blank database

You're anxious to create your first table, but before learning how to create a table, let's create a blank database first and then create a table for the blank database.

I show you how to create a blank database in Chapter 1, but a quick refresher is helpful at this point. To create a blank database, follow these steps:

1. Start Access 2007.

2. Click Blank Database (see Figure 4.1) in the center pane of the Getting Started with Microsoft Office Access screen.

3. Change the name of the database, if you want.

4. Change the folder for the database, if you want.

5. Click Create to create the database (see Figure 4.2).

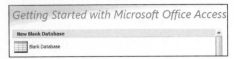

Figure 4.1. Create a blank database.

Blank Database

Create a Microsoft Office Access database that does
not contain any existing data or objects.

File Name:

Database1

C:\Documents and Settings\Owner\My Documents\

| Create | | Cancel |

Figure 4.2. Enter the name of the database and then click Create to build it.

Creating a table

In Chapter 3, I discuss that a business system consists of entities such as a customer, an order, and a product. Each entity has information associated with it such as a customer name. Information is decomposed into data — customer first name, customer last name.

Like data — customer data — are placed into the same group. Now it is time to transform the group into a table of your Access 2007 database.

You can create a table two ways:

- Datasheet view resembles a spreadsheet because records and fields appear as rows and columns. At the top of each column is the field name and below it is data. You saw this in Chapter 1 when I gave you a tour of Access 2007.

- Design view shows each field and its description, but no data. You see a complete list of ways to describe the field in the Design view, which is not available in the Datasheet view.

Inside Scoop

Enter a database name that describes the kind of information that is being stored in the database. Place the database in its own folder rather than using the default folder designated by Access 2007.

So which view should you use to create your tables? I show you how to use both of them in this chapter, and then you can answer this question for yourself. The best way is always the one you find most comfortable to use.

Creating a table in the Datasheet view

Access 2007 automatically places you in the Datasheet view when a blank database opens. This is referred to as *design-in-browse* and is where you can perform some — not all — table design tasks.

Building a table using the Datasheet view is a good way to get started creating a table because Access 2007 helps you behind the scenes.

Access 2007 gives you the option to pick the data type for the field manually or by entering data. If you enter data without first picking the data type, Access 2007 determines the data type based on the data you enter. Enter a date and Access 2007 assumes you want a Date/Time field. Enter a person's name and Access 2007 surmises you want a Text field.

I show you how to use other features of design-in-browse in a moment. However, design-in-browse won't let you create an Attachment field or an OLE field and it won't let you start the Lookup Wizard from a field.

The Datasheet view layout

The blank table appears in the right pane under the Table1 tab. Access 2007 automatically inserts the first field, labeled ID, as the table's primary key. A unique numeric value is automatically entered into the ID field when a new record is inserted into the table (see Chapter 3).

Access 2007 seems to have entered a second field called Add New Field. However, this field isn't created until you either enter data into it or manually set its database.

The left pane lists tables that are part of the database. Only one table is listed until you create another table for the database, which I show you how to do later in this chapter.

The Datasheet tab is located at the top of the Ribbon. It contains all the tools you need to work with tables in the Datasheet view. I explain each tool later in this chapter.

Inside Scoop

Table1 is the default name for the table. Change the name to describe the kind of information stored in the table.

Setting the data type by entering data

The easiest way to set the data type for a field is to simply enter data into it. Access 2007 analyzes the data and then determines the best data type for the field. You can always change Access 2007 data type selection if you disagree with the type Access 2007 chooses. Follow these steps:

1. Place the cursor into Add New Field. This makes the Add New Field the current field.

2. Enter data. This is the data that is stored in the field when the table is saved.

3. Press Enter. Access 2007 creates a new record and prepares you to create another field in the table (see Figure 4.3).

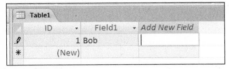

Figure 4.3. Access 2007 determines the data type for the field based on data you enter into it.

Setting the data type manually

As you hone your database design skills, you'll probably want control over setting the data type yourself. Don't fret because Access 2007 won't get insulted.

You select the data type from a list of data types shown in the Data Type combo box on the Datasheet tab at the top of the screen. To set the data type manually, you:

1. Highlight the Add New Field.

2. Click the down arrow in the Data type combo box on the Datasheet tab to see the list of data types.

3. Click the data type name. Access 2007 creates the field as that data type and prepares you to create another field in the table (see Figure 4.4).

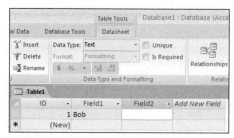

Figure 4.4. Select the field's data type from the Datasheet tab.

Changing the field name

You probably noticed that Access 2007 has it own, not-so-creative way of naming fields you created in the table. It labels them Field1, Field2, and so on. Think of these names as placeholders until you get around to giving them a more proper name.

Rename each field to something that describes the kind of data that will be stored there. (I discussed renaming fields in Chapter 3.) To rename a field:

1. Highlight the field you want to rename.

2. Click the Rename on the Datasheet tab. The field name becomes highlighted.

3. Type the new field name.

4. Click the cursor outside the field name and Access 2007 changes the field name (see Figure 4.5).

Hack

The data type of the highlighted field appears in the Data Type combo box in the Datasheet tab.

Inside Scoop

A shortcut to renaming the field is to double-click the field name and then enter a new field name.

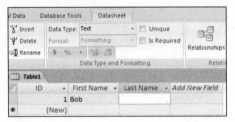

Figure 4.5. Click Rename on the Datasheet tab to change the field name.

Setting the format for the field

You may find yourself wanting to format many numeric fields that you create for your table. Some will be formatted as currency and others commas, and still others you'll want to set the number of decimal places that are displayed.

Use the Format tool on the Datasheet tab to set the format. You probably noticed that the Format tool might be grayed. As with other Windows applications, gray means the tool isn't available for the highlighted field unless the field is a numeric data type.

The Format tool is a combo box that displays a list of formats for the highlighted numeric field. Additional formatting is set by clicking one of the five buttons beneath the Format tool. These should be very familiar to you because they are the same as found on the Excel toolbar.

The dollar sign applies the currency format. The percent applies the percent format, and the comma inserts commas into the value of the field. The last two buttons set the number of decimal places shown in the value. Click to the left to increase the number of decimal places and to the right to decrease the number of decimal places.

Inside Scoop

Formatting a decimal value affects how the value is displayed, but doesn't change the decimal places stored in the value.

1. Highlight the field.

2. Set the field as a numeric data type.

3. Click the down arrow of the Format tool (see Figure 4.6) to display a list of formats or click an appropriate format button. Access 2007 applies the format to the value in the field.

Figure 4.6. The Format tool on the Datasheet tab sets the format for a field.

Unique and required fields

Some fields in your database must contain a unique value for each record such as order number in the orders table and customer number in the customer information table. These fields are usually, but not always, the primary key.

Other fields must have a value for each record such as a first and last name for records in the customer information table and a postal code for an address.

You can set these field attributes by selecting the Unique check box and Is Required check box on the Datasheet tab. Simply do the following:

1. Highlight the field.

2. Click the Unique check box (see Figure 4.7) to require that each value in the field be unique for each record.

3. Click the Is Required check box (see Figure 4.7) to make it a required field.

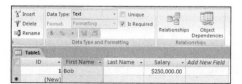

Figure 4.7. Click the check boxes to make the field unique and required.

Deleting and inserting fields

Don't fret if you entered an incorrect field because fields are easily deleted from the table by using the Delete tool on the Datasheet tab. Of course, data entered into the field is deleted, too. This shouldn't be a problem because at this point you're only creating the table. Deleting a field after your database is completely built and after it contains information is another story.

Create fields in a logical sequence such as first name, middle name, and last name. The sequence is important because Access 2007 uses it to display data in the Datasheet view, which can be a way users of your database interact with your table.

If you find that you forgot a field, you can always insert the field in the proper sequence using the Insert tool on the Datasheet tab. Access 2007 separates existing fields to make room for the new field. Do the following:

1. Highlight the field you want deleted.

2. Click the Delete tool (see Figure 4.8) on the Datasheet tab.

3. Access 2007 displays a warning message telling you that the field and its data are gone forever. Click Yes to go ahead and delete the field or No to leave the field as is.

4. Highlight the field where you want to insert the new field.

5. Click the Insert tool on the Datasheet tab (see Figure 4.8). Access 2007 moves the highlighted field to the right and inserts the new field in its place.

Figure 4.8. Click the Delete tool to delete the highlighted field and the Insert tool to insert a new field in the position of the highlighted field.

Inside Scoop

Delete multiple fields at the same time by highlighting all the fields that you want deleted. Hold down the Shift key and click the first field you want to delete and then click the last field you want to delete, and Access 2007 highlights all the fields between them.

Using the New Field tool

When you glance at the Datasheet tab, you notice the New Field tool. You probably gathered that this tool inserts a new field into the table. However, it does more than that.

The New Field tool lets you choose from a list of predefined field templates that are commonly used in tables. For example, selecting the Purchase Price field template inserts a currency field called Purchase Price and applies the currency format to its values.

Here's how to use the New Field tool.

1. Highlight the field position where you want to insert a field template.

2. Click New Field (see Figure 4.9) on the Datasheet tab to display field templates.

3. Double-click the field template you want inserted into the table and Access 2007 inserts it for you.

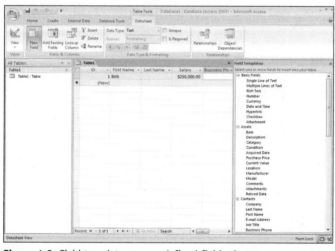

Figure 4.9. Field templates are predefined fields that are common to many tables.

Adding fields from another table

After you build a few tables, you discover that you'll use the same field in several tables. For example, the employees table, customers table, and vendors table probably have first name, middle name, and last name fields.

Instead of redefining these fields each time you insert them into a table, you can select a field from a field list and have Access 2007 copy it for you. Doing so saves time and eliminates errors introduced by rewriting the field definition.

The Add Existing Fields tool on the Datasheet tab displays a Field List that contains a list of tables in your database and its fields. You simply choose the field you need, and Access 2007 inserts it into the table. Access 2007 also creates a relationship between these tables.

Here's how to add a field from another table.

1. Insert fields into Table1.

2. Click Create on the Table Tools tab to open the Create tab (see Figure 4.10).

3. Click Table to create a new table called Table2 (see Figure 4.11).

4. Click Datasheet to open the Datasheet tab.

5. Click Add Existing Fields to display the Field List pane.

6. Click the plus sign to the left of Table1 to see a list of fields in Table1.

7. Double-click the field name to insert it into the table.

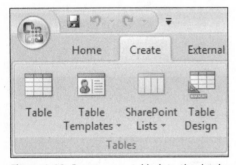

Figure 4.10. Insert a new table into the database.

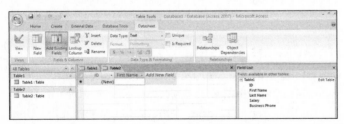

Figure 4.11. Double-click the field on the Field List that you want inserted into your table.

Creating a lookup column

You can enter a value into a field by picking it from a list. This field is called a lookup column. The Lookup wizard is used to create the list of values to pick from.

You create a lookup column by using the Lookup Column tool on the Datasheet tab to open the Lookup wizard. The Lookup wizard gives you three ways to create this pick list:

- Lookup values in a table. The list is built from values in a field in another table.

- Create a query. You request (query) Access 2007 to retrieve information that will be used to create the pick list.

- Type the value. Create your own pick list by entering values onto the pick list.

The way you use a lookup column (pick list) depends on the nature of your application. I try to avoid creating my own pick list because then I'd have to manually update it each time it changes. Instead I use a field in a different table as the pick list or generate a pick list using a query.

I show you how to build a lookup column using values in a different table and by writing your own list. I show you how to use a query in Chapter 8.

Create two tables before building a lookup column. The second table contains the lookup column that is used by the first table that you create. Table1 contains the ID, First Name, and Last Name fields. Table2 renames the ID field to Sales Rep ID and has First Name and Last Name fields. You'll insert Sales Rep field in Table1, making it the lookup column; the Sales Rep ID field in Table2 contains the lookup value.

Create a lookup column from a table

To create a lookup column from a table, follow these steps:

1. Click the Lookup Column tool on the Datasheet tab to run the Lookup wizard.

2. Select the I want the lookup column to look up the values in a table or query option and click Next.

3. Click Tables (see Figure 4.12) in the View box. Table2 is automatically highlighted because it is the only other table there. Highlight

the table that contains the field for the pickup list if more than one table is shown.

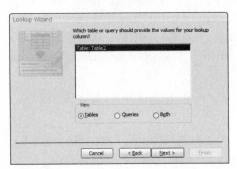

Figure 4.12. Select the table that contains the value for the pick list.

4. Click Next to see a list of fields in the table you selected (see Figure 4-13).

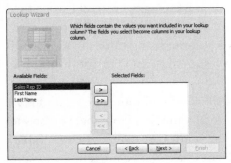

Figure 4.13. Select the fields that contain the value for the pick list.

5. Highlight the Sales Rep ID field and click the right arrowhead to use it as the pick list. You can create the pick list from multiple fields by selecting the other fields on the Available Fields list.

6. Click Next and decide the sort order for the pick list (see Figure 4.14).

Inside Scoop

Click Query if you want the pick list generated from a query. Access 2007 lists all the queries that you previously created. You learn how to do this in Chapter 8.

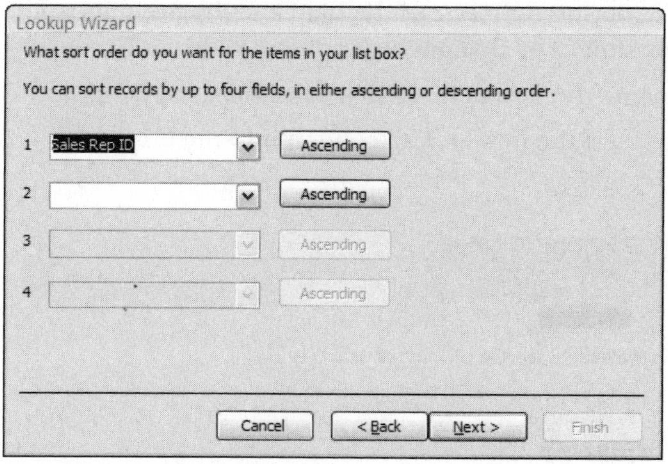

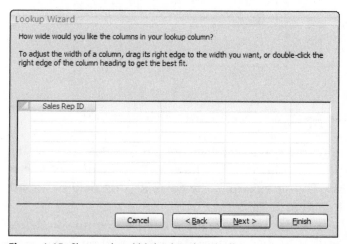

Figure 4.14. Select the fields that contain the value for the pick list.

7. Click the down arrowhead of the combo box to pick the selected field that will be sorted.

8. Click the Ascending button to change from an ascending sort to a descending sort.

9. Click Next to adjust the width of the column of the lookup field (see Figure 4.15).

Figure 4.15. Change the width by dragging the line.

10. Move the cursor on the right line of the field and drag the line to the desired size, similar to changing the column width in Excel.

11. Click Next to name the new field. I call it Sales Rep.

12. Click Finish to insert the new lookup column into the table (see Figure 4.16).

Figure 4.16. Click the arrowhead to see the pick list of sales rep IDs.

Maintain the relationship

Creating a lookup column using a value from a field in another table creates a relationship between these tables. You can see this relationship by clicking the Relationships tool in the Datasheet tab (see Figure 4.17).

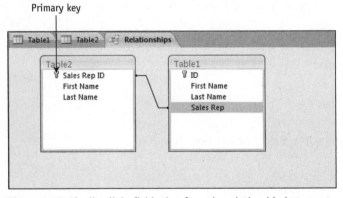

Figure 4.17. The line links fields that form the relationship between two Tables.

Each table is represented as a box that contains its fields. An icon of a key appears to the left of primary key. A line connects fields used to create the relationship. In this example, the Sales Rep ID field of Table2 links to the Sales Rep field in Table1.

You cannot delete fields that create the relationship until you delete the relationship itself; otherwise you would violate the database's data integrity. Data integrity assures that the relationships among tables remain intact.

Delete the relationship by:

1. Clicking Relationships on the Datasheet tab.

2. Right-clicking the line that shows the relationship between Table2 and Table1.

3. Clicking Delete from the pop-up menu.

4. Clicking Yes when Access 2007 asks if you want to permanently delete the relationship.

Create a lookup column from a list created by hand

Creating a lookup column using your own list is similar to the way you create it from a field in another table. Simply click the Lookup Column tool on the Datasheet tab to start the Lookup wizard.

1. Select the I will type in the values that I want option and click Next.

2. Enter the number of columns you want to appear in the pick list (see Figure 4.18). Usually one column is sufficient.

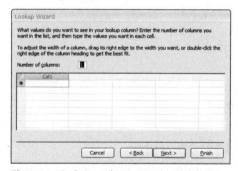

Figure 4.18. Enter values onto the pick list.

3. Enter the value.

4. Adjust the width of the value by dragging the line, similar to adjusting a column in Excel.

5. Click Finish to insert the field into the table and then change the field name.

6. Alternatively, click Next.

7. Enter the field name for the lookup column.

8. Click the Allow Multiple Values check box to store multiple values in the lookup.

9. Click Finish to create the lookup column (see Figure 4.19).

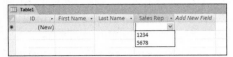

Figure 4.19. Values appear from a list rather than from a field in another table.

Modify the table design

You can modify the table created using the Datasheet view by changing to the Design view, where all the features are available to you to modify the table design.

To modify the table, click View from the Datasheet tab to enter the Design view.

Rename tables

Change the table name to something more meaningful by first closing the table and then renaming it. To do so, follow these steps:

1. Right-click the tab of the table.

2. Select Close to close the table.

3. Right-click the name of the table in the All Tables pane (left pane).

4. Enter the new name for the table.

Creating a table in the Design view

Some developers prefer to create a table in the Design view because doing so is more intuitive than using the Datasheet view. Either way works fine, so you'll have to decide which is best for you.

As you discovered, Access 2007 opens the Datasheet view when you create a new database. You switch to the Design view by clicking the View in the Datasheet tab, which I describe in the "Modify the table design" section.

The Save As dialog box appears, prompting you to accept Table1 as the table name or enter your own name. Use Table1 for now (because you're learning how to create a table) and click OK. You can change the table name at any time, which I show you how to do earlier in this chapter (refer to "Rename tables").

Exploring Design view

Defining a table using the Design view is intuitive, as you can tell by looking at the screen. Field names are entered in the Field Name column, and the field data type is placed in the Data Type column. The Data Type column is a lookup column. Click it, and you'll see a pick list of data types to choose from.

The bottom of the screen contains the field properties for the highlighted field. Notice that these properties change to reflect the data type of the field that you highlighted.

The value of many properties can be chosen from a pick list by clicking the value column (second column) on the field properties list. Other values such as Caption are entered manually.

Enter a New field

Access 2007 automatically inserts an AutoNumber field called ID and designates it as a primary key. Enter your own fields below the ID field by simply typing the name of the field in the Field Name column (see Figure 4.20).

When you move the cursor from the field name, Access 2007 automatically enters Text as the data type. Change the data type to a more appropriate one if necessary. To do so, follow these steps:

1. Click the Data Type column.

2. Click the down arrowhead to display the pick list.

3. Click the appropriate data type.

Add a field description

Right of the Data Type column is the Description column, where you can add a description of the field that will appear on the status bar when the field is selected on a form.

I use this to tell the user what he is expected to enter into the field during data entry. Rarely do you have to include a description for every field because the data required by many fields, such as first name and last name, is obvious.

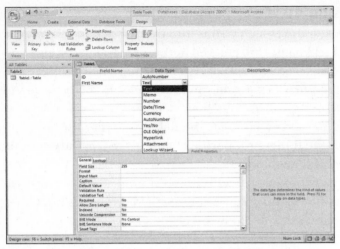

Figure 4.20. Enter a new field and select the field's data type.

Setting the primary key

You can create your own primary key and discard the primary key created by Access 2007. I prefer using a more meaningful primary key such as order number and customer number than the auto-generated numbers in the ID field.

There are a couple of techniques to create your own primary key.

One way is to simply rename the ID field and change its data type to an appropriate value. It remains designated as the primary key as noted by the key icon alongside the field name.

Another way is to delete the ID field by highlighting it and then clicking the Delete Rows tool on the Design tab. Access 2007 warns you that you're about to delete the primary key. Click Yes and then do the following:

1. Insert a field and designate the primary key.

2. Enter a field name such as Customer Number.

3. Choose a data type. Select Number to supply your own order number or AutoNumber to have Access 2007 automatically generate a unique sequential number that you can use as the order number.

4. Click the Primary Key tool on the Design tab and Access 2007 displays the key icon alongside the field name and changes the Indexed field property to Yes (No Duplicates).

5. Change the Required field property to Yes using the pick list.

Setting field properties

Setting the field properties is intuitive (except for a few properties) because you either type a value or choose one from a pick list. The value itself you'll find on your database design (refer to Chapter 3).

For example, field size is the maximum number of characters that is permitted to be stored in a Text field or a value on a pick list for a Number field.

There are a few field properties in the Design view that are new to you since I didn't discuss them in Chapter 3. These field properties include:

- Validation Text is the text that Access 2007 displays when the user attempts to enter a value that violates the validation rule. Think of this as your own warning message.

- Unicode Compression tells Access 2007 if it should compress Text, Memo, and Hyperlink fields. Unicode is a code that assigns a unique number to each character in a language. Years ago ASCII code was used, but simply ran out of numbers for non-English languages. Unicode expanded the range of numbers to represent characters from all languages. However, each character takes up approximately double the storage space. Setting Unicode Compression to Yes reduces the space taken up by these fields.

- IME properties refer to the Input Method Editor tool that is used for the English version of Access 2007 with files created in Japanese or Korean. It is best to accept the default values for these properties.

Using the Expression Builder

Default Value and Validation Rule properties offer you two options — enter the default value or validation rule manually or use the Expression Builder. For default values you probably want to manually enter the default value into the field property such typing "US" as the default value of the country field. Text values must appear within quotations.

Inside Scoop

Make sure you set the Show Date Picker property to For dates. This setting enables the user to pick the data from a calendar.

If you create complex default values, then you probably want to use the Expression Builder.

Click the ellipsis (...) icon at the end of the Default Value and Validation Rule properties to display the Expression Builder (see Figure 4.21).

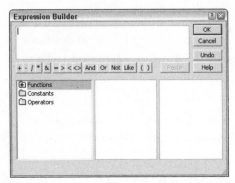

Figure 4.21. Use features of the Expression Builder to create sophisticated expressions.

Think of an expression as a statement that tells Access 2007 the default value, or how to validate a value entered into the field.

The term *expression* probably brought to mind high school math. The Expression Builder is used to create math expression and logical expression. The result of a logical expression is either true or false, such as A = B. If A is equal to B, then the expression is true; otherwise it is false.

Don't become overly concerned if math isn't your strongest skill because most expressions you build are simple ones.

Exploring the Expression Builder

The empty box at the top of the Expression Builder is where you enter the expression. Below it are commonly used operator buttons that are no doubt familiar to you.

- The left four buttons are for arithmetic.

- The ampersand is to join together two subexpressions such as A = B & C = D. A = B is a subexpression as is C = D. Both subexpressions must be true for the expression to be true.

- The next four buttons are comparison operators. Alongside the equal sign is the greater-than (>) operator. It asks Access 2007 to determine if the value on the left is greater than the value on the right such as A > B. This asks, "Is the value of A greater than the value of B?" Next is the less-than (<) operator and is used such as A < B. It asks, "Is the value of A less than the value of B?" When both operators are used (<>), Access 2007 is asked if the values are not equal to each other such as A <> B, where the value of A is not equal to the value of B.

■ The And and Or operators join subexpressions. The And operator requires both subexpressions to be true for the expression to be true. The Or operator requires only one subexpression to be true for the expression to be true.

■ The Not and Like operators are used to determine if a value is similar (Like) to another value or not similar (Not Like) to another value.

■ The parenthesis is used to explicitly set which operation is performed before another operation in the expression. Suppose you enter the expression 5 + 5 * 5. Is the answer 30 or 50? It depends if you add or multiply first. Access 2007 follows standard rules when evaluating the expression. This is referred to as the order of operation. In doing so Access 2007 arrives at 30 because multiplication is performed before addition. You can change this by using parentheses such as (5+5)*5. The calculation or subexpression within parentheses is performed first.

Below the buttons is a list of functions, constants, and operators. Click them and a list of built-in functions, values, and operators are displayed in the center and right panes. These are used to create sophisticated expressions. In this chapter, I focus on creating expressions that you'll use frequently; I show you how to create sophisticated expressions using the Expression Builder in Chapter 9.

Common Expressions

When creating an expression as the default value or validation rule, you'll come across a few common situations where it isn't obvious how to create the expression.

For example, you may want to use the current date as the default value or you may want Access 2007 to prevent a zero value from being entered into a field.

Inside Scoop

The In operator tells Access 2007 to compare a value to each item in the list of values within the parentheses.

Here are expressions I use to set default values and set validation rules.

- Numeric default value: 54.
- Text default value: "text".
- Empty field: " ".
- Today's date: Date().
- The value of the field is equal to the sum of the Subtotal field and the Tax field: = [Subtotal] + [Tax].
- Enter a non-zero value: <>0.
- The value must be zero or more than 100: 0 Or >100.
- The value must have five characters beginning .with C: Like "C????".
- Enter a date before 2000: <#1/1/2000#.
- Enter a date in 2007: >=#1/1/2007# And <#1/1/2008#.
- Invalid if the value of the Country field is Russia and Germany: = [Country] In ("Russia", "Germany").
- Invalid length: Len([Social Security Number]) <> 8.

Using the Input Mask wizard

The Input Mask wizard helps you define the pattern for values entered into a field such as the format of a phone number, Social Security number, and postal code.

Hack

Access 2007 uses wildcard characters to represent unknown characters and for pattern matching. ? is used for a single character; * is used for zero or more characters; # is used for a single digit; [A-Z] is used for any uppercase character from A through Z; [a-zA-Z0-9] is used for any lowercase or uppercase character to digits; ! means not one of characters in the pattern.

1. Click the ellipsis (...) icon at the end of the Input Mask property to display the Expression Builder (see Figure 4.22). Access 2007 lists the most commonly used input masks.

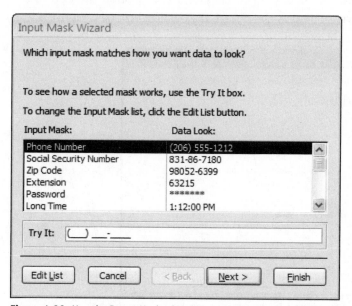

Figure 4.22. Use the Input Mask wizard to create an input mask for a field.

2. Click EditList to change the way Access 2007 defines it or enter your own to the predefine input.

3. Highlight an input mask.

4. Click the Try It box to see and try the input mask.

5. Click Finish to apply it to the field.

If you're not satisfied and want to tweak it a little, click Next and the Input Mask wizard walks through steps to modify the input mask. This modification applies to this field and doesn't affect the predefined input masks.

Using Smart Tags

A Smart Tag task does something with the value that is entered into the field such as copying the value to another field or application. This sounds a bit unusual at first, but consider how a person uses information stored in the database.

Information about a new customer is placed in the customer information table and into a contact list. A stock symbol in a table could display information about the company from MSN MoneyCentral.

Create a Smart Tag for a field by clicking the ... icon at the end of the Smart Tag property to display the Smart Tags dialog box (see Figure 4.23).

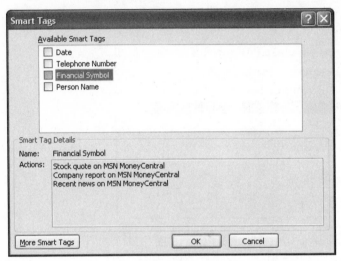

Figure 4.23. Assign a field a Smart Tag by selecting a Smart Tag from the list.

Click as many Smart Tags as you want applied to the field. Click More Smart Tags and visit the Microsoft Web site to see if any others have been created since you installed Access 2007. Then click OK to apply it to the field.

Creating a lookup list

The Lookup tab in Field Properties is used to create a lookup list for Text and Number fields nearly identical to the one you built previously in this chapter when creating a table from the Datasheet view.

Click the Lookup tab (see Figure 4.24) and you'll see Text Box as the Display Control. This simply means that the lookup appears as a text box. Click the down arrowhead to switch to a List Box or a Combo Box. Each has its own set of properties.

Display control

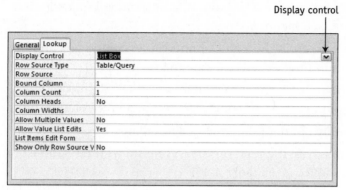

Figure 4.24. Use the Lookup tab to create a lookup list for the field.

Select the source of the lookup list by clicking either the down arrowhead in the Row Source property to choose a table that contains values, or click the ... icon to open the Query Builder to create the lookup list from values through your database. I show you how to use the Query Builder in Chapter 8.

Creating relationships

In Chapter 3, you learn the importance of relationships to a relational database such as Access 2007. A relationship joins together two tables with a common value creating one virtual table that contains fields from both tables. Fields from both tables can be used once the relationship is created.

Before learning how to create the relationship, create two tables. I created Table1 that has a Customer Number field, which is the primary key, and a First Name field. My second table is called Table2 and uses the default ID field as the primary key, and I've added the Customer Number field, which I'll use to join Table2 to Table1.

1. Click the Database Tools tab.

2. Click the Relationships tool on the Database Tools tab to display the Show Table dialog box. This is where you select the tables you want to relate.

3. Click Edit Relationships on the Design tab. This displays the Edit Relationships dialog box.

4. Click Create New to display the Create New dialog box.

5. Click the down arrow in the Left Table Name combo box and select the table name (see Figure 4.25).

6. Click the down arrow in the Left Column Name combo box and select the column that is used to create the relationship.

7. Click the down arrow in the Right Table Name and Right Column Name and pick the table and column to complete the relationship.

8. Click OK to return to the Edit Relationships dialog box.

9. Click Create to create the relationship. A line shows the relationship between these tables (see Figure 4.26).

Figure 4.25. Select the table and fields to form the relationship.

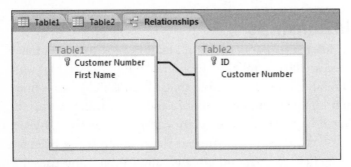

Figure 4.26. A line shows fields that form the relationship.

Just the facts

- Create a table in the Datasheet view or the Design view.
- Start by creating a blank database.
- Access 2007 automatically places you in the Datasheet view referred to as the design-in-browse.
- Enter a value in a field and Access 2007 determines the best data type for the field.

- Set the format for the field using the Format tool on the Datasheet tab.

- Click the New Field tool on the Datasheet tab to insert a field using a field template.

- Click the Lookup Column tool on the Datasheet tab to create a lookup field in the table.

- Click the Primary Key tool on the Design tab to set the primary key for a table.

GET THE SCOOP ON...
Using a form and a datasheet ▪ Cascading updates
Finding and replacing records ▪ Handy shortcuts for
data entry

Entering and Editing Data

What's the big deal about entering and editing data in an Access 2007 database? Entering data? Click the mouse in a field and begin typing. Editing data? Double-click the mouse in a field and begin typing.

The big deal isn't about how to enter and edit data. You enter and edit data in Access 2007 just as you do in Excel, Word, and other Office applications.

The big deal is that Access 2007 has improved, moving to Ribbons that contain tabs of useful tools that make your job of entering and editing data into an Access 2007 database application a breeze.

In this chapter, I show you the smart way to do this using tips and tricks that I picked up from using Access 2007.

Forms and datasheets

You enter and edit data in two places — a form and a datasheet.

A form is used to interact with data the way you expect to when using a professional database application. The screen is dressed up and check boxes, radio buttons, text boxes, and combo boxes are used to enter and edit.

A datasheet is used to interact with data the way you expect to when using a spreadsheet. Although you could find a combo box in a field (see Chapter 4), most data is entered and edited by typing in a field.

These should be old hat to you by now after reading previous chapters in this book.

Advantages of using a form

An advantage of using a form over a datasheet is that a form can interact with multiple tables simultaneously, something that can't be done using a datasheet.

Think of a form as your plate at a buffet — it has a few fields from this table and some from that table. When you look at the plate — I mean the form — it seems that everything came from the same table.

Using a form for data entry and editing is better than the datasheet if your data is being entered or modified in more than one table.

To see how to use a form, begin by creating a database from the Contacts template. Follow these steps:

1. Click the Featuring subcategory of the Template Categories on the Navigation pane of the Getting Started with Microsoft Office Access screen. This displays the list of templates.

2. Click Sales Pipeline (see Figure 5.1) in the center pane and create the database as you learned in Chapter 1.

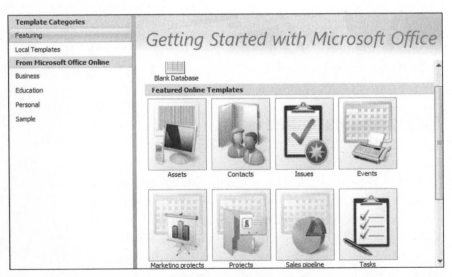

Figure 5.1. Click Sales Pipeline to create the Sales Pipeline database.

3. Click New Opportunity (see Figure 5.2) to display the Opportunity Details form. You'll be prompted to enter information about the form.

Figure 5.2. Click New Opportunity to enter information about a new sales opportunity.

4. Enter the customer name and press Enter. Access 2007 detects that it is a new customer and prompts you to enter detailed information about the customer.

5. Click Yes and enter information about the new customer on the Customer Details form (see Figure 5.3).

6. Click Save and New to save this information.

7. Click Close to return to the Opportunity Details form.

Figure 5.3. Enter new information, click Save and New to save it, and click Close to close the form.

8. Enter the name of an employee. Access 2007 detects this is a new employee and prompts you to enter information about the new employee.

9. Click Yes and enter information about the new employee on the Employee Details form.

10. Click Save and New to save this information and then click Close to return to the Opportunity Details form.

11. Enter the remaining information about the new opportunity.

12. Click Save and New to save this information and then click Close to close the Opportunity Details form.

13. Click the shutter bar at the top of the Navigation Pane to open the Navigation Pane (see Figure 5.4).

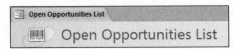

Figure 5.4. Click to open the Navigation pane.

14. Click the double arrowhead alongside the Supporting Objects heading to display supporting objects.

15. Double-click Employees to see the Datasheet view of the Employees table. Notice that employee data entered into the Opportunity Details form appears in the table.

16. Double-click Customers to see the Datasheet view of the Customers table. Notice that customer information entered into the Opportunity Details form appears in the table.

Tabbing through the form

Some believe that the mouse revolutionized the way data is entered into a form. Point, click, and then type away. Repeat these steps and in no time the form is completed.

That's not necessarily true if you have to enter lots of data onto a form. Point, click, and type impede progress because you take your fingers off the keyboard.

Using the Tab key is more efficient. The cursor automatically moves to the next logical data-entry object on the form when you press the Tab key. That is, assuming the form is designed for efficiency.

Access makes the distinction between the next data-entry object and the next logical data-entry object on the form.

A form is assembled by dragging and dropping form objects onto the form. A form object is a text box, check box, and other items you find on the form.

Inside Scoop

Access 2007 saves data automatically after the cursor is moved to a new field in the same row or when the cursor is moved to another row.

Access 2007 sets the Tab Stop property for each data-entry object to Yes. Think of the Tab Stop property as a flag that tells Access 2007 to stop at this object when the Tab key is pressed.

Access 2007 also assigns a Tab Index value to each data-entry object. The Tab Index value determines the sequence in which the data-entry object gets focus when the Tab key is pressed. Focus is placing the cursor into a text box or highlighting a radio button.

The first data-entry object placed on the form is assigned the Tab Index value of 0 and the second data entry object has a Tab Index value of 1, and so forth.

You can see this by placing the Opportunity Details form in the Design view and then clicking the Customers combo box. The Other tab on the property sheet shows the Tab Stop property set to Yes and the Tab Index set to zero (see Figure 5.5).

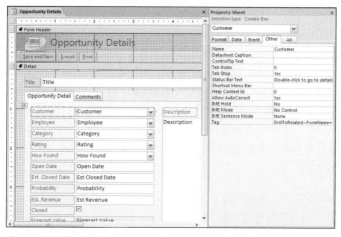

Figure 5.5. The Tab Stop is set to Yes and the Tab Index is set to 0.

The form's designer changes the sequence of Tab Index values to conform to the logical way a person enters data into the form. When the

Inside Scoop

Press Shift Tab to move to the previous Tab stop.

Tab key is pressed, focus is given to the next logical data entry object — not necessarily the next data-entry object.

For example, the designer may have dropped the last name text box and first name text box onto the form and then rearranged them to read first name and last name.

Access 2007 assigns the last name text box the key stop value of 0 because it is the first data-entry object placed on the form and the first name text box is assigned key stop value 1.

The problem is that the person is prompted to enter last name and then first name, which isn't the way most of us expect to enter data. The solution: Switch the key stop values to enable the form to be filled out in a logical sequence.

In Chapter 12, I show you how to change the sequence of the Tab stops, which is when you'll learn to design your own forms.

Picking dates

Dates are always a challenge to enter. Do I enter the century or just the year? Do I put a zero in front of the day or month when it's a single-digit month?

A clever forms designer takes the guesswork out of entering a date by setting the Show Date Picker property to Form dates. This causes the calendar icon to be displayed when a date field receives focus.

You can see this by clicking the Open Date field in the Opportunity Details form. Click the calendar icon to open the calendar and pick the date (see Figure 5.6).

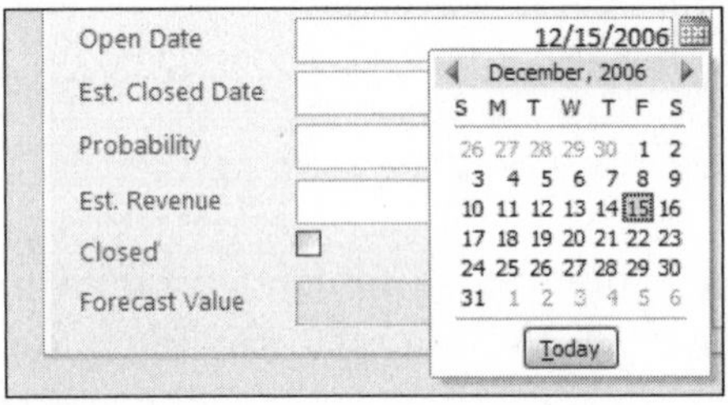

Figure 5.6. Pick a date from a calendar.

Inside Scoop

Setting the Input Mask also enforces the date format for a date field.

Advantages of using a datasheet

Although arguably less attractive than a form, the datasheet is the choice of many to enter and modify data because it is less cumbersome to use than a form.

The datasheet presents data spreadsheetlike, making it familiar to everyone who has used a spreadsheet. No training is needed. All records appear on the screen or are accessible by scrolling the vertical scroll bar.

A blank record always appears as the last record. Click a field and begin entering new data to create the new record. Press Enter to move to the next field.

Data is automatically saved when data is entered into a field of a new record or when a value is changed in an existing record.

Many time-saving features found on a form area are also available in the datasheet. When you enter new data into a combo box, such as a new customer in the Opportunities table, Access 2007 prompts to you enter details into a corresponding form (Customer Details form, for example). Dates can be picked from a calendar rather than entered manually into a date field.

Hide and display columns

The datasheet offers flexibility not found on a form. A field can be hidden from view, yet still not deleted from the table.

To hide a field, follow these steps:

1. Right-click the field to be hidden to display a pop-up menu.
2. Select Hide Columns (see Figure 5.7).

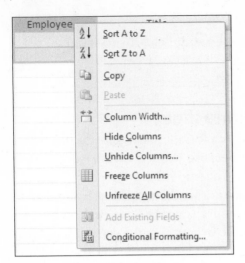

Figure 5.7. Click to hide the column.

To display some or all hidden fields, follow these steps:

1. Right-click any field to display a pop-up menu.

2. Select Unhide Columns to display the Unhide Columns dialog (see Figure 5.8).

3. Select the column you want to appear in the datasheet.

4. Click Close to make the column visible.

Figure 5.8. Click columns that you want to appear in the datasheet.

Freeze and unfreeze a field

A common frustration occurs when using the datasheet — not all fields fit on the screen. Scrolling brings them into view, but also scrolls other fields off the screen.

Stop pulling your hair out and simply freeze fields you want displayed with those that are off the screen. Freezing tells Access 2007 not to scroll the frozen field off the screen.

To freeze a field, follow these steps:

1. Right-click the field you want to freeze to display the pop-up menu.
2. Select Freeze Columns (see Figure 5.9) and the frozen field is moved to the first field in the datasheet.
3. Scroll using the horizontal scroll bar and you'll notice the field not moving. It is frozen.

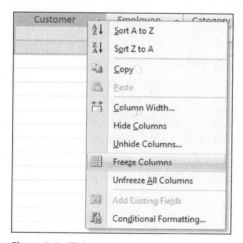

Figure 5.9. Click Freeze Columns.

To unfreeze a field, follow these steps:

1. Right-click any field to display the pop-up menu.
2. Select Unfreeze All Columns and the field is unfrozen. The field remains in the first field position.
3. Scroll using the horizontal scroll bar and you'll notice the field moves. It isn't frozen.

Inside Scoop

Select multiple fields by clicking a field and then dragging over other fields. Select a range of fields by clicking the first field in the range and then Shift-clicking the last field in the range.

Moving fields

Another convenience when using the datasheet is that you can reposition fields. You'll love this feature when you need to enter or modify three or four fields that are located throughout the table.

To move a field, follow these steps:

1. Place the cursor on the bottom line of the field name. A four-arrowhead cursor appears.

2. Drag and drop the field into its new position in the datasheet. Access 2007 automatically moves other fields aside to make room for the field.

Using grid lines and changing colors

The datasheet has gridlines that can be distracting when you modify a field or modify the entire record.

Here's a trick I used to help me focus on the field or record I'm changing. Hide gridlines that are distracting and change the color of rows to make them pop out.

To change the gridline style follow these steps:

1. Click the corner arrowhead icon in the upper-left corner of the datasheet to highlight the entire datasheet or click the cursor into a field.

2. Click the Gridlines tool on the Home tab to display a list of grid options.

3. Click the grid option that best fits your situation and Access 2007 applies it to the datasheet (see Figure 5.10).

To change the gridline color, follow these steps:

1. Click the corner arrowhead icon in the upper-left corner of the datasheet to highlight the entire datasheet or click the cursor into a field.

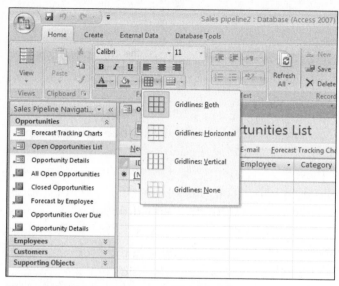

Figure 5.10. Click the grid to apply to the datasheet.

2. Click the Alternate Fill/Back Color tool on the Home tab to display a list of color options. Colors are listed as Automatic (default), Access theme Colors (coordinated colors), Standard Colors, Recent Colors, No Color, or More Color (see additional colors).

3. Click a color to apply it to the datasheet (see Figure 5.11).

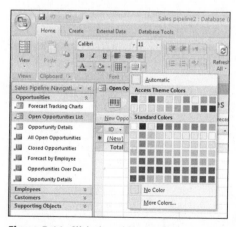

Figure 5.11. Click the grid to apply to the datasheet.

The Home tab

The Home tab contains many tools that make it easy to enter and modify data. Some I touched on previously in this chapter, so I'll simply mention them here and others you'll learn about in the next chapter. The rest I explore in detail.

The View tool changes between Form View, Datasheet View, Layout View, and Design View, which you've already used in the last chapter.

Cut, copy, and paste

The Clipboard tool is used to cut, copy, and paste data. Here, I explore a few less-obvious things you can do with the Clipboard tool.

The last 24 items that you cut or copy remain on the Clipboard, enabling you to repeatedly paste the same value into multiple fields without having to recopy them.

To repeat pasting, follow these steps:

1. Copy two or more data to the Clipboard by highlighting the data and pressing Ctrl+C.

2. Click the angled arrow on the Clipboard tool to display the Clipboard pane.

3. Click the cursor into the field that you want to paste the data.

4. Select the data from the Clipboard pane that you want to paste (see Figure 5.12).

To remove an item from the Clipboard, do the following:

1. Click the angled arrow on the Clipboard tool to display the Clipboard pane.

2. Move the cursor over the item in the Clipboard pane to display a combo box.

3. Click the down arrow of the combo box.

4. Click Delete (see Figure 5.13).

Inside Scoop

The Clipboard pane is used amongst all Windows applications, so don't be surprised to find items that you cut or copy from other applications on the Clipboard pane.

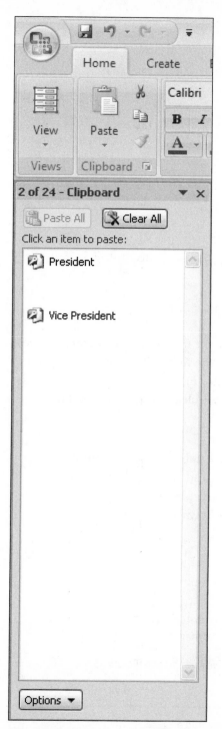

Figure 5.12. Click data on the Clipboard that you want to copy to the field.

Figure 5.13. Click Delete to remove the item from the Clipboard.

The Clipboard tool has a Format Painter that pastes the format of a field and not the value of the field. Highlight the field whose format you want to copy and click the Brush icon (see Figure 5.12). Place the cursor into the field you want to apply the format and double-click the Brush icon.

Dress up the datasheet

The Font group of tools on the Home tab is probably familiar to you because they are used in Excel, Word, and other Office applications to change the appearance of information displayed on the screen.

You can use these tools to do the following:

- Change the font and size.
- Position data within a field.
- Change the back color and font color.
- Make the font bold, italics, or underlined.

Inside Scoop
Right-click an item on the Clipboard pane to display the combo box.

However, the Font group of tools also enables you to modify the appearance of the datasheet using the Datasheet Formatting dialog box.

To change the format of the datasheet, use these steps:

1. Click the angled arrow in the Font tool group to display the Datasheet Formatting dialog box.

2. Change the settings and view these changes in the sample grid (see Figure 5.14).

3. Click OK to apply the changes to the datasheet.

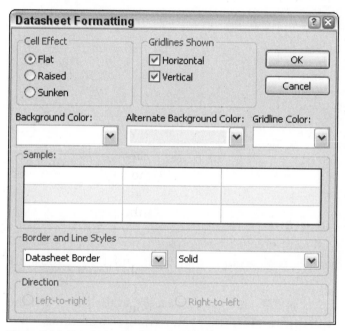

Figure 5.14. Set changes and see them in the Sample grid.

Special treatment for Rich Text fields

A Rich Text field (see Chapter 4) has its own formatting tools (see Figure 5.15) used to format text as you enter it or modify the format of existing text.

The Decrease and Increase indent tools automatically indent the data. The Numbering and Bullets tools enable you to automatically number lines in a Rich Text field or make them bulleted, similar to how you do it in Word and other Windows applications.

Inside Scoop

Only Rich Text can be highlighted. Plain text and other fields cannot be highlighted.

The Left-to-Right tool is a combo box that lets you set whether the text is entered from the left (standard for text) or right (standard for numbers) side of the field. These are the same as the Align Left and Align Right tools in the Font tool group.

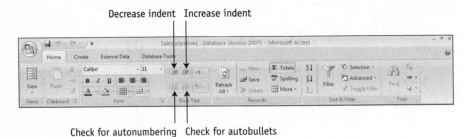

Figure 5.15. Rich Text tools work only on a Memo field where the Text Format property is set to Rich Text.

The Records tool group

All the tools you need to interact with records when you enter or modify data are in the Records tool group. New, Save, and Delete tools are self-explanatory.

- Click New, and Access 2007 opens a new record at the bottom of the datasheet or displays a empty form if you're in the Form view.

- Click Save to save changes made to the datasheet or form.

- The Delete tool is grayed until you select a record to delete. Click the leftmost column of the record you want deleted in the datasheet and then click Delete. The Form View always displays a record. Simply click Delete to remove the record.

- The More tool displays the Hide Columns, Freeze, and other tools that you learned previously in this chapter.

Totals

At first the Totals tool may not seem important during data entry. However, I use it to check my data entry. Click the Totals tool, and Access

2007 places a Total row at the bottom of the datasheet. Each field in the Total row is a combo box that lets you select the type of total for the field. There are two values for data entry.

These are:

- Click Count and Access 2007 displays the total number of values entered into the field.

- Click Sum (only for numeric fields) and Access 2007 totals values entered into the field.

Count is perfect to determine if you enter a value for all fields. Suppose you're entering information about 50 new customers. Insert a Total row and set it to Count. Each field should be 50. If not, then you left out data.

Sum is ideal way to find out if a wrong number was entered into the datasheet. Suppose you enter salaries of 50 employees from a printed document into a datasheet. Use Sum to tally the salaries in the table then compare the total with the total salaries on the printed document. Any difference indicates that an incorrect salary was entered into the datasheet.

Check spelling

I wasn't the last one standing in a spelling bee. But that doesn't bother me today because Access 2007 has a Spelling tool that compares the value of text and memo fields against the Office 2007 dictionary and then displays the Spelling dialog box when the value isn't found in the dictionary.

The Spelling dialog box is familiar because it contains features that you've seen in other Windows applications (see Figure 5.16).

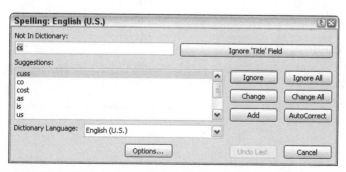

Figure 5.16. Pick the correct spelling and Access 2007 makes the changes to the field.

Inside Scoop

The record counter located at the bottom of the datasheet is another way to determine if you entered all the records that you wanted to enter into the datasheet.

The Refresh tool

Although the database you're using to learn Access 2007 is probably located on your hard drive, the Access 2007 applications that you built are likely to run over a computer network, so you can share data among your colleagues.

Access 2007 automatically updates the screen each time a change is made to the related table in the database. However, sometimes you want to make sure that what you're seeing on the screen is actually the latest information.

Instead of waiting for Access 2007 to update your screen, click the Refresh tool in the Records tool group to tell Access 2007 to update it now.

Cascading updates

The primary key uniquely identifies each row in the table and links tables together, which you can learn about in Chapter 3 and Chapter 4.

When you change the value of a primary key, Access 2007 performs a cascading update. This means that Access 2007 finds all the tables where the primary key value is used as a foreign key and changes them too. As you'll remember from Chapter 3, a foreign key is the primary key of another table used as the shared value used to link two tables.

A cascading update is performed only on primary key fields that are Text or Number data types. It cannot be used for AutoNumber data type fields.

Inside Scoop

The value of a primary key is changeable, but change its value sparingly.

Cascading updates are used only for tables that have a one-to-many relationship (refer to Chapter 3).

The cascading update feature must be turned on, otherwise Access 2007 will not automatically update foreign keys. In this example I use the Assets database to show you how to turn on cascading updates, but the same technique can be used for any database that has two related tables.

1. Create the Assets database from the Featuring subcategory of templates. (You learn how to create databases this way in Chapter 1.)

2. Click the Database Tools tab.

3. Click the Relationships tool to display the relationship between the Contacts table and the Assets table.

4. Right-click the line that connects the two tables to display a popup menu (see Figure 5.17).

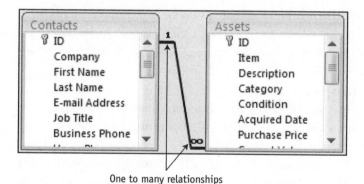

One to many relationships

Figure 5.17. Right-click the line to display the pop-up menu.

5. Click Edit Relationship to display the Edit Relationships dialog.

6. Click the Cascade Update Related Fields check box (see Figure 5.18).

7. Click the Cascade Delete Related Fields check box and then click OK.

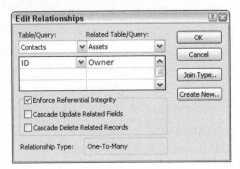

Figure 5.18. Select two check boxes to enable cascading updates and deletes.

Finding records

Locating a specific record in a table is easy by using the Find and Replace dialog box.

All right, the Find and Replace dialog box isn't new to you because it is practically the same as you use in other Office applications. However, the Access 2007 Find and Replace dialog box has features specially designed to help you quickly locate records in a table or query.

Access 2007 uses pattern matching to find the search criteria in a table or in the results of a query (see Chapter 8). It simply compares each character in the search string against values in a table or query result and returns records that match the pattern.

Access 2007 returns values that partially or completely match the search pattern. If you searched for "man," you'll see records that have the value "man" and "Manhattan."

The Find and Replace dialog box does not search a database. Instead, it searches the current datasheet or the table associated with the current form. You need to create a query to search multiple tables in the database.

Searching

Access 2007 can search one or more fields except for a lookup field or the complete table, depending on the selection you make in the Find and Replace dialog box.

To begin searching:

1. Open a datasheet or form that you want to search. (See Chapter 8 if you want to search the results of a query). I'm using the Customers Datasheet from the Northwind 2007 database (see Chapter 1).

2. Click the field or control you want to search. I clicked Last Name.

3. Press Ctrl+F to open the Final and Replace dialog box. Alternatively, click the Find tool on the Home tab.

4. Click the Find tab. This is the default setting.

5. Type the search string in the Find What box. I'm looking for Bagel.

6. Select the field you want to search on the Look In list. This defaults to the field that you clicked before opening the Find and Replace dialog box.

7. Select the table name from the Look In list if you want Access 2007 to search the entire table rather than a field.

8. Click the Search Fields As Formatted check box. This is the default setting.

9. Select Whole Field (default), Start of Field, or Any Part of Field in the Match list.

   ■ When Whole Field is selected, Access 2007 returns records when a value in the field completely matches the search criteria. A record is not returned if it contains at least one character that is different from the search criteria.

   ■ When Start of Field is clicked, Access 2007 begins pattern-matching with the first characters in the field. A record is returned if at least the first character and subsequent characters match the search criteria. A record is not returned if the first character is different from the search criteria, even if all the other characters in the field match.

   ■ When Any Part of Field is selected, Access 2007 returns a record when the search criteria appear anywhere in the field.

   ■ Select All (default), Up, or Down in the Search combo box. All tells Access to search all the rows. Up tells Access 2007 to search only rows above the current row. Down tells Access 2007 to search rows below the current row.

Inside Scoop

You can select other fields to search by clicking them on the datasheet without having to close the Find and Replace dialog box.

10. Click Find Next to find the next record that contains the search criteria (see Figure 5.19). The next record that contains the search criteria becomes the current record. Click Find Next to continue the search to determine if the search criteria is in other records. Access 2007 displays a message telling you if the search criteria wasn't found.

Figure 5.19. Click Find Next to begin the search.

Wildcard characters

A wildcard character is used in a search string to locate partial matches to the search pattern. For example, the asterisk (*) wildcard character is used if you're searching for a customer's last name but are unsure if it is Smith, Smite, or Smithson. Write the search string as "Smith"[*].

Wildcard characters must be placed in brackets ([]) except for the exclamation point wildcard character and the closing bracket wildcard character.

Table 5.1 contains wildcard characters that you can use in your search string. Any combination can be used to help find the field or record you need.

Table 5.1 Search string wildcard characters

Wildcard Character	Description	Example
*	Matches one or more characters anywhere in the search string	T* finds Tom, tent but not at

Wildcard Character	Description	Example
!	Matches any character not within the brackets	T[!e] finds Tom but not tent
[xy]	Matches any single character within the brackets	T[ai]ll finds tall and till, but not tell
?	Matches any single alphabetic character	T?ll finds tall, till, and tell
-	Matches any one of a range of characters specified in ascending order.	T[a-z]ll finds tall, tell, till, tom
#	Matches any single numeric character	22# finds 220 through 229
%	Matches any number of characters	T%ll finds tall, till, and tell
_	Matches any single alphabetic character	T_ll finds tall, tell, and till
^	Matches any character not in brackets	T[^oa] finds till, tell, tent but not tall or Tom

Find blank values

Probably one of the more common searches you make is to find records that have empty fields. These are referred to as blank fields or null fields.

Type either Null or Is Null into the Find What text box and then click Find Next to locate the next blank field.

Empty text, memo, and hyperlink fields are said to contain a zero-length string. Type a pair of double quotations ("") in the Find What text box to find an empty text, memo, and hyperlink field.

Some fields are formatted to display a value when they are empty. The value is set when the field is created (refer to Chapter 4). Type this value in the Find What text box to find such a field.

Replace values automatically

Click the Replace tab to have Access 2007 find and replace values the same way as you use this feature in other Windows applications. Enter the search criteria in the Look In text box and type the new value in the Replace

With box. Click Find Next to locate the search criteria and then click Replace or Replace All to update the field with the replacement value.

Use caution because you can make some awful mistakes using find and replace (see Figure 5.20). Remember when using wildcard characters that the next match could be a partial match — and not the value you want replaced. If you're in a rush and click Replace All, you might replace a lot of data you do not want replaced.

Don't use wildcard characters in the Replace With text box because Access 2007 doesn't recognize them as wildcards and considers them replacement values. It replaces the value in the field with wildcard characters that you typed into the Replace With box.

Figure 5.20. Make sure the search criteria is correct before clicking Replace All.

Handy shortcuts for data entry

Admit it, you were probably amazed the first time you saw someone copy and paste an entire page with three magic keystrokes — Ctrl+A, Ctrl+C, and Ctrl+V. Now you know that Windows applications are loaded with shortcuts that seem to cut data entry in half.

Access 2007 is no exception. Table 5.2 contains noteworthy short cuts to keep in mind when entering new data or updating existing data.

Table 5.2 Data-entry shortcuts	
Shortcut	**Description**
F1	Display help
F2	Display the insertion point, highlights data in the field so you can overwrite it
F4	Open a combo box
F5	Go to the first field of the first record
F6	Go to next control on the screen

Shortcut	Description
F7	Check spelling
F9	Recalculate fields, refresh a list box or combo box
F10	Display shortcut keys
F11	Open/closes left pane
F12	Save As
Shift+F10	Display the shortcut menu
Right Arrow	Move the insertion point one character to the right
Ctrl+Right Arrow	Move the insertion point one word to the right
Left Arrow	Move the insertion point one character to the left
Ctrl+Left Arrow	Move the insertion point one word to the left
End	Move the insertion point to the end of the field in a single line field or end of the line in a multiline field
Ctrl+End	Move the insertion point to the end of the field in a multi-line field
Home	Move the insertion point to the beginning of the field in a single line field or to the beginning of the line in a multiline field
Ctrl+Home	Move the insertion point to the beginning of the field of the line in a multiline field
Tab	Move to next field
Shift+Tab	Move to the previous field
Ctrl+Down Arrow	Move to the current field in the last record
Ctrl+End	Move to the last field in the last record
Ctrl+Up Arrow	Move to the current field in the first record
Ctrl+Home	Move to the first field in the first record
Spacebar	Switch between check boxes or option buttons
Ctrl+C	Copy to the Clipboard
Ctrl+X	Cut the selection and copy it to the Clipboard

continued

Table 5.2 *continued*

Shortcut	Description
Ctrl+V	Paste from the Clipboard to the insertion point
Backspace	Delete the character to the left of the insertion point
Delete	Delete the character to the right of the insertion point
Ctrl+Delete	Delete all characters to the right of the insertion point
Ctrl+Z	Undo typing
Esc twice	Undo changes in the current field or current record if both have changed
Ctrl+; (semicolon)	Insert the current date
Ctrl+Shift : (colon)	Insert the current time
Ctrl+Alt Spacebar	Insert the default value for the field
Ctrl+' (apostrophe)	Insert a value from the same field in the previous record
Ctrl+Enter	Enter a new line
Ctrl+ +	Add a new record
Ctrl+ -	Delete the current record
Shift+Enter	Save changes to the current record
Ctrl+S	Save
Ctrl+P	Print

Just the facts

- There are two places to enter and edit data – a form and a datasheet.
- A form can interact with multiple tables simultaneously.
- The Tab Stop property of a control on a form determines if the control receives focus when the Tab key is pressed.
- The Tab Index value determines the order in which a control on a form receives focus when the Tab key is pressed.
- The first Tab Index value is 0.

GET THE SCOOP ON...
Ready-to-use filters ▪ Filter By Form ▪ Modifying the
filter criteria ▪ Reusable Filter By Form forms ▪ Advanced
filter/sort

Filtering and Sorting Data

Chapter 6

Picture this: A datasheet with thousands of customers' names. You want the names of the handful of customers who are located near your next business trip destination. Don't search each record; use a filter instead and have Access 2007 create a list of customers for you. It takes seconds to do.

A filter is like the colander that a chef uses to filter pasta from water. A filter separates things you want from things you don't want. However in the case of your table, unwanted records are not flushed down the drain — Access 2007 simply hides them from view.

Learn how to create simple and complex filters in this chapter and how to sort records trapped by the filter.

Examining filters

A filter changes the selection of data that appears in a datasheet, form, report, or Layout view based on your filter criteria, but leaves other data intact and out of sight.

The filter criteria consist of one or more values that Access 2007 compares to one or multiple fields in the underlying table. Think of the filter criteria as holes in a colander. The size of the hole determines the pasta that remains after drainage.

There are five ways to create a filter — Selection, ready-to-use filters, Filter By Form, Advanced Filter/Sort, and the Filter tool.

Inside Scoop

Fields whose values are determined by an expression cannot be filtered.

The Selection tool

The fastest way to filter records is by using the Selection tool on the Home tab. You'll find a handful of the most commonly used filters ready to be applied at the click of the mouse.

You can choose Equals or Does Not Equal and other filters that relate to the data type of the field you use to filter records. Text, number, and date/time fields each have their own filter selection.

Access 2007 uses the value of the field you pick as filter value. I'm going to filter all the records that have Northwind Traders Chocolate as the value in the Product ID field.

Here's how I'm going to do this:

1. Open the Northwind 2007 database. I showed you how to Open the Northwind 2007 database in Chapter 1.

2. Double-click Inventory Transactions under Supporting Objects to display inventory transactions.

3. Click a row in the Product ID field that has the value Northwind Traders Chocolate.

4. Click the Selection tool.

5. Click Equals Northwind Traders Chocolate to apply the filter to the datasheet. Notice that Access 2007 automatically uses the value in the field you selected as the filter value.

6. Click the Toggle Filter tool on the Home tab to see all the records again. Click again to apply the filter.

Ready-to-use filters

Ready-to-use filters are built-in filters created by the Access 2007 folks and picked from a pop-up menu by right-clicking a field in a datasheet, form, report, or Layout view.

The types of ready-to-use filters that appear on the menu depend on the field's data type and values stored in the field, although you'll find many of these common among all data types.

Inside Scoop

Access 2007 fills a field with pound (#) signs when the field is too small to display its value. Fix this by dragging the right border of the field until values appear.

You can take a closer look by opening the ready-to-use filters pop-up menu. I'm using the Northwind 2007 database.

1. Open the Northwind 2007.

2. Double-click Inventory Transactions under Supporting Objects.

Inventory Transactions table is a good example because it contains text, number, and date fields, each of which has a slightly different set of ready-to-use filters.

Common filters

Each ready-to-use filters pop-up menu has two common filters at the bottom of the menu. These are:

- Equals (shows rows that have exactly the same value)
- Does Not Equal (shows rows that don't have the exact same value)

Alongside each is the value of the current cell. Click one of these, and Access 2007 displays only those records that match your selection. The other records are hidden from view.

To do this, right-click Northwind Traders Chocolate in the Product ID field to display the ready-to-use filters pop-up menu (see Figure 6.1). Then click Equals to filter the records (see Figure 6.2).

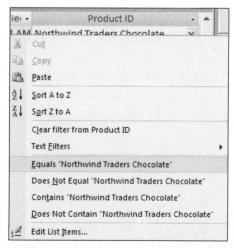

Figure 6.1. Click the type of filter that you want applied to the table.

Inventory Transactions						×
Transactio ▾	Transaction Typt ▾	Transaction Created Date ▾	Transaction Modifie ▾	Product ID	▾	C
50	Purchased	3/22/2006 4:04:31 PM	3/22/2006 4:04:31 PM	Northwind Traders Chocolate	▾	
70	Sold	3/22/2006 4:11:56 PM	3/24/2006 10:59:41 AM	Northwind Traders Chocolate		
74	Purchased	3/24/2006 10:53:13 AM	3/24/2006 10:53:13 AM	Northwind Traders Chocolate		
75	Sold	3/24/2006 10:53:16 AM	3/24/2006 10:55:46 AM	Northwind Traders Chocolate		
99	Sold	4/3/2006 1:50:08 PM	4/3/2006 1:50:15 PM	Northwind Traders Chocolate		
123	Sold	4/4/2006 11:37:45 AM	4/4/2006 11:37:49 AM	Northwind Traders Chocolate		
124	Sold	4/4/2006 11:38:07 AM	4/4/2006 11:38:11 AM	Northwind Traders Chocolate		
(New)		7/15/2006 11:07:14 AM	7/15/2006 11:07:14 AM			

Figure 6.2. Records that don't meet the filter criteria are hidden from view.

Bet you're wondering how to make the other records visible again. There are three ways to do this:

■ The Toggle Filter tool in the Sort & Filter tool group on the Home tab changes color whenever a filter is applied to a table.

■ You can also find filter the icon by right-clicking the column head.

■ You also get the filter icon at the column header, which reminds you which column(s) are being filtered.

This serves a reminder that you're not seeing all records in the table. Click the Toggle Filter tool (see Figure 6-3) to see the other records. The Toggle Filter tool returns to its normal color, and the table is full again.

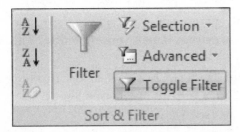

Figure 6.3. The Toggle Filter tool is used to remove and apply a filter to a table.

Click the Toggle Filter tool another time to apply the same filter to the table.

The color of the Toggle Filter tool isn't the only reminder that a filter is applied to the table. There's another indicator at the bottom of the pane (see Figure 6.4) that changes from "Unfiltered" to an orange color "Filtered" when the table is filtered.

Figure 6.4. Filtered signals that a filter is applied to the table.

The filter can be applied to the table until you select Clear filter from the ready-to-use filters pop-up menu. This option deletes the filter.

Text ready-to-use filters

Text fields have additional options available on the ready-to-use filters pop-up menu. You probably noticed two of them in Figure 6.5. These are Contains and Does Not Contain.

- Click Contains and Access 2007 includes records that have an exact match or records that have the value somewhere in the field.

- Click Does Not Contain and those records that have the value at least somewhere in the field are not displayed.

To test the ready-to-use filter, do the following:

1. Right-click Northwind Traders Chocolate.

2. Click Contains and Access 2007 displays records that have Northwind Traders Chocolate and Northwind Traders Chocolate Biscuits Mix because the filter criteria "Northwind Traders Chocolate" is contained in the Product ID field in these.

The Text Filters option on the ready-to-use filters pop-up menu has a full list of ready-to-use filters specifically designed for text fields. In addition to the filters you already learned, the list includes:

- Begins With (the field must begin with the filter criteria)

- Does Not Begin With (the field must not begin with the filter criteria)

- Ends With (the field must end with the filter criteria)

- Does Not End With (the field must not end with the filter criteria)

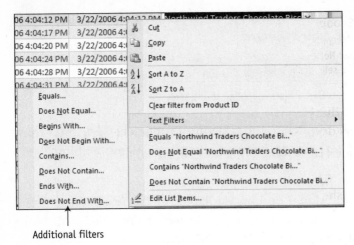

Additional filters

Figure 6.5. A full list of filters is available by clicking the Text Filters option.

Number ready-to-use filters

Number fields also have additional options available on the ready-to-use filters pop-up menu besides Equals and Not Equal. These are:

- Less Than or Equal To (shows rows that are equal to or less than the value)

- Greater Than or Equal To (shows rows that are equal to or greater than the value.)

   To test this, do the following:

1. Move the horizontal scroll bar to the right until the Quantity field is displayed.

2. Right-click the first record that has a quantity of 100 to display the ready-to-use filters pop-up menu.

3. Click Less Than or Equal To and Access 2007 shows records that have a quantity of 100 or less.

Inside Scoop

Filtered records are automatically sorted by their primary keys.

Inside Scoop

The Equal To and Not Equal enable you to enter a search value. The quick pick Equal To and Not Equal are found on the bottom of the first menu default to the value of the selected record.

Click Number Filters on the ready-to-use filters pop-up menu to see the full list of filters designed for number fields. These are:

- Less Than (shows rows that have less than the value, but not the value)

- Greater Than (shows rows that have greater than the value, but not the value)

- Between (displays the Between Numbers dialog box where you specify a range of values. Records that contain those values and values between them are displayed.)

Date/Time ready-to-use filters

Date/Time fields have additional options available on the ready-to-use filters pop-up menu too. These are:

- On or Before (shows rows that have exactly the same date/time or a date/time before it)

- On or After (shows rows that have exactly the same date/time or a date/time after it)

To check this out:

1. Right-click the record in the Transaction Created Date field that has the date 3/24/2006 to display the ready-to-use filters pop-up menu (see Figure 6.6).

2. Click On or After and Access 2007 shows records that have a transaction modification date of 3/24/2006 or later.

Inside Scoop

A check mark appears next to the active filter on the Number Filters list.

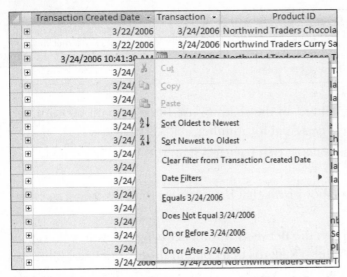

Figure 6.6. The ready-to-use filters pop-up menu has filters designed specifically for the Date/Time field.

Here's how to use the ready-to-use date filter:

1. Click Date Filters on the ready-to-use filters pop-up menu to see the full list of filters designed for date fields. All of these are self-explanatory except for All Dates In Period.

2. Click the All Dates In Period to see a list of common date periods (see Figure 6.7). These are quarters of the year and months. The quarters are a calendar quarter. The first three months is the first quarter, the second three months is the second quarter, and so on.

3. Click a quarter, and all records in that quarter are displayed. Likewise, click a month and all records in that month are displayed.

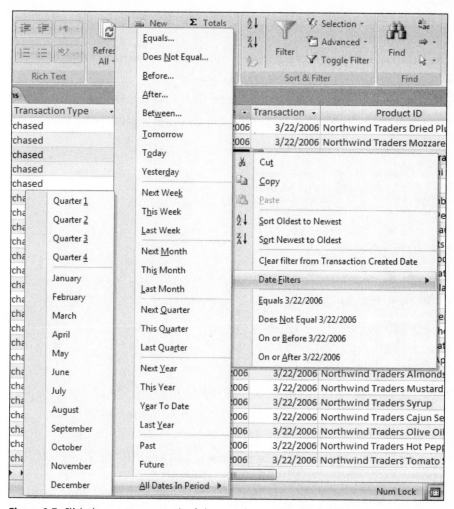

Figure 6.7. Click the quarter or month of the records you want displayed.

Using Filter By Form

The easiest and fastest way to create a filter is to use ready-to-use filters; however, sometimes you'll need more-complex filters than those available in the ready-to-use filter. In such a situation you'll need to use a Filter By Form.

Although the designers of Access 2007 placed this under the Advanced tool on the Home tab, Filter By Form is simple to use because the filter criteria is entered directly into fields on a form.

Let's create a filter for the Inventory Transactions datasheet using the Filter By Form.

1. Double-click Inventory Transaction under Supporting Objects to open the Inventory Transactions datasheet.

2. Click Advanced in the Sort & Filter group on the Home tab.

3. Click Filter By Form (see Figure 6.8) to open the Filter By Form form.

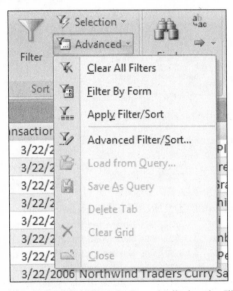

Figure 6.8. Click Filter By Form to display the Filter By Form form.

You'll see all fields that are in the table along with what appears to be a blank record. The blank record is not really a record. It is simply the place where you enter values for the filter criteria. Enter values by picking them from a list of values already in the field.

Here's how to do it.

1. Click the Transaction Type column.

2. Click the down arrowhead to display the list of values in the underlying field.

3. Click Sold.

4. Click the Product ID column.

Bright Idea

Remove the filter criteria from the Filter By Form form by clicking Clear Grid from the Advanced tool on the Sort & Filter group on the Home tab.

5. Click the down arrowhead to display the list of values in the underlying field.

6. Click Northwind Traders Chocolate.

7. Click Toggle Filter in the Sort & Filter group on the Home tab to apply the filter.

Modifying the filter criteria

Clicking Toggle Filter while in the Filter By Form form applies the filter to the underlying table. Click Toggle Filter again and all the hidden records appear.

What happened to the Filter By Form form?

Don't worry, it didn't disappear. Simply click Filter By Form in the Advanced tool on the Home tab to see it again. When you do, you'll notice that the filter criteria remain intact. This is a good thing because you can easily modify it if the original filter criteria didn't return the records you expected it to return.

There are three ways to modify this filter:

■ Click Clear Grid from the Advanced tool to remove all the values and then enter a completely new filter criteria.

■ Click a new value for fields you need.

■ Remove all values from a field by highlighting them and then press the Delete button.

Using the Or tab

Glance at the bottom of the Filter By Form form and you'll notice the Look for and Or tabs. The Look for tab is used to enter filter criteria that matches one value in each field of the filter. You learned to use this in the previous section.

Suppose that you want to filter on two or more values in the same field. Although you can't do that in the Look for tab, you can do it by using the Or tab. As the name implies, the Or tab is where you enter alternative filtering values.

The Look for tab is on top and ready to be used when you open the Filter By Form form. The Or tab is on the bottom and grayed, indicating it isn't active and won't be until you enter a filter value in the Look for tab (see Figure 6.9).

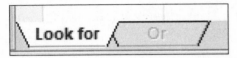

Figure 6.9. The Or tab is used to enter alternative filter values.

Let's open the Filter By Form form for the Inventory Transaction datasheet. (You learned how to open this in the previous section.)

1. Select Northwind Traders Chocolate as the Product ID. Notice that the Or tab becomes active.

2. Click the Or tab. It contains another blank filter form.

3. Select Northwind Traders Chocolate Biscuits as the Product ID.

4. Click Toggle Filter to apply the filter and see only records that have a Product ID of Northwind Traders Chocolate or Northwind Traders Chocolate Biscuits.

Each time you click an Or tab another Or tab is automatically created. It remains grayed until a value is entered into the active Or tab. You can use multiple Or tabs to enter additional alternative filter criteria for the same field.

Modifying the Or tab

Modify the filter criteria in the Or tab the same as you do in the Look for table (see "Modifying the filter criteria" section). There is also another technique that I find handy to use when the filter criteria in the Or tab is no longer needed. Instead of clearing its filtering values, I simply remove the Or tab.

Here's what I do:

1. Click the Or tab that is to be removed. This brings it to the top.

2. Click the Delete tab in the Advanced tool on the Home tab to remove the Or tab. The tab on the left then becomes the active tab.

Reusable Filter By Form forms

Filters created by using Filter By Form are reusable: Create it, save it, and use it again and again without having to reenter the filter criteria. This is a valuable time-saver. If you're like me you routinely look for the same information.

The Filter By Form can be saved as a query. Think of a query as a request to Access 2007 to do something, such as show all records that have Northwind Traders Chocolate or Northwind Traders Chocolate Biscuits as its Product ID. The query is loaded and then executed each time you want to make the same request to Access 2007.

To save a Filter By Form form:

1. Click Advanced on the Home tab.

2. Click Save As Query (see Figure 6.10).

3. Click OK (see Figure 6.11).

Figure 6.10. Click Save As Query to save the query.

Figure 6.11. Enter a name for the query and click OK to save it.

Inside Scoop

The filter is automatically added to the Unassigned Objects category in the left pane.

To load a Filter By Form form:

1. Click the Advanced tool on the Home tab.

2. Click Filter By Form to open a new Filter By Form form.

3. Click the Advanced tool on the Home tab again.

4. Click Load from Query to display the Applicable Filter dialog box (see Figure 6.12).

5. Double-click the filter name to load the filter.

6. Click Toggle Filter on the Home tab to apply the filter.

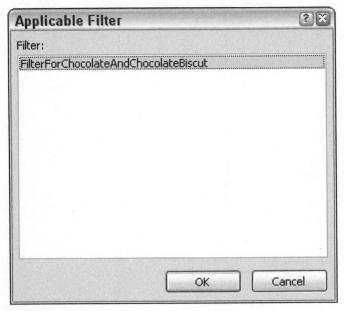

Figure 6.12. Double-click the filter name to load the filter.

You can modify the filter as described previously in this chapter and save it again either under its current name or under a new name using the Save As Query option on the Advanced tool.

Hack

Access 2007 combines values on the Or tab with values on the Look for tab when saving the query. These values appear in the field of the Look for tab when the query is loaded. Each value is within quotations and separated by the Or operator. The Or tab contains blank columns.

Advanced Filter/Sort

Filter By Form has advantages over using the ready-to-use filters because you can choose multiple values for the same field and save the filter as a query.

Ready-to-use filters and Filter By Form solve most of your filtering needs — most, but not all. You may find a need to filter records using an expression. Using expressions are as familiar to you as your telephone number because you create expressions every day — probably without realizing it — when you add numbers and perform simple math.

The Advanced Filter/Sort option in the Advanced tool on the Home tab enables you to create a complex filter using an expression.

Here's how it is done.

1. Double-click Inventory Transaction under Supporting Objects to open the Inventory Transactions datasheet.

2. Click Advanced in the Sort & Filter group on the Home tab.

3. Click Advanced Filter/Sort (see Figure 6.13).

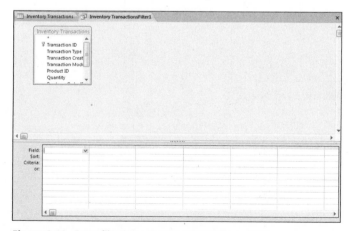

Figure 6.13. Enter filtering criteria at the bottom of the screen.

Access 2007 displays a query form, which you learn how to use in Chapter 8. At the top of the screen is a box that represents the table that is being filtered. The box lists all the fields of the table.

At the bottom of the screen is a grid that resembles a spreadsheet. Think of each column as a field and its rows as the filtering criteria.

- The first row is the name of the field.
- The second row is the sort order.
- The third row is the filter criteria for the field.
- The fourth and subsequent rows are alternative filter criteria for the field.

Let's get started by creating a simple filter using Advanced/Sort.

- Double-click Transaction Type in the table box. This places the field name in the first column.
- Enter 3 in the Criteria row (see Figure 6.14). This tells Access 2007 to use the third item on the pick list for that field, which is On Hold. You can view the pick list by opening the combo box for that field on the datasheet.
- Click Toggle Filter on the Home tab to apply the filter (see Figure 6.15).

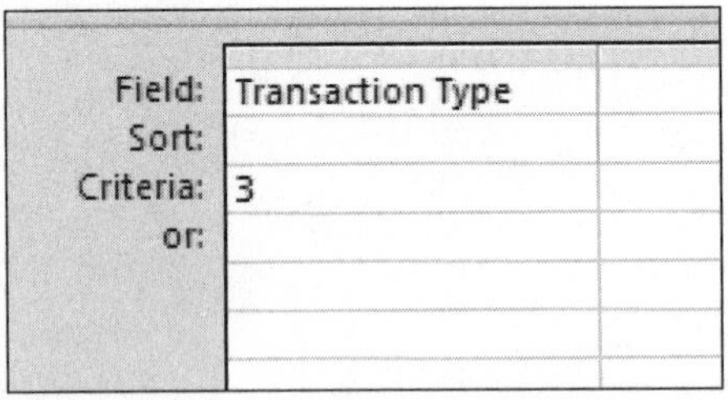

Figure 6.14. Enter the field name and criteria.

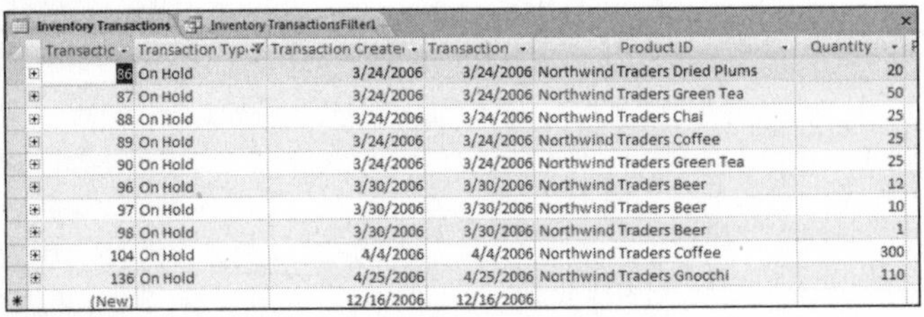

Transactic	Transaction Typ	Transaction Create	Transaction	Product ID	Quantity
86	On Hold	3/24/2006	3/24/2006	Northwind Traders Dried Plums	20
87	On Hold	3/24/2006	3/24/2006	Northwind Traders Green Tea	50
88	On Hold	3/24/2006	3/24/2006	Northwind Traders Chai	25
89	On Hold	3/24/2006	3/24/2006	Northwind Traders Coffee	25
90	On Hold	3/24/2006	3/24/2006	Northwind Traders Green Tea	25
96	On Hold	3/30/2006	3/30/2006	Northwind Traders Beer	12
97	On Hold	3/30/2006	3/30/2006	Northwind Traders Beer	10
98	On Hold	3/30/2006	3/30/2006	Northwind Traders Beer	1
104	On Hold	4/4/2006	4/4/2006	Northwind Traders Coffee	300
136	On Hold	4/25/2006	4/25/2006	Northwind Traders Gnocchi	110
(New)		12/16/2006	12/16/2006		

Figure 6.15. Records with On Hold are displayed.

Inside Scoop

You can toggle to Filter By Form, select a value, and return to the dialog box and the selected value is automatically entered into the dialog box.

Using the Expression Builder

The real power of using Advanced Filter/Sort comes from expressions. An expression lets you fine-tune the filter to display exactly the records that you need to see.

Expressions may not be your forte and could bring back the nightmares of math homework. Those days are long gone, thanks to the folks who developed Access 2007. They make creating expressions easy by using the Expression Builder.

You'll learn the ins and outs of using the Expression Builder in Chapter 9, but I'll give you a look here by modifying the filter created in the previous section. Our objective is to see all the On Hold transactions that have a quantity greater than 25.

Here's what to do.

1. Click the Inventory Transactions Filter1 tab under the Home tab to display the filter.

2. Double-click Quantity in the table box. This places the field name in the second column.

3. Right-click the Criteria row in the second column to display the pop-up menu.

4. Click Build to display the Expression Builder (see Figure 6.16).

Figure 6.16. Click Build to open the Expression Builder.

The top box is where the expression is displayed. Below it are operators that are probably familiar to you. I explain how to use each of them in Chapter 9.

Below the operators are three panes. The left pane contains objects that can be part of the expression. We're interested in tables of the Northwind 2007 database because that's where we'll find the Inventory Transaction datasheet.

1. Double-click Tables and a list of tables appears in the left pane.

2. Click Inventory Transaction and fields in the Inventory Transaction table are displayed in the center pane.

3. Double-click Quantity, and the Expression Builder inserts the table and field into the expression in the expression box.

4. Click the greater than operator, and the Expression Builder inserts it into the expression.

5. Type 25 to the right of the greater than operator in the expression to completes the expression (see Figure 6.17).

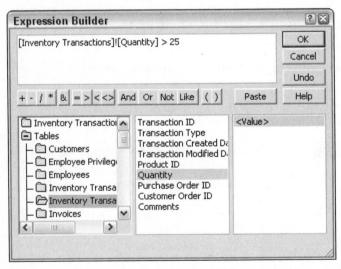

Figure 6.17. Use controls in the Expression Builder to create the expression.

6. Click OK to enter the expression into the filter.

7. Click Toggle Filter in the Home tab to apply the filter (see Figure 6.18).

Transactic ▪	Transaction Typ▪	Transaction Create ▪	Transaction ▪	Product ID	▪	Quantity ▪
87	On Hold	3/24/2006	3/24/2006	Northwind Traders Green Tea		50
104	On Hold	4/4/2006	4/4/2006	Northwind Traders Coffee		300
136	On Hold	4/25/2006	4/25/2006	Northwind Traders Gnocchi		110
(New)		12/16/2006	12/16/2006			

Figure 6.18. Records the are On Hold with a Quantity of greater than 25 are displayed.

Using the Filter Tool

The Filter tool is the big Filter icon in the Sort & Filter group on the Home tab and is a fast way to filter for multiple values in the same field. Say you want to see records that have Northwind Traders Beer and Northwind Traders Almonds as the Product ID. The Filter tool displays them within a few clicks.

Here's how it works:

1. Click the mouse in the Product ID field.

2. Click the Filter tool to display the pop-up menu containing a check box for each value in the Product ID field (see Figure 6.19).

3. Click Select All to uncheck all fields.

4. Click the check box of Northwind Traders Beer and Northwind Traders Almonds.

5. Click OK to apply the filter (see Figure 6.20).

Inside Scoop

Use the Filter tool to find records with blank fields by clicking the Blank check box.

Figure 6.19. Click values to include in the filter criteria.

Inventory Transactions					
Transactio ▾	Transaction Typ ▾	Transaction Created Date ▾	Transaction Modifiec ▾	Product ID	
52	Purchased	3/22/2006 4:04:41 PM	3/22/2006 4:04:41 PM	Northwind Traders Almonds	▾
60	Purchased	3/22/2006 4:05:51 PM	3/22/2006 4:05:51 PM	Northwind Traders Beer	
82	Purchased	3/24/2006 10:54:58 AM	3/24/2006 10:54:58 AM	Northwind Traders Beer	
83	Sold	3/24/2006 10:55:02 AM	3/24/2006 11:03:00 AM	Northwind Traders Beer	
96	On Hold	3/30/2006 4:46:34 PM	3/30/2006 4:46:34 PM	Northwind Traders Beer	
97	On Hold	3/30/2006 5:23:27 PM	3/30/2006 5:23:27 PM	Northwind Traders Beer	
98	On Hold	3/30/2006 5:24:33 PM	3/30/2006 5:24:33 PM	Northwind Traders Beer	
102	Purchased	4/4/2006 11:01:14 AM	4/4/2006 11:01:14 AM	Northwind Traders Beer	
107	Purchased	4/4/2006 11:02:17 AM	4/4/2006 11:02:17 AM	Northwind Traders Beer	
108	Sold	4/4/2006 11:02:19 AM	4/4/2006 11:08:14 AM	Northwind Traders Beer	
117	Sold	4/4/2006 11:04:55 AM	4/4/2006 11:05:04 AM	Northwind Traders Beer	
130	Sold	4/4/2006 11:40:32 AM	4/4/2006 11:40:38 AM	Northwind Traders Almonds	
(New)		7/16/2006 7:18:53 PM	7/16/2006 7:18:53 PM		

Figure 6.20. Here are the records that meet the filter criteria.

Sorting records

Sorting records is easy, which is why I left this topic for the end of the chapter. Simply select the field to sort, click a sort button, and Access 2007 rearranges records.

You'll find sort buttons in the Sort & Filter group on the Home tab (see Figure 6.21) and items on pop-up menus that you used in this chapter. There are two sets of sort buttons — ascending/descending and smaller to larger/larger to smaller. Ascending/descending is used for text fields and smaller to larger/larger to smaller is used for number and date/time fields.

Figure 6.21. Sort in ascending or descending order with a click of the mouse.

Sorting multiple fields

Sometimes you'll want to sort using more than one field. You might have last name and first name fields, for example, and you want to sort by last name and then by first name within the same last name. That is, sort first names for everyone whose last name is Smith.

Inside Scoop

The sort affects how records are displayed and doesn't have an effect on the underlying table. You click the Clear All Sorts to see records as they were before the sort.

This is possible by selecting more than one field. You'll probably need to move fields so they appear alongside each other. I showed you how to do this in Chapter 5.

Access 2007 sorts using the leftmost field to the rightmost field that you select. This means if you have last name, first name, Access 20007 sorts the last name and then the first name.

Watch out for strange sorts

You won't experience any surprises when sorting numbers, currency, dates, and time fields. However, text fields are another thing if they contain numbers and special characters such as blanks, punctuation, and symbols (i.e. %, &).

Access 2007 sorts numbers in a text field as single digits. It knows to place 4 before 5, but 44 is a little confusing because Access 2007 doesn't recognize 44 or other multiple-digit numbers as a single number. Instead, 44 is treated as two fours and is sorted as 4, 44, 5.

You're probably scratching your head wondering why this happens. Access 2007 is following the sorting rule for text, which is different than the sorting rule for numbers, currency, dates, and time. And that's why you place text in a text field and numbers in number, currency, and date/time fields.

Table 6.1 shows the sorting rules for special characters. Don't memorize this list. No one does. Instead, sort a field to see the order. Just keep in mind that the order may be different than you expect.

Table 6.1. Sorting rules in ascending order for special characters

Blank (null)
Space
|
"

#
%
&
(
, (comma)
. (period)
[
^
~
Letters (Case is ignored when sorting)
Numbers

Just the facts

■ A filter changes the selection of data that appears in a datasheet, form, report, or Layout view based on your filter criteria but leaves other data intact and out of sight.

■ The filter criteria consist of one or more values that Access 2007 compares to one or multiple fields in the underlying table.

■ There are five ways to create a filter — Selection, Ready-to-Use Filters, Filter By Form, Advanced Filter/Sort, and the Filter tool.

■ The fastest way to filter records is by using the Selection tool on the Home tab.

■ Ready-to-Use Filters are built-in filters picked from a pop-up menu by right-clicking a field in a datasheet, form, report, or in the Layout view.

GET THE SCOOP ON...
Importing/exporting essentials ▪ Importing/exporting
from SharePoint list ▪ Importing/exporting from Excel,
Word, XML, and PDF

Importing and Exporting Data

Hey, want to trade some data? Granted, no one asked you this recently, but data is traded all the time — not at the local swap meet but among colleagues in the office and between business partners.

Pawning off data entry on the unsuspecting new guy is passé, thanks to techniques that let you trade data in Access 2007 electronically with practically any application.

Officially this is called *importing and exporting data,* but I like to think of it as my own office grunt who takes the drudgery out of exchanging data.

Examining importing and exporting data

Importing and *exporting* are terms you have heard used to explain how goods made abroad are sold here (importing) and goods made here are sent abroad (exporting).

This same concept holds true with databases with one exception: The exchange occurs between databases, not countries. The exchange involves more than data. It also includes tables, queries, forms, reports, macros, modules, and relationships among tables. All of these are objects of the database.

Inside Scoop

Any data-entry errors in the original database are copied when the data is imported.

You can import/export an entire database, a table with or without its data, or just data, depending on your needs.

Save time

Importing/exporting data avoids the distasteful job of data entry. It simply doesn't make sense to enter data that is already available electronically when Access 2007 can do this for you.

I like to think of importing/exporting as a double time-saver.

Access 2007 loads a table with data in seconds, which might otherwise take a week of data entry.

There are no data entry errors! You don't have to spend time proofreading imported data because, unlike mere mortals, Access 2007 doesn't make typos.

Database applications are similar to each other. One is pretty much like another except for some tweaking. This is why Microsoft provides a bunch of database templates with Access 2007 (see Chapter 1).

When creating a new database application, look for a similar database application and import its objects into a new database. The data is left behind because data is usually different among database applications.

Table definitions, forms, reports, and queries are modified to conform to requirements of the new database application. Once tweaking is done, the new database application is ready for testing.

Enhance existing database applications quickly

Grab a feature from another user's application and save it to your system by importing the feature's objects then linking those objects to your database application. Objects such as a forms, controls, and tables are exchangeable between applications using Import and Export tools that are available on the External Data tab.

Avoid the pitfalls of importing/exporting

Importing/exporting does have traps, especially when borrowing a database. Make sure you avoid these common problems:

- **Excess baggage.** More database objects than needed are imported, resulting in a waste of resources.

- **Poor design.** The imported database application is not efficient

- **Time consuming.** Modifying the imported database takes longer than if it were built from scratch.

- **Lack skills to make modifications.** It is difficult to make modifications if you are unfamiliar with the workings of the imported database application.

- **Maintenance headache.** You know how the database application works to maintain it because someone else built it.

Importing and exporting essentials

Get ready to trade data! Well, not quite yet. I need to go over a few basics before you can import/export data and objects into your database.

It gets a little confusing when talking about where something comes from (exporting) and where it is going (importing). So to avoid any confusion I call the database where data or objects come from the *source* database and where it is going the *destination* database.

Another thing that's bound to confuse you is when I use the term *importing/exporting*. Is it importing or exporting? Actually, the action involves both terms, because often you do them at the same time. I'll use importing or exporting when I'm talking about doing these separately and importing/exporting when they are performed in the same process.

Think of importing/exporting as al a carte. If you import a form, report, query, and modules, you must also import tables and records it uses unless you import the complete database.

Therefore, if you import a report that lists customers, you get the report — not the customers. Customer data must also be imported. Don't be overly concerned because multiple database objects can be imported at the same time.

Preparing the database

You can export data from any Access database; however there are some restrictions for importing database objects into an Access 2007 database. Tables, queries, forms, reports, macros, and modules can only be imported if the source database has either the MDB or ACCDB file format. If it doesn't, then you're limited to importing data only.

No doubt at some point you'll run into this problem. The destination database already has an object with the same name as an object being imported from the source database. That is, both databases have a table called Customers.

The imported object does not overwrite the existing object. Each import operation creates a new object. The folks at Microsoft who design Access 2007 address conflicts by appending a number to the name of the duplicate object. This means that the imported Customer table is called Customer1. You can rename it.

Before importing/exporting:

1. Log onto the source and destination databases. Sometimes a user ID and password protects these.

2. Close the source database. The source database needs to be closed in order to import data from it and will be opened by the Import wizard.

3. Open the destination database. Make sure you have read/write access and permission to add data and objects to the database, otherwise you won't be permitted to import data or database objects from the source database.

4. Create a blank database (see Chapter 1) if you want to import data or database objects into a new database.

Importing/exporting records

Importing/exporting records is an all-or-nothing proposition. All records and fields must be exported from the source database and imported into the destination database. You cannot pick and choose records or fields.

Records cannot be imported directly into an existing table. Instead, records are copied into a new table and then you can append those records using an append query into an existing table. I'll show you how to do this later in this chapter.

Importing/exporting tables

You can import/export a table with all its data or simply the table definition. The table definition contains the same field definition as the table in the source database, except without the data.

Sometimes a table is a *linked* table. A linked table looks like the table it is linked to in another application except that its fields are linked to cells in another application, such as a spreadsheet. Changes made to the cell automatically appear in the field. (I show you how to link tables in this chapter.) When importing a linked table, you are importing the link.

Remember from Chapter 4 that tables are related to each other using foreign keys. These relationships are not automatically imported unless the whole source database is imported. However, you can import the relationship separately. You find out how this is done later in this chapter.

Another twist happens if the table you're importing has a lookup field. In Chapter 2, I discuss that a lookup field displays a list of values contained in another table or generated by a query. Access 2007 doesn't automatically import the table or query that contains values for the lookup field. You must import these separately; otherwise the lookup field displays only the lookup IDs.

Importing/exporting forms and reports

As you find out in Chapter 12 (forms) and Chapter 16 (reports), forms and reports can contain subforms and subreports. For example, say a form shows a list of customers. Selecting a customer from the list opens a subform that contains orders placed by that customer.

When a form or report is imported into the destination database, its subforms and subreports and its data are left behind in the source database. You must import subforms, subreports, and their data, too. Access 2007 doesn't automatically import these for you.

Importing/exporting queries

A query is a request to Access 2007 to retrieve data and place it into a datasheet. I like to think of this datasheet as a temporary table because the datasheet looks like and acts like a permanent table.

Inside Scoop

Remember that tables used by the query are not automatically imported.

Depending on the needs of your Access 2007 database, when importing/exporting a query you choose to import/export:

- The query.
- The data the query generates.
- Both, depending on the needs of your Access 2007 database application.

   Keep these points in mind when importing/exporting a query:

- If you import the query, then you don't get the data. You'll have to run the query in the destination database to generate the data.
- If you import the data, then the data is placed into a new table in the destination database, but you don't get the query.
- If you import both, then you get the query and the data is automatically inserted into a new table in the destination database.

Importing/exporting data using Copy and Paste

Get ready to trade data! Yes, it's time! The easiest, fastest way is to copy and paste, but you probably figured that out on your own.

   You can copy data from many applications including Excel and Word and paste it into a field or an entire record in a datasheet, depending on the requirements of your Access 2007 database application.

Importing from Excel

Try this by copying data from an Excel spreadsheet and pasting it into a datasheet. You can copy a cell, a complete row, or the entire spreadsheet.

   I'll be using the Customers Datasheet in the Northwind Traders database to illustrate how to copy and paste data into a table of your database. You'll find the Customers Datasheet in the Support Object section of the database.

To copy a cell:

1. Highlight a cell in the spreadsheet.

2. Press Ctrl+C or right-click the cell and click Copy to copy it to the Clipboard.

3. Double-click a field in a table.

4. Press Ctrl+V or right-click the field and click Paste to copy the data from the Clipboard into the field.

To copy a row to a record of an existing table:

1. Make sure the sequence of columns in the spreadsheet matches the sequence of fields in the datasheet. Insert a blank column as the first column. Access 2007 replaces the blank with the primary key when entering a new record into the table.

2. Click the row number to highlight the entire row (see Figure 7.1).

3. Press Ctrl+C or right-click the cell and click Copy to copy it to the Clipboard.

4. Click the leftmost column in the (New) record of the datasheet. This is where you enter a new record.

5. Press Ctrl+V or right-click the field and click Paste to copy the data from the Clipboard into a new row in the table (see Figure 7.2).

Figure 7.1. Highlight the row you want to copy.

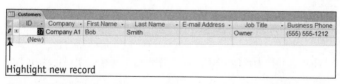

Figure 7.2. Select the (New) record and paste data from the Clipboard.

To copy multiple rows to multiple records an existing table:

1. Make sure that the sequence of columns in the spreadsheet matches the sequence of fields in the datasheet.

2. Highlight all the rows.

3. Press Ctrl+C or right-click a cell and click Copy to copy it to the Clipboard.

4. Click the leftmost column in the (New) record of the datasheet. This is where you enter a new record.

5. Press Ctrl+V or right-click the field and click Paste to copy the data from the Clipboard into new rows of the table. Access 2007 asks you to confirm that you want to paste four records. Click OK.

To copy an entire spreadsheet into a new table:

1. Enter column names in the first row of the spreadsheet. These become field names.

2. Leave the first column blank. This becomes the primary key field that Access 2007 automatically populates.

3. Highlight all rows in the spreadsheet.

4. Press Ctr+C or right-click a cell and click Copy to copy it to the Clipboard.

5. Click the Create tab to open the Create tab in Access 2007.

6. Double-click Table to create a new table.

7. Click the leftmost column in the (New) record of the datasheet.

8. Press Ctrl+V or right-click the field and click Paste to copy the data from the Clipboard into the table. Access 2007 asks you to confirm that you want to paste four records. Click OK.

Exporting to Excel

Exporting data from a datasheet to Excel using copy and paste is straightforward. Do the following:

1. Drag the cursor down the first column of the datasheet to highlight records you want to copy.

2. Press Ctrl+C or right-click a cell and click Copy to copy it to the Clipboard.

Inside Scoop

Access 2007 determines the data type of fields copied from Excel based on the kind of data appearing in the cell. You can modify the field definition after saving the new datasheet (see Chapter 4).

Inside Scoop

Access 2007 exports field names that become the first row of the spreadsheet.

3. Click the first cell of the spreadsheet.

4. Press Ctrl+V or right-click the field and click Paste to copy the data from the Clipboard into the spreadsheet.

Importing from Word

There are two situations when you'll want to import data from Word — when copying free-form data in a Word document or data stored in a Word table. *Free-form* data is any data that isn't in a Word table (see Figure 7.3).

Free-form data must be copied into a single field, even though it may contain data designated for more than one field. Access 2007 doesn't know how to break up the data. If you want free-form data imported into separate fields, then convert it to a Word table.

Copying data from a Word table is the same as copying data from an Excel spreadsheet.

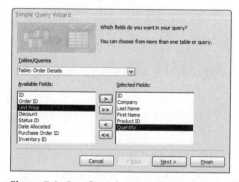

Figure 7.3. Free-form data must be imported into one cell.

Inside Scoop

If you try importing free-form data into a complete record, Access 2007 places the free-form data into the first field and then overwrites the first field with the primary key. As a result, no data is imported into the datasheet.

Inside Scoop

All data in a Word table is treated as text.

Exporting to Word

Exporting records from a datasheet into Word is basically the same as processing as exporting a record to Excel. Access 2007 copies the field names and selected records from the datasheet and places them on the Clipboard.

Word creates a Word table that corresponds to the data on the Clipboard and then places the table name in the first row of the Word table, adds field headers to the second row, and then populates other rows with the remaining data from the Clipboard.

Copying and pasting into another table

The copy/paste technique also works to copy data from a datasheet to another datasheet. The definition of the destination datasheet must match that of the source datasheet, unless the destination datasheet is a new datasheet. In this case, Access 2007 copies the definition of the source datasheet to the new datasheet and then fills it with data that you're copying.

Here's how to do it:

1. Drag the cursor down the first column of the datasheet to highlight records you want to copy.

2. Press Ctrl+C or right-click a cell and click Copy to copy it to the Clipboard.

3. Click the leftmost column in the (New) record of the datasheet.

4. Press Ctrl+V or right-click the field and click Paste to copy the data from the Clipboard into the table. Access 2007 asks you to confirm that you want to paste four records. Click OK.

Exploring the Import and Export wizards

Copy and pasting is fine when you need to quickly trade data. It's easy and quick to do, but limiting, too. You can't import/export forms, reports, and other database objects by copying and pasting.

The pros prefer to use the Import wizard and Export wizard for trading data and database objects.

The Import wizard is used to import an object from another database into the destination database. It is also used to convert data from one format into the Access 2007 format and store the data in the destination database. Use the Import wizard to import from:

- Access database
- Excel
- Text file
- XML file
- SharedPoint List
- ODBC database
- HTML document
- Outlook Folder

The Export wizard is used to copy a database object from the source database to the destination database and to convert data from the Access 2007 data form to another format so the data can be directly used by another application. Use the Export wizard to export to:

- Access database
- Excel
- Text file
- XML file
- SharedPoint List
- ODBC database
- HTML document
- Word RTF file
- PDF or XPS
- DBASE file
- Paradox file
- Lotus 1-2-3 file
- Merge with Microsoft Office Word file

Using the Import wizard

Okay, you didn't buy this book to learn how to use a wizard. After all, the wizard is designed to walk you through the process. However, there are a few hints that I can give to make using the wizard easier to use.

First, create a blank database so that you have a destination database. I called mine Destination Database. (This isn't very creative, but it will do for our examples.)

To import from an Access database, follow these steps:

1. Click the External Data tab.

2. Click Access (see Figure 7.4).

Figure 7.4. External Data tab.

3. Click Browse to display the File Open dialog box (see Figure 7.5).

Figure 7.5. Click Browse and select the source database.

4. Double-click the name of the source database. The name appears in the filename text box. I selected Northwind 2007.

5. Click the Import tables, queries, forms, reports, macros, and modules into the current database radio button. This is the default setting.

6. Click OK to display the Import Objects dialog box (see Figure 7.6).

7. Click the Tables tab (default) or the tab containing the database objects that you want to import into the destination database.

8. Click the table(s) you want to import. Click it a second time to deselect it. I clicked both tables. You can also click Select All if you want to import all the tables.

Figure 7.6. Click objects to import into the destination database.

9. **Click OK.** Access 2007 asks if you want to save these import steps. If this is a one-time import, then leave the Save import steps check box unchecked. If you plan to import that same data or objects from the source database, then click the check box. Access 2007 creates a shortcut for importing the source database to the destination database (see "Creating an import shortcut").

10. **Click Close** to import the source database into the destination database. The names of the imported objects appear in the All Tables pane (see Figure 7.7).

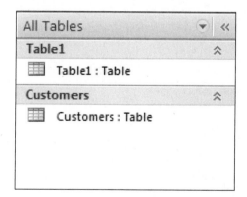

Figure 7.7. Imported objects are displayed in the All Tables pane of the destination database.

Creating an import shortcut

At one point in my career, it was my job to import sales data each week from the corporate sales database into an Access database so that I could use macros I wrote to analyze the sales data.

Access has a great feature to streamline this process. Instead of using the Import wizard, you can click a button and Access 2007 imports the data. This is an import shortcut.

All right, it is slightly more involved than clicking a button because you have to create the import shortcut.

Follow these steps to create the shortcut:

1. Select items to import using the Import wizard, like I showed you in the previous section.

2. Click the Save the import steps check box when prompted. Access 2007 displays the Save Import Steps dialog box (see Figure 7.8).

3. Click Create Outlook task if you want Outlook to remind you to import the data.

4. Click Save Import to create the shortcut and import the selected database objects into the destination database.

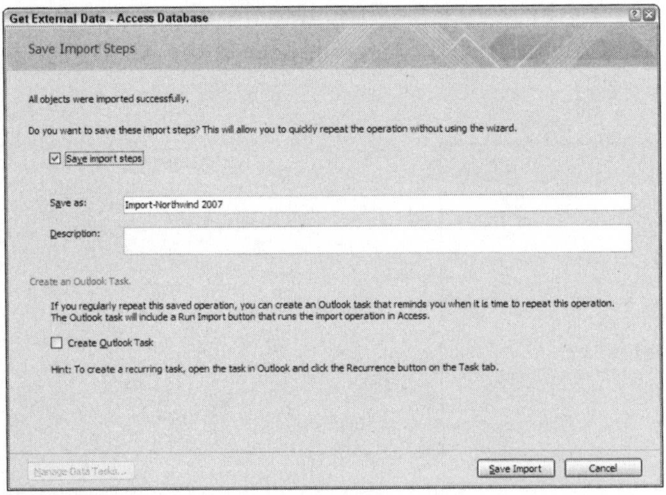

Figure 7.8. Enter a name for the shortcut.

Inside Scoop

The Outlook task includes a Run Import button so that you can run the import right from Outlook. Click the Reoccurrence button in Outlook to make the import task recurring.

Running an import shortcut

After the import shortcut is created, you can run it — and any other import shortcut — from the External Data tab.

Here's what you need to do:

1. Click the External Data tab.

2. Click Saved Import to display the Manage Data Tasks dialog box (see Figure 7.9).

3. Click the Saved Imports tab (default).

4. Click the shortcut.

5. Click the Run button to import the data.

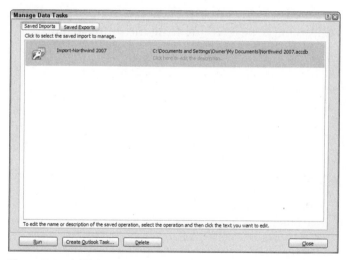

Figure 7.9. Highlight the shortcut and click the Run button to import the data.

Using importing options

The folks who designed Access 2007 turned on the commonly used import options for you. However, occasionally you want some of those options turned off and others turned on. After you save the import, you can't go back and adjust the options.

Here's how you turn on and off import options:

1. Click Options at the Import Objects when you're importing data or database objects to see your options (see Figure 7.10).

2. Select the Relationships check box if you don't want to import relationships among database objects such as tables. This is turned on by default because it makes sense to maintain relationships in the destination database after objects are imported.

3. Select the Definition Only option if you want to import only the table definition and not the data, too. Choose this if you are replicating tables but not the data.

4. Select the As Tables option if you want to import data generated by queries and not the query. Access 2007 runs each query in the source database. Data the query generates is imported into a new table in the destination database.

5. Select the Menus and Toolbars, Import/Export Specs, and Nav Pane Groups if you want to import everything from the source database.

Figure 7.10. Click options to tailor the import to your needs.

Importing from Excel into a new table

Colleagues of mine are always providing an Excel spreadsheet that I have to load into my Access 2007 application. This is easy to do if you use the Import wizard for Excel.

Here's how to import the Excel spreadsheet into a new table:

1. Open the database (see Chapter 1).

2. Click the External Data tab.

3. Click Excel in the Import group to open the Import wizard for Excel.

4. Click the Browse button to display the File Open dialog box.

5. Double-click the name of the Excel file. The name appears in the filename text box (see Figure 7.11).

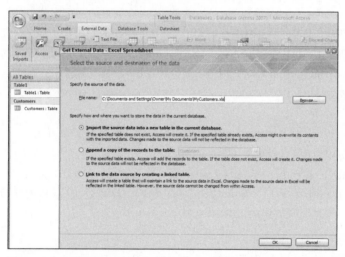

Figure 7.11. Click Browse and select the Excel spreadsheet to import.

6. Select the Import the source data into a new table in the current database (default).

7. Click OK to display the Import Spreadsheet wizard (see Figure 7.12). The Import Spreadsheet wizard shows you worksheets in the Excel Workbook and can show Named Ranges.

8. Click the Worksheet or Named Range you want to import.

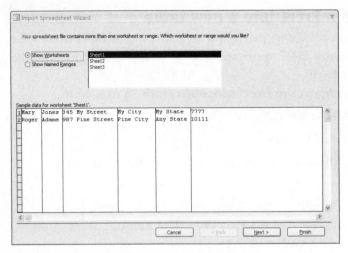

Figure 7.12. Select the Worksheet you want to import.

9. Click Next to refine the import specifications or click Finish to begin importing the Worksheet.

10. If you clicked Next, select the First Row Contains Column Headings if the first row in the spreadsheet is column headings; otherwise leave this unchecked.

11. Click Next to refine the import specifications or click Finish to begin importing the Worksheet.

12. If you clicked Next, enter the field options. This becomes the field definition (see Figure 7.13). Select the Do not import field (Skip) check box if you don't want to import this column.

Figure 7.13. Enter options for the field.

13. Click Next to refine the import specifications or click Finish to begin importing the Worksheet.

14. If you clicked Next, an ID column is inserted into the Worksheet for the primary key (see Figure 7.14). You are given three options: have Access 2007 insert the primary key, choose your own primary key, or don't have a primary key for the table. I prefer to have Access 2007 insert the primary key.

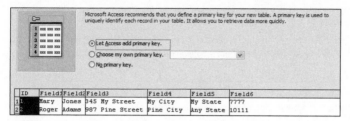

ID	Field1	Field2	Field3	Field4	Field5	Field6
1	Mary	Jones	345 My Street	My City	My State	7777
2	Roger	Adams	987 Pine Street	Pine City	Any State	10111

Figure 7.14. Choose specifications for the primary key.

15. Click Next to refine the import specifications or click Finish to begin importing the Worksheet.

16. If you clicked Next, the wizard is ready to import the Worksheet. You'll find two check boxes. One has the wizard analyze the new table after the data is imported. The other displays help after the wizard is finished. Click these if you wish.

17. Click Finish to import the data into a new datasheet. You'll also prompted to save the import steps in a shortcut, which I showed previously in this chapter.

18. Click Close and the new table appears in the All Tables pane under the name Sheet1. Double-click it to open it in a datasheet and then rename the fields to an appropriate name. Access 2007 calls them Field1, Field2, etc.

Importing from Excel into an existing table

Appending rows from an Excel spreadsheet directly into a datasheet is the best way to add data from the spreadsheet to an Access 2007 table. There are alternatives but few developers use them, so it's not worth mentioning them here.

Follow the same steps as you do to import rows into a new table, except click the Append a copy of the records to table radio button instead of clicking Import the source data into a new table in the current database.

After clicking the radio button, select the destination table from the list of tables in the combo box (see Figure 7.15). Click OK to start importing the data. You'll see the same screens as you do when importing the spreadsheet into a new table.

Watch Out!

Make sure that columns in the spreadsheet coincide with the destination table and close the destination table before you attempt to append records to it.

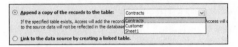

Figure 7.15. Choose the destination table and click OK to append records from the spreadsheet.

Importing a text file

A text file is the fallback file format used to trade data if Access 2007 doesn't understand another application's file format. You probably heard the term *text file* used as a format for saving a document such as a Word doc without formatting and other special characters you don't see in a document.

You can also save data in a text file; however, you'll need to tell Access 2007 or other applications that read the text file where records and fields begin. Otherwise, Access 2007 tries to squish all the data into one field. It uses line breaks to separate records, which is probably not what you wanted.

Access 2007 starts reading a text file at the beginning of the text file. All right, it didn't take a rocket scientist to figure that out.

Access 2007 keeps reading until it encounters the end-of-line character or the end of the file, whichever comes first. Characters up to this point are considered data of one record. The end-of-line character is inserted into the text file when you press the Enter key or by the application that exported the file.

Fields within a record are identified in one of two ways: by delimiter or by fixed width. A delimiter is a character used as a marker to tell Access 2007 where a field ends and another begins. The end-of-line character is a delimiter that tells Access 2007 where a record ends and another begins.

Delimited versus fixed width

A comma or tab is common delimiter for a field, although any character could be used. If a comma is used, the file is said to be comma delimited. If a tab is used, the file is called a tab-delimited file.

Inside Scoop

Each line you see on the screen may not be considered a record. Word and other applications use word wrap that takes a long line of text and wraps it around on the screen, giving the appearance of many lines when in fact there is one line.

Fixed width is where fields within the text file are defined by a specific number of characters, such as 2 characters for a state abbreviation, or 20 characters for a first name. Data that is shorter than the fixed width for the field are padded with spaces. So if the first name has 15 characters, 5 spaces are added at the end to fill out the field.

Delimited or fixed width, which should you choose? You probably don't have a choice because the person who exports the text file makes that decision, although you could request one or the other.

Creating a delimited text file

You can begin by creating a delimited text file. The easiest way to create a delimited text file is to use Excel. Here what to do:

1. Create an Excel spreadsheet where columns correspond to fields in a table. I'm using the Customers spreadsheet and table that I created previously in this chapter.

2. Enter data into the spreadsheet.

3. Click File ⇨ Save As.

4. Select the Save as type. You'll see tab delimited, space delimited and comma delimited. I picked comma delimited.

5. Click Save.

Importing a delimited text file

Importing the delimited text file is straightforward because Access 2007 has a Text File Import wizard that walks you through the process. Do the following:

1. Click the External Data tab.

2. Click Text File to start the Text File Import wizard. Looks familiar? It should because the opening screen is the same as the other Import wizard you saw previously in this chapter.

3. Select the text file and click either Import to a new table or Append to an existing table.

4. Click OK to display the Import Text wizard (see Figure 7.16).

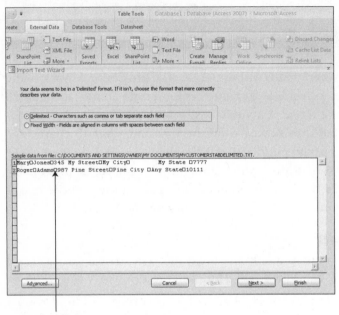

Comma delimiters

Figure 7.16. Access 2007 is smart and scans the text file to determine if it is delimited or fixed width.

5. Click Finish, if it looks like Access 2007 correctly read the delimiters in the same data. This begins importing the text file.

6. Click Next, if you need to tweak the importing specification (see Figure 7.17).

If you clicked Next, click the character used as the delimiter character. The person who created the delimited text file can tell you which character to use or you can display the text file in Notepad or another text editor and look for yourself.

7. Click the character used as the Text Qualifier.

8. Click Finish if it looks like Access 2007 correctly read the delimiters in the same data. Doing this begins importing the text file.

9. Click Next, if you need to tweak the importing specification.

If you click Next, you see the same options are you saw with the other Import wizard.

Hack

The application that created the text file might use a Text Qualifier character to distinguish between text and nontext data, such as numbers. Usually single or double quotation marks are used as the Text Qualifier and are used to enclose text data in the file. Numbers, dates, and other kinds of files are not enclosed with the Text Qualifier.

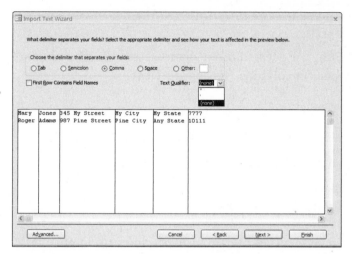

Figure 7.17. Click the character used as the delimiter in the text file.

Importing a fixed width text file

Importing a fixed width text file is nearly the same as importing a delimited text file, but with a twist. Before showing you how this is done, create a fixed width text file by following these steps:

1. Save an Excel spreadsheet as a tab-delimited text file.

2. Open the tab-delimited text file in Notepad. Data seems to be separated by spaces, but they're really tab characters.

3. Place the cursor at the start of each data (except the first because its at the beginning of the line) and press Backspace to remove the tab character.

4. Press the spacebar several times until data on each line forms a column. Make sure the font is Courier New or other fixed-width font.

5. Save the file.

Now that you have the fixed-width text file, it's time to show you how to import it into Access 2007.

6. Click Text File on the External Data tab to open the Text File Import wizard.

7. Select the fixed-width text file as I showed you previously in this chapter.

8. Click OK. The Text File Import wizard reads the file and guesses it is a fixed-width text file.

9. Click Fixed Width, if it guessed other than fixed width. The sample data should appear in columns (see Figure 7.18).

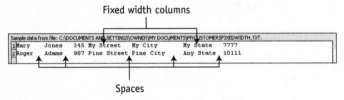

Figure 7.18. Columns are defined by a fixed width.

10. Click Finish, if data seems to line up properly, to begin importing the data.

11. Click Next, if the data seems out of alignment or if you want to see where the wizard thinks each field begins. The wizard draws a line showing where each field begins.

12. Modify the field alignment by dragging and dropping each line into the proper position (see Figure 7.19).

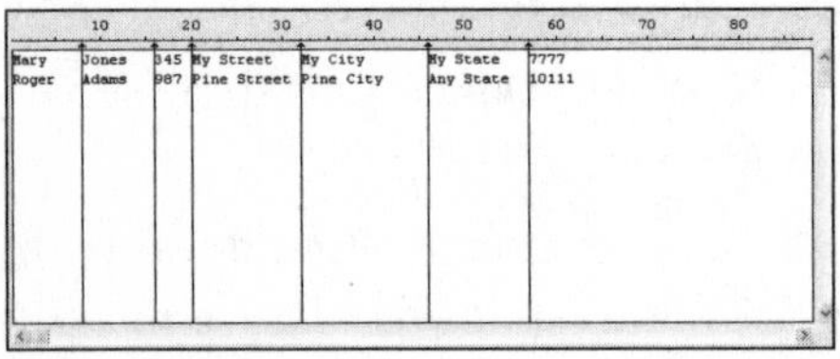

Figure 7.19. Drag and drop each line to define fields.

13. Click Finish, if you are satisfied with the realignment, to begin importing the data.

14. Click Next, if you wish to set the other importing options that I told you about previously in this chapter.

Importing from an XML file

XML is gaining popularity as a way to describe data in an XML document using a standard set of symbols called a *markup language*. Think of XML as a way to write a field name and data itself in a text file that contains the .xml file extension.

Use these steps to create an XML document before I show you how to import it into a table:

1. Open Notepad.

2. Enter the following:

```
<?xml version="1.0" encoding="UTF-8"?>
<dataroot xmlns:od="urn:schemas-microsoft-com:officedata"
generated="2006-08-07T15:16:40">
<Customer>
<ID>1</ID>
<FirstName>Bob</FirstName>
<LastName>Smith</LastName>
</Customer>
</dataroot>
```

3. Save the file as customername.xml.

Now you can import this XML document. Here what you need to do.

4. Click XML File on the External Data tab to start the XML File Import wizard.

5. Select the XML document as the source of the data as I showed you previously in this chapter.

6. Click OK and the wizard loads data from the XML document into a new table.

Importing from a SharePoint list

SharePoint is one of the strange-sounding features that most of us rarely use outside of work. It's a Microsoft tool, referred to as a service, which lets you and your colleagues collaborate on the same information without losing track of who changed what. SharePoint keeps track of versions of the information and checks it in and out like a librarian.

You can import a SharePoint list into Access 2007 using the SharePoint List Import wizard. In doing so, the wizard converts SharePoint list data types to Access 2007 data types. Table 7-1 shows the data type conversions.

Here's how to import a SharePoint list:

1. Click SharePoint List on the External Data tab to start the SharePoint List Import wizard

2. Enter the SharePoint site into the SharePoint List wizard and click Next.

3. Select the SharePoint list that you want to import.

4. Click Finish to import the SharePoint list.

Table 7.1. Data type conversions from SharePoint list to Access 2007

SharePoint Data Type	Access Data Type
ID	AutoNumber
Modified, Created	Date/Time (Read-only)
Modified by, Created by	Text
Single line of text	Text
Multiple Lines of text	Memo
Number	Number
Currency	Currency
Date/Time	Date/Time
Lookup	Number
Choice (single)	Text
Choice (multiple)	Memo (Read-only in a linked table)

SharePoint Data Type	Access Data Type
Grid Choice	Memo (Read-only in a linked table)
Yes/No	Yes/No
Hyperlink	Hyperlink
Attachment/Picture	Hyperlink (Read-only)
Computed	Any one of the following: Text Number Currency Date/Time Yes/No The field is Read-only
Rich Text	Memo

Importing from an HTML document

Occasionally, you may want to import an HTML document such as a Web page into your database so that you can make it part of a form or report. You do this by using the HTML Import wizard.

An HTML document contains HTML markup code that describes information in the HTML document. The wizard strips the HTML markup code from the information and stores only the information in the database.

Here's how to do this.

1. Click More on the External Data tab to see a list of import wizards.

2. Click HTML Document to start the HTML Import wizard.

3. Enter the name of the HTML document similar to when you imported other files into Access 2007.

4. Click OK. The HTML Document Import wizard loads any table in the HTML document into the same data area of the wizard.

5. Click Finish to import the data.

6. Click Next to fine-tune the import specifications as I showed you previously in this chapter.

Importing from an Outlook folder

Outlook contains a lot of contacts and other important information that you might want to store in an Access 2007 database. This is easily accomplished by using the Outlook Folder Import wizard.

Here's what you need to do to import an Outlook Folder:

1. Click More on the External Data tab to see a list of import wizards.

2. Click Outlook Folder to start the Outlook Folder Import wizard.

3. Click the Outlook Folder that you want to import (see Figure 7.20).

4. Click Finish to import the Outlook Folder into an Access 2007 table.

5. Click Next to fine-tune the import specifications.

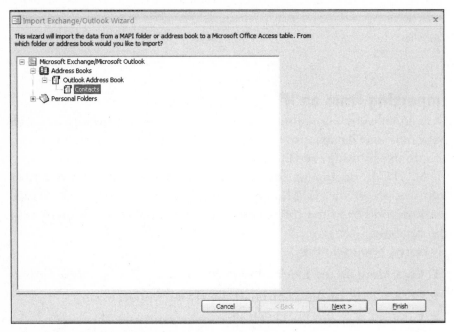

Figure 7.20. Click the Outlook Folder that you want to import.

Importing from an ODBC database

What the heck is ODBC, you're probably asking. ODBC is Open Database Connectivity standard developed back in the early days of PC databases. This standard's purpose is to make it possible to access any data from any application.

Access 2007 can import data from any ODBC database; however, it is more involved than importing data from other database formats that I showed you so far in this chapter.

Refer to Windows online help to learn how to set up an ODBC database connection. It isn't difficult to do, but more involved than I have space to explain in this book.

After the connection is established, then do the following:

1. Click More on the External Data tab to see a list of import wizards.

2. Click ODBC Database to start the ODBC Database Import wizard.

3. Click Import the source data into a new table in the current database.

4. Click OK.

5. Select the ODBC Database from the Select Data Source dialog box.

6. Click OK to import the ODBC Database.

Import dBase, Paradox, Lotus 1-2-3

The folks who design Access 2007 didn't forget the old-timers. I'm talking about the granddaddies of databases, dBase and Paradox and the granduncle of spreadsheets, Lotus 1-2-3.

Access 2007 has an import wizard for each. You can find them by clicking More on the External Data tab. These import wizards work the same as the others that I showed you earlier in the chapter, so I won't bore you with going over something you already know.

Using the Export wizard

What comes into an Access 2007 database can also be exported into another file format by using one of the many export wizards that you'll find on the External Data tab.

Exporting is fairly straightforward as you probably imagined after learning how to import data into an Access 2007 database. The Export wizard knows the format of the source file, so it can handle nearly all exporting chores without your help.

Exporting to Excel

Begin exporting an Access 2007 table to Excel by opening a database and then clicking the name of the Access 2007 table in the All Tables pane. You don't have to open the table.

Here's what to do next:

1. Click Excel in the Export group of the External Data tab. This starts the Excel Export wizard.

2. Enter a name for the Excel spreadsheet. The wizard uses the Access 2007 table name by default.

3. Select the Excel Workbook format. Use the default unless an older version of Excel is going to read the spreadsheet.

4. Click Export data with formatting and layout if you want to preserve the format or layout of the table. I usually leave this unchecked.

5. Click OK to export. The wizard asks you if you want to save the export steps, which I explained previously in this chapter.

6. Click Close.

Exporting to a text file

Exporting a table to a text file is almost as easy as exporting to Excel. Here's how to do it:

1. Click Text File in the Export group of the External Data tab. This starts the Text File Export wizard.

2. Enter a name for the text file. The wizard uses the Access 2007 table name by default.

3. Click Export data with formatting and layout if you want to preserve the format or layout of the table. I usually leave this unchecked.

4. Click OK. The wizard gives you the choice to export as a delimited text file or fixed-width text file. These are the same choices you have when importing a text file. Your choice depends on the format requested by the person who is going to use the text file. When in doubt I always use the default choice, which is Delimited.

5. Click Finish to export the table.

6. Click Next to fine-tune the export specifications. I showed you how this is done when you learned how to import a text file.

Exporting to a PDF or XPS file

A popular request these days is to export an Access 2007 database object as a PDF or XPS file, so Adobe Reader can read it. Here's how to export it:

1. Click PDF or XPS in the Export group of the External Data tab. This starts the PDF or XPS Export wizard.

2. Enter a name for the PDF or XPS file. The wizard uses the Access 2007 table name by default.

3. Click Publish to export.

Exporting to a SharePoint list

You can share your table or database object with your colleagues by exporting it as a SharePoint list to a SharePoint site. The SharePoint List wizard converts Access 2007 data types to SharePoint data types (see Table 7.2). Here's how its done:

1. Click SharePoint List in the Export group of the External Data tab. Doing this starts the SharePoint List Export wizard.

2. Enter the name of the SharePoint site.

3. Enter a name for the SharePoint list. The wizard uses the Access 2007 table name by default.

4. Enter a description for the SharePoint list. This is optional but I usually describe the table and how it relates to what we're doing at work.

5. Click Open the list when finished. This is the default setting. I leave this checked because this is a fast way to verify that the SharePoint list was exported.

6. Click OK to export.

Table 7.2. Data type conversion from Access 2007 to a SharePoint list

Access Data Type	SharePoint Data Type
Text	Single line of text
Memo	Multiple lines of text
Number	Number
Date/Time	Date/Time
Currency	Currency
AutoNumber	Number
AutoNumber where the Field Size property is set to Replication ID	Single line of text
Yes/No	Yes/No
OLE Object	The field is not exported
Hyperlink	Hyperlink

Exporting to an XML document

There is an increasing demand to export data and database objects as XML documents. Exporting is fairly easy.

1. Click More in the Export group on the External Data tab to see a list of export wizards.

2. Click XML Document.

3. Enter a name for the XML document. The wizard uses the Access 2007 table name by default.

4. Click the XML format. Use the default selections.

5. Click OK to export.

Exporting to an HTML document

You can create an HTML document from a table with three clicks of the mouse. Four, if you want to export the format or layout.

Here's how:

1. Click More in the Export group on the External Data tab to see a list of export wizards.

2. Click the HTML Document link.

3. Enter a name for the HTML document. The wizard uses the Access 2007 table name by default.

4. Click Export data with formatting and layout if you want to preserve the format or layout of the table. I usually leave this unchecked.

5. Click OK to export.

Exporting to dBase, Paradox, Lotus 1-2-3

Exporting an Access 2007 to these old-timers requires three clicks of the mouse.

1. Click More in the Export group on the External Data tab to see a list of export wizards.

2. Click dBase or Paradox or Lotus 1-2-3 Document.

3. Enter a name for the table or spreadsheet. The wizard uses the Access 2007 table name by default.

4. Select the format from a list of versions of dBase or Paradox or Lotus 1-2-3. Use the default format when in doubt.

5. Click OK to export.

Exporting to an ODBC database

The ODBC Database Export wizard can export a table to any application that uses the ODBC standard. Here's how.

1. Click More in the Export group on the External Data tab to see a list of export wizards.

2. Click ODBC Database.

3. Enter a name for the table. The wizard uses the Access 2007 table name by default.

4. Click OK.

5. Select the ODBC database to export to.

6. Click OK to export.

Merge with Word

Merge with Word is very similar to mail merge that you probably used in Word to create personalized form letters and envelopes. The main difference is the contact information is contained in an Access 2007 database.

Here's how this is done:

1. Open a database.

2. Click the table in the All Tables pane. You don't have to open it. The table contains data you want to merge with a Word document.

3. Click More in the Export group on the External Data tab to see a list of export wizards.

4. Click Merge it with Microsoft Office Word.

5. Click Link your data to an existing Microsoft Word document, if you already have one created. You'll then be prompted to select the name of the document.

6. Click Create a new document and then link the data to it, if you don't have a document created. This is what I selected.

7. Click OK. An empty document opens in the window with Mail Merge already running (see Figure 7.21).

8. Click Insert Merge Field to see a list of fields from the Access 2007 table.

9. Click a field and the field appears at the cursor position in the document.

10. The Word Mail Merge wizard walks you through creating the rest of the Mail Merge document.

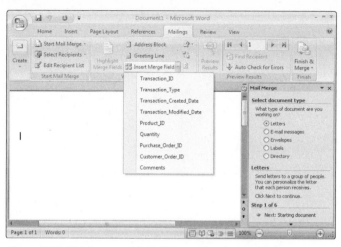

Figure 7.21. Word opens with Mail Merge already opened.

Just the facts

- The source database contains data or other database objects that are inserted into Access 2007.

- The destination database is the Access 2007 database that receives data and other database objects from the source database.

- Importing is copying data or database objects from the source database to an Access 2007 database.

- Exporting is copying data or database objects from an Access 2007 database to a source database.

- An Import wizard is a tool in Access 2007 that walks you through the steps of importing data or database objects into an Access 2007 database.

- An Export wizard is a tool in Access 2007 that walks you through the steps of exporting data or database objects from an Access 2007 database to a source database.

PART III

Creating Queries

GET THE SCOOP ON...
Ad hoc query ▪ Using summary options ▪ Querying
a query ▪ Mastering the Query Design tool ▪
Fine-tuning the Query wizard

Creating a Query

Access 2007 can tell you the product that will make you the most money — assuming the right data is in the database.

Ask the question correctly and Access 2007 answers it in seconds.

In this chapter, I show you how to write questions and ask Access 2007 to answer them.

Asking a query

A query is a request for data stored in the database or for data that can be calculated using information stored in the database. For example, you can write a query asking to see all the orders for John Smith and Access 2007 rummages through the database and returns John Smith's orders. Likewise, you can ask for the number of orders that have been placed for this month. Access 2007 counts this month's orders and returns the total to you.

A query is written using the Query wizard or the Query Design tool found within the Other group on the Create tab. These let you create your query with as little actual writing as possible. It is breeze, so don't sweat thinking that you have to learn another language. You don't because the

Chapter 8

Inside Scoop

Take a look at the SQL generated by Access 2007. Right-click anywhere in the Query Design tool and click SQL View from the pop-up menu. Look but don't touch unless you know SQL. If you do, then feel free to use the SQL View to write a query using SQL.

Query wizard and the Query Design tools translate your request into Structured Query Language (SQL), which is the language that Access 2007 and other database software understand.

Ad hoc query

An ad hoc query is the kind you create when you need that last bit of information before your next meeting — the one that starts in five minutes. An ad hoc query is also used for the one-off requests that will never be made again.

You create and run the query, make note of the information, and exit without saving the query.

Saved queries

A saved query is a request that is made often. Create the query once and save it, and then recall and run the query whenever the information is needed.

I find myself writing more saved queries than ad hoc queries because a saved query is a timesaver — and makes me a whiz kid to my buddies.

My boss goes crazy waiting for the guys in IT to write a report. The report is too simple for IT to make it a priority and too complicated for Excel.

That's when I get the call. I use either Query wizard or the Query Design tool to extract information and then save the query. A saved query can be linked to a report or to other Access 2007 objects.

Inside Scoop

Access automatically removes unused fields from the query before saving it. An unused field is a field that isn't used in the query criteria or isn't selected to be shown in the results.

Complex queries

Some queries are simple to write, such as a query asking to see Bob Smith's address. I show you how to do this in the next section of this chapter.

Many queries that you write are complex and designed to provide information to answer tough questions such as, show me:

- The buying patterns of the top ten customers.
- The inventory that needs to be ordered for the Christmas season.
- How much profit we'll make this year.

Don't get excited. Access 2007 isn't a crystal ball. Experts in your organization tell you the information you need and the formulas to apply to answer questions like these. Your job is to create a query that selects the information and use it in the formula to generate a response to the request.

Types of queries

Access 2007 identifies queries by their function. The types that you'll use the most are:

- **Select.** Filters information from one or more tables.
- **Total.** Calculates values using information from one or more tables and returns the result of the calculation. (See Chapter 9.)
- **Action.** Performs an action such as appending, updating, and deleting records from a table. (See Chapter 10.)
- **Crosstab.** Summarizes information in one or more tables into a spreadsheet called a cross-tabular form. (See Chapter 11.)
- **Top(n).** Displays the top n number of rows and is used in conjunction with one of the previous query types.

Running a query

Think of running a query as sending a streamlined e-mail — minus the addressing. With a click of the mouse, Access 2007 hears, "You've Got Mail" and then reads the query and gets right to work generating a response.

The query automatically runs when you click Finish on the Query wizard. Clicking Run in the Results group of the Design tab runs a query from the Query Design tool.

A query can be linked to a button on a form or an event, such as when a report opens.

Getting results

The result is returned as a *dynaset*. Think of a dynaset as a temporary table. You don't see the dynaset; instead Access 2007 displays the results in a datasheet. This datasheet is like others you learned about in previous chapters. The datasheet generated by a query contains information that you requested in the query.

The dynaset is not stored in the database even if you save the query. Only the query is saved. Access 2007 re-creates the dynaset each time the query is run. This is important to remember because the data might change the next time you run the query.

If you want to save the data, you need to create an action query. I describe how to do this later in this chapter.

Querying a query

Access 2007 has the capability to query the results of another query. At first, this might sound strange, but you'll find this a handy feature if you become baffled writing a complex query.

You could break down the complex query into a series of small queries, each querying the result of the previous query. Suppose that you want to see the customer names and their orders for the top 20 orders for the month.

There are a number of ways of doing this, one of which is a series of queries. The first query results in a list of customers and their orders. The next query returns orders for the selected month from the result of the first query. And a third query returns the top 20 orders from the results of the second query.

The pros laugh at this approach because it can be written in one query, but querying a query is a life-saving option for the semi-pro who is under the gun to produce a quick result.

Mastering the Query Wizard

With all the preliminaries out of the way, you can now create a query. The easiest way is to use the Query wizard. The Query wizard prompts you to make selections and answer questions, and at the end the Query wizard, creates and runs the query for you.

I'm using the Northwind Traders database to show you how to create a query. (You learned how to open this database in Chapter 1.) Open it now.

1. Double-click Customers in the Supporting Objects section of the Northwind Traders panel. Alternatively, highlight the table you want to query.

2. Click Query wizard on the Create tab to start the Query wizard.

3. Double-click Simple Query wizard (see Figure 8.1). This is at top of a list of queries that the Query wizard can create.

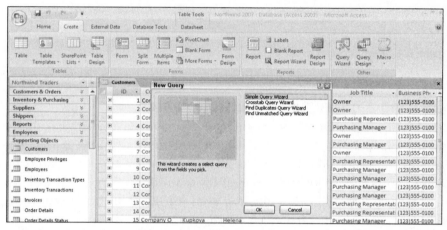

Figure 8.1. Double-click Simple Query Wizard to get started.

4. Double-click the field names in the Available Fields list that you want to query (see Figure 8.2). The Query wizard moves them from the Available Fields list to the Selected Fields list.

5. Click Finish to run the query. You'll see a datasheet containing the contents of the ID, First Name, and Last Name fields.

Hack

Double-click a field on the Selected Fields list to remove it from the query. The field is returned to the Available Fields list.

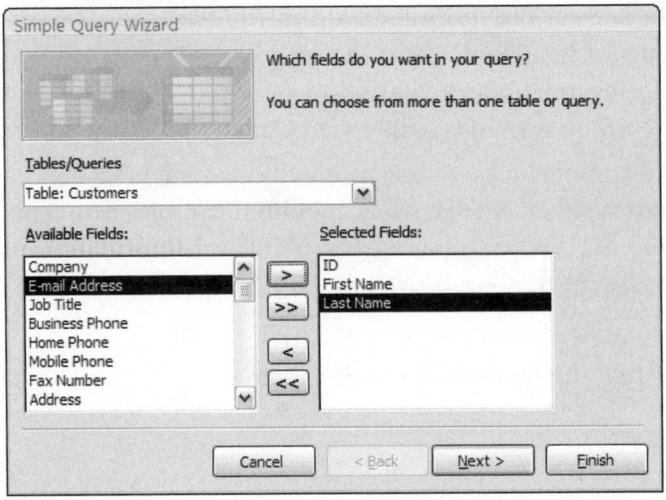

Figure 8.2. Select the fields to query.

Creating a query using multiple tables

Maybe this query didn't wow you, but you now have your first query under your belt. Now you can move on to something a little more challenging. Show me all the names of all our customers and their company name, along with the name and quantity of products they purchased.

This takes some head scratching even for me to plan how to create this query. At first this request is confusing, but here's a trick to simplify it. Identify what data you need and where it is located.

The data can be plucked from the request:

▪ Company

▪ First Name

▪ Last Name

▪ Product name

▪ Quantity

Finding it takes some knowledge of the database's organization. You probably remember from Chapter 3 that data is placed into multiple tables. Tables can be linked together to form one imaginary table using a primary key.

Hack

Close the previous query by right-clicking the datasheet containing the query result and select Close from the pop-up menu.

I've already identified that the data in this example is in the Customers table and the Order Details table. With this information in hand, you're ready to start the Query wizard.

1. Click Customers in the Supporting Objects section of the Northwind Traders panel.

2. Click Query wizard.

3. Double-click Simple Query wizard.

4. Double-click ID, Company, First Name, and Last Name.

5. Click the down arrow to open the Tables/Queries combo box.

6. Click Order Details. Fields in the Order Details table appear in the Available Fields list.

7. Double-click Product ID, Quantity in the Available Fields column. Product ID identifies the product (see Figure 8.3).

8. Click Finish to run the query. A datasheet containing customers and the products they purchased is displayed.

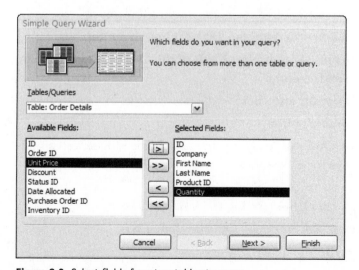

Figure 8.3. Select fields from two tables to query.

Using summary options

Access 2007 can do more than simply present information. It can also answer questions about the information, which is a time-saver because you won't have to analyze the information yourself.

The Query wizard lets you ask Access 2007 to summarize information. These include:

- Sum
- Average
- Minimum value
- Maximum value
- Count records

Suppose that you need to know the number of items purchased by each customer regardless of the number of orders they placed. You could run the query that you created in the previous section and then calculate the sum yourself. Alternatively, you can ask Access 2007 to perform the calculations to show you the results.

Here's how this is done:

1. Click Customers in the Supporting Objects section of the Northwind Traders panel.
2. Click Query wizard.
3. Double-click Simple Query wizard.
4. Double-click ID, Company, First Name, and Last Name.
5. Click the down arrow to open the Tables/Queries combo box.
6. Click Order Details. This displays fields of the Order Details table in the Available Fields column.
7. Double-click Quantity and click Next.
8. Select the Summary option.
9. Click Summary Options. A list of calculable fields is displayed alongside check boxes for each calculation Access 2007 can perform on the field.
10. Select the Sum check box(see Figure 8.4).
11. Click OK to close the Summary Options dialog box.
12. Click Finish to run the query.

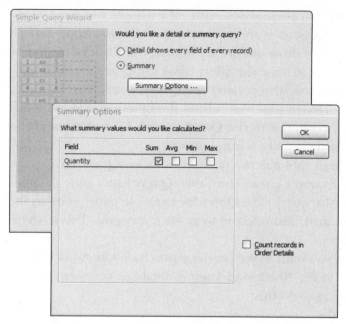

Figure 8.4. Click the type of summary calculation that you want Access 2007 to perform.

If you compare the previous query with this one, you'll notice dramatic differences.

The previous query shows a row for each order that was placed. A customer can appear in multiple rows if he or she placed multiple orders.

This query shows fewer rows because Access 2007 summarized the quantity field for each customer.

Fine-tuning the Query wizard query

By now your brain is probably spinning with other ways that you'd like to see or analyze information stored in the database. It is at this point when I find myself asking, "I wonder if Access 2007 can show me. . ." and then I come up with all data manipulations that would have made my job a lot easier in the past.

Hack

Complex calculations can be performed using the Query Design tool.

Yes, Access 2007 can present you with information you need to do your job, if the information is in the database and if you know how to write the query. Many of those queries are beyond the scope of the Query wizard and require you to write the query using the Query Design tool.

The folks at Microsoft who created the Query wizard enable you to jump to the Query Design tool from within the Query wizard to modify the query that you created with the Query wizard. I use this feature to fine-tune what started out to be a simple query.

The Query Design tool has two panes: the Table/Query Entry pane and the Query By Example pane. The Table/Query Entry pane contains tables selected for the query. The Query By Example pane contains the Query By Example grid, also referred to as the query grid. This is where you build your query.

For example, if you want to see products purchased by Anna Bedecs, who is a customer in the Northwind Traders database, you need to fine-tune a previous query to do this.

Here's what to do:

1. Click Customers in the Supporting Objects section of the Northwind Traders panel.

2. Click Query wizard.

3. Double-click Simple Query wizard.

4. Double-click ID, Company, First Name, and Last Name. These fields are selected for the query.

5. Click the down arrow to open the Tables/Queries combo box. This enables you to select another table for the query.

6. Click Order Details. This displays fields of the Order Details table in the Available Fields column.

7. Double-click Product ID, Quantity. This selects the Product ID, and Quantity fields for the query.

8. Click Next. The Detail radio button should be the default selection. Then click Next.

9. Enter a title for the query.

10. Click Modify the query design. (This tells the Query wizard to open the Query Design tool when you click Finish.)

11. Click Finish. The Query Design tool opens. At first this appears overwhelming, but it is easy to understand. At the top are tables used in the query. Lines connect fields used to join these tables. At the bottom is a spreadsheet where columns are fields in the query and rows describe what you want to do with the field (more on this when I show you how to use the Query Design tool later in this chapter).

12. Type **Anna** in Criteria row of the First Name column. Access 2007 isn't concerned about the case of the criteria. Uppercase and lowercase — it's all the same to Access 2007 when it comes to criteria for a query.

13. Type **Bedecs** in the Criteria row of the Last Name column.

14. Click Run (see Figure 8.5) in the Results group of the Design tab to run the query.

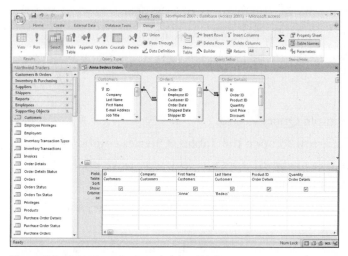

Figure 8.5. Enter the criteria and then click Run.

After running this query, you may notice that only orders placed by Anna Bedecs appear in the datasheet. Keep the datasheet on the screen because you'll use it in the next section.

Hack
The Query Design tool automatically places quotations around text used as the criteria for a query.

Creating a query from the results another query

So far you learned how to use the Query wizard to query a table. You can also use the Query wizard to create a subquery that queries the results of another query. Access 2007 places the results of a query in a temporary table that is displayed in the Datasheet view. It's temporary because the table isn't part of the database design and goes away when you close the datasheet.

However, until you close it, you can use the datasheet as if it is a permanent table. That is, you can query it.

You should have the datasheet containing Anna Bedecs's orders on the screen. If you don't, then simply run the query from the previous section.

You can summarize the quantity of products that she purchased. Select everything except Product ID and summarizing by customer.

Here's how to summarize the quantity of products.

1. Click the Create tab to display the Create tab.

2. Click Query wizard. You'll be prompted to save the Anna Bedecs Orders query.

3. Click Yes.

4. Double-click Simple Query wizard.

5. Click the down arrow to open the Tables/Queries combo box.

6. Click Anna Bedecs Orders if the Query wizard hasn't selected it as the default target for the new query.

7. Double-click ID, Company, First Name, and Last Name, and Quantity (see Figure 8.6).

8. Click Next to move to the next step in the Simple Query wizard.

9. Select Summary.

10. Click Summary Options.

11. Click Sum, Avg, Min, and Max (see Figure 8.7).

12. Click OK to close the Summary Options dialog box.

13. Click Finish. Access 2007 summarizes the purchases made by Anna Bedecs.

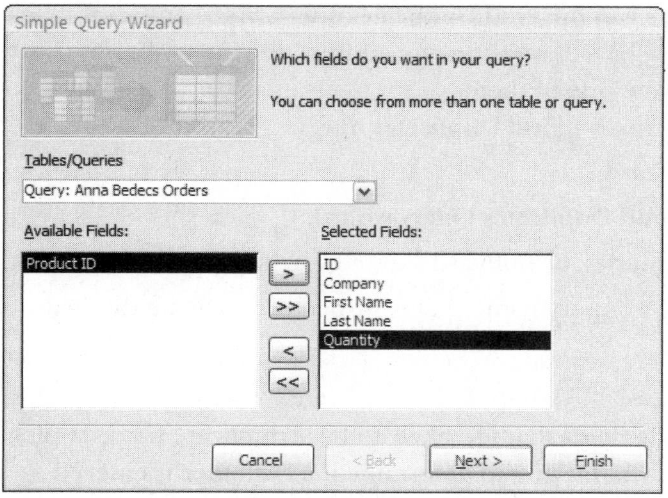

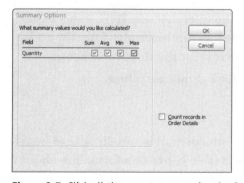

Figure 8.6. Choose fields from the Anna Bedecs Orders query for use in the new query.

Figure 8.7. Click all the ways to summarize the Quantity field.

Find Duplicates query

The Find Duplicates query creates a query that returns records that have at least one duplicate value in a table or in the result of another query. I use this all the time to clean up customer names in a table.

You might experience this problem I often encounter. I enter a customer as New York University. Weeks later, I try recalling information about the customer by typing NYU. Access 2007 tells me the customer isn't in the table. I then proceed to enter the same customer information except that I use NYU as the customer name.

Once a month, I run the Find Duplicates query. Since entries for New York University and NYU have the same address, the query displays both records. I then delete one of them.

Here's how to create a Find Duplicates query.

1. Click Query wizard.

2. Double-click Find Duplicates Query wizard.

3. Click Tables, Queries, or Both as I showed you in the previous section.

4. Click the table or query name that is suspected as having duplicate rows.

5. Click Next.

6. Double-click the fields that are likely to have duplicate values. I pick street and city when trying to determine if a customer is entered multiple times.

7. Click Next.

8. Double-click fields to display in the query. Access 2007 shows fields that you suspect have duplicate values automatically. I usually pick customer name since this is incorrect for the duplicate record.

9. Click Finish to see records that have duplicate values.

Find Unmatched query

Back in Chapter 3 you learned that information is usually spread across multiple tables, such as the Customers table contains information about a customer and the Order Details table contains information about orders placed by the customer.

Say that you need to find customers that haven't placed an order. You do this by using the Find Unmatched query. The Find Unmatched query returns records of one table that has no related record in another table.

Here's how to create the Find Unmatched query:

1. Click Query wizard.

2. Double-click Find Unmatched Query wizard.

3. Click Tables as I showed you in the previous section.

4. Click the table or query name that is suspected as not having referential integrity. I usually pick Customers table.

5. Click Next.

6. Click Tables, as I showed you in the previous section.

7. Click the table or query name that should relate to the first table or query that you selected. I usually pick the Order Details table.

8. Click Next.

9. Double-click fields used to join these tables. Usually the default setting chosen by the Query wizard is fine.

10. Click Next.

11. Double-click fields that you want displayed in the results. I choose ID and Customer Name because this is enough information to investigate any problems with the relationship.

12. Click Next.

13. Click Finish to see unmatched records.

Mastering the Query Design tool

The Query Design tool is used to create complex queries that are beyond the range of the Query wizard. It contains all of the features you need to get the job done efficiently.

With that said, you'll find the Query Design tool less friendly than the Query wizard, simply because the Query Design tool doesn't walk you through the process of creating a query.

Don't look at this as a disadvantage. After you get used to the Query Design tool — and no longer require hand-holding — you'll find that the Query wizard is slow to use anyway.

Getting started

Start by opening the Northwind Traders database and then clicking the Query Design on the Create tab. This displays the Show Table dialog box and the query grid.

Hack

Right-click the Query Design tool and click Show Table to display the Show Table dialog box if it isn't displayed.

The Show Table dialog box is used to select tables and queries that are used by the query that you're creating. It contains three tabs:

- **Tables.** Lists all tables in the database.
- **Queries.** Lists all queries in the database.
- **Both.** A complete list of tables and queries that are in the database.

Selecting tables and queries

Double-click the table or query, and Access 2007 displays the table or query depending on what you selected at the top of the Query Design tool as a box containing its field names. You'll use the table or query to choose the fields for your query.

Here are the fields you need to select.

1. Click Customers.
2. Click Orders.
3. Click Order Details.

Notice that three boxes appear at the top of the Query Design tool and each connects to the other by a line. The line indicates fields used to join together the tables.

The ID field in the Customers table is used to join the Customer ID field in the Orders table. Both fields have the same value. Likewise, the Order ID field in the Orders table is joined to the Order ID field in the Order Details table. The Order ID fields have the same value in both tables.

Relationships

The line joining together tables also indicates the type of relationship that exists between these tables (see Figure 8.8).

In this example, 1 appears near the Customers table, and the infinity symbol (the eight lying down) is near the Orders table. This indicates a 1 to many relationship. That is, each customer (record in the Customers table) can have zero, one, or many orders (records in the Orders table).

Hack

Right click the table and then click Remove Table to remove the table from the query.

Primary key   One-to-many relationship

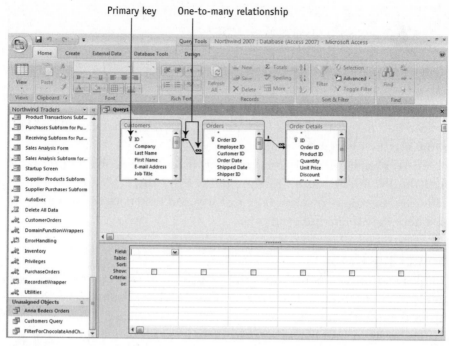

Figure 8.8. Lines show fields used to join tables and the relationship between tables.

Missing lines

Unbeknownst to you, the Query wizard watches your back. The Query wizard is smart enough to perform steps that you might have overlooked. However, that's not the case with Query Design tool.

Using the Query wizard in a previous example, you picked Company from the Customers table and Product ID and Quantity from the Order Details table. The problem is there isn't a direct relationship between the Customers table and the Order Details table.

The Query wizard realized this and knew to join the Customers table to the Orders table and then to join the Orders table to the Order Details table. When these tables are joined, Access 2007 can display the products and the quantity each customer ordered.

Hack

Reposition a table by dragging and dropping it into its new position.

Watch Out!

Always use related tables in a query.

The Query Design tool doesn't watch your back. Access 2007 doesn't draw a line between the Customers table and the Order Details table if those are the only tables selected.

You can include the ID and Company fields from the Customers table and the Product ID and Quantity fields from the Order Details table. However, the query displays values of selected fields but those values are not necessary related to each other.

Selecting fields

You'll need to pick fields you want to include in your query. These are fields you want displayed and the fields to which you want Access 2007 to apply the query criteria.

There are a number of ways to include fields in the query, but the fastest way is to double-click fields in the table. Access 2007 automatically enters the field you select in the query grid. The first field is placed in the first column, the second field in the second column. You get the picture.

Beneath the field name in the query grid is the table name. This comes in handy when the same field name appears in multiple tables.

Double-click the asterisk above the fields list if you want all fields in the table added to the query. I find myself doing this whenever I use one table for the query.

Displaying fields

Tell Access 2007 the fields you want displayed in the query result by clicking the Show check box beneath each field that you selected for the query. Fields left unchecked remain part of the query but will not appear in the result.

Suppose that you want to see a list of customers who purchased Northwind Traders Beer. You'll need to include the Product Name field and the Company field in the query; it makes sense to display only the Company field because you know the product name.

Inside Scoop

You'll probably find the need to change or remove a field as you refine your query. The Field cell is a combo box. Click and then pick another field name if you want to change the current field. To remove the field, place the cursor anywhere in the column and then click Delete Columns in the Query Setup group of the Design tab.

Sorting results

Use the Sort combo box under each field in the query grid to set the sort order for that field. You have three options:

- Ascending. ABC
- Descending. CBA
- Not sorted. No sort order

You can set the sort order for multiple fields; however, Access 2007 sorts the results in left-to-right order beginning with the leftmost field that has a sort order of Ascending or Descending. Subsequent fields are sorted within sorted leftmost field.

Say that you have:

Last Name	First Name
Smith	Mary
Jones	Tom
Smith	Bob
Jones	Anne

You sort Last Name in ascending order and First Name in ascending order. This is referred to as a sort order precedence. The result is:

Last Name	First Name
Jones	Anne
Jones	Tom
Smith	Bob
Smith	Mary

Hack

Memo and OLE object fields cannot be sorted.

Setting the query criteria

The workhorse of the Query Design tool is the Criteria line in the query grid. The Criteria line is where you tell Access 2007 how to choose records you want to see. I think of the criteria as the shopping list that my wife gives me. It tells me exactly what to buy.

You were introduced to writing the criteria in "Fine-tuning the Query wizard query" section of this chapter when you displayed Anna Bedecs' orders. This was a simple criteria that told Access 2007 to return records where the First Name field equals Anna and the Last Name field equals Bedecs.

You use basically the same technique to write complex criteria — except now you must also use operators, wildcards, and other elements.

Equals

More times than not, you'll want Access 2007 to find a particular value in a specific field, such as Anna in the First Name field. The expression is, First Name = "Anna."

If you enter a value on the Criteria line of a field, Access 2007 assumes you want to find the value in the field. This means that you don't have to write the equals expression.

Or

You may want Access 2007 to find multiple values in the same field, such as Anna or Roland or Peter. The easiest way to write this is to use one of the Or lines in the query grid.

You might be doing a little head-scratching about now because it seems there is only one Or line beneath the Criteria line. Actually, there are nine Or lines. The first is labeled Or, and the remaining eight are right below it.

Inside Scoop

The Show/Hide group on the Design tab has toggle buttons that display and hide lines on the query grid and the Property Sheet and Parameter Sheet.

When matching alternative values, place each alternative value on a separate line in the query grid.

Enter each value you want matched on its own line (see Figure 8.9).

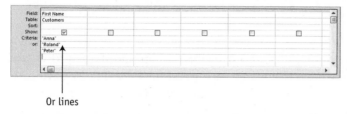

Or lines

Figure 8.9. Enter alternative values to match in an Or line.

Another way to set multiple values in a field is to use the Or operator, which is simply the word *Or*. Write the expression the way you say it. That is, "Anna" Or "Roland" Or "Peter."

Enter the expression on the Criteria line (see Figure 8.10) and on the Or lines if necessary.

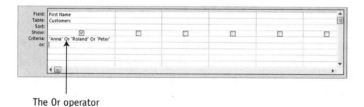

The Or operator

Figure 8.10. Using the Or operator lets you specify more than nine alternative values.

 Inside Scoop

Scroll down to bring the other Or lines into view.

Bright Idea

When the result is returned by the query, you can switch between the Query Designer tool and the Datasheet view by clicking the Views group on the Home tab and then clicking the view that you want to see.

And

And is used to link together two expressions just as it is used in an English sentence. You've done this in a previous example by saying to yourself, First Name = "Anna" and Last Name = "Bedecs."

Translated into terms that Access 2007 understands, you wrote on the Criteria line "Anna" in the First Name column and "Bedecs" in the Last Name column.

Access 2007 assumes that you want records returned that have values matching the criteria in each column on the Criteria line without having to use And.

When a record must match multiple values, place each value on the same line in the query grid.

Mixing it up with Or

Now, I'm going to mix things up a little. In the real world, you'll be expected to write a query that has some fields that must match a required value and other fields that must match one of the alternative values.

Suppose that you know the customer as Carlos, but his last name could be Grilo, Ramos, or Lee. The value of the First Name field must match Carlos and the value of the Last Name field must match one of three values.

The required value must appear on the Criteria line of the First Name field. The alternative last names each must appear in their own Or line (see Figure 8.11).

Figure 8.11. Required values must appear on the Criteria line and alternative values on an Or line.

Inside Scoop

Remember that a record must match all values on the Criteria line to be returned by the query.

Multiple Or values

When several Or values are used across more than one field, you must place each on its own Or line. This is important to remember when you experience a senior moment and lose track of information.

Suppose that you want to contact, you know, that guy, what's his name? It was Grilo or Ramos. He works for Company A or was it Company AA? It's one of them.

Access 2007 can help you out. Grilo and Ramos are placed on its own Or line in the Last Name field. Company A and Company AA are also placed on their own Or line. It is critical that each Or line has either no value or one value regardless of the column.

Not

You've heard an expression like, "You're getting the big corner office — not!" The word *not* negates the previous statement. This holds true for using NOT in a criteria except NOT precedes the criteria value.

Say you want a list of all customers except Grilo. You'd write NOT "Grilo" in the Criteria line of the Last Name field. Access 2007 compares Grilo to the value of the Last Name field in each record. The record is added to the dynaset only if there isn't a match.

In

You can link together a bunch of Or expressions to search for multiple values in the same field. (I showed you how to do this previously in this chapter.)

Use the In operator instead of several Or expressions. It is easier to use and does the same job. The In operator accepts a list of values to compare to the value in the field. Values on the list are separated with a comma.

Suppose you want records that have Anna or Roland or Peter in the First Name field. Previously, I showed you how to do this using a series of Or operators. Here's how to do it using the In operator. On the Criteria line in the First Name field type in("Anna", "Roland", "Peter") (see Figure 8.12).

This is quicker to write and easier to read than a series of Or expressions.

Figure 8.12. Enter multiple values in the In operator.

Between

Show me orders that that have a quantity between 20 and 50. If you get a request like this, then use the Between operator to retrieve the information from the database.

As the name implies, the Between operator is used to specify a range of values. Access 2007 selects records that fall within the range for the dynaset.

Place Between 20 And 50 on the Criteria line of the Quantity field. Orders with a quantity between 20 and 50, including those orders that have 20 and 50, are returned.

The Between operator can be used for any range of values.

Like

Her name is Ann. No, Anna. Wait, I'm sure it is Annie or maybe Anne. Definitely it started with Ann.

This is frustrating to everyone except Access 2007 because Access 2007 can find records that have values that are alike — but not exactly the same.

Use the Like operator when you are sure of some but not all characters in the value of a field. Use wildcard characters in place of unknown characters. Table 8.1 lists wildcard characters to use with the Like operator.

Write the Like operator on the Criteria line of the field followed by known characters and wildcard characters such as:

Like "Ann*".

The asterisk is a wildcard for one or more characters.

Inside Scoop

When searching for a character that is also a wildcard character, place the character within square brackets such as "Ann[*]". This searches for the value Ann* in the field.

Bright Idea

If you want to find fields that are empty, use Is NULL. NULL means empty.

Table 8.1. Wildcard characters

Wildcard Character	Description
?	A single character (A to Z, 0 to 9, or any character)
*	Any number of characters (0 to n)
#	Any single digit (0 to 9)
[list]	Any single character in the list. A hyphen can be used to define a range [A-Z]

Using the Query Setup

The Query Setup group on the Design tab lets you modify the query grid and the number of rows returned by the query. Here are ways to modify a row:

- **Insert Row.** Inserts a row in the query grid.
- **Delete Rows.** Removes a row from the query grid.
- **Insert Column.** Inserts a column into the query grid.
- **Delete Columns.** Removes the selected column from the query grid.

You can modify the number of rows returned by the query by using the Return tool. The Return tool gives you the option to:

- **All.** Returns all rows.
- **5.** Returns the first five rows.
- **25.** Returns the first 25 rows.
- **100.** Returns the first 100 rows.
- **5%.** Returns the first 5 percent of the rows.
- **25%.** Returns the first 25 percent of the rows.

Bright Idea

Select 5 or 25 while refining your query. This reduces the risk of running a runaway query. A runaway query is a miswritten query that returns an unexpected very large number of rows.

Creating a Parameter query

Here's a feature that lets me wow my colleagues with little or no effort. You probably use a computer application that prompts you to enter a person's name. When you click OK, the computer application displays information about that person.

You can create this same kind of application with a Parameter query. Think of a parameter as a box in your computer's memory. You give that box a name using the Query Parameter Sheet. I'll show you how to do this a little bit later. The name of the box is used in the query criteria in place of the actual value.

When the query runs, Access 2007 prompts the user to enter a value into a dialog box. Access 2007 then places the value in the box you created in memory and then replaces the name of the box in the query criteria with the value that is placed in the box. This has the same effect as if you enter the value directly into the Criteria line in the query grid.

Let's build a parameter query. I want Access 2007 to prompt the user to enter a customer's first and last name and then have Access 2007 display orders placed by that customer.

Begin by creating a query using the Query Design tool. You learn how to do this throughout this chapter. I'm using the First Name and Last Name columns from the Customers table and Product ID and Quantity fields from the Order Details, as I did in other examples.

Creating query parameters

Next, create parameters by doing the following:

1. Click Parameters in the Show/Hide group of the Design tab. This displays the Parameters dialog box.

2. Click the first column on the first line.

3. Type **Enter the customer's first name**. This is the name of the first parameter.

4. Click the Data Type column and click the Text from Data Type combo box. This is the default setting.

5. Click the first column on the second line.

6. Type **Enter the customer's last name**. This is the name of the second parameter.

7. Click the Data Type column and click Text from Data Type combo box.

8. Click OK to close the Query Parameters dialog box.

Using query parameters

You can use both parameters in the criteria. Here's what you need to do:

1. Type **Like [Enter the customer's first name]** in the Criteria line of the First Name column in the query grid. This tells Access 2007 to search for first names that are like the first name that the user entered.

2. Type **Like [Enter the customer's last name]** in the Criteria line of the Last Name column in the query grid. This tells Access 2007 to search for last names that are like the last name that the user entered (see Figure 8.13).

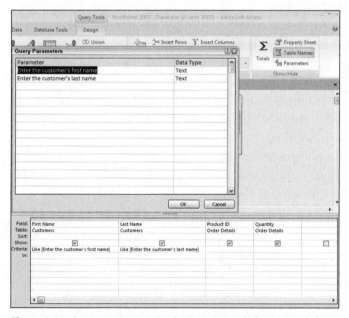

Figure 8.13. Create parameters in the Parameters dialog box and then use them in the query.

Bright Idea

You can enter values on the Criteria line in addition to using query parameters just as you did earlier in this chapter.

When the query runs, Access 2007 uses the name of the query parameter as the prompt in the Enter Parameter Value dialog box, telling the user to enter information (see Figure 8.14). The value the user enters is the criteria Access 2007 uses to select records from the database.

If the user leaves the parameter empty and clicks OK, Access 2007 treats it as if the parameter doesn't have a value.

If the user clicks Cancel, Access 2007 stops running the query.

Figure 8.14. The user is prompted to enter values when the query runs.

Creating a Union query

A Union query isn't the easiest query to create because the query is written using the Structured Query Language (SQL) rather than interacting with the Query Design tool or using the Query wizard.

With that said, a Union query is invaluable when you need to combine records from multiple tables. This happened to me when my company merged with another company and I had to combine our customer tables. The Union query did this for me.

Although I don't have room to teach you SQL in this book, I'll show you enough of SQL so you can write a Union query, but first let's create the Union query by following these steps:

1. Click Query Design in the Other group on the Create tab.

2. Click Close when the Show Table dialog box appears.

3. Click Union in the Query Type group of the Design tab. This displays an empty sheet like you find when opening a new document in Word.

4. Enter statements (see Figure 8.15). Replace field names within the brackets with fields in your tables. Replace the table names myCustomers and their Customers with your table names.

5. Click Run in the Results group of the Design tab to run the query.

Figure 8.15. The Union query uses SQL to combine records of two or more tables.

And now for SQL 101:

6. Select identifies fields that are returned by the query. This is similar to clicking Show in the query grid.

7. From identifies the table that contains these fields. This is like the Table line in the query grid.

8. Union tells Access 2007 to compare records of both tables and return nonduplicate records. Records that have the same contents in all fields identified by Select are considered duplicates.

Creating a Pass-Through query

The Pass-Through query is probably a query you won't be using much unless you use Access 2007 to interact with a database located on a database server. A database server is special computer connected to a computer network that is used to store databases that are shared throughout a company. Sometimes this is referred to as a remote database because the database is somewhere other than on your computer.

Inside Scoop

You can learn more about SQL by creating a query using the Query Design tool and then click View in the Results group of the Design tab and click SQL View to convert the query into SQL.

My company uses an Oracle database on a database server and my friend's company uses Microsoft SQL Server. Access 2007 doesn't care what kind of database or database server is used because Access 2007 simply takes the Pass-Through query and sends it to the database server where the Pass-Through query runs. The result is then passed back to Access 2007 where it is displayed in a datasheet.

In order to create and run a Pass-Through query, you need a remote database server that is connected to the same network as is connected to your computer. In addition, you must set up an Open Database Connectivity (ODBC) entry using the appropriate operating system utility for the remote database.

If you don't have these, then you can't run a Pass-Through query.

If you have them, then:

1. Click Pass-Through in the Query Type group on the Design tab. This displays the same empty sheet as when you click Union to create a Union query in the previous section of this chapter.

2. Write SQL statements in the empty sheet. The SQL statements must conform to the dialect of SQL understood by the remote database. Think of this as the difference between American English and British English. You can learn the proper SQL by reading a book that is specific to that database.

3. Click Property Sheet in the Show/Hide group of the Design tab to display the properties for the query.

4. Enter the ODBC Connect Str property. This is information needed for Access 2007 to connect to the remote database server. It is unique to your remote database, so I can't show you what to type, but usually it contains a user ID and password.

5. Click Run to execute the Pass-Through query.

Hack

Use a Pass-Through query to send SQL statements, retrieve data from an external database, and work with the data in Access 2007.

Creating a Data Definition query

A Data Definition query is used to modify the database definition such as to create, modify, or remove a table on your database, however you'll find it easier to do this interactively using techniques I showed in Chapter 4.

Here's how to create a Data Definition query:

1. Click Data Definition in the Query Type group of the Design tool. This displays an empty sheet as you saw when you created a Union query.

2. Enter SQL statements to create, modify, or drop a table.

3. Click Run to execute the query.

I'll show you how to write SQL statements in Chapter 26. Here are statements I used to create a table using a Data Definition query. You'll need to modify this query for the table and fields used in your query. Here's what you have to modify.

■ Replace mytable with the name of the new table.

■ Replace field1 and field2 with the name of fields for the table.

■ Replace integer and text with the data type that is appropriate for your fields.

■ Replace field1 with the field name of the primary key for the table.

```
Create Table mytable
    ([field1] Integer, [field2] Text Primary key
    ([field1]) );
```

And to remove a table use:

```
Drop Table mytable
```

Query properties

A query property is a setting that affects the entire query such as the Top Values query property that sets the number of rows a query returns. Query properties are set on the Query Properties Sheet. Open the Query Properties Sheet by clicking Property Sheet in the Show/Hide group of the Design tab.

Here is a list of query properties:

- **Description.** A description of the query.

- **Default View.** Determines if the result is displayed in a Datasheet, Pivot Table, or Pivot Chart.

- **Output All Fields.** Determines if the results display all fields from the table being queried.

- **Top Values.** Number of rows to return.

- **Unique Values.** Determines if only unique values are returned.

- **Unique Records.** Determines if only unique records are returned.

- **Run Permissions.** Determines if the person who created the query (owner) or any user can access the query.

- **Source Database.** Identifies the external database to use for the query.

- **Source Connect Str.** Contains the connection string used to connect to a remote database server.

- **Record Locks.** Determines if records are locked while an action query runs.

- **Recordset Type.** Determines which records can be edited.

- **ODBC Time-out.** The amount of time in seconds Access 2007 waits to connect to an external database before reporting an error.

- **Filter.** The name of the filter that is automatically loaded with the query.

- **Order By.** The automatic sort used with the query result.

- **Max Records.** Maximum number of records returned by ODBC (external) database.

- **Orientation.** Determines if the view order is left to right or right to left.

- **SubDatasheet Name.** Identifies a subquery.

- **Link Child Fields.** Field names in subuery.

- **Link Master Fields.** Field names in main table.

- **Subdatasheet Height.** The maximum height of a subdatasheet.

- **Subdatasheet Expanded.** Determines if records are expanded in a subdatabasheet.

- **Filter On Load.** Determines if a filter is loaded automatically when the query runs.
- **Order By On Load.** Determines if the results are automatically sorted.

Joining tables

Access 2007 automatically joins tables when you select them for a query if:

- A relationship was created between them when the database was created.
- Both tables have a field with the same name and data type and one is a primary key.

Sometimes you come across a situation in which two tables need to be joined, but Access 2007 hasn't joined them. You must do it yourself by creating a query join.

Joins that Access 2007 create are called Self-joins. There are three other types of joins that you can create in the Query Design tool: Equi-join, Outer join, and Cartesian join.

Equi-join

An Equi-join (also known as an inner join) selects records from both tables that have the same value in the field used to join the tables. Records that don't match are not selected. This is the default join.

Outer joins

An outer join selects all the records of one table and records from the second table that have the same value in the field used to join these tables. There are two kinds of outer joins. These are:

- **Left Outer Join.** All rows from the left table and matching rows in the right table are selected.
- **Right Outer Join.** Matching rows from the left table and all rows in the right table are selected.

Inside Scoop

I like to use the Find Unmatched Query wizard to find records that don't have a matching record in the other table or neither table.

Cartesian join

Cartesian join selects records from both tables. Don't be surprised to discover more records than you imagined when running a query using tables that have a Cartesian relationship.

Create a query join

A query join is easy to create. Before doing so, make sure that fields used to join these tables have the same value. They can have different field names.

Here's what you need to do:

1. Drag and drop the field from the left table to the field in the right table that is used to create the join. For example, you can join the Order ID field of the left table to the field in the right table that contains order IDs. Access 2007 connects these fields with a line.

2. Right-click the line.

3. Click Join Properties from the pop-up menu. This displays the Join Properties dialog box. The Join Properties dialog box contains three types of joins that are self-explanatory.

4. Click the join.

5. Click OK. Access 2007 applies the join to the tables. You can always repeat these steps to change the join type.

Delete a query join

Deleting a query join is easy. Follow these steps:

1. Right-click the line indicating the join between two tables.

2. Double-click Delete from the pop-up menu.

Inside Scoop

You won't find a Cartesian join as an option. Create a Cartesian join by adding the fields of both tables to the query grid.

Just the facts

- A query is a request for data stored in the database or for data that can be calculated using information stored in the database.

- A query is written using the Query wizard or the Query Design tool.

- An ad hoc query is a one-off request that will never be made again.

- A saved query is a request that is made often.

- Select query filters information from one or more tables.

- Top(n) query displays the top n number of rows and is used in conjunction with one of the previous query types.

- The result of a query is returned as a dynaset.

- A dynaset as a temporary table.

- The dynaset is not stored in the database, even if you save the query.

GET THE SCOOP ON...
Creating a calculated field in a query ▪ Specifying tables
and fields in an expression ▪ Zooming into a cell on the
query grid ▪ Using built-in functions

Creating Calculation Queries

You still have the chore of writing the calculation in a query, but Access 2007 has plenty of tools to help. Access 2007 has built-in functions to make those frequent calculations a breeze to write. You can also use the Expression Builder to interactively create complex expressions. And with a click, the expression is automatically inserted in your query.

In this chapter, I show you how to master the calculation capabilities of a query.

Creating a calculated field in a query

Calculations are performed in calculated query fields. A calculated query field is an empty field on the query grid that contains a mathematical expression describing the calculation. The mathematical expression is entered on the Field line. As long as you can build the expression, Access 2007 can calculate it.

You probably recall from your school days that an expression consists of an operator and operands. An operator tells Access 2007 the operation to perform using the operands. For example, the expression 2 + 4, + is an operator for addition and 2 and 4 are operands.

Specifying tables and fields

Expressions that you'll write probably use field values and parameters (see Chapter 8) besides using literal values. A field value and parameters are referenced within an expression by using the field name or parameter name within square brackets as shown here where the value of the SubTotal field is multipiled by the value of SalesTax field.

```
[Orders!SubTotal]  *  [Taxes!SalesTax]
```

- ■ If one table is used in the query, then you don't have to reference the name of the table in the expression. Access 2007 assumes you are using the current able.

- ■ If multiple tables are used in the query, then specify the name of the table by placing the table name, an exclamation, and the field name into the expression.

Zooming into a cell on the query grid

Right about now you're probably staring at the Field line on the query grid wondering how you can write an average-size expression into that relatively small space. I had that thought when I was introduced to calculated query fields.

If you start typing, Access 2007 automatically scrolls the cell to accommodate the expression, but that means you won't be able to see the entire expression.

The better way is to zoom into the cell. You're not actually zooming into the cell. Instead a dialog box opens where you'll have plenty of room to write the expression.

Here's how to do this:

1. Click Query Design in the Other group on the Create tab. The Show Table dialog box appears.

2. Click any table. I'm using Customers.

3. Right-click the Field line in the first column. A pop-up menu displays.

4. Click Zoom. The Zoom dialog box opens. This is where you enter an expression.

5. Click OK. The Zoom dialog box closes and the expression appears on the Criteria line.

Creating a Total query

A Total query is a calculation query that summarizes records in one or more tables, such as calculating the sum of values in a field or determining the number of records in a table.

You create a Total query by first creating a Select query, which I showed you how to do in Chapter 8. After the Select query is created, click Totals in the Show/Hide group in the Design tab. This inserts a Totals line in the query grid.

Finding out about built-in functions

The Totals line contains a combo box for each query field that lists built-in functions. A built-in function performs a calculation without you having to create an expression.

Built-in functions are:

- **Sum.** Calculates the sum of values in the field.
- **Avg.** Calculates the average value in the field.
- **Min.** Returns the minimum value in the field.
- **Max.** Returns the maximum value in the field.
- **Count.** Counts the number of records in the field.
- **StDev.** Calculates the standard deviation of values in the field.
- **Var.** Calculates of variance (the square of the StDev) in the field.
- **First.** Returns the first value in the field.
- **Last.** Returns the last value in the field.

Using built-in functions

After you learn how to use one built-in function, you know how to use all of them. You simply select the built-in function from the combo box on the Totals line of the query.

Suppose that you want to know the number of records in a table. Here's how to calculate it:

1. Click Query Design in the Other group on the Create tab. The Show Table dialog box appears.
2. Click a table. I'm using Customers.

3. Double-click the ID field. Doing this adds the ID field to the query grid.

4. Click Totals. This inserts a Totals line in the query grid.

5. Select Count from the Totals combo box in the first column (see Figure 9.1).

6. Click Run. Access 2007 displays the total in a datasheet.

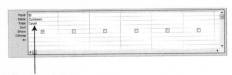

Select counter

Figure 9.1 Select the Count built-in function to count the number of records.

Setting criteria for a built-in function

At some point, you will want a built-in function to use some, but not all, records in a table. You can do this by setting criteria on the Criteria line. Access 2007 applies the criteria and then executes the built-in function.

Suppose that you want to know how many orders Elizabeth Andersen placed. Here's how to do this:

1. Click Query Design in the Other group on the Create tab. The Show Table dialog box appears.

2. Click the Customers table and the Orders table.

3. Double-click the First Name field and Last Name field in the Customers table and double click the ID field in the Orders table. This adds these fields to the query grid.

4. Click Totals. Doing this inserts a Totals line in the query grid.

5. Select Count from the Totals combo box in the ID query field.

6. Select Where in the Totals line of the First Name and Last Name query fields. This step tells Access 2007 that a criteria is used to select records.

7. Type **Elizabeth** in the Criteria line of the First Name query field.

8. Type **Andersen** in the Criteria line of the Last Name query field (see Figure 9.2).

9. Click Run. Access 2007 counts the number of records that have Elizabeth as the first name and Andersen as the last name and displays the count in a datasheet.

Figure 9.2 Count records based on a criteria.

Using GroupBy

Here's a task I come across frequently. I'm often asked to organize orders by customers. You may have a similar situation where you have to group records.

The solution is straightforward because the Totals combo box has a GroupBy built-in function. The GroupBy built-in function groups records using the field you specify and then totals values.

Here how this is done:

1. Click Query Design in the Other group on the Create tab. The Show Table dialog box appears.

2. Click the Customers, Orders, and Order Details tables.

3. Double-click Company, First Name, and Last Name from the Customers table and Product ID and Quantity from the Order Details table. This step adds these fields to the query grid.

4. Click Totals. Doing this inserts a Totals line in the query grid.

5. Select GroupBy. Access 2007 automatically selects GroupBy for all the fields.

6. Click Run. Access 2007 groups the records and displays them in a datasheet.

Concatenate text

You're bound to become frustrated trying to combine a person's first name and last name when each is in a separate field in a table. Stay cool, because Access 2007 can do this for you.

Watch Out!

Access 2007 doesn't place a space between the text — you need to do it yourself.

When I hear the term *calculations*, right away I think about numbers. However, calculations can also be performed with text and you can set up an expression to concatenate two text fields. *Concatenation* means combine.

You use the concatenation operator to do this. The concatenation operator is an ampersand (&). The concatenation operator tells Access 2007 to place the beginning of one text at the end of another text.

Here's how to combine values of the first name and last name fields using the concatenation operator.

1. Click Query Design in the Other group on the Create tab. The Show Table dialog box appears.

2. Click the Customers table.

3. Enter [First Name] & " " & [Last Name} on the Field line in a empty query field (see Figure 9.3).

4. Click Run. Access 2007 creates a single column datasheet that contains the combine first and last names of each customer.

Figure 9.3 Combine the first and last names into a datasheet using the concatenation operator.

Using the inline If statement

Access 2007 can choose which expression to execute depending on a condition that you write on the Criteria line. The decision is made using an inline If statement.

An If statement tells Access 2007, if this condition is true then do this otherwise do that. The condition is one you set, "this" is an expression and "that" is another expression.

It's called an inline If statement because the If statement is written all on one line. The inline If statement is written as:

```
IIf( condition, expression1, expression2)
```

Expression1 is calculated only if the condition is true, otherwise expression2 is calculated.

Try using this expression to apply different discounts depending on the customer. Here's how to do it:

1. Click Query Design in the Other group on the Create tab. The Show Table dialog box appears.

2. Click the Order Details table.

3. Click Zoom on the Field line. The Zoom dialog box opens.

4. Type **IIf([Quantity]>50,[Unit Price]*1.1,[Unit Price]*1.5)**. This tells Access 2007 to determine if the value of the Quantity field is greater than 50. If so, then increase the Unit Price by 10%. If not, the increase the Unit Price by 5%.

5. Click OK. The Zoom dialog box closes and the expression appears on the field line (see Figure 9.4).

6. Click Run. Access 2007 applies the criteria in the inline if statement to the Quantity field of each record and then calculates either the first or second expression. The result is displayed in a datasheet.

Condition

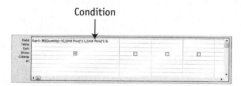

Figure 9.4 Access 2007 decides which expression to calculate based on the condition in the inline If statement.

Using the Expression Builder

The Expression Builder is an interactive tool for writing complex expressions. Using the Expression Builder for creating simple expressions is a bit cumbersome, in my opinion, but nothing is stopping you from doing so.

Create a Select query first and then place the cursor on the Field line of a empty column on the query grid. This is where the Expression

Builder will place the finished expression. Open the Expression Builder by clicking Builder in the Query Setup group on the Design tab. You can also right-click the Field line and click Build from the pop-up menu.

The Expression Builder is divided into several sections. At the top is the expression window where the expression is entered. This window is similar to the Zoom dialog box. You can type the complete expression or use the interactive tools to let Access 2007 help you build the expression.

The folks who designed the Expression Builder use buttons for the more commonly used operators. Simply click the button to insert the operator at the cursor in the expression.

The real power of the Expression Builder is with the folders in the left column. Each folder contains elements that can be used in the expression.

Click Tables and you'll see a list of tables from the current database. Click a table and you'll see fields of that table appearing in the second column. Double-click a field and the table, and field is added to the expression at the cursor position. The field is placed in the expression and the value of the field is referenced when the expression is calculated.

The Queries, Forms, and Reports folders are used the same way, except references to elements of those objects are displayed.

The Functions folder contains references to built-in functions and functions that are unique to the current database. These are likely functions you or your colleagues build (see Chapter 19). The number of built-in functions seems limitless. There are too many to discuss here. Most are self-explanatory and the others you look up using the Access 2007 Help button, which is the question mark in the upper-left corner above the Ribbon.

The Constants folder contains constants as the name implies. Constants are True, False, Null, and "". Null means nothing such as a field without a value. Double quotations "" is an empty string. Sometimes you'll need these when building advance queries.

The Operator folder contains a complete list of operators much more than what is on the button row.

The Common Expressions folders has built-in expressions that you'll use a lot such as Page Number, Current Date, and Current User.

Try using the Expression Builder to create an expression that displays orders for Elizabeth Andersen. Here's what you need to do:

1. Click Query Design in the Other group on the Create tab. The Show Table dialog box appears.

2. Click the Customers, Orders, and Order Details tables.

3. Place the cursor on the Field line in the first column of the query grid.

4. Click Builder in the Query Setup group on the Design tab. This displays the Expression Builder.

5. Double-click the Tables folder. A list of tables appears.

6. Double-click the Customers table folder. A list of fields in the Customers table appears.

7. Double-click First Name. Access 2007 displays the First Name field in the expression window.

8. Type = " **Elizabeth**" in the expression window to the right of the First Name field.

9. Click the And button. This joins together two subexpressions telling Access 2007 that both subexpressions must be true for the overall expression to be true.

10. Double-click Last Name. Access 2007 displays the Last Name field in the expression window.

11. Type = " **Andersen**" in the expression window to the right of the Last Name field (see Figure 9.5).

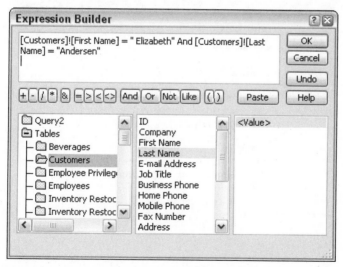

Figure 9.5 Create the expression interactively using the Expression Builder.

12. Click OK to insert the expression on the Field line in the first column.

13. Double-click Product ID in the Order Details field.

14. Click the Show box for the Product ID and deselect the Show box for the expression (see Figure 9.6).

15. Click Run. Access 2007 displays products purchased by Elizabeth Andersen in a datasheet.

Figure 9.6 Add the Product ID field from the Order Details table.

Operator precedence

Access 2007 calculates an expression according to the operator precedence, commonly called the order of precedence. This is simply a list of what to do first.

Table 9.1 contains the operator precedence used by Access 2007.

Table 9.1. Operator precedence	
Mathematical	
	Exponetiation
	Negation
	Multiplication or division (left to right)
	Integer division
	Modulo
	Addition and/or subtraction (left to right)
	String concatenation

Comparison	
	Equal
	Not equal
	Less than
	Greater than
	Less than or equal to
	Greater than or equal to
	Like
Boolean	
	Not
	And
	Or
	Xor
	Eqv
	Imp

Just the facts

- A calculated query field is an empty field on the query grid that contains a mathematical expression describing the calculation.
- Field names must be enclosed within square brackets in an expression.
- Expressions must be entered into the Field line of the query grid.
- Use Zoom to zoom into a cell on the query grid which makes it easier to enter an expression.
- Total query calculates values using information from one or more tables and returns the result of the calculation.
- Built-in functions perform a calculation without you having to create an expression.

GET THE SCOOP ON...
Action queries ▪ Setting criteria for appending and
updating records ▪ Creating an Update query ▪ Creating a
Delete query ▪ Creating a Make Table query

Creating Action Queries

Typing 500 new customer names into a table is usually a chore assigned to the summer intern. But not anymore, because after reading this chapter you'll know how to ask Access 2007 to handle this grunt work for you.

I show you how to create an action query to enter new information, update existing information, or remove information currently in the database. You can also transform a dynaset into a new table at a blink of an eye.

The Jeanie is an action query. You learn how to master the action query in this chapter.

Finding out about action queries

In Chapter 8, I showed you how to create a query that looks up information in a database. You select tables, fields, and set criteria and then have Access 2007 return records that match your criteria. Records are returned in a dynaset, which is a temporary table, and displayed in a datasheet.

An action query is similar to the queries you already know how to build and execute except, as the name implies, an action query does something besides simply look up information. Instead, an action query can change records and add a new table to the database.

Chapter 10

There are four kinds of action queries that you can create. These are Append, Update, Delete, and Make Table.

- The Append action query copies records from one or more tables into another table. Use it to avoid having to re-enter data that is already electronically available.

- The Update action query changes values of existing records in one or more tables. I use this whenever I'm asked to apply a price hike to the unit price in the Products table.

- The Delete action query removes records from a table. No matter how careful I try to be, sometimes erroneous data sneaks into the table. I don't sweat this problem because I create a Delete action query to quickly remove them from the table.

- The Make Table action query transforms a dynaset into a new table and adds it to the database. A dynaset is a snapshot of values in field of one or more tables when the query runs. You can save the query, but the dynaset disappears. The data might have changed by the time you rerun the query. Creating a Make Table action query saves the dynaset as a table and thereby retains its values.

Using action queries

A colleague devised a clever way to use action queries with Excel. She was always asked to be the point person in the office to collect data and then maintain the data using Access 2007.

It was an important role — and one no one else wanted because the data was delivered in various formats, none of which could be automatically processed electronically.

She spent hours entering the data by hand until she had this brilliant idea — use Excel. Everyone in the office knew how to use Excel, so my colleague created three Excel spreadsheets: one for new information, another for updates of existing information, and a third for information that should be deleted from the Access 2007 database.

Each person entered their changes to the appropriate spreadsheet and e-mailed it back to my colleague. She imported each of them (see Chapter 7) and then used the appropriate action query to modify information in the database. It took seconds instead of days to keep the database current.

Getting ready to use action queries

Before showing you how to create action queries, let's create another table for the Northwind 2007 database and populate it with a few records. You'll append these records to the Customers table of the Northwind database and then update and finally remove them using action queries.

Here's a refresher from Chapter 4 on how to create a table:

1. Click Table Templates in the Tables group of the Create tab.

2. Click Contacts. Doing so creates a new contacts table.

3. Right-click the table to display a pop-up menu.

4. Click Save. The Table Name dialog box appears.

5. Enter a name for the table. I call it New Customers.

6. Click OK.

7. Enter values for Company, First Name, Last Name, and E-mail Address fields.

8. Enter another record for the same fields.

9. Right-click the tab. This displays a pop-up menu.

10. Click Close. This removes the datasheet from the screen.

Turning off disable mode

You're about to go crazy. Bet you're wondering how I know this. It's because you're about to make the same mistake I did when I first started using Access 2007.

You probably noticed a Security Alert when opening the Northwind Traders database. It gave you two options: Enable Content and Trust Center. And like me, you clicked Enable Content and the Trust In Office dialog box popped on the screen showing two options:

- Leave this content disabled (recommended)
- Enable this content

And like me you took the recommended advice and clicked OK. Wrong!

In doing so, action queries are blocked. They won't work. Click Enable this content to remove this block — and don't think that you're going crazy when running an append query.

Creating an Append query

The Append query requires two tables:

- **Source table.** Contains records to append.

- **Destination table.** Where records are appended to.

In this example, the source table is New Customers and the destination table is the Northwind Traders database Customers table.

First you create a Select query, which you learned to do in Chapter 8. The Select query selects fields you pick from the source table when you run the query.

Next, you'll transform the Select query into an Append query by clicking Append. This inserts an Append To line in the query grid and prompts you to enter the name of the destination table.

The destination table can reside in the current database or in another database. You get to choose. If the destination table isn't in the current database, then you'll need to provide the name of the database.

The final step before running the query is to match fields from the source table to the destination table by entering the field name of the destination table in the corresponding column in the query grid.

Access 2007 inserts them for you if both tables use the same field names and the same data type. I always double-check to assure that Access 2007 makes the right choice by comparing the contents of each field.

Now that you know what has to happen to create an Append query, let's create one:

1. Click Query Design in the Other group on the Create tab. The Show Table dialog box appears.

2. Click the table that contains records you want to append (source table). I'm using New Customers because I want to append records from the New Customers table to the Customers table.

3. Click Add. The New Customers table appears in the Query Design tool.

4. Click Close. The Show Table dialog box closes.

5. Double-click the fields you want to append. I picked Company, First Name, Last Name, and E-mail Address.

6. Click Append in the Query Type group of the Design tab. The Append dialog box appears.

7. Type the name of the destination table in the Table Name combo box or select the table from the combo box list. I entered Customers (see Figure 10.1).

8. Click Current Database. This is the default setting because Access 2007 assumes that the destination table is in the current database. If it isn't, then click Another Database and enter the filename of that database in the File Name text box.

9. Click OK.

10. Type the field name on the Append To line of the query grid. Match fields of the New Customers table (source table) with fields of the Customers table (Append to table) (see Figure 10.2).

11. Click Run in the Results group of the Design tab. Access 2007 copies the value from the selected fields of all the records in the New Customers table and appends them to the Customers table.

12. Click Yes when you see a warning message saying that you are about to append rows to the table.

13. Double-click Customers under the Supporting Objects group in the Northwind Traders pane. The Customers Datasheet displays, showing the appended records at the bottom of the datasheet.

Figure 10.1. Enter the name of the Append To table.

Field:	Company	First Name	Last Name	E-mail Address			
Table:	New Customers	New Customers	New Customers	New Customers			
Sort:							
Append To:	Company	[First Name]	[Last Name]	[E-mail Address]			
Criteria:							
or:							

Figure 10.2. Match fields from the source table to the Append To table.

The previous example shows how to append all records from one table to another table. However, you can easily have Access 2007 append selected tables by setting a query criteria.

Create the Append query as in the previous section and then enter a criterion on the Criteria line. In this next example, I'm appending only records that have Jim Keogh as the customer's name.

Modify the Append query like this:

1. Type **Jim** on the Criteria line in the First Name column on the query grid.

2. Type **Keogh** on the Criteria line in the Last Name column on the query grid.

3. Click Run.

Creating an Update query

The Update query requires a source table and destination table. The source table contains values that update values in the destination table. In this example, I'm changing the e-mail address of the two records that I previously appended to the Customers table.

Before showing you how to create an Update query, change the values of the E-mail Address field in the New Customers table.

Here's what to do:

1. Double-click New Customers under the Unassigned Objects group in the Northwind Traders pane. This displays the New Customers table in a datasheet.

2. Change jk@someplace.org to jim@someplace.org.

3. Change ac@someplace.org to anne@someplace.org.

4. Right-click the tab. A pop-up menu is displayed.

5. Click Close. The datasheet closes.

Several steps are necessary to create an Update query. First select the source table and destination table from the Show Table dialog box. This step places both tables on the Query Design tool.

Then join these tables. I use the First Name and Last Name fields because I know there are only two records in both tables with customers Jim Keogh and Anne Code. Be sure to join your tables using fields that identify comparable records.

Place the field name of the field you're updating on the query grid. This is the Customers E-mail Address field. And then insert the Update To line into the query grid by clicking Update. This is the line used to tell Access 2007 where to get the updated values.

You tell Access 2007 the values to use by specifying the table name and the field name that contain these values. Both table names and field names must be enclosed within square brackets and an exclamation point separates the table name from the field name.

Here's how to create an Update query:

1. Click Query Design in the Other group on the Create tab. The Show Table dialog box appears.

2. Click the table being updated (destination table). I'm using Customers because I want to update values from the New Customers table to the Customers table.

3. Click Add. The Customers table appears in the Query Design tool.

4. Click the table that contains the updated values (source table). I'm using New Customers.

5. Click Add. The New Customers table appears in the Query Design tool.

6. Click Close.

7. Drag and drop the First Name field from the Customers table to the First Name Field of the New Customers table. This step joins the tables by first name.

8. Drag and drop the Last Name field from the Customers table to the Last Name Field of the New Customers table. This step joins the tables by last name.

9. Click Update in the Query Type group of the Design tab. Doing this inserts the Update To line in the query grid.

10. Double-click E-mail Address in the Customers table. The E-mail Address appears in the first field on the query grid.

11. Type [New Customers!E-mail Address] in the Update To line in the first column of the query grid (see Figure 10-3). This tells Access 2007 to update the value of the E-mail Address field in the Customers table with the value of the E-mail Address field in the New Customers table.

12. Click Run.

13. Click Yes when you see a warning message saying that you are about to append rows to the table.

14. Double-click the Customers table in the Supporting Objects group of the Northwind Traders pane to display the Customers datasheet. You'll notice that the e-mail address for two records you added previously is updated.

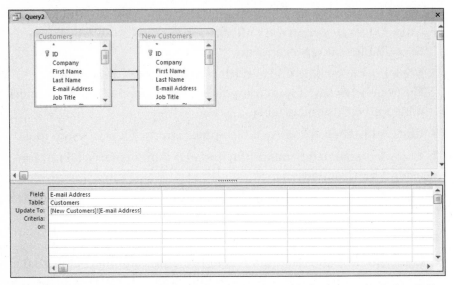

Figure 10.3. Enter the name of the field that contains the updated values on the Update To line.

Joining tables sets the relationship between the source and destination tables sufficient for Access 2007 to identify destination records to update. However, sometimes you'll want to set additional criteria to identify records to update.

You do this by adding fields to the query grid and then specifying the criteria on the Criteria line. You learned how to do this in Chapter 8. Access 2007 then updates those records that meet the criteria and skips other records in the destination table.

Creating a Delete query

The delete query requires one table — the table that contains records you want to delete. Identify those records by specifying a query criteria, which you learned how to do in Chapter 8.

You create a Delete query by first creating a Select query and then once you select the table, transforming the Select query to a Delete query by clicking Delete in the Query Type group of the Design tab.

This places a Delete line in the query grid. The Delete line contains a combo box for each column where you select the Where clause. The Where clause tells Access 2007 that the Criteria line contains the conditions that a record must meet before it can be deleted.

In this example, I'm deleting the records that have Jim Keogh as the customer name.

After you run the query, you cannot undo the deletions.

Here's how to create a Delete Query.

1. Click Query Design in the Other group on the Create tab. The Show Table dialog box appears.

2. Click the table from which records are being deleted. I picked the New Customers table.

3. Click Add. The New Customers table appears in the Query Design tool.

4. Click Close. The Show Table dialog box closes.

5. Double-click the First Name field. This adds the First Name field to the query grid.

6. Double-click the Last Name field. This adds the Last Name field to the query grid.

7. Click Delete in the Query Type group of the Design tab. This inserts the Delete line in the query grid.

8. Select Where from the combo box on the Delete line for each column. This tells Access 2007 to delete records where the value of the First Name field and the value of the Last Name field equal the query criteria.

9. Type **Jim** on the Criteria line in the first column. You are deleting records that have the value Jim in the First Name field.

10. Type **Keogh** on the Criteria line in the second column. You are deleting records that also have the value Keogh in the Last Name field.

11. Click Run.

12. Click Yes when you see a warning message saying that you are about to append rows to the table.

Inside Scoop

Always use the criteria for selecting records in an Update and Delete query in a Select query before using them in the Update and Delete query so you're sure that the criteria selects records that you want updated or deleted.

13. Double-click the New Customers table in the Unassigned Objects group of the Northwind Traders pane to display the New Customers Datasheet. You'll notice that the record containing Jim Keogh is deleted.

Creating a Make Table query

Begin to create a Make Table query by creating a Select query. You pick the tables and fields and then set the criteria for selecting records for the dynaset.

Transform the Select query to a Make Table query by clicking Make Table in the Query Type group on the Design tab. Access 2007 then prompts you to enter a name for the new table and decide to add the new table to the current database or another database of your choosing.

When the query runs, Access 2007 creates the dynaset. Fields and values in the dyanset are transformed into a new table. It's just as if you created the table yourself. You'll find the table listed in the Unassigned Objects category on the Northwind Traders pane.

Here's how to create a Make Table query:

1. Click Query Design in the Other group on the Create tab. The Show Table dialog box appears.

2. Click the table(s) for the query. I'm using the Products table from the Northwind Traders database.

3. Click Add. The Products table appears in the Query Design tool.

4. Double-click fields to select for the new table. I picked Product Code, Product Name, Description, Standard Cost, List Price, and Category.

5. Click to add the Show check boxes.

6. Type **Beverages** on the Criteria line in the Category column of the query grid.

7. Click Make Table in the Query Type group of the Design tab. This displays the Make Table dialog box.

8. Enter a name for the new table. I call the new table Beverages (see Figure 10.4).

9. Click Current Database unless the new table is going to be added to a different database. If so, then click Another Database and enter the name of the database in the File Name text box.

10. Click OK.

11. Click Run.

12. Click Yes when you see a warning message saying that you are about to paste rows into the new table.

13. Double-click the Beverages table in the Unassigned Objects group of the Northwind Traders pane to display the Beverages Datasheet. You'll notice that it contains only beverage products.

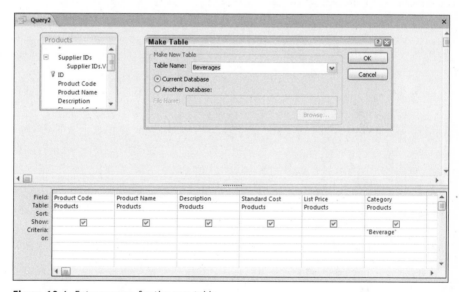

Figure 10.4. Enter a name for the new table.

Just the facts

- An action query performs an action such as appending, updating, and deleting records from a table.

- The Append action query copies records from one or more tables into another table.

- The Update action query changes values of existing records in one or more tables.

- The Delete action query removes records from a table.

- The Make Table action query transforms a dynaset into a new table and adds it to the database.

- Turn off disable mode so that other action queries won't run.

GET THE SCOOP ON...
Using the Crosstab wizard ▪ Working around limitations
of the Crosstab wizard ▪ Creating a Crosstab using the
Query Design tool ▪ Creating a PivotTable

Working with Crosstabs and PivotTables

Chapter 11

If you like working with spreadsheets, then you're bound to fall in love with the Access 2007 Crosstabs and PivotTables features because they transform a datasheet into a spreadsheet.

Hold on. I know what you're thinking. Didn't I learn to export a table to an Excel spreadsheet in Chapter 7? Yes you did, but this is different because you create the spreadsheet's columns, rows, and values using values of fields in the datasheet.

This sounded confusing to me until a friend showed me an example and then everything fit into place. I now use these features to solve challenging problems in no time.

In this chapter, I pass along tips on becoming more productive by using Crosstab and PivotTables.

All about Crosstabs

A Crosstab is a specialized Total Query in the form of a spreadsheet where some fields of a table are column headings and other fields are row headings. Cells contain summaries of the fields.

You choose the field used as the columns and rows. Access 2007 then calculates the totals and displays them in the cells.

Suppose that you want to see how many of each product was purchased by each customer. Column heads are product names. Row headings (the first cell in each row) are company names. Each cell is the total of each product purchased by that company.

Create a Crosstab, drag and drop the product name to the column heading, and then drag and drop company names to the row heading. Access 2007 uses values of the product name field as headings for the columns and values of the company names field as headings for the row. Access 2007 then calculates the total of each product purchased by each company and places the total in the appropriate cell.

Using the Crosstab wizard

The fastest way to create a Crosstab is to use the Crosstab wizard.

A Crosstab query uses one table or the result of another query. If you need to create a Crosstab query using multiple tables, then you must create a simple query first to combine those tables into one temporary table. This is an extra step, but you're an old hand at creating these because you've been creating simple queries throughout this book.

You'll need to create a simple query in this next example since fields from three tables are used to create the Crosstab. These are:

- **Customers table.** ID, Company.
- **Order Details table.** Product ID, Quantity.
- **Products table.** Product Name.

The ID in the Customers table joins with the customer's order in the Order Details table. The Product ID in the Order Details table joins with the Product Name in the Products table.

To create the simple query, do the following:

1. Double-click Customers in the Supporting Objects section of the Northwind Traders panel.
2. Click Query wizard in the Other group on the Create tab.
3. Double-click Simple Query wizard.
4. Double-click ID and Company.
5. Click the down arrow to open the Tables/Queries combo box.
6. Click Order Details.
7. Double-click Product ID, Quantity.

8. Click the down arrow to open the Tables/Queries combo box.

9. Select Products.

10. Double-click Product Name.

11. Click Next twice.

12. Type a title for the query. I titled this as: Customer Orders By Product Name.

13. Click Finish to view the results in a datasheet.

14. Right-click the datasheet.

15. Click Save.

Now you're ready to create the Crosstab query. You can create a Crosstab query by following these steps:

1. Click Query wizard.

2. Double-click Crosstab Query wizard.

3. Select Queries (see Figure 11.1). If you were using one table, you would click Tables or Click Both if the Crosstab query uses both tables and the results of a query.

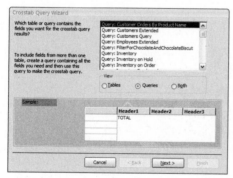

Figure 11.1. Select the query to use as the basis for the Crosstab.

4. Double-click Query: Custom orders By Product Name.

5. Double-click Company in the Available Fields column (see Figure 11.2). The field you select becomes the row headings, which you'll see in the Sample box.

6. Click Next.

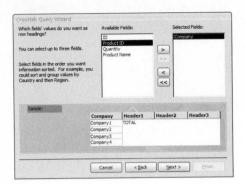

Figure 11.2. Select the field used as the row headings.

7. Select Product Name (see Figure 11.3). The field you select becomes the column headings.

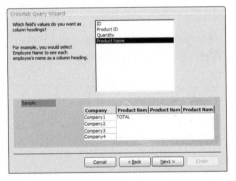

Figure 11.3. Select the field used as the column headings.

8. Click Next.

9. Select Quantity (see Figure 11.4). This field is used in the calculation. The result of the calculation appears in each cell under the column headings.

10. Select Sum in the Functions column. This is the calculation Access 2007 performs on the selected field.

11. Click Next.

12. Click Finish to run the query.

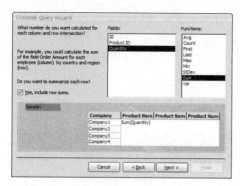

Figure 11.4. Select the field to calculate and the calculation to perform.

Access 2007 displays a datasheet that shows company names in the first column; total quantity ordered for each company in the second column; and a breakdown of total by each product (see Figure 11.5).

Total column

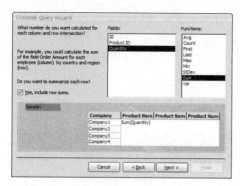

Figure 11.5. Access 2007 calculates totals and displays the crosstab.

Working around limitations of the Crosstab wizard

The Crosstab wizard has limitations. However, there are known ways to workaround some of these. Here's what to do:

- **One Table.** The Crosstab wizard works with one table. The workaround is to create a simple query that uses tables that you want used in the Crosstab wizard. Save this simple query and use the simple query in the Crosstab wizard. I showed you how to do this in the previous section.

- **No calculated fields.** You can't use a calculated field in the Crosstab wizard. The workaround is to use the calculated field in the simple query, save the simple query and use the simple query as the source for the Crosstab.

- **Ordering column headings.** The Crosstab wizard places column headings in the order values that appear in the field. You can't change this order. The workaround is to set the order using a simple query, save the simple query and use it as the source for the Crosstab.

Creating a Crosstab using the Query Design tool

There will be instances when the Crosstab you want to build is beyond the capabilities of the Crosstab wizard. When this happens, I use the Query Design tool because it provides the flexibility needed to create simple and complex Crosstabs.

The Crosstab is created similar to how you create other queries using the design tool in Chapter 8 with a few additional steps.

Here's how to do it:

1. Click Query Design in the Other group on the Create tab. Doing this starts the query design tool and displays the Show Tables dialog box.

2. Click the tables for the query. I selected Customers, Orders, and Order Details. These tables appear in the Query Design tool, each joined together by a line.

3. Click Close to close the Show Tables dialog box.

4. Click Crosstab in the Query Type group on the Design tab. This inserts the Total and Crosstab lines in the query grid.

5. Double-click Company in the Customers table. Access 2007 displays Company in the Field line in the first column of the query grid and places Group By on the Total line.

6. Double-click Product ID in the Order Details table. Product ID appears in the second column and Group By is placed on the Total line.

7. Double-click Quantity in the Order Details table. Quantity appears in the third column and Group By is placed on the Total line.

8. Click the Total line in the third column and select Sum. This summarizes values in the Quantity field.

9. Click the Crosstab line in the first column and select Row Heading. This makes values in the Company field row headings for the Crosstab.

Inside Scoop

Sometimes you want empty cells to show a zero instead of being empty. Change empty cells to show zero by placing 0;;;0 in the Format property of the field used as the value for the Crosstab.

10. Click the Crosstab line in the second column and select Column Heading. This step makes values in the Product ID field column appear as headings in the column headings for the Crosstab.

11. Click the Crosstab line in the third column and select Value. This makes values in the Quantity field values for cells in the Crosstab (see Figure 11.6).

12. Click Run. Access 2007 creates the Crosstab.

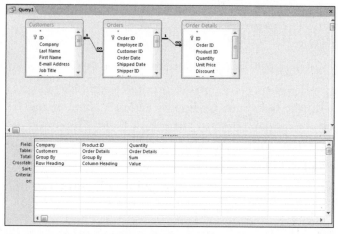

Figure 11.6. Creating a Crosstab using the Query Design tool gives greater flexibility in the design than using the Crosstab wizard.

Creating a PivotTable

A PivotTable is similar to a Crosstab because you define values for rows, columns, and totals. However, I've found that a PivotTable is more versatile than a Crosstab.

Before you drive yourself crazy, make sure that the table or form used for the PivotTable has fields that lend themselves to a PivotTable. The value of one field is used as column headings and the value of another field is used as row headings. The value of another field is summarized.

Let's re-create the Crosstab example to illustrate how to create a PivotTable. The Crosstab summarized orders per product name by each company. We need a table that has company names, product names, and quantity for each order.

Right away there's a problem. There isn't one table or form that contains all the information. We have to create the form using the query that we used in the Crosstab (see the "Creating a Crosstab using the Query Design tool" section).

Create and run this query, and then save the result in a form. I called it Company Orders By Product Name. Access 2007 places it in the Unassigned Objects category on the Northwind Traders pane.

Now that you have one table with all the necessary information, you can create the PivotTable by following these steps:

1. Highlight the Company Orders By Product Name form and click More Forms in the Forms group on the Create tab. Doing this displays a list of forms.

2. Click PivotTable. Access 2007 displays a template for the PivotTable.

3. Click Field List in the Show/Hide group on the Design tab to show the list of fields on the Company Orders By Product Name form. Drag and drop the Company field to Drop Row Fields Here area of the template. Access 2007 displays values of the Company field as row headings (Figure 11.7).

4. Drag and drop Product Name to the Drop Column Fields Here area of the template. Access 2007 displays values of the Product Name field as column headings.

5. Drag and drop the Quantity field to the Drop Totals or Detail Fields Here area of the template. Access 2007 calculates total of order placed by company and product and places the total in the corresponding cell.

You can insert a Totals column as we did in the Crosstab by clicking Add To. The Totals column becomes the first column and shows the total orders for each company.

You'll notice + and - signs in column and row headings. These signs are used to hide (-) and display (+) details of the column or row. The details are visible after dragging and dropping to column and row headings. I usually leave it this way unless I need to focus on specific data in the table.

Drag and drop

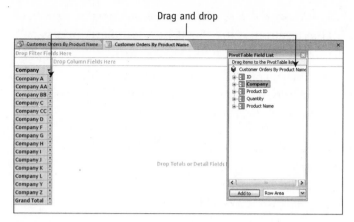

Figure 11.7. Drag and drop fields from the PivotTable Field List to the PivotTable.

Cells contain the sums of the corresponding column and row. Sometimes you don't want to see some but not all totals. Click the combo box at the top of each column to filter these values. The combo box displays a check box for each value displayed in the detail area of the PivotTable. Select the values you want displayed in the PivotTable.

Creating a PivotChart

A PivotChart is similar in concept to a PivotTable, except that information is depicted graphically rather than in numbers. I find a PivotChart useful when analyzing information for trends or when explaining my analysis to someone who finds it easier to read graphs than a table of numbers.

As with a PivotTable, you'll need to start with a table or form that lends itself to being pivoted, otherwise creating a PivotChart is straightforward.

Let's create a PivotChart that graphically shows sales of each product. I'm using the Company Orders By Product Name that I used for the PivotTable.

1. Click the Company Orders By Product Name.

2. Click PivotChart in the Forms group on the Create tab. Access 2007 displays a template for a column graph and displays the PivotChart Field List.

3. Click Field List in the Show/Hide group on the Design tab to display a list of fields contained on the Company Orders By Product

Name table. Drag and drop the Product Name field to the Drop
Category Fields Here section of the PivotChart template. Access
2007 displays the Product Name combo box.

4. Drag and drop the Quantity field to the Drop Data Fields Here section of the PivotChart template. Access 2007 displays a column
graph of the totals for each product (see Figure 11.8).

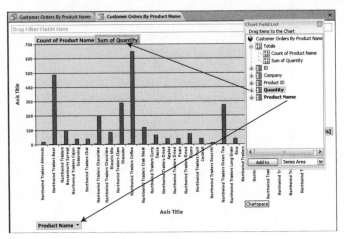

Figure 11.8. Drag and drop the Quantity field, and Access 2007 draws
a column graph of totals for each product.

Changing the type of PivotChart

If a column graph doesn't do justice to your data, then change from a
column graph to another type of graph.

Here's how to do it:

1. Click Change Chart Type in the Type group on the Design tab.
   Access 2007 displays the PivotChart's properties sheet opened to the
   Type tab, where you'll see a list of types and styles to choose from.

2. Click a type of PivotChart in the first column, and Access 2007
   shows you available styles.

3. Click a style. Access 2007 draws the PivotChart using that type and
   style (see Figure 11.9).

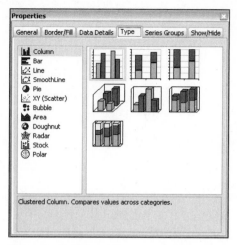

Figure 11.9. Click a chart type in the first column and then click a chart style.

Insert titles

You'll probably want to dress up the PivotChart by adding titles for the two axes and for the chart itself. Here's how to do it.

To add a title to the chart:

1. Click Property Sheet in the Tools group on the Design tab. This displays the PivotChart's properties.

2. Click the General tab. This displays general properties.

3. Click the first button under the Add section of the General Table. Access 2007 displays Chart Workspace Title at the top of the chart.

4. Click the Chart Workspace Title. Access 2007 displays a text box in which you enter the title.

5. Click the Format tab.

6. Enter the title in the Caption text box. Access 2007 displays the caption at the top of the chart (see Figure 11.10).

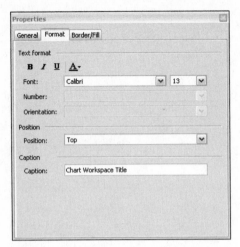

Figure 11.10. Enter a caption for the chart.

To add a title to an axis:

1. Click Property Sheet in the Tools group of the Design tab.

2. Select Category Axis 1 Title from the Select combo box in the General tab.

3. Click the Format tab.

4. Enter the title in the Caption text box. Access 2007 displays it on the chart. Do the same for each axis.

Add a legend

A legend identifies each series of data in the graph using a color or symbol. You probably won't need a legend unless the graph displays more than one data series.

Insert a legend by clicking Legend in the Show/Hide group on the Design tab. Follow these steps:

1. Click the Property Sheet.

2. Select Legend in the Select combo box on the General tab.

3. Click the Format tab.

4. Click the Position combo box and the set the location of the legend on the chart.

Changing the calculation

The PivotChart displays the total purchases of each product. You can change the calculation to another calculation by clicking:

- Sum of Quantity field button at the top of the chart.

- AutoCalc in the Tools group on the Design tab. This displays a list of calculations.

- A calculation. Access 2007 redraws the chart by using the recalculated data.

Insert values to the chart

Don't get me wrong. Sometimes a chart is the best way to communicate data, but at times I find it difficult to read the exact value depicted on the chart when the value is between those marked on the chart.

Here's a trick a colleague showed me to take away guessing. Place the exact value on the chart. Here's how to do this.

1. Click Property Sheet.

2. Select Series in the Selection combo box on the General tab.

3. Click the first button in the Add section. This inserts exact values for each item on the chart.

Just the facts

- A Crosstab is a specialized Total Query in the form of a spreadsheet where some fields of a table are column headings and other fields are row headings. Cells contain summary of the fields.

- The fastest way to create a Crosstab is to use the Crosstab wizard.

- The Crosstab wizard works with one table. The workaround is to create a simple query that uses tables that you want used in the Crosstab wizard. Save this simple query and use the simple query in the Crosstab wizard.

- You can't use a calculated field in the Crosstab wizard. The workaround is to use the calculated field in the simple query and use the simple query in the Crosstab wizard.

- The Crosstab wizard places column headings in the order values appear in the field. You can't change this order unless you use a simple query.

- Create a Crosstab using the query designer if you want to build a Crosstab.

Using Forms

GET THE SCOOP ON...
Using the Form Designer ▪ Using the Form wizard ▪
Modifying a built-in form ▪ Creating controls ▪
Converting a form to a report

Designing and Using Forms

Every database application has a face — that's what I call forms used to enter and display information stored in the application's database. And like a face, a form projects a database application's persona. Glance at a form and you get the impression that the database application is user friendly or hard to use leaving you shaking your head as you continue searching for an easy-to-use application.

By now designing and creating a database is a cinch. Data entry and creating queries are no-brainers. It's time to dress up your database application. Think of this as dressing for success.

In this chapter, I show you how to design and create forms and add bells and whistles that you expect in a professional database application.

Figuring out forms

A *form* is the user interface to your Access 2007 database application. The term *user interface* is probably familiar to you. A user interface is the way someone interacts with a computer program. Throughout this book you use the Access 2007 user interface to build databases and queries and to enter and display information from a database. In this chapter you build a user interface for your database application.

With a form, you can:

▪ Display information
▪ Enter information

- Modify information
- Delete information
- Create dialog boxes
- Provide navigation throughout your database application

Differentiating between a form and a datasheet

The Datasheet that you've been using throughout this book is similar to a built-in form, but it really isn't a form. A datasheet is a temporary view of data that provides basic functionality of a form — data entry, data editing, and data display.

No doubt you already stumbled across the datasheet's limitation. You have little control over how information is displayed in a datasheet. You can change the font and modify columns, but that's about all you can change. This limited control is fine for a quick view of information, but unacceptable for a professional database application.

A form provides greater flexibility than a datasheet because you can place information anywhere on a form and dress up its appearance using color, shading, graphics, and special effects. There can be one or multiple records displayed on a form at one time.

You can create a form that lets the user of your database application enter and maintain information in multiple tables — something that can't be done with a datasheet. In addition, you can enhance a form to perform data validation, assuring the accuracy of the information before information is entered into the database.

The feature I like best is the ability to display pictures and other Object Lining and Embedding (OLE) objects (see Chapter 4) on a form. You probably saw this feature used when you were getting a photo ID card. Your photo and your information both appeared on the screen at the same time. After reading this chapter, you could probably build that application.

Types of forms

Access 2007 lets you create forms in all shapes and sizes; however, each falls into one of six types of forms. These are:

- **Columnar.** A columnar form shows one record at a time as is used most commonly for data-entry forms, dialog boxes, message boxes, and for navigating through your database application. Sometimes a columnar form is referred to as a full-screen form.

- **Datasheets.** A datasheet form is the same as the datasheets that you've been using throughout this book; however, a datasheet form is a permanent datasheet that displays multiple records in a spreadsheetlike format.

- **Tabular.** A tabular form combines features of columnar and datasheet forms. I like calling this a free-form form because you use it to create any form you can imagine.

- **Main/Subforms.** The main/subforms form consists of two forms that have a parent/child relationship. The parent form might have a list of customers. Double-clicking a customer name displays a subform containing detailed information about the customer (see Chapter 14).

- **Pivot Table.** A Pivot Table displays data in a cross-tabulation view. You learned how to create this type of form in Chapter 11.

- **Graphs.** A graphs form displays information as a bar chart, pie chart, line graph, or other kinds of graphical format (see Chapter 14).

Ways to create a form

Access 2007 provides several ways to create a form, and you can find them in the Forms group on the Create tab. You can create a form by using built-in forms, the Form wizard, and the Forms Design tool.

Built-in forms are commonly used form designs built for you that can be easily modified to meet your requirements. I use these all the time rather than building a form from scratch.

Built-in forms are available either as buttons in the Forms group or from a list displayed by clicking More Forms.

Here are the built-in forms that you'll find in the Forms group.

- **Form.** Creates a single record form.

- **Split Form.** Splits a form into two sections. The top section contains multiple records and the bottom section contains single records. I use this to display a list of records on top and then let the user click one of them to see details of the record at the bottom of the form.

- **PivotChart.** Displays data in a graph. You learned how to do this in Chapter 11.

- **Blank Form.** Creates an empty form.

- **Datasheet.** Displays data in spreadsheet-like format.

- **Modal Dialog.** Creates a dialog box that when opened blocks interaction with the rest of the application until the person responds to the modal dialog box. This is like the Save As dialog box used in many Windows applications to save a file.

- **PivotTables.** Lets you define data values for rows and columns. (I go over how to do this in Chapter 11.)

The Form wizard walks you through the process of building a form. You can find the Form wizard on the More Forms list. You'll probably create your first form using the Form wizard, but like me you'll find it cumbersome to use and probably will use one of the built-in forms for most of your work.

Form Design in the Forms group opens the Form Designer tool where you can build any form. I use this to build complex forms and forms that are faster to build from scratch than to modify one of the built-in forms.

Sections of a form

A form is divided into five sections. Some sections appear when a form is viewed on the screen and printed, while others are used only when a form is printed.

These sections are:

- **Form Header.** This section is at the top of each page when the page is viewed on the screen and on top of the first page if the form is printed.

- **Page Header.** This section is used only when the form is printed and appears after the form header is printed.

- **Details.** This section is the body of the form.

- **Page Footer.** This section is used only when the form is printed and appears before the form footer.

- **Form Footer.** This section is displayed at the bottom of each page when the form is viewed and printed at the bottom of the form when printed.

Inside Scoop

Although a form can be printed, forms are designed to be viewed on the screen. Reports are designed to print information.

Controls for forms

Each element on a form such as a label, a text box, or a check box, is called a control. Access 2007 has a variety of controls that you can use to build your form. I show you how to use each in Chapter 13 and Chapter 14.

Controls are found in the Controls group on the Design tab. Click the control, click the form, and then drag the control into position. You can position controls in any section of the form, although most times controls are placed in the details section of the form.

A control can be bound or unbound, depending on the nature of the control. *Bound* is the term that describes a link between a control and a field in a table. A control is bound if it is linked to a field; otherwise the control is called unbound.

Any control can be unbound although many, such as a text box, a check box, and other controls used for data entry, are usually bound to a field. In this way, Access 2007 automatically saves information to the field once you move it to a different record.

Some controls are always unbound because they are not associated with information. These include lines and rectangles that are used to visually organize the form.

Creating controls from fields

A control can also be added to a form by double-clicking a field on the field list. The field list shows all tables and queries in the current database and its fields. I show you how to create this association later in this chapter.

Access 2007 uses the default control for a field, which is usually a text box, and automatically bounds the control to the field. This is the way I create most controls for my forms when I'm modifying a built-in form. It eliminates the extra step of binding the control to the field.

However, it sometimes adds another step to change to a different control. You'll see how this is done later in this chapter.

You probably remember from Chapter 4 that a label can be created for a field when the field is created. The label becomes the default label used to describe the contents of the field.

Access 2007 uses the text of this label as the text for a label control that is automatically placed on the form when you create a control by double-clicking on the field list.

Both controls are linked — move the control bound to the field and the label goes along for the ride. This is a good thing most times because they are used as a couple. Occasionally, you'll want to break the link and move them separately. This is a cinch to do — I show you how later in this chapter.

Calculating controls

A calculated control is an unbound control that displays the result of calculating an expression such as the total number of orders that a customer placed.

The expression is entered as the Control Source property for the control. Access 2007 automatically calculates the expression and displays the result in the control each time the form is viewed.

Modifying properties

You can change the default characteristics of a form or a control by modifying its properties. As you can imagine, there are many properties dealing with nearly every aspect of the form or control such as colors and special effects.

I show you how to modify important characteristics later in the chapter when you learn how to create a form and control.

Data sources for a control

There are two potential data sources for a control: a field and a query.

The major disadvantage of using a query is that the form can't be used to update the data. You'll remember from Chapter 8 that data filtered by a query is placed in a dynaset. A dynaset is a temporary table.

Using the Form wizard

Reading about how forms are built is interesting, but you probably want to jump in and build your own. The quickest way to get started is to use the Form wizard. The Form wizard, as with any wizard, walks you through the entire process, so I'll point out the highlights and let the Form wizard explain each step of the process.

I'm using the Northwind Traders database for this example. Here's what you need to do to build a form using the Form wizard:

1. Click More Forms in the Forms group of the Create tab. Doing this displays a menu that contains the Form wizard.

2. Click Form wizard to run the Form wizard.

3. Click the Tables/Queries combo box and click the table or query for the form. The Form wizard automatically displays its fields in the Available Fields column of the Form wizard dialog box.

4. Double-click the name of the field(s) that you want to appear on the form. The Form wizard automatically moves the field name to the Selected Fields column (see Figure 12.1).

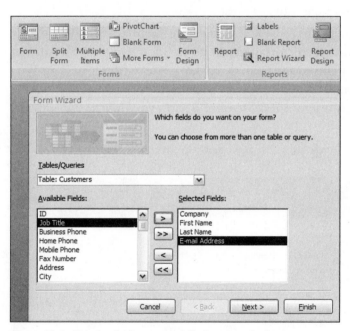

Figure 12.1. Pick the fields you want displayed on the form.

Inside Scoop

You can choose a different table or query if you want to use fields from multiple sources. The Form wizard retains the selected fields and displays fields from another table or query in the Available Fields column.

5. Click Finish. The Form wizard creates the form.

6. Click Next, if you wish to fine-tune the form. The Form wizard asks you to pick a layout for your form.

7. Select a form layout. The Form wizard shows you the layout and then click Next.

8. Select the style for the controls. The Form wizard applies your selection to a sample control. Click another style if you don't like the style that you selected.

9. Click Next to continue to fine-tune the form or click Finish to create the form.

10. Enter a title for your form. The Form wizard creates a title for you, but it's best to enter your own title.

11. Click Open the form to view or enter information. This tells the Form wizard to create and open the form when you click Finish. You can further fine-tune the form by clicking Modify the form's design. When you click Finish, the Form wizard creates the form and opens it in the Form Designer tool, which I'll show you how to use later in this chapter.

12. Click Finish. The form is created and opened (see Figure 12.2).

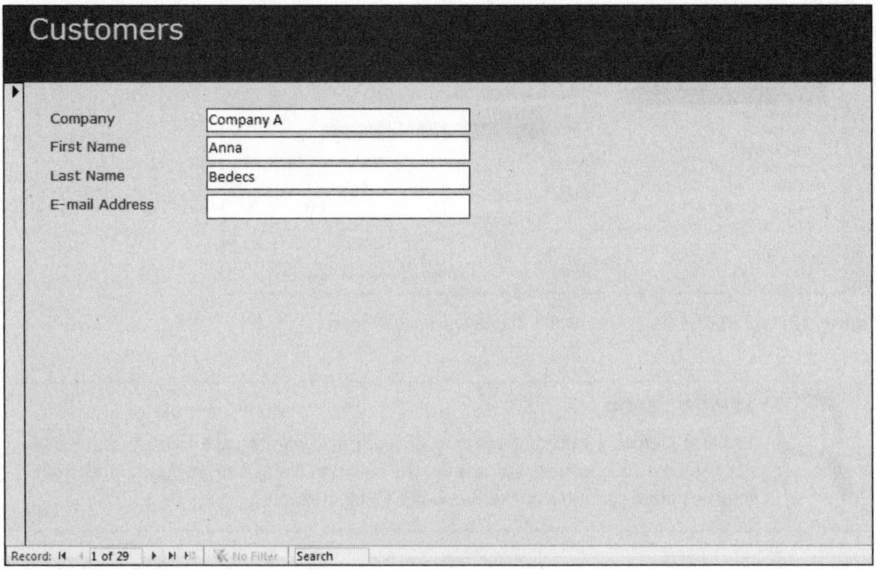

Figure 12.2. The Form wizard creates and opens the form.

Inside Scoop

The form appears in the Unassigned Objects group in the Northwind Traders pane. Double-click it to display the report. Highlight the name and click Form Design in the Forms group on the Create tab to modify the report.

Access 2007 automatically displays the first record in the form. The record navigation bar at the bottom of the form is used to move to another record. This is the same as the record navigation bar that you've used in other Windows applications.

Besides scrolling through records, you can use the record navigation bar to search for a particular record. Here's how to do this:

1. Click the text box control that is bound to the field you want to search.

2. Enter the search criteria in the search box on the record navigation bar. Access 2007 begins searching when you enter the first character and displays the matching record in the form.

Using built-in forms

Are you ready for a little magic? Click the Customers table and then click Form in the Forms group on the Create tab.

Magically, right before your very eyes a completed form appears ready to be used to look up customer information or enter information about a new customer. Here's how to do it:

1. Click Form to create a single record form.

2. Click Split Form to create a form split into a multiple record and single record form.

3. Click Multiple Items to create a multiple record form.

4. Click Blank form to create your own form by double-clicking fields from the Field List.

5. Click More Forms and the datasheet to create a datasheet form.

One of the built-in form probably serves most of your needs, but you can always modify a built-in form if it doesn't.

Modifying a built-in form

Access 2007 automatically binds controls to fields from the table and uses the default label for the field as the text for the Label control on the form. Text for the title of the form comes from the table name.

Choices that Access 2007 made for you may not be to your liking, but that isn't a problem because you can modify the form using tools on the Formatting tab.

When Access 2007 created and opened the built-in form, it also made the Formatting tab the current tab. The Formatting tab contains an assortment of tools, many of which are the same formatting tools available in Microsoft Word or Microsoft Excel.

Click a control or element of the form that you want changed and then click the tool in the Formatting tab to apply to modify its format.

Changing the appearance of text

An assortment of tools in the Font group can be used to change the appearance of text on the form. You can change the font, the size, make text bold, italic, or underlined, and align text within the control. You can also change the color of the text and that color of the background. These tools work the same way as they work in Word and Excel.

Changing the text conditionally

The Conditional tool within the Font group is used to change the appearance of text based on a condition that you specify. Why would you want to do this? You may want to show critical values such as a decline in revenue in red and bold type and noncritical values in black.

Click the Conditional tool, and Access 2007 displays the Conditional Formatting dialog box where you can specify the default appearance of the text and the appearance when a condition you specify occurs.

The Conditional Formatting dialog box is divided into two groups of controls:

- **Default Formatting.** These controls set the format for text when the condition isn't met. These are the same controls used to change the appearance of the font in Word and Excel.

- **Condition 1.** These controls set the format for text when the condition is met and lets you specify the condition. One condition is shown, but you can specify other conditions by clicking Add.

Here's how to use the Conditional tool. I'm using the Customers table from the Northwind Traders database. I clicked Customers table in the Supporting Object section of the Northwind Traders pane and then clicked Form in the Forms group on the Create tab to display the built-in form:

1. Click a control whose text will be affected by the condition. I selected the Zip/Postal Code text box control.

2. Select Conditional in the Font group of the Format tab to display the Conditional Formatting dialog box.

3. Click formatting tools in the Default Formatting group to set the appearance of the text if no condition is met. The format is applied to the sample text. If the sample text is grayed, then click the Enabled button, which is the last button in the Default Formatting group. The Enabled button activates the default formatting.

4. Click Field Value Is in the first combo box. Selecting this tells Access 2007 to apply the format when the value of the Zip/Postal Code field is the value specified in the expression. You could also select Field Has Focus, which means the format is applied when the cursor is placed in the field. Another choice is Expression. This is used when an expression specifies when a condition exists.

5. Select Between in the second combo box. The combo box lists operators you can use to define the condition.

6. Enter 07660 in the next text box and 08660 in the second text box. Records that have a zip/Postal Code value between 7660 and 08660 triggers the conditional format change to the text.

7. Open the font color combo box and click red. The sample text changes from black to red (see Figure 12.3). Click the Enabled button (last button) if the sample text is grayed.

8. Click OK to apply the condition.

Inside Scoop

The number of text box controls that appears to the right of the second combo box in the Condition group depends on the operator. Some operators require one text box control.

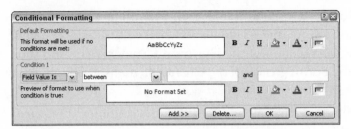

Figure 12.3. Pick the fields you want displayed on the form.

Formatting numbers

Tools in the Formatting group on the Formatting tab are used to format numbers. These probably look very familiar to you because they are the same as you use in Word and Excel.

The Formatting group is grayed if you selected a control that is bound to other than a number field.

Formatting the grid

The Gridlines group contains tools used to format the grid that is drawn around controls on the form. These tools are also familiar because they are the same used in Word and Excel to set the format of a table and spreadsheet.

You choose what lines, if any, in the grid are visible on the form, as well as the thickness, style, and color of the lines.

Adding bound controls

Remember that a bound control is a control that is bound to a field in the table. Access 2007 automatically places controls bound to the table you selected before creating the form.

You can insert additional fields from the Field List. Open the Field List by clicking Add Existing Fields from the Tools group of the Formatting tab.

The Field List (see Figure 12.4) is divided into three sections. The top section contains fields from the current table. The middle section contains related tables. The bottom section contains a list of other tables in the database. Click the plus sign to see fields available in other tables.

Double-click the field name.to insert a field. If the field is from the table that is bound to the form, Access 2007 creates a Label and Text Box control and places it at the bottom of the form. If the field is from a different table, the Specify Relationship dialog box is displayed and prompts you to identify the fields used to join together these tables. You are also prompted to select the type of join (see Chapter 8).

Changing the logo

Access 2007 displays a default logo for the report. Change this by clicking the Logo tool in the Controls group of the Formatting tab. Doing this displays the Insert Picture dialog box.

Select the file that contains the image of the logo and click OK. Access 2007 then uses it as the logo.

Changing the title of the form

There are two ways to change the title of the form. You can double-click the title and begin typing. Or you can click Title in the Controls group on the Formatting tab and then begin typing.

Inserting date and time

Click the Date and Time tool in the Controls group on the Formatting tab and Access 2007 displays the Date Time dialog box. Click the check box if you want the date and or the time displayed on the form and click the style to use.

Click OK and Access 2007 displays the current date or time or both, depending on your choice in form's header.

Changing lines on the form

Some controls have lines. You can change the characteristic of the line by using the line tools in the Controls group of the Formatting tab. There are three tools that affect lines.

- The thickness tool is used to set the thickness of the line.
- The style tool is used to select the line's style (i.e. solid, dotted).
- The color tool is used to select the line's color.

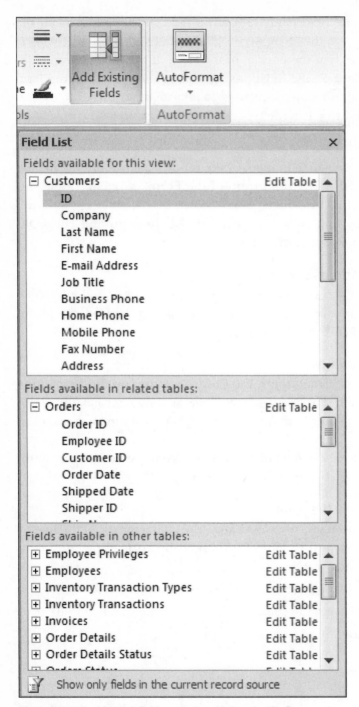

Figure 12.4. Double-click field names to add them to the form.

Watch Out!
Delete with caution because you cannot undo the delete.

Using AutoFormat

In a pinch use the AutoFormat tool in the Quick Format group of the Formatting tab to apply one of the many built-in formats to the form.

1. Click AutoFormat to see the built-in formats.

2. Double-click a built-in format to have Access 2007 apply it to the form.

3. Click Style at the bottom of the AutoFormat list to see a listing of styles that can be applied to the form.

4. Select a style in the form AutoFormats column, and Access 2007 applies it to the sample control displayed in the center of the AutoFormat dialog box.

5. Click OK to apply the style to the form.

Deleting a control

Remove a control by selecting the control you want to remove and then pressing Delete. Access 2007 removes the control from the form.

Repositioning a control

Reposition a control by clicking the control and then dragging the move handle into the new position. Access 2007 might place several controls in a block. You can only move the block and not controls within the block.

Creating a modal dialog

A modal dialog is a dialog box that requires the user to respond to it before accessing other parts of the application. The Save As dialog box that you use to save a file is a modal dialog. You can still access other applications, but not other parts of the application that display the modal dialog.

Inside Scoop
Automatically convert an existing form or report to a built-in form by clicking the form or report and then clicking the built-in form.

Inside Scoop

Dialog? Dialog box? What's the difference? There isn't any difference. The term dialog box was used with early version of Windows and has since evolved to simply dialog. Both terms are still used today.

Create an empty modal dialog by:

1. Click More Forms in the Forms group of the Create tab to display a pop-up menu.

2. Select Modal Dialog from the pop-up menu. This displays an empty modal dialog and makes the Design tab the current tab. The Design tab contains controls and other tools needed to create the modal dialog box.

3. The empty modal dialog consists of a grid filled with tiny dots. Scroll to the end of the modal dialog and you'll find the traditional OK and Cancel buttons already placed on the modal dialog for you.

Using the grid and dots

Grid lines and dots are guides for you to position controls and don't appear on the modal dialog. After placing a control on the modal dialog, drag the control into alignment with other controls on the modal dialog by using either grid lines or dots as a guide.

The edge or order of the new control is positioned along the same grid line or row or column of dots at the edge of an existing control. This ensures that your modal dialog has a professional flair about it.

Sometimes I find the grid and dots distracting when designing the modal dialog. I remove this distraction by hiding the grid and dots and then continue to design the modal dialog.

Here's how I remove the grid and dots. Right-click the modal dialog to display a pop-up menu. Click Grid. The grid is hidden or the grid is displayed, if the grid is already hidden.

From time to time, I want to view the modal dialog the way the user will see it. To do this I click the Form View button, which is the left button in the lower-right corner of the Access 2007 window. Then I return to the Design View by clicking the right-most button (see Figure 12.5).

Line control

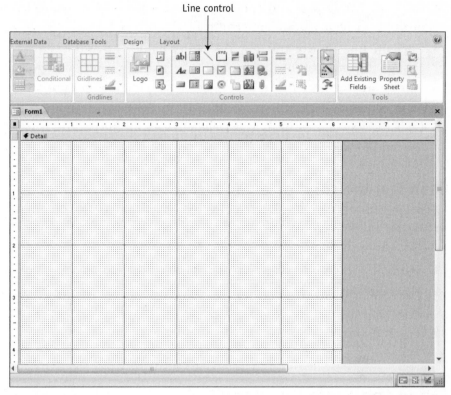

Figure 12.5. Toggle between Form View and Design View to see how the modal dialog looks to the user of your application.

Placing and removing controls on the modal dialog

The Controls group on the Design tab contains controls that give the modal dialog functionality. I show you how to use each of them in Chapter 13 and Chapter 14.

For now let's see how to place a control on the modal dialog.

1. Click the Line control. This is the line drawn on an angle in the Controls group.

2. Click the modal dialog. Access 2007 draws the line control.

3. Drag and drop the line control in the position where you want it in the modal dialog.

4. Click the line control and drag a handle at either end to change left or right the length of the line control.

5. Click the line control and drag the center handle up or down to change the angle of the line control. Alternatively, you can drag the handle at either end of the line control on an angle to produce the same results.

6. Click the line control and press Delete to remove the control from the modal dialog.

Changing the color of the modal dialog

Liven up your modal dialog by changing its color from gray to something snazzy. Access 2007 provides an assortment of colors to choose from.

Here's how to change the color:

1. Right-click the modal dialog. This displays a pop-up menu.

2. Move the cursor over the Fill/Back Color. A palette of colors is displayed.

3. Select the new color. Access 2007 applies the color to the modal dialog.

Using the Form Designer

The Form Designer is a tool that lets you build a form from scratch. Open it by clicking Form Design in the Forms group on the Create tab. This looks familiar because it's the same grid and dots you use when creating a modal dialog.

The grid is the form's workspace. This is where you place controls. The nongrid area is outside the form's workspace. However, place a control outside the grid and Access 2007 expands the workspace to hold the control.

Resizing the form

Access 2007 uses the default 5" x 2" for the form's workspace, which is probably not the right size for your form. The size of the workspace depends on your design for the form. You resize the form by grabbing the border of the workspace and dragging it into position. You also need to move the controls out of the way.

Inside Scoop

Grab the upper-right corner and drag toward the lower-left corner to resize the form proportionally.

Don't make the size larger than 7.5" x 4.5", otherwise scroll bars are displayed because the form is larger than the screen, which forces the user to scroll to the hidden area of the form.

If you need more space, use the Tab control (see Chapter 13) or a form/subform (see Chapter 14). The Tab control is similar to tabs on file folders and creates overlapping pages of a form. Pages are accessed by clicking the tab.

It goes without saying that you've seen countless forms in the many Windows applications that you use. Try to mimic the design of forms that you found easy to use and avoid those designs that were difficult to use.

Adjust your screen resolution

If you're like me, you'll base your design on what you see on the screen. And if you're like me, you'll quickly discover doing so is not a good idea because the resolution of the computer screen alters the way a form appears on the screen. The resolution on your computer could be different from the resolution on the computer of users who run your Access 2007 database application.

What resolution should you use? There isn't an easy answer. However, professional developers use the resolution that is most commonly used by whoever is going to use the application.

What resolution is most commonly used? I set the resolution of my computer screen to 1024 x 768 because this seems to be the most commonly in use.

Selecting a resource source for a form

A form can be bound to a table, a query, or an SQL Select statement by setting the form's Record Source property. You do this by clicking Property Sheet in the Tools group of the Design tab to display the form's properties.

The Record Source property is the first property on the Data tab. Click the Record Source property, and Access 2007 displays a combo box of tables and queries that are part of the current database. Select the one that you want bound to the form.

You'll see a button displaying three dots to the right of the combo box in the Record Source property. Click it, and Access 2007 opens the Query Designer (see Chapter 8). Use the Query Designer to create a new query and bound it to the form. This is referred to as an SQL Select statement because the Query Designer translates your query design into an SQL Select statement that is used to select records for the form.

Creating the form

Use methods that you learned previously in this chapter to create the form.

Click Add Existing Fields in the Tools group on the Design tab to display the Field List and then double-click the fields you want bound to controls on the form.

Click controls in the Controls group on the Design tab to place controls on the form. I show you how to use each control in Chapter 13 and Chapter 14.

Using the form property

Click Property Sheet in the Tools group on the Design tab to display the form's property. Properties are organized into categories, each appearing on its own tab. Use the combo box at the top of the form's property sheet to select an area of the form, and Access 2007 displays its properties.

Table 12.1 contains form properties that are commonly changed depending on the needs of your Access 2007 database application.

Table 12.1. Properties to change

Property	Description
Caption	Text for the title bar.
Auto Resize	Resizes the form to display a complete record.
Auto Center	Centers the form on the screen.
Border Style	Sets the border for the form.
Picture	The name of the bitmap image for the background of the form.

Property	Description
Grid X and Grid Y	Sets the number of dots in the work area.
Record Source	The name of the record source.
Filter	Sets the filter used to filter records shown in the report.
Order By	Sets the order in which records appear in the report.
Allow Edits	Prevents or enables a user to edit data in the form.
Allow Deletions	Prevents or enables a user to delete data in the form.
Allow Additions	Prevents or enables a user to insert data in the form.
Pop up	Display form as a pop-up that floats above other objects on the screen.
Modal	Determines if the form is a modal dialog.

Inserting headers and footers

A form consists of a detail area. This is the second area of the form that contains the majority of controls and is the area displayed when you create a new form using the form designer.

You can add a form header and footer and a page header and footer and then place controls in those areas. For example, you'll probably place the time and date control in the form header and page number control in the form footer.

- **Form Header.** Is displayed at the top of each page when viewed and at the top page when the form is printed.
- **Page Header.** Is displayed after the form header only when the form is printed.
- **Page Footer.** Is displayed before the form footer only when the form is printed.
- **Form Footer.** Is displayed at the bottom for each page when viewed and at the bottom of the form when the form is printed.

You add a form header/form footer and page header/footer by right-clicking the form and then clicking Form Header/Footer or Page Header/Footer from the pop-up menu. Access 2007 inserts them into the form.

Hack

Press Crl+PgDn to move to the current field in the next record. Press Ctrl+PgUp to move to the current field in the preceding record.

Using a form

You'll be testing the form as you build it. Each time you move from the current record, Access 2007 saves changes to field that are bounded to the record. Changes are also automatically saved when the form is closed.

At the bottom of the form are navigation buttons that are used to navigate through the records. You are probably familiar with these because they are the same navigation buttons found on most Windows applications.

Access 2007 displays a record number for the current record. This is a virtual record number and not the record's record number in the table. There is absolutely no relationship between these record numbers.

Whenever you view the form, Access 2007 loads records from the data source and assigns each record a virtual record number. Many times records loaded into the form are filtered or sorted and therefore are not in the same order as they appear in the table.

Virtual record numbers are a good reference while viewing the form, but should not be used a reference from one viewing to the next because the order might have changed, causing the record to be assigned a different virtual record number.

Controls on a form function the same way as they do in any Windows application, so don't expect surprises simply because you built the form. Table 12.2 contains a few shortcuts that I use when modifying data using a form.

Table 12.2. Shortcuts to editing data in a form

Shortcut	Description
F2	Selects the entire content of a field.
Ctrl+' (single quote)	Replaces the content of the field with the content of the previous field.

Shortcut	Description
Ctrl+Alt+Spacebar	Replaces the content of the field with the default value.
Ctrl+; (semicolon)	Replaces the content of the field with the current date.
Ctrl+: (colon)	Replaces the content of the field with the current time.
Ctrl+Enter	Inserts a line break in a memo or text field.
Ctrl++	Inserts a new record.
Ctrl+-	Deletes the current record.
Shift+ Enter	Saves the current record.
Move to a different record	Saves the current record.
Esc	Undoes change.

Printing a form

A form can be printed by using the Print option on the File menu or by pressing Ctrl+P. This is the same way as you print any document. The printed version looks nearly the same as the screen version, although some minor adjustments are necessary depending on the printer.

The font used for the printed version of the form depends on fonts available at the printer. Usually there is a printer equivalent to the screen font.

Colors are transformed into shades of gray called a gray scale if you are not using a color printer.

Converting a form to a report

Expect this to happen to you — because it happened to me more than once. You create a dynamite form that meets all your requirements. Then someone asks you to modify it slightly to include features that are available only in a report, such as adding group sections and additional ways to tally the data.

Don't scream. Convert the form to a report instead. Once converted, open it in the Report Designer tool (see Chapter 15) and insert the new features without starting over from scratch.

Here's how to convert a form to a report:

1. Right-click the form name. This displays a pop-up menu.

2. Click Save As. This is displays the Save As dialog box.

3. Change the file type to report.

4. Click Save. Access 2007 converts the form to a report and saves the new report.

Just the facts

- A form is the user interface to your Access 2007 database application.

- A datasheet is a temporary view of data that provides basic functionality of a form — data entry, data editing, and data display.

- A columnar form shows one record at a time as is used most commonly for data entry forms, dialog boxes, message boxes, and for navigating through your database application. Sometimes a columnar form is referred to as a full-screen form.

- A datasheet form is the same as the datasheets that you've been using throughout this book, however a datasheet form is a permanent datasheet that displays multiple records in a spreadsheet like format.

- A tabular form combines features of columnar and datasheet forms.

- The main/subforms form consists of two forms that have a parent/child relationship.

GET THE SCOOP ON...
Grouping controls ▪ Creating an input mask ▪ Using
Label and Text Box controls ▪ Working with memo fields
▪ Using Image and OLE object controls

Chapter 13

Using Controls on a Form

For those of you who are control freaks, you'll love this chapter because I show you how to create controls for your forms. Think of a control as something that makes your form become functional. It is used to display information, input information, and to make your form interactive.

Controls are not new to you since you've probably used most of them when interacting with Windows applications. In this chapter, I take you behind the scenes and show you how to use these same controls to enhance the performance of your own Access 2007 application.

I'll cover basic controls in this chapter and then show you how to create more advanced controls in Chapter 14. After reading both chapters, you'll be able to create a form that has many features found in your favorite Windows application.

Choosing the right control

As you noticed in Chapter 12, the Controls group on the Design tab contains nearly all the controls you need to create a professional, working form for your Access 2007 application.

Your choice of a control determines how easy the form is to use and increases the accuracy of information entered into it. Think of how the form is going to be used before picking a control.

Available controls

In this chapter, I'm going to tell you how controls work in general and show you how to create simple controls for your form. You'll learn how to create more advanced controls, controls that I call intelligent controls, in the next chapter. Intelligent controls do more than display information and collect information from the person using the form. They also reduce the risk of data-entry errors. More on this in the next chapter. For now, here are all controls that you can choose for your form (see Figure 13.1):

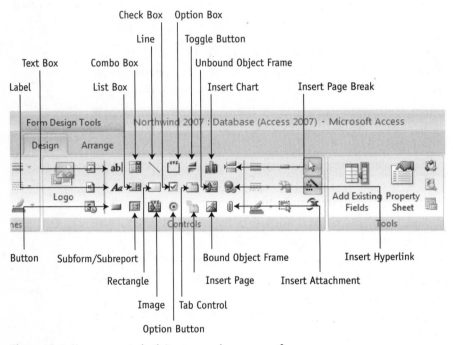

Figure 13.1. Here are controls that you can place on your form.

- ■ **Label.** Displays text.
- ■ **Text Box.** Used to input free-form data.
- ■ **Option Group.** Visually organizes controls into a group on the form.
- ■ **Toggle Button.** A two-state button used for data display and data input. Limits data input one of to two values — on/off.

- **Option Button.** This radio button is used for data display and data input. It limits data input to one of two values. These are on/off. An Option Button is usually grouped with other Option Buttons in an Option Group. Only one Option Button within the group can be on. Access 2007 automatically turns off other Option Buttons in the group.

- **Check Box.** This is used for data display and data input. It limits data input to one of two values — on/off.

- **Combo Box.** This control is similar in appearance and function to a Text Box except the user has a choice of entering a value into the Combo Box or selecting a value from a pop-up list.

- **List Box.** This control displays a list of items. One or multiple values can be selected for data input.

- **Command Button.** This control is a push button that when clicked runs a macro or Visual Basic program that is associated with the Command Button.

- **Subform/Subreport.** This control creates a subform within the current form or a subreport within the current report.

- **Tab.** This control displays multiple pages of a form as tabs of a file folder.

- **Image.** This control efficiently displays a bitmap picture.

- **Unbound Object Frame.** This control displays an OLE object or embedded picture that is not associated with a field in the database. Use this for graphs, video, pictures, and sound files.

- **Bound Object Frame.** This control is similar to the Unbound Object Frame control except it displays OLE objects and embedded pictures that are associated with a field in the database.

- **Line.** This control places a single line on the form.

- **Rectangle.** This control places a rectangle on the form.

Making tough decisions

Suppose that you're creating an order form and you need a control for the customer to use to enter the product he's purchasing. Here are some controls that you could use for the product — a Text Box, List Box, Combo Box, and Check Boxes.

- A Text Box enables the customer to type the name of the product, but the customer may not know the product's name or could misspell it.

- A List Box shows the customer all products and lets him pick one or several from the list. However, the List Box requires a relatively large space on the form, which may not leave room for other controls.

- A Combo Box also displays all products and lets the customer select the product he wants to purchase — and takes up less room on the form than a List Box.

- A Check Box shows one product. The customer can easily click the product he wants to purchase without having to look up the product on a list of products. However, you'll need too many Check Boxes if you offer a lot of products for sale.

Which control should you choose? It depends on the number of products being offered. The Check Box control is ideal if you have a handful of products — and your product line isn't expected to grow. A Combo Box makes sense if many products are offered and if your line of products is likely to increase in the future. However, for a really long list use a List Box control instead, because a List Box control is easier to scroll than a long list in a Combo Box control.

Using Windows standards

Besides picking the control that works best for your form, you must also consider how the control is used in other Windows applications. Over decades, developers have standardized the way controls are used in the Windows graphical user interface (GUI).

This standard makes it a no-brainer for us to learn how to use any Windows applications because all controls work the same way, regardless of who built the application. Windows standards dramatically reduce the learning curve.

You don't have to learn this standard, but you should use controls in your form in the way that you've seen them used in other Windows applications.

Conforming to the Windows look

Access 2007 gives you the latitude to add your personal touch by changing the appearance of a control. You can change the font, color, and style. I'll show you how to do this later in this chapter and in Chapter 14.

However, developers tend to adhere to a standard style so not to confuse anyone who uses the application. Here is the style standard for a Windows application.

- Tahoma font for all controls that are 12 points or smaller.
- Verdana font for all font sizes about 12 point.
- Etched line rectangles.
- Gray form backgrounds.
- Flat label controls.
- Sunken text box with white backgrounds for data input.
- No bold text except for a label control at the top of the form.

Placing a control onto a form

Click the control you want in the Controls group on the Design tab and then click the form. Access 2007 displays the control at the point on the form where you clicked the mouse.

I never get the control positioned correctly the first time. You might experience this same problem. Don't be concerned because you can easily reposition the control on the form.

You do this by clicking the control and then dragging the move handle of the control and dropping it into the new position. Access 2007 automatically aligns the control to the nearest grid line or dot if you have the grid displayed (see Chapter 12).

Working with a Label control and input control

Don't be puzzled if two controls pop on the form when you selected one of them. Access 2007 likes to think ahead and add a control that you'll probably want.

This is the situation when you add a Text Box control to the form. Each Text Box control usually has a Label control associated with it. The Label control describes the content of the Text Box control.

From Chapter 12 you might recall that double-clicking a field on the Field List caused Access 2007 to create a Label control and a Text Box control that is bound to the field.

Practically the same happens when you create a Text Box control from the Design tab. Access 2007 also creates a Label control on the form without you having to ask.

The Label control and the input control are a pair. Reposition the input control and the Label Control follows. You can break up this pair by using the move handle of the Label control to drag and drop the Label control into a new position on the form. Only the Label control is repositioned. The move handle is the large box in the upper-right corner of the control.

Changing characteristics of a control

Although the folks at Microsoft who built Access 2007 decide how a control works, you can modify a control's characteristics by changing the control's properties.

Changing the value of a control's property is no different than changing a property for a form or properties of other database objects that I showed you how to do in previous chapters.

Click the control and then click Property Sheet in the Tools group of the Design tab to see properties for the control. I'll show you properties that I change when I introduce you to each control later in this chapter and in the next chapter.

Sizing a control

Here's a problem that I'm always encountering — and I'm sure you will too. I place controls on a form, move them into position, and adjust the size. However, the form looks terrible. Controls are not evenly sized. Some are larger than they should be and others shorter. Tweaking their size makes matters worse.

The solution is to have Access 2007 adjust the size for you. Here's how to do this:

1. Select controls that you want to be the same size by dragging the mouse around them. The controls are selected when you release the mouse button.

Hack

Another way to select multiple controls is to hold down the Shift key and click Controls.

2. Right-click a control. This displays a pop-up menu.

3. Move the cursor over Size. A list of size options appears.

4. Click the appropriate size option (see Figure 13.2).

- **To Fit.** Adjust the size of the control to fit the text it contains.

- **To Grid.** Move the control to the nearest points on the grid.

- **To Tallest.** Make the control as high as the tallest selected control.

- **To Shortest.** Make the control as short as the shortest selected control.

- **To Widest.** Make the control as wide as the widest selected control.

- **To Narrowest.** Make the control as narrow as the narrowest selected control.

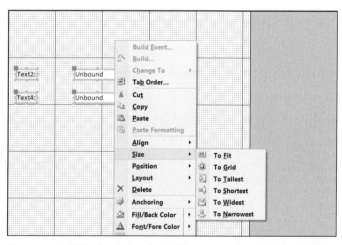

Figure 13.2. Click the size option and Access 2007 resizes the selected controls.

Aligning controls

Aligning controls on the form can be tricky. You can spend hours doing it unless you let Access 2007 help you. Access 2007 can align controls in the blink of an eye.

Here's how to align controls using the Align options:

1. Drag the mouse around controls you want aligned. The controls are selected when you release the mouse button.

2. Right-click a selected control. This displays a pop-up menu.

3. Move the cursor over Align. A list of alignment options is displayed.

4. Click the appropriate alignment (see Figure 13.3).

   - Left. Controls are aligned to the left edge of the leftmost control that you selected.

   - Right. Controls are aligned to the right edge of the rightmost control that you selected.

   - Top. Controls are aligned to the top edge of the topmost control that you selected.

   - Bottom. Controls are aligned to the bottom edge of the bottommost control that you selected.

   - To Grid. Controls are aligned to the top left corner of the nearest grid position.

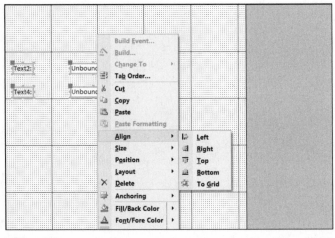

Figure 13.3. Click the alignment option and Access 2007 aligns the selected controls.

Copying and deleting a control

Here's another time-saver when creating unbound controls. Sometimes you'll find yourself creating multiple versions of the same control such as the Text Box control used for a person's name and address. You must create and format each version of the control.

A better approach is to create and format one control and then copy and paste the control on the form as many times as you need.

1. Click the control and press Ctrl+C to copy the control from the form to the Clipboard.

2. Press Ctrl+V to paste the control from the Clipboard to the form.

Don't fret if you make an error. Simply click a control and press Delete to remove it from the form.

A Label control is sometimes displayed automatically with an input control such as a Text Box control. Make sure both controls are selected if you want to delete both of them.

Naming controls

When I bring up the topic of naming a control, I usually get strange looks from some of my colleagues who are not familiar with creating macros (see Chapter 18) or interacting with forms using Visual Basic. Each control already has a name. That is, Text Box control is the name of the Text Box control. That's true, but each instance of a control has a unique name too.

Think of a control in the Controls group on the Design tab as a template that describes the control. It isn't actually a control. When you click the control onto the form, Access 2007 uses the template to create an instance of the control.

Hack

Copying a control is a way to make sure similar controls have a uniform appearance and size. Create one control, and then resize it and change its properties as necessary so it has the characteristics you want to see. Copy the control, and the copy has the same size and property setting as the original control.

So the Text Box control in the Controls group describes a Text Box to Access 2007. It's like a blueprint for creating a Text Box control. When you click the Text Box control on the form, Access 2007 uses this blueprint to create a real Text Box control, sometimes referred to as an instance of the Text Box control.

Each instance is given a unique name by Access 2007. The first Text Box you create is called Text1 and the next Text2. The names aren't very creative nor does it indicate the nature of the control, but it is the easiest names that Access 2007 can generate.

You should give each instance of a control a more informative name, a name that implies the content of the control, if the control is used in a macro or Visual Basic program.

A macro and Visual Basic program have instructions that tell Access 2007 to do something, which might be to read or write a value to a control or read or set a property of a control. The instruction might say, "Read the value of Text1 and write the value to Text2."

Access 2007 has no problem identifying Text1 and Text2 as long as there are controls with those names. However, anyone reading the instructions will have to examine the form to know how these Text Box controls are used in the form.

A better approach is to give each an informative name. Naming conventions specify two parts to a name — the prefix and the name. The prefix is a three letter abbreviation that describes the type of control (see Table 13.1) and the name describes the contest of the control.

For example, txtCustomerFirstName is the name of the instance of the Text Box control that contains the first name of a customer. You'd write txtCustomerFirstName when referring to this control in a macro or Visual Basic program.

To enter a name, do the following:

1. Click the control.

2. Click Property Sheet in the Tools group on the Design tab. This displays the control's properties.

3. Click the All tab. This displays all the properties for the control.

4. Enter the name in the Name property (see Figure 13.4).

Bright Idea

It's a good idea to name all your controls. You may change your mind or get new requirements that later require you to use it in a macro. You don't need to name things like simple labels and such, but input controls should be named with something that makes sense.

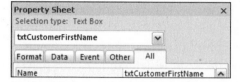

Figure 13.4. Enter the name of the control in the Name property.

Table 13.1. Prefixes for naming controls

Prefix	Description	Prefix	Description
frb	bound object frame	lst	list box
cht	chart	opt	option button
chk	check box	grp	option group
cbo	combo box	pge	Page (tab)
cmd	command button	brk	Page break
ocx	ActiveX Custom Control	pft	Page Footer (section)
det	detail (section)	phd	Page Header (section)
gft[n]	footer (group section)	shp	Rectangle
fft	form footer section	rft	Report footer (section)
fhd	form header section	rhd	Report Header (section)
ghd[n]	header (group section)	sec	Section
hlk	hyperlink	sub	Subform/Subreport
img	image	tab	Tab Control
lbl	label	txt	Text Box
lin	line	tgl	Toggle Button
		fru	unbound object frame

Setting the tab order

One thing that's irritating is to enter information into a text box, and then press the Tab key and have the cursor move somewhere other than to the next text box.

Everyone expects that pressing the Tab key moves the cursor to control for the next piece of information that needs to be entered into the form. You can assure this happens by properly setting the tab order on your forms.

The tab order is the order in which controls are selected using the Tab key. The default tab order is the order in which controls are placed on the form, however rarely is the order that information is entered into the form.

There are two decisions to be made regarding the tab order of controls on your form.

■ Should the control be a tab stop? Access 2007 places the cursor on a control when the Tab key is pressed only if the control is designated as a tab stop, otherwise Access 2007 skips the control and moves to the next control that is a tab stop.

■ What is the tab index if the control is a tab stop? The tab index is a value that specifies the position of the control in the tab order. The first control in the tab order has the lowest tab index value.

Set the tab order by:

1. Clicking the control.

2. Clicking Property Sheet. This displays the control's properties.

3. Change the Tab Stop property to Yes. This means that at some point Access 2007 places the cursor on the control when the Tab key is pressed.

4. Enter a value in the Tab Index property. This is the position of the control in the tab order (see Figure 13.5).

The fastest way to set the tab order when you have a lot of controls on the form is to use the Tab Order dialog box. The Tab Order dialog box lists all controls on the form by name left to right, up and down as each control appears on the form.

Inside Scoop

The position of controls on the form are unaffected by changing the tab order in the Tab Order dialog box.

Figure 13.5. Enter the position in the tab sequence of the control.

Display the Tab Order dialog box by right-clicking the form to display a pop-up menu and then click Tab Order.

Do the following to change the tab order:

1. Drag and drop controls in the Tab Order dialog box into the tab order.

2. Click OK. Access 2007 sets the tab index for each control based on its position on the list.

3. Click Auto Order. Access 2007 rearranges the list and tab index according to the order in which controls are placed on the form.

Using the Label control

The Label control is used to display text on a form — like you didn't know that already. Typically a Label control is used to describe an input control such as a Text Box, but it can also be used to identify sections of the form and instructions for using the form.

Click the Label control in the Design tab and then click the form and Access 2007 displays the Label control on the form. Begin typing the text that you want to appear on the form. Access 2007 automatically adjusts the size of the Label control to fit the text.

Text should be consistent throughout your form. I usually capitalize the first letter for each word except for *the, an, and, or,* and other articles and conjunctions. I don't use bold, italic, or underline because I want my forms to blend with other professional Windows applications.

There may be occasions when you want to dress up the Label with special effects, color, and in other ways. You'll find these features on the Label control's property sheet.

1. Click the Label control.

2. Click the Property Sheet in the Tools group on the Design tab to see its properties.

3. Click the Format tab to see formatting options (see Figure 13.6).

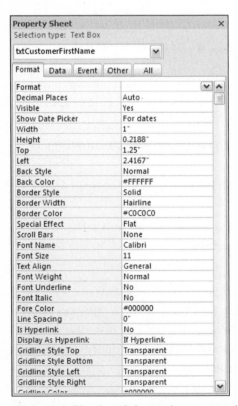

Figure 13.6. Give the Label control your personal touch by changing its format properties.

Using the Text Box control

The Text Box control is used to enter, modify, and display information. The information is usually the value of a field in a table or query, but can be associated with a calculation.

To create an unbound Text Box, do the following:

1. Click the Text Box control in the Controls group on the Design tab.

2. Click the form and Access 2007 displays an unbound Text Box control. An unbound Text Box control is not linked to a field. Anything entered into it isn't saved to the database.

To create a bound text box, double-click a field in the Field List. Access 2007 displays a Label control and a Text Box control and binds the Text Box control to the field. The label that is associated with the field in the database is used as the text for the Label control.

Changes made to the value of a text box that is bound to a field in a table are automatically saved when the cursor moves to another record. However, the same isn't true if the text box is bound to a field in a query. In this case, the changes are not saved to the underlying fields in the table that were used in the query.

Using calculations

The value of a Text Box control can be used as an operand in an expression or used to display the result of Access 2007 calculating the expression. You'll remember that an operand is a value used by an operator in an expression.

Let's say you want the form to calculate a price increase. Three text boxes are required: One to hold the price; another to hold the percentage increase, and a third to hold the increased price.

I'll name these controls txtPrice, txtIncrease, and txtNewPrice. The value of txtPrice and txtIncrease are entered when the form runs, so for now leave them empty.

The value of the txtNewPrice control is the expression used to calculate the new price. Place the expression in the Control Source property of the Text Box control.

Here's what to enter:

```
= txtPrice * (1 + (txtIncrease))
```

When calculating this expression, Access 2007 multiplies the value of the txtIncrease Text Box by 1. So if the value of txtIncrease is 0.05 (the decimal equivalent of a 5 percent increase), then 1 + txtIncrease is 1.05. Next, Access 2007 multiplies the value of the txtPrice Text Box by 1.05 and then displays result in txtNewPrice with the value.

You can also use the Expression Builder (see Chapter 9) to create an expression for the Text Box control. Click the Text Box control's Control Source property and then click the ... small button to display the Expression Builder.

Working with Memo fields

You'll remember from Chapter 4 that a table can have a Memo field that holds up to 65,536 bytes of text to store free-form text such as comments. A Memo field is displayed on a form using a multiline Text Box control.

If you double-click a Memo field on the Field List, Access 2007 creates a multiline Text Box control on the form. Adjust the size of the Text Box control to fit comfortably on the form. Don't try to display the entire value of the Memo field at one time. Scroll bars automatically appear to display parts of the Memo field that are hidden from view.

Creating an input mask

An input mask inserts formatting characters into the text in the text box. This is handy to use when the Text Box control is used for telephone numbers (i.e. (201) 555-1212) and Social Security numbers (i.e. 111-11-1111). The parentheses and hyphens are format characters. Format characters are not saved to the Text Box control's bound field in the database. They are used only during data input and data display.

Follow these steps to create an input mask:

1. Click the Text Box control on the form.

2. Click Property Sheet in the Tools group on the Design tab. This displays the Text Box control's properties.

3. Click the Input Mask property. Access 2007 displays the Input Mask wizard.

Inside Scoop

Be sure to set the Allow AutoCorrect property to Yes. Access 2007 then applies the same autocorrections that Word performs.

Inside Scoop

Access 2007 automatically applies to the Text Box control the input mask that is associated with the field that is bound to the Text Box control if the field has an input mask.

4. Click one of the many built-in input masks in the Input Mask column.

5. Enter sample data in the Try It text box and confirm it is right for your form.

6. Click Finish. Access 2007 displays the input mask in the Text Box Control (see Figure 13.7).

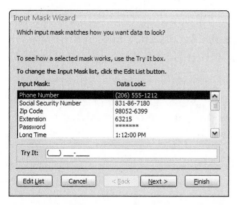

Figure 13.7. Select the input mask to use for the control.

See Chapter 4 for more tips on using the Input Mask wizard.

Using the Tab control

The Tab control is my favorite because it gets me out of tight spaces. There are practical limitations on the number of controls you can place on a form. There's a point when you can't squeeze any more controls onto the form.

Before reaching this point, consider inserting the Tab control. Think of the Tab control as a screen-stretcher. It doesn't really stretch the screen size, but it does add pages to the form as tabs.

Use tabs to organize your form. Each tab can contain related controls. The first tab could have a customer name. The second tab the customer's address. The third tab the customer's telephone numbers and e-mail address. And the fourth tab comments about the customer.

Watch Out!
Only the Tab control can be resized. You cannot resize each tab on the Tab control.

Place a Tab control on your form first, and then place other controls on a tab. Here's how to create the Tab control:

1. Click the Tab control in the Controls group on the Design tab.

2. Click the form. Access 2007 displays the Tab control showing two tabs labeled Page1 and Page2. This is a counter. The number is an increment of the last one inserted in your form.

3. Drag the size handles to resize the Tab control. Give yourself enough room for the other controls. Access 2007 automatically resizes the Tab control to fit new controls added to the Tab Control.

4. Place controls on the Page 1 tab. Do this the same way that you created the Tab control except this time click the tab page instead of the form. Access 2007 then places the control on the tab.

5. Click Page 2 to display the second tab page.

Place controls on Page 2 (see Figure 13.8).

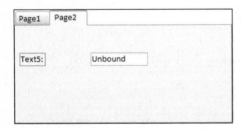

Figure 13.8. Add controls to a page the same way as you add controls to a form.

Inserting a new tab in the Tab control

Insert as many tabs as your form requires, but keep the tab page count to a reasonable number, otherwise you'll confuse the person who uses your form.

Here's how to insert a new tab to the Tab control:

1. Right-click the Tab control. This displays a pop-up menu.

2. Select Insert Page. Access 2007 inserts another tab and labels it as Page 3 or whatever is the next page number.

Hack

Delete a tab in a Tab control by selecting the tab you want deleted and press the Delete key.

Changing the label on the tab

Access 2007's choice of labels (i.e. Page 1, Page 2) is not very informative. That's why I always change them to a word or two that describes the contents of the tab. You should do the same.

To change the label on a tab:

1. Click the tab to make it the current tab.

2. Click Property Sheet.

3. Change the Name property to the new name of the tab.

Using Line and Rectangle controls

Line and Rectangle controls do more for your form than make your form look pretty. They are used to section the form. This helps the person using the form to focus on a set of controls at a time.

For example, I use Line controls to separate a customer name, customer telephone, and e-mail and customer address when I'm not using the Tab control for this purpose.

To create a Line control, follow these steps:

1. Click the Line control in the Controls group on the Design tab.

2. Click the form. Access 2007 displays the line.

3. Drag Line control into position.

4. Drag the sizing handles to resize the Line control.

5. Click Line Thickness in the Controls group on the Design tab to change the thickness of the line.

6. Click Line Type in the Controls group to change to a solid or dotted line.

7. Click Line Color in the Controls group to change the color of the line.

8. Click Special Effects in the Controls group to apply a special effect to the line.

Bright Idea

Drag the center size handle or the size handle on either end up or down to display the line on an angle.

Create a Rectangle control using the same steps as used to create the Line control, except select the Rectangle control.

Sometimes you'll want to increase or decrease the size of the Rectangle proportionally. The easiest way to do this is to drag the corner size handles. Access 2007 automatically adjusts the vertical and horizontal sides proportionally.

Using Image control

The best way I know to get a wow from anyone who sees your form is to place an image on it. This is very easy to do. The image can be a graphic such as a drawing or a photograph like they use in security systems — or shots you take on vacation.

The image is displayed using an Image control. Here's how you do it:

1. Click the Image control in the Controls group on the Design tab.

2. Click the form. Access 2007 displays the Insert Image dialog box.

3. Click the image you want to insert. Navigate the Image dialog box the same way as you find files using the File Open dialog box.

4. Drag the corner size handles to proportionally resize the Image control and the image itself.

Using OLE object controls

OLE is called object linking and embedding. Sounds a little too technical, but this is very easy to understand. An object is a file produced by an application other than Access 2007.

Inside Scoop

Don't use the side resize handles to resize the Image control. The image will probably appear distorted because you didn't proportionally resize it.

These include:

- PhotoShop
- Illustrator
- Flash
- Excel
- PowerPoint
- Word
- Microsoft Project
- MIDI software
- Video software
- Sound software

OLE tells Access 2007 that a program other than Access 2007 will display the file. For example, Access 2007 calls upon Excel to display the spreadsheet.

You could store an OLE object in a database, but that would make the database enormous. Alternatively you can reference the object in your form. This is called linking. Access 2007 then embeds the OLE object in your form.

It's like telling Access 2007 to display a Macromedia Flash Movie by giving Access 2007 the name and location of the Flash Movie file. Access 2007 finds Flash Movie and loads it into an OLE control on your form.

There are two types of OLE controls that you can create. These are:

- **Unbound.** This means that reference to the OLE object isn't in the database.
- **Bound.** This means that the reference to the OLE object is in a field in the database.

Here's how to create an Unbound OLE control:

1. Click the Unbound OLE control in the Controls group on the Design tab.

2. Click the form. Access 2007 displays the Microsoft Office Access dialog box.

3. Click Create From file.

4. Click Browse. The Browse dialog box is displayed.

5. Double-click the OLE file. Access 2007 returns to the Microsoft Office Access dialog box.

Click OK. Access 2007 creates the Unbound OLE control and displays the select file in the control.

Before I show you how to create a Bound OLE control, you need to have an OLE field in a table that contains references to an OLE object. Here's how to do this:

1. Double-click a table. Access 2007 displays the table in a datasheet.

2. Click View in the Views group on the Design tab. This changes to the Design view.

3. Enter the name of the OLE field.

4. Change the Data Type to OLE Object.

5. Click View. This changes back to the datasheet.

6. Right-click the OLE Object field in a row. This displays a pop-up menu.

7. Click Insert Object. This displays the Microsoft Office Access dialog box.

8. Click Create from File.

9. Click Browse and select the OLE file as you did when creating an Unbound OLE control.

Now that you have a table that contains reference to an OLE object, here's how to create a Bound OLE control:

1. Click Add Existing Fields from the Tools group on the Design tab. Access 2007 displays the Field List.

2. Click the table name that contains the OLE field. Access 2007 shows its field names.

3. Double-click the OLE field. Access 2007 creates a Bound OLE control and binds it to the OLE field.

4. Click View and Access 2007 displays the Form view and displays the OLE file in the OLE control.

Just the facts

- Label control displays text.
- Text Box control is used to input free-form data.
- Option Group control visually organizes controls into a group on the form.
- Toggle Button control is a two-state button used for data display and data input. Limits data input one of to two values — on/off.
- Option Button control is a radio button that is used for data display and data input. It limits data input to one of two values. These are on/off. An Option Button is usually grouped with other Option Buttons in an Option Group. Only one Option Button within the group can be on. Access 2007 automatically turns off other Option Buttons in the group.
- Check Box control is used for data display and data input. It limits data input to one of two values — on/off.
- Combo Box control is similar in appearance and function to a Text Box, except the user has a choice of entering a value into the Combo Box or selecting a value from a pop-up list.

GET THE SCOOP ON...
Looking at intelligent controls ▪ Choosing an intelligent
control ▪ Reacting to an event ▪ Selecting events ▪
Providing instructions for common events

Creating Intelligent Forms

Chapter 14

With the basics out of the way, it's time for you to learn how to create intelligent forms. These are forms that do more than save and display information entered into a control.

Intelligent forms reduce the opportunity for data-entry errors by using controls that limit choices of information that can be saved to the database. You've probably used many of these controls — combo boxes, list boxes, radio buttons, check boxes — in other Windows applications. Now you can learn how to create these controls.

Intelligent forms can also have multiple pages called subforms that open at the click of a button to collect or display information that doesn't fit on the form.

There's a lot you can do with intelligent forms. Rather than telling you about them, let's get down and dirty and build intelligent forms for your Access 2007 application.

Looking at intelligent controls

Say that a sales representative is placing an order for a customer. The order form requires the customer's name. You could use a text box control for this. However, when you use this method, you risk that the sales representative will mistype the customer's name.

A better way is to let the sales representative choose the customer name from a list of current customers using a combo box or list box control.

The sales representative also needs to enter products and quantities as well as calculate prices. This data entry exposes the company to risks, especially the risk of miscalculating prices.

Using a combo box or list box control and an expression in a text box control lowers this risk tremendously. Products are picked from a list, and Access 2007 uses the unit price from the product table and the quantity entered into the order by the sales representative to automatically calculate the price for the order.

Picking items from a list and automatic calculations are two of the many ways that you can build intelligence into a form.

Access 2007 provides a wide variety of intelligent controls to choose from, giving you the tools to meet any situation. You'll find these controls in the Controls group on the Design tab.

These are (see Figure 14.1):

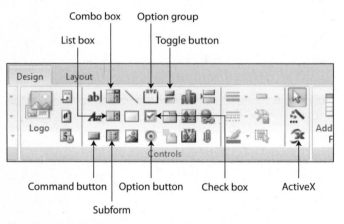

Figure 14.1. Here are intelligent controls that you can place on your form.

- **Toggle button.** Think of a toggle button control as the Caps Lock key on your keyboard. Press it once, and the button is on. Press it again, and the button is off. The toggle button control looks alike a button and changes appearance depending if it is on or off. It saves a True/False value if bound to a Boolean field in a table.

- **Option button.** You know this as a radio button. Click it once, and a dot appears in the center of the radio button. Click it again, and the dot disappears. It too saves a True/False value if bound to a Boolean field in a table.

Inside Scoop

Many people using a form expect only option buttons (radio buttons) in an Option Group control and expect check boxes and toggle buttons to work independently from each other.

- **Check Box.** Click it once, and a check mark appears in the box. Click it again, and the check mark disappears. And as with the toggle button and option button controls, the check box control saves a True/False value if bound to a Boolean field in a table.

- **Option Group.** An option group appears as a box around two or more toggle button, option button and/or check box controls. Only one control within the group can be selected. Others in the group are automatically deselected.

- **List box.** A list box control contains a list of items. The list always appears on the form. The items usually come from a query or a field in a table. The person using the form can select one or multiple items from the list.

- **Combo box.** A combo box control looks like a text box control and acts like a list box control by showing a list of items that can be selected by the person using the form.

- **Command button.** The command button control is better known as a push button. Click it and Access 2007 performs an action that you associate with the command button control, such as displaying the first record in a table or query.

- **Subform/Subreport.** The subform/subreport control creates a form or report that is related to the form or report that you're creating. I think of this as a form within a form.

- **ActiveX.** An ActiveX control is a control that isn't part of Access 2007, but instead is made by someone else to provide features that are not available in Access 2007. You'll find ActiveX controls available from many Web sites.

Reacting to an event

An event is something that happens when someone uses the form. The following are examples of events:

- Moving the cursor to a control is an event. The control is said to have focus.

- Moving the cursor away from a control is an event. The control is said to lose focus.

- Clicking the left mouse button when a control has focus is also an event.

Access 2007 ignores an event unless it has instructions to react to the event. The instruction is given to Access 2007 by the folks at Microsoft who built Access 2007 — and you.

- When a check box control has focus and the left mouse button is clicked, Access 2007 either displays a check mark in the box or removes it if the box checked. The folks at Microsoft told Access 2007 to do this.

- When an unselected options button labeled New Customer has focus and left mouse button is clicked, other controls on the form that are used to input information about a new customer become enabled. You tell Access 2007 to do this.

Enabled versus disabled

You probably experienced this. You're entering information into a form and some controls on the form are grayed, preventing you from entering data into it. The control is disabled. Controls that are functional — not grayed — are enabled and can be used for data entry.

A common practice is to place appropriate controls on a form and then disable those that are not necessary yet. When events occur that require data to be entered into a disabled control, intelligence that you build into the form enables that control.

A control is enabled or disabled by setting the control's Enabled property.

Hide versus visible

Having a bunch of disabled controls on a form is distracting to anyone using it. Some developers place related disabled controls toward the bottom of the form and then hide them unless they are needed.

Suppose you have a group of controls used to gather information about a new customer. You could place them near the bottom of the form and hide them. When the New Customer options button is selected, you can tell Access 2007 to make them visible.

A control is hidden or made visible by setting the control's Visible property.

Selecting events

Events differ depending on the object.. You can find a list of events for an object by following these steps:

1. Click the object.

2. Click Property Sheet.

3. Click Event tag on the property sheet.

Controls have similar events. Here are the events for a Check box control as an example. Which events your Access 2007 application reacts to depend on the nature of your form.

- **Before Update.** Before the value of the object is updated.

- **After Update.** After the value of the object is updated.

- **On Enter.** The object is enabled.

- **On Exit.** The object is disabled after being enabled.

- **On Got Focus.** The cursor is moved onto the object.

- **On Lost Focus.** The cursor is moved away from the object.

- **On Click.** The left mouse button is clicked.

- **On Dbl Click.** The left mouse button is double-clicked.

- **On Mouse Down.** The left mouse button is down (i.e. dragging).

- **On Mouse Move.** The mouse is moved.

- **On Mouse Up.** The left mouse button is up after being down (i.e. dropping).

- **On Key Down.** The user presses a key down on the keyboard.

- **On Key Up.** The user releases a key on the keyboard that was previously pressed.

- **On Key Press.** The user presses a key on the keyboard.

Providing instructions for common events

I can almost see the wheels turning in your head thinking about all the possibilities of creating a professional Access 2007 application now that you know the application can do things in response to events.

And I imagine that you're wondering how to make this happen.

Each event on the properties sheet can be assigned a macro, expression, and Visual Basic code.

These provide instructions that tell Access 2007 what to do when the event occurs with the object. I show you how to create macros in Chapter 18. You already learned to create expression in Chapter 9. Space doesn't allow me to teach you all of Visual Basic, but I'll give you a taste of what can be done with Visual Basic to illustrate how to react to events.

Enabling a control

Let's write Visual Basic code that enables a Check box control when someone selects another Check box control.

This is tricky because clicking a Check box control reverses its state. Click it once, and a check appears in the box (selected). Click it a second time, and the check is removed (deselected).

Obviously our instructions are assigned to the On Click event property; however Access 2007 must be told to examine whether the check box is selected or deselected.

We give Access 2007 instructions on how to make this decision by using an If Then Else statement. It tells Access 2007 that If this conditions exists (check box is selected), Then follow these instructions Else (check box is deselected) following these other instructions.

1. Create a simple form that contains two Check box controls. I named (the Name property) one of them chkProspectiveMember and labeled it Prospective member and the other chkSendApplication and labeled it Send me an application.

2. Change the Enabled property (Data tab) for the chkSendApplication Check box control to No. Access 2007 grays it on the form.

Inside Scoop

A statement is like a sentence in an Visual Basic instruction.

3. Click chkProspectiveMember and display the Event tab on the property sheet.

4. Click the second column on the On Click row.

5. Click the ... button. This displays the Choose Builder dialog box.

6. Click Code Builder. This runs the Visual Basic Code Builder and opens to the chkProspectiveMember_Click() subroutine. Think of a subroutine as a set of instructions that Access 2007 runs when your application calls the name of the subroutine, which is chkProspectiveMember_Click().

7. Type **If Form_Form1**. in the space between Private Sub and End Sub. The Code Builder displays a list of options, one of which is chkProspectiveMember, assuming your form has this name. The form name isn't necessary if you are in the context of the form.

8. Click chkProspectiveMember and type . (a period). The Code Builder displays another list of options.

9. Click Value.

10. Type = and you'll see two possible values False or True.

11. Click True.

12. Type **Then** and press Enter. This tells Access 2007 to determine if the Value property of the chkProspectiveMember Check Box control is true, which means that the person selected this check box.

13. Type **Else Form_Form1**. in the space between Private Sub and End Sub. The Code Builder displays a list of options, one of which is chkSendApplication.

14. Click chkSendApplication and type . (a period). The Code Builder displays another list of options.

15. Click Enabled.

16. Type = and you'll see two possible values False or True.

17. Click True and press Enter. This tells Access 2007 to enable the chkSendApplication Check Box control if someone selected the chkProspectiveMember Check Box control.

18. Type **Form_Form1**. in the space between Private Sub and End Sub. The Code Builder displays a list of options, one of which is chkSendApplication.

Inside Scoop

If you run into problems running a macro, go to the Trust Center and select enable macros by clicking the File icon in the upper-left corner of the screen, and then click Access Options where you'll find Trust Center.

19. Click chkSendApplication and type **.** (a period). The Code Builder displays another list of options.

20. Click Enabled.

21. Type = and you'll see to possible values False or True.

22. Click False. This tells Access 2007 to disable the chkSendApplication Check Box control if someone deselected the chkProspectiveMember Check Box control.

23. Type **End If** (see Figure 14.2).

24. Click the red box containing the X in the far right corner to close the Code Builder and return to the Form Design.

25. Click View to change to the Form view. You'll notice that the Send me an application check box is grayed and the Perspective member check box is black (see Figure 14.3).

26. Select the Prospective member check box and the Send me an application check box turns black, enabling a person to click it.

27. Deselect the Prospective member check box and the Send me an application check box turns gray, preventing a person from clicking it.

Figure 14.2. This instruction tells Access 2007 to enable the chkSendApplication when the chkPrspectiveMember Check Box control is selected and to disable it when the chkPrspectiveMember Check Box control is deselected.

Figure 14.3. The Send me an application check box remains disabled until the Prospective member check box is clicked.

Making a control visible

You can modify the previous example to hide the Send me an application check box and then make it visible only when the Prospective member check box is selected.

No doubt you can probably figure out how to do this.

Here's how:

1. Change the chkSendApplication's Visible property on the Format tab to No. This tells Access 2007 to hide the control when the form is displayed.

2. Replace Enabled in the statement between If Then and Else to Visible.

3. Replace Enabled in the statement between Else and End If to Visible.

If the chkProspectiveMember Check Box control is selected, then the ChkSendApplication Check Box control is visible; otherwise it is hidden on the form.

Using the Control wizards

Intelligent controls are more complicated to create than the basic controls you learned about in Chapter 13. You'll probably find it more efficient to use the Control wizard to create these controls rather than fine-tuning a control once it is placed on the form.

Each control has its own Control wizard; however you won't find them on the Design tab. Instead you'll find Control wizards in the Controls group on the Design tab. I show you the finer points of using each Control wizard later in this chapter when I show you how to create each control.

Here's how to start a Control wizard:

1. Click the Control wizard.

2. Select the control in the Controls group.

3. Click the form. Access 2007 displays the control and starts the Control wizard.

Using toggle button, option button, and check box controls

I've grouped these controls into one section because they basically do the same thing, although they look different. Toggle button, option button, and check box controls are used to identify one of two choices. Each choice is referred to as a state, such as yes or no.

A control can be set to a third state, which is referred to as the Null state. (Null means nothing.) Each control is in the Null state when it is initially displayed on the form unless a default value is set for the control. You can allow a Null state by setting the control's Three State property.

By default each of these controls is set up as two states — Yes or No. You can change the control's Three State property to yes.

When you bind the control to a Boolean field of a table using the control's Control Source property, Access 2007 stores -1 if the control is in the Yes state and 0 if it is in the No state. Nothing is saved if the control is in the Null state.

You can change the value that the control saves by setting the control's Format property. Your choices are:

▪ Yes/No

▪ On/Off

▪ True/False

Using toggle button controls

The toggle button control is easy to create — you won't need to use a Control wizard for this.

Inside Scoop

There are several ways to refer to a control when it is selected or unselected. I use Yes for selected and No for unselected, but you might hear others refer to this as True/False, On/Off or 1/0.

Inside Scoop

Always set the Default Value property of a control with the most commonly selected state. If most people select Yes, then set the default value to Yes.

Here's how to create it:

1. Click the toggle button control in the Controls group on the Design tab.

2. Click the form. Access 2007 displays the toggle button.

3. Drag and drop the move handle to reposition the toggle button. The move handle is in the upper right corner of the control.

4. Drag the size handles to resize the toggle button.

5. Click the toggle button on the form.

Here's how to display a picture on the toggle button:

1. Click Property Sheet in the Tools group on the Design tab. Access 2007 displays the toggle button's properties.

2. Click the Format tab.

3. Click the ... button on the Picture row. This displays the Picture Builder dialog box.

4. Click a picture in the Available Pictures column. The picture will be displayed on the toggle button (see Figure 14.4).

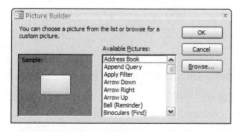

Figure 14.4. Click the picture you want displayed on the toggle button.

5. Alternatively, click Browse to display the Select Picture dialog box. Use this to select a picture that is available outside of the Available Pictures column, such as your picture.

6. Click OK on the Picture Builder dialog box to place the picture on the button.

Watch Out!

The caption doesn't appear if you already placed a picture on the button. Delete the reference to the picture from the Picture property and the caption appears on the toggle button.

Here's how to display a text on the toggle button:

7. Click Property Sheet in the Tools group on the Design tab. Access 2007 displays the toggle button's properties.

8. Click the Format tab.

9. Enter text in the Caption property that you want to appear on the toggle button.

Using option button and check box controls

You also won't need to use a Control wizard to create an option button or check box control unless you want to include it in an Option Group, which I'll show you how to do in the next section of this chapter.

Create these controls using the same steps to create the Toggle Button control. However, you don't have the option of putting your picture on it.

Double-click the label of the control and then enter text for the new label.

Turn the control initially on or off by clicking the Data tab on the control's property sheet and entering True (on) or False (off) as the value of the Default Value property.

Creating an Option Group

I find it easier to use a Control wizard when creating an Option Group than to change all the necessary setting by hand. Previously in this chapter your learned that the Option Group control is used to create a relationship among option button controls, toggle button controls, and/or check box controls. When one control in the group is set to True the others are automatically set to False.

Here's how to create an Option Group control:

1. Click Option Group in the Controls group on the Design tab.

2. Click the form. Access 2007 starts the Option Group wizard.

3. Enter text for Label Names. Each line in the Option Group wizard becomes a control within the group (see Figure 14.5).

Figure 14.5. Enter a label for each option. Press Tab to move to the next line.

4. Click Finish to create the Option Group control on the form.

5. Click Next to fine-tune the Option Group control. Access 2007 asks you to select a default control for the group.

6. Click the combo box and select the control that is the default control or click No and none of the controls in the group is the default control.

7. Click Finish to create the Option Group control on the form.

Alternatively, click Next to fine-tune the Options Group control. Access 2007 asks you to assign a value to each control in the group. This is the default value saved to the database when the control is selected. By default values are incrementally numbered.

8. Enter the default value for each control in the group.

9. Click Finish to create the Option Group control on the form.

Alternatively, click Next to fine-tune the Option Group control. Access 2007 asks you to choose the type and style of control. These are option buttons, check boxes, or toggle buttons. You are also asked to select a style for the control (see Figure 14.6).

10. Click type and style of the control to use in the Options Group control.

11. Click Finish to create the Option Group control on the form.

Alternatively, click Next to fine-tune the Option Group control. Access 2007 asks you to enter a title for the frame. By default, the title appears at the top of the Option Group control frame.

Inside Scoop

To bound the Options Group control to a field, click the Option Group control frame and click Property Sheet in the Tools group of the Design tab. Assign the field to the Control Source property.

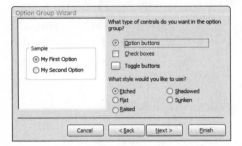

Figure 14.6. Enter a label for each option. Press Tab to move to the next line.

12. Enter a title that describes the group of controls.

13. Click Finish to create the Option Group control on the form.

Using combo box and list box controls

The Combo Box wizard and the List Box wizard ask basically the same questions and both come in handy whenever you create a Combo Box control or a List Box control because they make sure that you won't overlook any settings.

Click the combo box or list box control and place it on the form while the Controls wizard button is activated in the Controls group on the Design tab. I showed you how to do this in the "Using the Control wizards" section of this chapter. Access 2007 automatically starts the wizard.

You are asked if the values shown in the control will come from a table/query or if you'll enter them by hand. Your choice depends on the nature of your application.

I use values from a table/query if the information is going to change frequently. This way I don't have to manually update the control's values whenever the information is modified. This is a good choice if the control lists customers, products, or sales representatives.

I type in values if the values almost never change and there aren't a lot of values to type. If I wanted the combo box to display a list of common sizes, then I'd probably type those sizes directly into the combo box list because they rarely change. However, I'd use abbreviations for states from a table, probably a table I'd purchase from a vendor. These abbreviations don't change, but I also don't want to be typing 50+ abbreviations into the combo box list.

Type values displayed in a combo box or list box

If you select that you want to enter values for the control, you are prompted to enter the number of columns that should appear in the control. I usually leave this as 1 column unless the nature of the application warrants multiple columns.

Next, you are asked to enter values (see Figure 14.7). Type a value and then press the Tab key and enter the next value. Continue until all the values have been entered.

You're asked enter a label for the combo box. This is the same kind of label that appears in a Text Box control. Enter a label that describes the content of the control.

Click Finish. Access 2007 displays the combo box or the list box on the form.

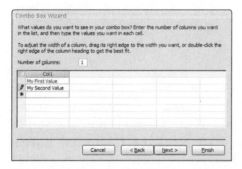

Figure 14.7. Enter values that you want to appear in the combo box list.

Use table/query for values displayed by a combo box or list box

Select that you want values for the combo box or list box to come from a table/query and you are presented with a list of tables that is associated with the current database. All tables are listed by default, but you can click Queries to see only queries or click Both to see a list of both tables and queries.

Next, you are prompted to select the field from the table or query whose values are displayed in the combo box or list box. You've learned how to do this in Chapter 8 when selecting fields for a query.

The wizard asks how you want these values sorted. The default setting of Ascending usually works well for most of my applications.

The drop-down list of the combo box or list box is then displayed, containing values from the field that you selected. Adjust the column width. This becomes the width of the combo box or list box.

The final step is to enter a label for the combo box or list box before pressing Finish and having Access 2007 create the combo box or list box on the form.

Using command button control

The command button control is a push button that causes Access 2007 to perform an action. There are many actions that can be assigned to the command button control. These include:

- Open Form
- Close Form
- Print Form
- Refresh Form Data
- Go to a particular record
- Add, delete, or save a record

There are so many actions. You can see a complete list in the Command Button wizard. Create the command button control as you've created other controls and Access 2007 starts the Command Button wizard.

Select the category of the action that you want the command button to perform and the Command Button wizard displays a list of actions in that category.

Select the action and then you are prompted to enter the text or picture to display on the command button. I usually accept either the default picture or the default text if I don't want to display the picture because I'm sure that these conform to Windows standards.

Next you're asked to give the command button a meaningful name. This is the name that is used to refer to the command button within your Access 2007 application. It isn't the text that appears on the command

Inside Scoop

You might wonder why this is called Subform/Subreport control when you're creating a form. Similar techniques are used to create a report that is used to create a form.

button. Give it a name based on the naming conventions I showed you in Chapter 13.

Click Finish and your command button appears on your form.

Using a subform/subreport control

Create a subform/subreport control by using a wizard. Start the wizard the same as you did the other controls that I showed you in this chapter. The wizard prompts you to create a new subform from an existing table/query or simply use an existing form as a subform.

I usually create a form outside of the SubForm wizard and then use the wizard to link it to another form.

Using an existing form as a subform

Click Use an existing form and then click the name of the form from a list of forms that are associated with the current database. Next you are prompted to enter a name for the form. I use the default name because that's always the name of the existing form.

That's about all you have to do. Click Finish, and Access 2007 creates the subform and displays it on the form (see Figure 14.8).

Using a table/query to create the subform

If you select to create the subform from a table/query, the SubForm wizard prompts you to select the name of the table/query and then select the fields you want to display on the subform. This technique is basically the same one you use to select fields for a query in Chapter 8.

You are then prompted to enter the name for the subform. Enter the name, press Finish, and the subform is created on your form.

Using an ActiveX control

An ActiveX control is a control that you can build or acquire from a third party other than Microsoft. It usually is a feature that isn't available in Access 2007.

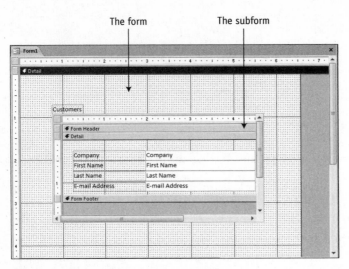

Figure 14.8. The subform is a form within a form.

To place the ActiveX control on your form, you first must make sure it is installed on your computer. If it is, then click the ActiveX control (the red X in the Controls group) and Access 2007 displays the Insert ActiveX Control dialog box.

Click the ActiveX control and then click OK. Access 2007 creates the control on your form. Refer to the third party that provided the ActiveX control for instructions on how to use it.

Just the facts

- Click a toggle button once and it is on. Click it again and the button is off.

- An option button is a radio button. Click it once and a dot appears in the center of the radio button. Click it again and the dot disappears.

- Click a check box once and a check mark appears in the box. Click it again and the check mark disappears.

- An Option Group appears is a box around two or more toggle button, option button, and/or check box controls.

Creating Reports

GET THE SCOOP ON...
Reports versus forms ▪ Choosing a report type ▪
Creating a report ▪ Designing the report ▪ Identify
printing requirements ▪ Understanding sections of a
report ▪ Setting the page headers and page footers

Creating a Report

L ook around. Notice something? The paperless office that so many of us expected hasn't materialized — at least not the way soothsayers forecasted.

Although e-mails dramatically reduce the demand for paper, I'm forever going to meetings and being handed a hardcopy of a report and then told the report is also being e-mailed to me.

Paper reports will be around for a while, and so you will your Access 2007 application to generate reports suited for viewing on the screen and printed on paper.

I hear you. Who needs a report? You can use a form to display information on the screen and printed on paper. True, but more information is provided in a report than on a form. I show you how to create a report in this chapter.

Reports versus forms

There are differences between a report and a form. Both do somewhat the same thing — display information on the screen and print information on paper. However, each can do things that the other can't do.

- A report prints information on paper better than a form because you can adjust the report to fit requirements of a printer.

- A form is used for data entry, but a report is not. A Text Box control on a form is used to display and input data. It is used only to display data on a report.

Hack

Convert a form to a report by saving the form as a report and then modify the report using the Report Design tool.

▪ Calculations that appear on a form are based on values in all the records that appear on the form. With a report, calculations can be based on groups of records.

Choosing a report type

At times I feel like a waiter when someone asks me to write a report.

I'd like apple pie a la mode. Heat the pie and I want the ice cream on the side — strawberry if you have it. If not, then no ice cream, just real whipped cream. If it's not real, then just the pie — not heated.

Uh?

You may find that colleagues are very particular when it comes to their reports and rightfully so, because the report is telling a story using information from the database.

It is your job to make their design a reality, regardless of the complexity. Fortunately, Access 2007 has all the tools you need to make this happen. You can create practically any report imaginable using Access 2007.

You can do the following:

▪ Group and sort records

▪ Calculate group totals

▪ Calculate page totals

▪ Calculate report totals

▪ Calculate any kind of summarization or statistics

▪ Create and print graphs

▪ Display and print pictures

▪ Mail merger

▪ Generate labels

Access 2007 gives you a leg up creating a report because it has five built-in reports that you can easily modify. These are:

- **Tabular report.** This report is sometimes called a groups/totals report. It presents information in rows and columns and is used to group by one or more fields and summarize information for numeric fields in each group. You can also create page totals and grand totals.

- **Columnar report.** This report is also known as a form report and is used to display one record on a page and resembles a data-entry form.

- **Mail-merge report.** This report combines information from a database with a block of text and is used to personalized form letters.

- **Mailing labels.** This report uses information in the database to create mailing labels. It offers a wide variety of label styles from Avery labels and other vendors. Select the style and Access 2007 makes sure addresses are printed properly on each label. This is very similar to printing labels in Microsoft Word.

- **Subreport.** This report is a type of columnar report. Think of this as a report within another report. You can use it to have customer contact information appearing at the top of the report and rows of orders in a subreport at the bottom of the report.

Creating a report

You can create a report in a few minutes using Access 2007. I show you how to do this shortly. However, reports that I've been asked to create requires forethought in order for the report to convey the message that my colleagues wants to deliver.

Begin creating a report by identifying the purpose of the report. Know the message that is being conveyed and then find the information used to convey the message.

There are three kinds of information that appear on a report.

- **Textual information.** This is text that appears on the form, such as labels, descriptions, and instructions.

- **Information in the database.** This is data in tables or the results of a query.

- **Calculated information.** This is information generated by the report by performing calculations.

Designing the report

I use the top-down approach when designing a report starting with what the person who receives the report sees and then assembling information for the report.

Expect to deal with fickle colleagues who know the report they want when they see it — and then leave you to read their mind. Avoid frustration by giving them a pencil and a blank sheet of paper and then ask them to sketch the report that they have in mind.

The sketch becomes your target. Create a report that looks similar to the sketch, and you'll be a hero.

Mapping information to the sketch

Analyzing the sketch gives you a clue to the type of information you need for the report. Mapping information to the sketch may seem easy to do, but it can be tricky.

First, a report is bound to the data source. You can choose fields from multiple tables or queries (see Chapter 8).

Most information on the sketch is available from the database — but not necessarily all the information. Your colleague knows the information needed for the report, but probably doesn't know or care if it is available from the database.

If the information isn't available from the database:

Ask your colleague for a sample of the information. You might be given a report or told to view a screen, which can be used to track down the source of the information and then import the information to the database (see Chapter 7).

Determine if the information can be derived from information already in the database. For example, you can concatenate (see Chapter 9) the customer first name field and customer last name field and display them as one name or calculate values.

Inside Scoop

Don't be afraid to tell your colleague that the information is not available from the database and cannot be derived from information in the database. Your colleague may decide that the information isn't required or will devote resources to generating the information.

Inside Scoop

Ideally you can use colors that provide the correct contrast when printed in black and white. This gives you the best of both worlds but you're still bound by the colors that give you this contrast.

Identify printing requirements

Reports are designed to be printed and not displayed on the screen. This is important to remember when designing the report because features that look great on the screen can be disastrous on paper.

Typically, reports are printed in black and white — not color. Although a colleague might use a color printer, printing in color is expensive for many organizations and requires employees to share a color network printer. Reports are not usually copied in color.

Use shades of gray instead of color. Shades of gray give the contrast that makes a report an eye-catcher. Black-and-white printers and copiers won't have a problem reproducing the report.

Design a report that fits on standard-size paper. I do my best to get the report to fit on letter paper because it is easy to handle and there is usually letter paper available on all printers.

Always test your report on the printer used to print the report to assure that the report is readable and looks good.

Test pieces before assembling

Some reports are simply too complex to wing it because they probably involve multiple queries and several calculations. The worst thing you can do is assemble all these pieces into the report and then test the report. Something is bound to go wrong and you'll spend hours trying to find the broken piece.

The best way to create complex reports is to test each piece separately and then assemble all the pieces when you know that each is working properly. If you do it this way, you know that everything worked before being placed in the report.

Create each query (see Chapter 8) independently of the report. Verify that the dynaset contains information required for the report.

Create expressions using a query (see Chapter 9) or a Text Box control in a datasheet and have Access 2007 calculate the expression. Tweak the expression until you get the desired result.

Place queries, calculations, and other pieces onto the report one at a time. Run the report and a verify information in the report each time. You'll know which piece caused a problem.

Understanding sections of a report

A report is divided into sections. My colleagues refer to these as bands. Each section — except one — is defined by a header and footer. A header contains information that is printed at the beginning of the section. Information in the footer is printed at the end of the section. The detail section is the exception. It contains detailed information such as customer orders.

Report and page headers and footers are inserted into the report as pairs.

Place any control in these sections. However, be sure that you understand how Access 2007 processes each section; otherwise, you might experience unexpected results when the report prints.

Here are sections of a report:

- **Report Header.** Typically contains the title page and is printed once at the beginning of the report. My colleagues use this section as cover page, and I use it as a cover letter in a mail-merge report.

- **Page Header.** This section is where I place column headers or the title of the report. In this way if a sheet is misplaced my colleague will know which report it belongs to. The Page Header section prints at the time of each page.

- **Group Header.** Here's where you identify the group of information that appears in the Detail section. I place the customer name and customer number here if I'm grouping customer orders. The orders appear in the Detail section. The Group Header prints before the first record in the group is processed.

Bright Idea

Break up the Report Header into two or more pages by setting the Force New Page property to After Section.

Bright Idea

You can insert multiple levels of Group Headers and Group Footer such as orders by customer by month. The first group is by customer and within that group orders are grouped by month.

■ **Detail.** This section is where the bulk of the information appears. The Detail section contains each record within the group of records.

■ **Group Footer.** This section prints after the last record of a group is processed. This is where you'll insert subtotals of numeric fields. You might also want to insert a line to separate groups in the report.

■ **Page Footer.** Here is where you'll probably insert the page number because this section prints at the bottom of each page.

■ **Report Footer.** This section prints once at the end of a report. I use this section to display the grand total of numeric fields in the report.

You're going to thank me for this advice because you'll avoid countless frustrating hours when you test your report. The Page Header prints on every page including on the first page, which is where the Report Header prints. Likewise, the Page Footer prints on the same page as the Report Footer.

Sometimes this doesn't look right, and you'll want the Report Header and Report Footer to print on pages that don't have the Page Header and Page Footer.

Access 2007 lets you pick where the Page Header and Page Footer are printed in the report by choosing one of four settings in the properties sheet:

■ **All Pages.** Both are printed on every page

■ **Not with Report Header.** Neither prints on a page with the report header.

■ **Not with Report Footer.** The Report Footer prints without the Page Header.

■ **Not with Report Header/Footer.** Page Header and Page Footer are not printed on the Report Header and Report Footer pages.

Understanding how reports are printed

Access 2007 knows to print a section when a certain condition exists in the report. These are referred to as triggers because the event triggers Access 2007 to do something.

It is helpful to understand these triggers when you test your report and discover that data isn't appearing where you want it to appear on the report. When this occurs — and it will occur — you'll probably find the problem by reviewing how Access 2007 processes the report.

The Report Header begins when the first record in encountered. Likewise the Report Footer starts after Access 2007 reaches the last record.

The first Page Header section prints once the Report Header prints. When Access 2007 comes near the end of the page, it prints the Page Footer. Subsequent Page Header sections print after the end in the page, which is called a page break.

When Access 2007 sees the first record in a group it prints the corresponding Group Header section and then the Group Footer is printed after the last record in the group is printed.

After the Group Header section is printed, Access 2007 prints the Detail section for that group.

Using the Report wizard

The quickest way to produce a report is to use the Report wizard. It'll walk you through the steps of several commonly used report styles. These reports may be all you need, depending on the nature of your Access 2007.

At times the Report wizard creates a report that almost meets your needs. That's all right because you can always fine-tune the design by using the Report Design tool.

And if tweaking the Report wizard's report doesn't do the job, then create the report from scratch using the Report Design, which I show you how to use later in this chapter.

For now, let's take a look at the important points on using the Report wizard. Before beginning, you need a table or dynaset for the report. I'm using a dynaset that contains customer orders by product. I call the query Customer Orders By Product Name.

You learned how to create this query in Chapter 8 by joining together the Customers, Orders, and Orders Details tables in the Northwind Traders database.

Here are the fields that you'll need in the dynaset:

- ID
- Company
- Product ID
- Quantity
- Product Name

Creating a report

The Report wizard is located in the Reports group on the Create tab (see Figure 15.1). Before starting the Report wizard, select the table or query for the report. You can select other tables and queries from within the Report wizard.

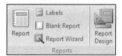

Figure 15.1. Click to start the Report wizard.

Don't be concerned if you selected the wrong table or query or didn't select any because you can make this selection after the Report wizard starts.

Here's how to create a report:

1. Click Customer Orders by Product Name in the Unassigned Objects group of the Northwind Traders pane. This is the query I'm using, but replace this with your own table or query.

2. Click Report wizard. No doubt the screen that appears is very familiar because it is basically the same screen used in the Query wizard (see Chapter 8) to select tables/queries and fields for the query.

3. Click the Tables/Queries combo box and choose the table/query you want to use for the report. Customer Orders By Product Name is already selected if you highlighted it before starting the Report wizard. The first column shows the list of fields for the selected table or query.

4. Double-click fields in the Available Fields list that you want to appear on the report. Selected fields are removed from the Available Fields column and placed in the Selected Fields column. I'm using Company, Quantity, and Product Name (see Figure 15.2).

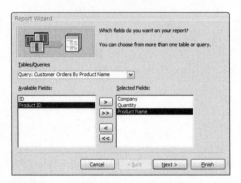

Figure 15.2. Double-click the fields you want on the report.

5. Click the Tables/Queries combo box and choose a different table/query you want to use for the report, if you wish. Names of its fields appear in the Available Fields column. Move the fields you want to the Selected Fields column.

6. Click Finish, if you're done. The Report wizard generates the report.

7. Click Next to fine-tune the report. You are asked how you want to view the data in the report. Each field is listed in the first column beginning with the first field selected for the report. The Report wizard draws a diagram of the report based on your selection (see Figure 15.3).

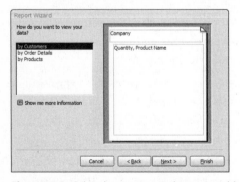

Figure 15.3. Select how you want data grouped in the report.

8. Select how you want to view the data. I selected by Customers because I want to see Products and Order Details by customer.

9. Click Finish, if you're done. The Report wizard generates the report.

10. Click Next to fine-tune the report. You select grouping levels based on the remaining fields.

11. Double-click Product Name. This groups together records by customer, by products, and then by quantity for each product. The Report wizard adjusts the diagram of the report to reflect your selection.

12. Click Grouping Options. You are prompted to select Grouping Intervals. A grouping interval specifies how the Report wizard groups records within the group. The Grouping Interval combo box gives you options. I selected Normal, which is the default selection. Click OK and then click Finish in the dialog box and the Report wizard generates the report.

13. Click Next to fine-tune the report. Select the sort order for the detail records. I'm using the default setting.

14. Click Summary Options. You'll find various calculations that the Report wizard can build into your report (see Figure 15.4). It lists names of numeric fields and types of calculation that Access 2007 can perform. The Show group is used to show the detail and summary or simply the summary, which is what you'll pick if you want only summary data on the report. There is even a check box to have Access 2007 calculate percentage of total for the sum. I'm not using any summary options for this report.

15. Click OK.

16. Click Finish, if you're done. The Report wizard generates the report.

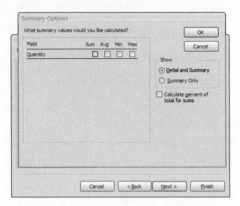

Figure 15.4. Click the calculations that you want to appear on the report.

17. Click Next to fine-tune the report. Choose from three layout options: Stepped, Block, and Outlined. Try each one so that you can see which layout looks best. The Report wizard displays the layout in a diagram; however, I prefer seeing the real report in each layout by clicking Finish. Also choose the orientation of the report — Portrait or Landscape. The Report wizard automatically adjusts the field width to fit all the fields on the page. I leave this option checked and then tweak the design using the Report Design tool if necessary. I selected Stepped and Portrait.

18. Click Finish, if you're done. The Report wizard generates the report.

19. Click Next to fine-tune the report. Select the report style from a list of available styles. The Report wizard displays the style you select in the sample window. There is no easy way to make your selection. I simply click each style until one catches my eye. I've selected no style for this report.

20. Click Finish, if you're done. The Report wizard generates the report.

21. Click Next to fine-tune the report. Here's where you enter a title for the report. I call it My First Report. You can also choose to preview the report or open the report in the Report Design tool. You'll probably want to see your report so select the Preview.

22. Click Finish. The Report wizard generates the report.

Adjusting the report

The report isn't perfect. You'll notice that the customer is truncated, and the quantity appears on its own row (see Figure 15.5), but this isn't a problem because you can fix it using the Report Design tool.

Figure 15.5. The report created by the Report wizard may need adjustments.

Here's how to make adjustments:

1. Right-click the My First Report tab. A pop-up menu is displayed.

2. Click Layout view. Access 2007 lets you modify the layout of the report.

3. Click the Company column. The column is selected.

4. Drag the right column edge until the entire name of the company appears.

5. Right-click a Quantity cell. A pop-up menu is displayed.

6. Click Layout. Another pop-up menu is displayed.

7. Click Move Up a Section. All the Quantity cells are aligned with its corresponding product on the same row.

8. Right-click the My First Report tab. A pop-up menu is displayed.

9. Click Report view. Now the report looks presentable.

Using a Blank Report

Another easy way to create a report is to use the Blank Report. The Blank Report lets you create report using the Layout view. I think of this as a blank sheet of paper. It is less confusing to use than the Report Design tool — and more robust than the Report wizard. Best of all, you see data as you create the report.

You'll find the Blank Report in the Reports group on the Create tab right above the Report wizard. Click it, and Access 2007 displays a blank report and a Field List that contains all the tables in the database. Click a table to see a list of fields in the table.

If you need a reminder of the type of data that is in the field simply click Edit Table to the right of each table name and Access 2007 displays data in a datasheet.

Double-click fields on the Field List that you want on the report and Access 2007 displays the field in a column. The column header is the field name and cells contain values of the fields.

The Field List expands automatically to show you tables that are related to the table you selected for the report (see Figure 15.6). This means you can use fields in the Field List. Access 2007 uses the relationship among tables to associate field values with records in the table selected for the report.

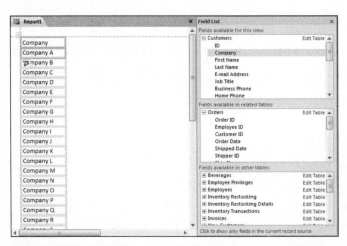

Figure 15.6. The Field List contains fields that you can insert into the report.

Hack

Click Add Existing Fields in the Controls group on the Formatting tab if you don't see the Field List displayed.

Now that you have an idea of how the Blank Report is used, let's build a report using the Blank Report. I show you the fundamentals here and then show you how to spruce up your reports in Chapter 16.

Follow these steps to create a blank report:

1. Click Blank Report. Access 2007 displays the Field List.

2. Click Customers. This expands the Customers table and lets you see its fields.

3. Double-click Company. Access 2007 places the fields in the first column of the form and displays values of its field.

4. Click Orders in the Fields available in related tables section of the Field List. You'll see the fields in the Orders table.

5. Double-click Order ID. The Order ID field and its values are placed in the second column on the form and a new list of tables appears in the Fields available in related table section of the Field List. Tables are related to the Orders table. Access 2007 also moves the Orders table to the Fields available for this view section of the Field List.

6. Click Order Details in the Fields available in related tables section of the Field List. You'll see a list of fields for the Order Details table.

7. Double-click Product ID. Access 2007 displays the Product ID field and its values in the third column on the form. It also moves the Order Details table to the Fields available for this view section of the Field List.

8. Double-click the Quantity field from the Order Details table. This becomes the fourth column on the report.

9. Click the X in the right corner of the Field List to close the Field List.

10. Right-click the Company column. This displays a pop-up menu.

11. Click Group On Company. Access 2007 groups orders by company (see Figure 15.7).

12. Double-click Order ID. This displays a pop-up menu.

13. Click Layout. (Delete is on the first pop-up menu.)

14. Click Delete. Access 2007 deletes the column from the report. The column was needed to relate the Order Details table to the Customers table, but is otherwise meaningless to someone reading the report.

15. Click each column and then drag the right side of the column to resize it so all the data appears on one line.

16. Right-click the report. A pop-up menu is displayed.

17. Click Properties. This displays the Property Sheet for the report.

18. Click the Format tab.

19. Enter a value for the Caption property. This becomes the text for the report tab when you leave the Caption property. I entered My Second Report.

20. Click the X in the right corner of the Property Sheet to close the Property Sheet.

21. Click Title in the Controls group on the Formatting tab. Access 2007 inserts a title on the report and uses the value of the Caption property as text for the title. Double-click the title and enter the next text if you wish.

Figure 15.7. Right-click the Company column and then select Group On Company.

Hack

Click View in the Views group on the Design tab and select Design View to view the Blank Report in the Report Design tool where you can fine-tune the report.

Using the Report Design tool

The Report Design tool provides all the options you need to create complex reports. Clicking Report Design in the Reports group on the Create tab displays the Report Design tool.

You can see a grid that is identical to the Form Design tool you learned about in Chapter 12. The grid is divided into three sections — Page Header, Detail, and Page Footer. (I discuss these earlier in this chapter.)

You drop controls from the Design tab and fields from the Field List into sections of the report the same way as you do when creating a form using the Form Design tool. However, remember to use controls such as Labels, and Text Boxes that are designed to display data and not those used for data entry. And as with the Form Design tool, you can drag controls anywhere on the report.

The size of a section can be adjusted by clicking the section bar and then dragging the edge of the section to give it more or less space. The size of the Detail section plays an important role in determining the number of records that appears on each page of the report. This puts less space between the records. You'll want this to be a minimum size so you can fit as many records as possible on one page.

Creating a report using the Report Design tool

To create a report using the Design tool, click the Report Design tool and then click Add Existing Fields in the Tools group on the Design tab to display the Field List.

Now let's create the report.

1. Click Customers in the Field List to display its fields.

2. Double-click the Company field. Access 2007 places a Label control and Text Box control on the report just like when you created the form.

3. Double-click the Order ID field in the Orders table as you did for the Blank Form.

4. Double-click the Product ID and Quantity fields in the Order Details table.

5. Highlight the Label control for each field and press Delete to remove the labels.

Inside Scoop

You may inadvertently place a control too close to a section bar, causing Access 2007 to increase the size of the section. Fix this by dragging the section bar back into position.

6. Highlight the Order ID Text Box control and press Delete to remove it from the report.

7. Drag each Text Box control to the top of the Details section right below the Page Header section.

8. Drag the Page Footer section bar directly below the Text Box control.

9. Click the Label control in the Control group on the Design tab of the Tab and then click the Page Header section. You need to increase the size of the label box. Access 2007 places the Label control in the Page Header.

10. Type Company in the Label control.

11. Drag the Company Label control above the Company Text Box control.

12. Create a Label control for Product and Quantity and position them in the Page Header section above their respective Text Box controls (see Figure 15.8).

13. Click View in the Views group and click Report View. Access 2007 displays the report, giving you a chance to see your handiwork. Expect that you'll need to tweak the report, such as stretching a Text Box control so its value isn't truncated.

Figure 15.8. Position each Label control over its corresponding Text Box control.

Inserting a Group Header and Footer

You probably noticed that there isn't a Group section in the form. This isn't a problem because you can insert a Group section in the report. Here's how to do it:

1. Right-click the Detail section. A pop-up menu is displayed.

2. Click Sorting and Grouping. The Group, Sort, and Total pane opens.

3. Click Add Group. You're prompted to select the field to group on.

4. Click Company. Access 2007 inserts a Group header and names it Company.

5. Drag the Company Text Box control to the Company Group section (see Figure 15.9). By doing this, the company name appears once at the beginning of each Group section rather than having the company name appear on each row in the Details section.

6. Click More in the Group, Sort, and Total pane to fine-tune the Group section.

   ▪ **By entire value.** Determines how Access 2007 knows if a record belongs to the group. Access 2007 compares characters in the value. All the characters in the field must match to make it part of the group. You can choose the number of characters to match by clicking by entire value combo box.

   ▪ **With no totals.** Determines if Access 2007 displays totals for the group. This is set to No Totals, but you can choose to total the field value, grand total, group as a percentage of grand total, display the total in the Group Header section or the Group Footer section. Make your choice by clicking the with No Totals combo box.

   ▪ **With title click to add.** This inserts a title for the Group section. Access 2007 displays the Zoom dialog box for the title cell, which is where you enter the title. I usually don't enter a title because I place the Company Text Box in the Group section, which serves as a title.

   ▪ **With a header section.** This tells Access 2007 to include or not include a Group Header section in the report.

   ▪ **With a footer section.** This tells Access 2007 to include or not include a Group Footer section in the report.

   ▪ **Do not keep group together on one page.** This lets Access 2007 print the Group section on multiple pages if it runs out of space on a page. You can keep the whole group on one page or keep the header and first record on one page. Click the do not keep group together on one page combo box to make your selection.

- **Less.** Click Less to hide this options.

- Click the X in the right corner of the Group on Company line in the Group, Sort, and Total pane if you want to delete the Group section from the report.

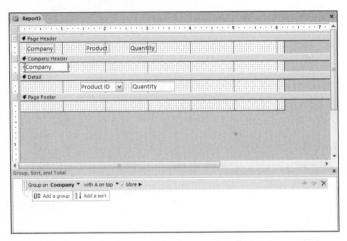

Figure 15.9. Drag the Company Text Box control to the Group section.

Inserting a Report Header and Footer

Access 2007 doesn't display a Report Header or Report Footer. This is fine because some reports that you create don't require these. However, you can easily insert them by:

1. Right-click the grid. A pop-up menu is displayed.

2. Click Report Header/Footer. This is a toggle option. Click it once and Access 2007 inserts them into the report. Click it a second time and Access 2007 removes them from the report.

3. Click the Label control.

4. Click the Report Header section. Access 2007 displays the Label control.

5. Enter a title for the report.

Inserting page numbers

A report wouldn't be complete without inserting page numbers in either the Page Header or Page Footer. There are two styles used to display page numbers. Your choice is the number of the current page or the page-of-pages, which indicates the total number of pages in the report such as 3 of 10.

- Use [Page] in the report when you want to refer to the current page number.
- Use [Pages] in the report when you want to refer to the total number of pages in the report.

Here's how to insert page numbers in your report:

1. Click the Text Box control.
2. Click the Page Header or Page Footer, depending on where you want the page number to appear in the report.
3. Enter =[Page] in the Text Box control if you want the page number to appear in the report.
4. Enter =[Page] & " of " & [Pages] in the Text Box control if you want to display page-of-pages displayed.

Entering a date and time

I find it very useful to insert the date and time that the report was printed in either the Report Header or Report Footer. By referring to the date and time on the printed report, everyone reading it will know that they are reading the same version of the report.

This is particularly useful as you develop the report and require several of your colleagues to approve it. Each draft of the report has its own date and time, so you're sure that a colleague is seeing the latest draft.

I also include date and time in the Page Header or Page Footer if the content of the report is time sensitive, such as reports containing financial information.

Here's how to insert the date and time on your report:

1. Click the Text Box control.
2. Click the Report Header or Report Footer, depending on where you want the date and time to appear in the report.

Inside Scoop

Use the Date() function if you don't want to include the time that the report is generated.

3. Enter =Now() in the Text Box control. Now() is a built-in function that tells Access 2007 to insert the current date and time that appears on the computer that generates the report. It looks like 01/01/2009 10:00 P.M. You'll probably have to increase the size of the Text Box control to display the date and time.

Growing and shrinking controls

One of the most frustrating aspects of designing a report is sizing Text Box controls. Adjusting the size isn't a problem. It's knowing what size to make them that's the problem.

I'd set the size and preview the report. The first few pages look fine, but then there's a page where a value is truncated because the Text Box control is too small. Then, it's back to the Report Design tool to stretch to the Text Box control. You can imagine that this could go on forever because values change constantly once the report is given to my colleagues.

Access 2007 has a solution. Each Text Box control has Can Grow and Can Shrink properties.

- Can Grow, if set to Yes, tells Access 2007 to increase the size of the Text Box control to the size of the value.

- Can Shrink, if set to Yes, tells Access 2007 to decrease the size of the Text Box control to the size of the value.

Inside Scoop

Use the field size of the field bound to the Text Box control as a guide for determining the size of the text box. Values cannot exceed the size of the field.

Just the facts

- A report prints information on paper better than a form because you can adjust the report to fit the requirements of a printer.

- A form is used for data entry, but not a report. A Text Box control on a form is used to display and input data. It is used only to display data on a report.

- Tabular report is sometimes called a groups/totals report. It presents information in rows and columns and is used to group by one or more fields and summarize information for numeric fields in each group. You can also create page totals and grand totals.

- Columnar report is also known as a form report and is used to display one record on a page and resembles a data-entry form.

- Mail-merge report combines information from a database with a block of text and is used to personalize form letters.

- Mailing labels is a report that uses information in the database to create mailing labels. It offers a wide variety of label styles from Avery labels and other vendors. Select the style and Access 2007 makes sure addresses are printed properly on each label. This is very similar to printing labels in Microsoft Word.

- Subreport is a type of columnar report. Think of this as a report within another report. You can use it to have customer contact information appearing at the top of the report and rows of orders in a subreport at the bottom of the report.

GET THE SCOOP ON...
Creating labels ▪ Customizing labels ▪ Creating a mail
merge report ▪ Setting the page layout and size ▪ Using
images on a report ▪ Modifying the image control's
settings

Enhancing and Printing a Report

Blah...dull...not impressive at all. These are probably a few words that cross your mind when looking at a report that you learned to create in the previous chapter.

That's fine because in this chapter I show you a few ways to insert pizzazz into your report. Stop! Don't go looking for the Pizzazz icon on the Ribbon. You won't find it.

You will find Labels, Page Setup, Formatting, lines, rectangles, images, and more of these features that enable you to transform a drab, plain-Jane report into one that gets you a *wow* from everyone who sees it.

Creating labels

Printing names, addresses, and other information is easy, thanks to the Access 2007 Labels wizard. Access 2007 has built-in templates for labels made by 40 manufacturers. These include sheet-feed labels, continuous labels, and labels sized in inches and millimeters.

And if the built-in templates don't meet your needs you can enter dimensions for customized labels, which Access 2007 saves, so you only need to enter these dimensions once.

Chapter 16

Inside Scoop

Select the label before preparing a label report so you'll know which built-in label template to use for the report.

Here's how to create labels.

1. Click the table or query that contains information for the label. I selected Customer Details in the Customers & Orders group in the Northwind Traders pane.

2. Double-click Labels in the Reports group on the Create tab. Access 2007 starts the Label wizard.

3. Click the filter by manufacturer combo box and pick the manufacturer of your labels. A list of built-in templates for their products is displayed.

4. Click the product number of your labels.

5. Click the appropriate Unit of Measurement. I use the default setting, which is English, except when I worked for a foreign auto manufacturer who used Metric because labels were supplied by their headquarters in Germany.

6. Click the appropriate Label Type. Use Sheet feed if you are using sheets of labels. Select Continuous if you are using a roll of labels such as those used by printers specially designed for printing labels (see Figure 16.1). Click Next.

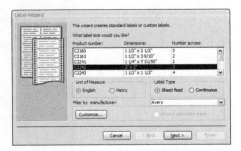

Figure 16.1. Select the type of label that you want to create.

Inside Scoop

Consider that labels might be printed on a black-and-white printer when choosing color for the text. Although Access 2007 converts color to shades of gray, you should test-print labels to make sure that you are satisfied with the color.

7. Select the appearance of the text. The same options are used for the report and form. The Label wizard shows a sample of the label as you change the appearance of the text.

8. Click Next. The Label wizard prompts you to select and position fields for the label.

9. Double-click fields to insert it on the label. The Label wizard places them in the Prototype label column. I selected First Name, Last Name, Job Title, and Company. Format text on the label by pressing Enter to position the cursor on a new line in the label and then continue to insert fields (see Figure 16.2).

10. Click Finish. The Label Wizard displays the Print Preview of the labels.

11. Click Next to fine-tune the labels. The Label wizard prompts you to sort the labels.

12. Double-click the field(s) you want to sort by. The Label wizard presents you with all the fields in the table. This enables you to sort the labels on a field that doesn't appear on the label. For example, you could sort by sales region, but not show the sales region on the label. I sorted by Last Name.

13. Click Finish.

14. Click Next to fine-tune the labels. The Label wizard shows you the same dialog box as you saw when you used the Report wizard. Here is where you can enter a name for the report and then choose to see a preview of the report or open the label report in the Report Design tool. I title this My First Label Report and preview the report.

Inside Scoop

You can enter text directly into the prototype label and the text will appear on every label.

Inside Scoop

You can change the font and layout of text by opening the label in the Report Design tool.

15. Click Finish.

16. Click Print on the Print Preview tab of the Ribbon to print the labels.

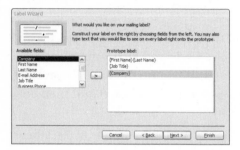

Figure 16.2. Insert fields and text on the label.

If you can't find a built-in label template, then create your own by clicking Customize in the first dialog box presented by the Label wizard. It is easier to use a built-in label template; however, the Label wizard makes creating your own template easy.

Here's how to do this:

1. Click Customize when the Label wizard displays the first dialog.

2. Click New. The Label wizard displays the New Label dialog box. This looks imposing at first, but the Label wizard is asking for dimensions for the label and the position of the label on the paper.

3. Enter a name for label template in the Label Name text box.

4. Click the Unit of Measure. This tells the Label wizard if you're going to enter measurements using inches or millimeters.

5. Click the Label Type. These are Sheet feed or continuous, which I explained in the previous section. The Label wizard changes the image of the sheet to reflect your choice.

6. Click Orientation. These are Portrait or landscape. Your choice depends on the labels you are using.

7. Enter the number of labels that are going across the page.

8. Measure the actual labels using the sample image as a guide (see Figure 16.3).

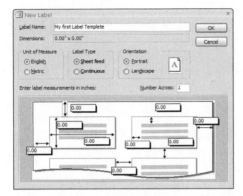

Figure 16.3. Enter dimensions for the new label template.

9. Enter the dimension for the new label template in the corresponding text boxes in the sample.

10. Click OK. The Label wizard enters the new label template in the New Label Size dialog box.

11. Highlight the label name and click close. The Label wizard uses this as your choice of label.

Creating a mail merge report

Be prepared to send personalized letters to customers, employees, and anyone else whose information is in an Access 2007 database. This is referred to as mail merge, which is probably familiar to you if you use Word.

In Word, information such as names and addresses is entered into columns of a table. The column name is then used in place of the information in the mail merge document. Word inserts the actual information when the mail merge document prints.

You can export (see Chapter 7) information from an Access 2007 database to a Word table or link Word directly to the Access 2007 database and then use information in the database for the Word mail merge document.

Alternatively, you can create a mail merge document directly in Access 2007 as a mail merge report. You won't find a mail merge button on any tab on the Ribbon; however, by using the techniques I showed you in the last chapter, you can easily create a mail merge document.

Let's say you want to send an invitation to customers who are listed in the Customers table of the Northwind Traders database. Here's what you need to do.

1. Click Report Design in the Reports group on the Create tab. This displays the Report Design tool.

2. Click the Label control in the Controls group on the Design tab.

3. Click the Page Header. Access 2007 displays the Label control in the Page Header.

4. Type your name or the name of your company. This is information that you find at the top of the letterhead. I typed My Company.

5. Insert other Label controls in the Page Header to complete the letterhead information. I typed street, city, state, and postal code.

6. Click Property Sheet in the Tools group of the Design tab. This displays the Property Sheet.

7. Click the Selection Type combo box at the top of the Property Sheet and click Report. This shows properties for the report.

8. Click Record Source in the Data tab and select the table or query that contains information for the mail merge document. I selected Customers.

9. Click the Textbox control in the Controls group on the Design tab on the Ribbon.

10. Click the Detail section. Access 2007 displays the Textbox control.

11. Click the Textbox control. Access 2007 shows its properties in the Property Sheet.

Bright Idea

Alternatively you can use one label with multiple lines. Press Shift+Enter to insert a new line.

Watch Out!

Make sure you turn the Can Shrink and Can Grow Textbox properties to Yes, otherwise values might be truncated or there might be too much space between values, text, and punctuation.

12. Change Can Grow and Can Shrink to Yes in the Format Tab. Access 2007 automatically adjusts the size of the textbox to reflect its value.

13. Click the label portion of the Textbox control and press Delete. This removes the label. You won't need a label.

14. Type = **[First Name] & " " & [Last Name]** in the Textbox control. This begins the return address section of the mail merge document. [First Name] and [Last Name] are fields in the Customers table. Field names are placed within square brackets when referenced in an expression. The ampersand (&) is an operator that joins two strings. The first ampersand joins the value of the First Name field to a space that is contained within quotations. The second ampersand joins the space to the value of the Last Name field.

15. Insert addition Textbox control and assign it the customer's:

   ▪ Company by typing = **[Company]**

   ▪ Street by typing = **[Address]**

   ▪ City, state and zip code by typing = **[City] &", " &[State/Province] & " " & [ZIP/Postal Code]**

16. Click the Textbox control and insert it in the salutation or greeting section of the mail merge document.

17. Type in the Textbox control = **"Dear " & [First Name] & ","**

18. Insert Label controls for text that remains constant for each copy of the mail merge document.

19. Click Insert Page Break in the Controls group on the Design tab.

20. Click the line following the last Label control. Access 2007 inserts a page break (see Figure 16.4).

21. Right-click the Report tab for the mail merge document. Access 2007 displays a pop-up menu.

22. Click Print Preview to see the mail merge document.

23. Right-click the Report tab again.

24. Click Layout View. Access 2007 displays the mail merge document in the Layout View where you can reposition controls and tweak the layout of the document.

Insert line break

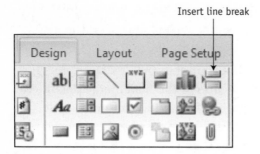

Figure 16.4. Insert a line break to separate each copy of the mail merge document.

Setting the page layout and size

Unlike a form, what you see on the screen is not necessarily what you get when the report is printed because the screen is different in size than the paper. This difference caused me headaches when I first learned to print reports in a much earlier version of Access. The report looked great on the screen but missed its mark when printed.

Avoid frustration by setting the page layout characteristics of your report and then designing your report within the page layout. Page layout characteristics define the paper used to print the report. This is probably not new to you because it's the same settings used to define the paper in Word.

Access 2007 can print a report on practically any paper that your printer can handle. Once, I was required to use Mail Merge to print invitations using Access 2007. At first, I thought my colleague was crazy, but an invitation is really a report on smaller paper.

You'll find page layout tools in the Page Setup tab and when you click print.

Inside Scoop

As a general rule, I use standard letter or legal paper. Letter is my preference because it is easy to handle and fits neatly into the most commonly used binders and folders. This is something to consider when designing your report.

1. Click the File icon in the upper-left corner of Access 2007. This displays the File pop-up list.

2. Click Print. Access 2007 displays the Print dialog box.

3. Click Setup to fine-tune the layout of the printed report. The Page Setup dialog box is where you set print options and column settings (see Figure 16.5).

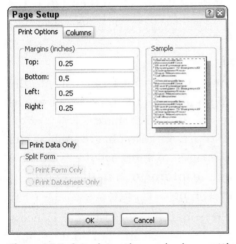

Figure 16.5. Set print options and column settings.

4. Click OK.

5. Click Properties. Access 2007 displays properties that you can set for your printer. Properties vary depending on the printer you selected for the report. You can select paper quality, poster printing, print on both sides of the paper, printing built-in watermarks (my favorite is Top Secret), and color adjustments.

6. Click OK. This returns you to the Print dialog box.

7. Click OK to print the report.

Bright Idea

Save a tree and use Print Preview to review how your report will appear on paper. Access 2007 simulates the printed page as if it is printed by the active printer on your computer.

Adjust the size of the report by dragging the rightmost edge of the report. Avoid exceeding the width of the printed page. You're probably thinking that this is obvious; however Access 2007 increases the size to accommodate controls that you insert into the report. I'm always bumping controls into borders of sections of the report as I tweak the layout. Access 2007 conveniently increases the size of the section.

You know you've exceeded the page width when every other page is blank. I usually pick up on this during Print Preview and then I drag the report back onto the page.

Using images on a report

The best way to spiff up a dull report is by inserting an image into the report. An image can directly relate to numbers in the report such as pictures of products in a report that talks about market share.

However, designers frequently use representative images such as clip art, clip photos, and other generic images to help set the tone of a report, while not necessarily clarifying the information in the report.

There are four ways to insert an image into a report:

- **Field List.** Dragging an image field from the Field List causes Access 2007 to create an Image control on the report and bound it to the image field in the table.

- **Image control.** An Image control is assigned an image associated with a field (bound) or the name of an image file (unbound).

- **Logo.** A logo is an image that Access 2007 automatically places in the Report Header.

- **Watermark.** A watermark is a background image that lightly appears on each page of the report.

Hack

Bound images reflect the value of their corresponding field, so the image can change each time the report runs. Unbound images remain the same each time the report runs.

Modifying the Image control's settings

It takes a few clicks of the mouse to insert an image into your report. An image is contained within an Image control. Think of the Image control as a container into which you place the image.

First create the Image control on the form and then assign the image to the Image control.

Here's how this is done:

1. Click Report Design in the Reports group on the Create tab on the Ribbon.

2. Click Image control in the Controls group on the Design tab on the Ribbon.

3. Click the Detail section of the report. Access 2007 displays the Image control on the report.

4. Click the Image control. This displays the Insert Picture dialog.

5. Click the image file you want displayed in the report.

6. Click OK. Access 2007 displays the image in the Image control.

7. Drag the corner size handles to proportionally adjust the size of the image.

8. Change the Size Mode property to the setting that is appropriate for your report.

   ▪ **Clip.** Displays the picture at actual size and trims the image to fit the Image control.

   ▪ **Stretch.** Changes the size of the picture to fit the Image control. The image may be distorted.

   ▪ **Zoom.** Keeps the image correctly proportional even if you resize it.

9. Click the Label control and click the report to enter text that describes the image (see Figure 16.6).

Hack

Change the Picture Type property from Embedded to Link if you want the report to link to the image.

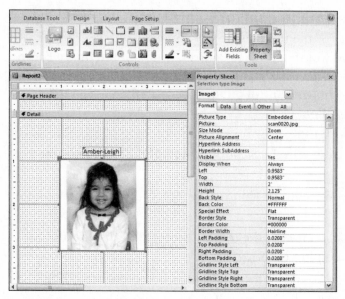

Figure 16.6. Drag the corner size handles to resize the image and then enter text to describe the image.

Inserting a logo

Inserting a logo into your report is very similar to inserting an image. In fact, the only difference is Access 2007 automatically displays the logo in the Report Header and Page Header.

Here's what you need to do:

1. Click Logo in the Controls group on the Design tab on the Ribbon. Access 2007 displays the Insert Picture dialog.

2. Select the image that you want used for the logo.

3. Click OK. Access 2007 positions the logo on the report. You can resize and reposition the logo the same way as you do with other controls.

Inserting a watermark

A watermark is an image that appears beneath other objects on a page. Previously in this chapter, I showed how to use the built-in watermarks by selecting the Properties in the Print dialog box. The watermarks are contained on the Effects tab.

Inside Scoop

Watermarks are designed to be nearly invisible. Therefore, select an image that displays in light gray and that doesn't distract the reader from controls on the report.

Here's how to create your own watermarks.

1. Click Report Design in the Reports group on the Design tab on the Ribbon.

2. Click Property Sheet in the Tools group on the Design tab on the Ribbon.

3. Click Report in the Selection type combo box.

4. Click the ellipsis button in the Picture property. Doing so displays the Insert Picture dialog.

5. Click the image to use as the watermark.

6. Click OK. Access 2007 places the image on the report.

7. Click the Picture Alignment property and select the alignment for the image. I select Center.

8. Click the Picture tiling property and choose whether or not to title (repeat) the image. I select No.

Using Snapshot Reports

Shortly after I began developing Access applications I discovered that only someone who has Access could view my reports. It was a bummer after spending days carefully building and tweaking the report.

Then a colleague told me about Snapshot Reports. A Snapshot Report is a version of an Access report that can be read using the Snapshot Viewer, which can be downloaded at no cost from www.microsoft.com.

It's easy to create a Snapshot Report. After you're finished designing the report, click the File icon and then Save As. Access 2007 displays the Save As dialog box and prompts you to enter the name of the report.

Then click the As combo box and choose Snapshot as the file type. This creates the Snapshot version and gives it the file extension .snp. Give your colleague this file.

E-mailing your report

E-mail your report directly from Access 2007. It is easy to do. Click the File icon and the click Email. Access 2007 displays the Send Object As dialog box where you can choose the format for your report. You can choose from:

- HTML
- PDF Format
- Rich Text format
- Snapshot Format
- Text Files
- XPS Format

After making your selection and clicking OK, Access 2007 prompts you to select output options that are unique for each format. Click OK, and Access 2007 opens your default e-mail program, creates a new e-mail, and attaches the report to the e-mail. You provide the e-mail address, subject, and text.

Creating a PDF file

PDF is a popular format for exchanging documents electronically. You can create a PDF version or the relatively new XPS version of your report. XPS is Microsoft's format that is similar to PDF.

Create a PDF or XPS version by clicking the File icon and then clicking the right arrow on the Save As option. Doing this opens a menu, and you'll find the PDF and XPS options toward the end of this list. Click it, and Access 2007 prompts you to enter the name for the file, the same prompt you see the first time that you save the report.

Inserting page numbers, date, and time

In the last chapter, I showed you how to insert page numbers, date, and time on your report. Access 2007 has two controls that let you tailor these options further to meet the need of your report.

Here's how to insert page numbers:

1. Click the Insert Page Number control. Access 2007 displays the Page Numbers dialog box.

2. Select the Format for the page number. Your choices are inserting the current page number or the current page number followed by the total number of pages in the report.

3. Select the Position of the page number. You can place the page number in the Page Header or the Page Footer.

4. Select the Alignment combo box. Choose where the number should appear within either the Page Header or the Page Footer.

5. Select Show Number on First Page if you want the page number to appear there. Some reports don't have a page number on the cover page.

6. Click OK. Access 2007 then inserts the page number in the report (see Figure 16.7).

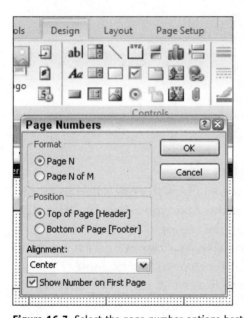

Figure 16.7. Select the page number options best suited for your report.

Here's how to insert the date and time.

7. Click the Insert Date and Time control. Access 2007 displays the Date and Time dialog box.

8. Click whether you want to include the Date and/or the time.

9. Click the date and time format. Access 2007 displays a sample of how your selections will appear in the report.

10. Click OK. Access 2007 inserts the date and/or time into the report (see Figure 16.8).

Figure 16.8. Select the date and time options for your report.

Using lines and rectangles

Admittedly, you don't need me to tell you how to draw a line and a rectangle on your report. Simply click the Line control or the Rectangle control and then click and drag it on the report.

Lines and rectangles are used to make your report easier to read and to help focus on important parts of the report. For example, I place a rectangle around key performance indicators on my weekly sales report. This becomes the first place everyone looks when they receive the report.

Lines are a great way to visually separate records. I find lines especially useful when each record is displayed on several rows in the report. Lines help the reader differentiate when one record ends and another record begins.

Aside from using lines and rectangles as visual cues, you can also enhance their appearance by changing their thickness, style, and color using tools available in the Controls group on the Design tab on the

Ribbon. These are the same controls that you use in Word, Excel, and other Microsoft Office products to change the characteristics of lines and rectangles.

I find the Special Effects control particularly useful when trying to get a wow from readers of my report. The Special Effects control is also in the Controls group on the Design tab on the Ribbon and it contains a selection of effects that give lines and rectangles character and dramatically change their appearance.

The best way to explore these special effects is to try each of them by clicking the Special Effects control, clicking a special effect, and then drawing a line or rectangle on your report.

Just the facts

- Access 2007 has built-in templates for labels made by 40 manufacturers. These include sheet-feed labels, continuous labels, and labels sized in inches and millimeters.

- You can create customized labels if one of the built-in template labels is insufficient for your report.

- A mail merge report is used to personalize form letters by combining values in a database with text.

- The ampersand (&) operator is used to concatenate two strings that can be either text of a label or values of fields.

- Field names must appear in square brackets ([]) when used in a expression in a Text control on a mail merge report.

- Set the page layout characteristics of your report and then design your report within the page layout.

GET THE SCOOP ON...
Choosing the right chart and graph ▪ Identifying your
message ▪ Avoiding common mistakes ▪ Focusing on
your message ▪ Creating charts and graphs

Generating Charts and Graphs

The invitation read, "We look forward to meeting with you at our regional meeting. Your presence is required."

I hate invitations that end with "your presence is required" because I know that I'm in for hours of sitting through presentations trying to make sense out of confusing charts — and I can't avoid the meeting.

It dawned on me that others have the same feeling when I invite them to my presentation or when I give them a report containing a chart. Knowing what to say is easy. Conveying it in a chart is difficult.

In this chapter, I show you how to use Access 2007 to generate charts that deliver your message clearly.

Choosing the correct chart and graph

Let's be honest. All of us have sat through a presentation where most of our time was spent trying to understand the graph on the screen — and not listening to a word said by the presenter.

A picture in the form of a chart or graph is worth a thousand words, only if it clearly tells the story, otherwise it is useless. I think of this as a joke. If you have to explain the joke, then you shouldn't have told the joke. The audience either gets the point immediately or you bombed.

There are many styles of charts and graphs to choose from — and Access 2007 has all of them built in, which I'll show you later in this chapter. Before you create a chart or graph, you'll need to choose the one that is best to get your message across to your audience.

The purpose of a chart or graph is to show visual relationships among data so that the audience can grasp the relationship at a glance. The graphical relationship and not the data delivers your message.

For example, the audience is not interested that sales rose by $4 million this quarter. They are interested in the magnitude of the sales increase, which can be clearly illustrated in a line graph that compares current and previous sales.

Identify your message

Before thinking about the kind of chart or graph to use, decide on the message you want to deliver. Your message must be a simple one that can be depicted graphically, such as sales are up $4 million.

Nothing is simple in the real world. My message is usually complex and can't be easily reduced to a few words. That is until a colleague gave me a few tips on how to simplify my message.

If I can't simplify my message, then how can I expect the audience, who is less familiar with the topic, to grasp it during the few minutes of my presentation?

Here's what she suggested:

1. Describe the most important point you want made in five words or less. Similar to a tabloid headline.

2. Describe the three important facts that support your main point each in five words or less. If these three facts don't convince your audience that your main point is correct, then neither will additional facts.

3. Stop. These are messages you need to convey to your audience.

Labeling the chart

Sometimes you need to use words in the form of labels on a chart or graph to help get your message across to the audience. Labels should tell the audience what to look for in the chart or graph.

Watch Out!
Make sure that text is displayed in a font and type size that is easy for the audience to read. Avoid fancy fonts, and when in doubt make the type larger.

It never fails. The regional sales manager displays a graph that is titled New York Regional Sales 2008. The graph does show a line chart of sales, but the regional sales manager hides the message. The title should say New York Regional Sales Up $4 Million.

The title and other labels should be an action statement that conveys a complete thought much like a news headline.

Keep in mind that labels help the audience understand the data.

Making your choice

Here are a few guidelines to use when making your decision on the type of chart or graph to use.

- **Line Charts.** Best to use when there are four or five data points and you want to emphasize continuity over several time periods. The slope of the line tells the direction of the trend at a glance. Look for words such as *grow, decline,* or *trend* in your message. They indicate a line chart should be used.

- **Vertical Bar Chart.** Use this chart when there are fewer than five data points and you want to emphasize quantity for periods of time. Vertical bars are less confusing than horizontal bars because audiences associate left-to-right with time periods rather than data points.

- **Horizontal Bar Chart.** This chart is used for comparing items or sets of items at the same point in time, such as sales representatives' dollar sales. Look for words such as *ranks* or *compare* in your message. They indicate a horizontal bar chart should be used. Rank data points from the largest to the smallest.

- **Pie Chart.** Use this chart to show proportion of items. Keep it to five items, otherwise the audience won't be able to grasp the information at a glance. Look for words such as *percentage, portion,* or *share* in your message. They indicate a pie chart should be used. Usually you'll want to highlight one item to emphasize it. Place this item at the top of the pie and make it stand out (explode) from the rest. I'll show you how to explode an item later in this chapter.

Avoiding common mistakes

All of us have sat through poor presentations. Chances are that the presenter made at least one of these common errors. Avoid these errors and your audience will be appreciative.

- No bells and whistles. The audience wants to understand your message and then move on. Your message gets lost if you try showing off your artistic skills in your charts and graphs.
- One slide per message.
- Use the type size of a label to convey its importance. The largest is the important message being conveyed to the audience.
- Eliminate clutter by avoiding using anything such as grid lines and boxes that make the chart or graph difficult to understand.

Focusing on your message

I design my charts and graphs the same way a news reporter presents a story — the most important information goes first.

A news reporter starts by telling you what you need to know and then tells you the details. This is contrary to what my English teacher told me. He said to begin with an introduction, followed by the details, and then end with a conclusion.

Remember the audience is looking at the chart or graph to ascertain information they need to make decisions. They're not there to hear your story.

Ask yourself what the audience needs to know, and then make that the headline with the chart or graph visually providing data to support that message. Only display information the audience needs to know.

Keep other supportive information on backup slides. A colleague of mine calls these slides his back pocket. He could always whip the slides from his back pocket at the end of the presentation to respond to questions from the audience. He didn't really keep them in his back pocket. They were in a different file on his computer.

- Keep patterns and color to a minimum. No more than four colors. No annoying fill patterns such as wave or crisscross patterns. Use colors and patterns to focus the audience on important points in your message.

- Write labels in uppercase and lowercase because they are easier for the audience to read rather than all uppercase.

Tell what your message means

Each chart or graph should put meaning behind data and not simply present data. For example, showing a trend line where the latest sales dropped by $500,000 for the quarter doesn't tell the audience what they really need to know.

It is better to project the trend to the next several quarters or to compare this year's trend to last year's actual results. The audience will then understand the importance of the drop in sales.

Charts and graphs should show what has happened, what is happening, and what is likely to happen in the future if the trend continues.

Creating charts and graphs

Access 2007 has a variety of choices when it comes to charts and graphs. I like to think that if Access 2007 doesn't have it, I don't need it.

Charts and graphs are used on forms (see Chapter 12) and reports (see Chapter 15). You create them by using the Chart control in the Controls group on the Design tab. Access 2007 refers to both charts and graphs as charts, so I'll do the same.

There are a lot of choices you have when creating a chart, so many choices that it is confusing at time to decide which is the best choice. Fortunately, Access 2007 starts the Chart wizard automatically when you place the Chart control on your form or report. The Chart wizard helps organize the decision you must make when designing a chart.

Getting started creating a chart

Begin by creating a new table (see Chapter 4) that you'll use to illustrate how to make a chart. The table I'm using is called Regional Sales and has two fields. These are Region and Sales. Here's the data that I inserted into these fields.

North	36
East	876
West	436
South	323

Next, create a new form or report. I'm going to create a new form to show you how to create a chart, but a similar technique is used to create a report.

1. Click Form Design in the Forms group on the Create tab. This opens a new form in the Form Design tools. Click Report Design if you are creating a report.

2. Click Insert Chart in the Controls group on the Design tab.

3. Click the Details area of the form. Access 2007 inserts the chart and runs the Chart wizard.

Building your chart

The Chart wizard prompts you to select the table or query as the data source for the chart. You'll remember seeing this screen (see Figure 17.1) because it's the same screen used by other wizards to select a table or query.

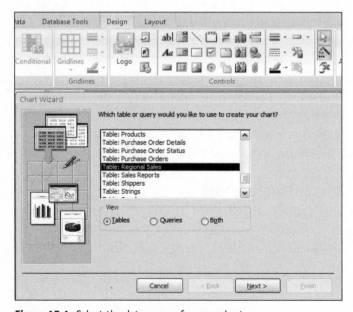

Figure 17.1. Select the data source for your chart.

The Chart wizard lists available tables, queries, or both, depending on your selection in the View options group.

Let's get started making a chart:

1. Click Tables in the View options group.

2. Select Table: Regional Sales. This is the table that you created in the previous section of this chapter.

3. Click Next. The Chart wizard displays fields in the table or query that can be used for the chart.

4. Double-click Region. The Region field moves to the Fields for Chart column.

5. Double-click Sales. The Sales field moves to the Fields for Chart column.

6. Click Finish, if you're done.

7. Click Next to fine-tune your chart. The Chart wizard display a selection of charts to choose from (see Figure 17.2).

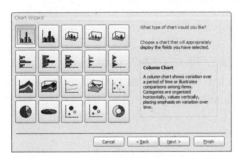

Figure 17.2. Select the style of chart.

8. Click Column Chart. This is the first chart.

9. Click Finish, if you're done.

10. Click Next to fine-tune your chart. The Chart wizard displays a preview of the chart and asks how you want the data to be laid out on the chart.

11. Drag the Sales button to the Series area of the same chart. Sales data is used as the series for the chart (see Figure 17.3).

12. Double-click SumOfSales. The Chart wizard displays a list of ways to summarize the series data; I'm using the default setting of Sum.

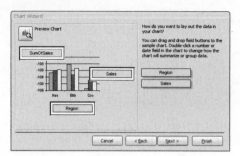

Figure 17.3. Select the data series for the chart.

13. Click Finish, if you're done.

14. Click Next to fine-tune your chart. The Chart wizard prompts you to enter the title for the chart. By default it uses the name of the table or query selected as the data source for the chart. You can also decide whether or not the legend is displayed. I've decided to use the default title and display the legend.

15. Click Finish. The Chart wizard displays the chart.

Editing the chart

You can edit data displayed in the chart. Access 2007 displays the data in a spreadsheet. Simply change values the same way as you change values in Excel, and Access 2007 automatically reflects those changes in the chart.

Here's how to do this:

1. Right-click the chart. Access 2007 displays a pop-up menu.

2. Move the cursor over Chart Object. Access 2007 displays a submenu.

3. Click Edit or Open. Access 2007 places data depicted in the chart in a spreadsheet.

4. Click the cursor in a cell and change the value. Access 2007 redraws the chart to reflect your changes. Those changes affect the chart and not the data in the underlying database. The data on the chart is now different from the data in the database.

5. Click the Close box (red X) to return to the form. The Data Editor dialog box closes.

Converting the chart to an image

The chart can be converted to an image. Once converted, the chart is treated like a picture and cannot be modified.

Here's how to convert to an image.

1. Right-click the chart. This displays a pop-up menu.
2. Move the cursor over to the Change To option. Access 2007 displays a submenu.
3. Click Image. Access 2007 warns that you cannot undo this action.
4. Click Yes. Access 2007 converts the chart to an image.

Modifying the chart

If the style of the chart doesn't suit your needs, you can modify the chart. It's easy to do. Access 2007 lets you change practically any characteristic of the axis, data series, or chart. This includes patterns, font, and colors.

Here's how this is done. First place the chart in edit mode. I showed you how to do this earlier in this chapter. Once in the edit mode, select the area of the chart that you want to change. Options that Access 2007 presents to you depend on the chart that you select. Here are the options for the Column style chart.

Double-click text in the X or Y axis. Access 2007 displays the Format Axis dialog box that contains five tabs of options. These are:

■ **Patterns.** This lists options that set the characteristics of lines and ticks used to mark the data series.

■ **Scale.** This is where you set the scale for the axis.

■ **Font.** This is where you set the font, font style size, effects, color, and background.

■ **Number.** This is where you set the format for numbers shown in the chart.

■ **Alignment.** This is where you set the direction of the text and the angle of the text.

Double-click the grid lines to display the Format Gridlines dialog box. This contains two tabs. These are:

■ **Patterns.** This sets characteristics of lines.

■ **Scale.** This sets the scale of the grid.

Double-click the data series to display the Format Data Series dialog box that contains five tabs. These are:

- **Patterns.** This is where you set borders and colors for the data series.
- **Axis.** This is where you plot the series on the primary and secondary axis.
- **Y Error Bars.** This is where you fine-tune the chart's error factor.
- **Data Labels.** This is where you set characteristics of the data labels.
- **Options.** This is where you set the gap between lines.

Another way to modify the chart is to right-click the chart and select:

- **Format Chart Area.** This is used to set patterns and fonts used on the chart.
- **Chart Type.** Lets you change the type of chart.
- **Chart Option.** Here is where you change the titles, data labels, the legend, and other elements of the chart.

Just the facts

- A picture in the form of a chart or graph is worth a thousand words only if it clearly tells the story; otherwise it is useless.
- The purpose of a chart or graph is to show visual relationships among data so that the audience can grasp the relationship at a glance.
- Before thinking about the kind of chart or graph to use, decide on the message you want to deliver.
- Labels should tell the audience what to look for in the chart or graph.

Working with Macros

GET THE SCOOP ON...

Looking at macros ▪ Setting conditions ▪ Embedding a macro ▪ Creating a macro ▪ Making a standalone macro ▪ Making a macro group ▪ Running a macro

PART VI

Creating a Macro

Push a button and have Access 2007 do all your work. You can, if you write a macro and assign the macro to a button. A macro is like a computer program that you write yourself. It tells Access 2007 what to do and when to do it.

Sounds complicated, but it isn't. If you can give directions to your house, then you can write a macro. You simply need to learn the language that Access 2007 understands.

That's where I come in. In this chapter, I show you how without having to learn a programming language. You find out how to use the Access 2007 Macro Builder to create a macro.

Finding out about macros

A macro is a set of instructions that tells Access 2007 to do something. Think of it as driving directions to your house that you save in a Word document.

When you want Access 2007 to do that something, you tell Access 2007 to run the macro. This is similar to your friend following directions in the Word document to find your house.

A macro can be run manually by clicking Run in the Tools group on the Design tab on the Ribbon or it can run when an event occurs. As you may recall from Chapter 14, an *event* is clicking a Button control, changing a value in a Text Box control, opening a report, and other activities that occur while your Access 2007 application runs.

An instruction is called an *action*. A macro is built by assembling one or more actions from an action combo box in the Macro Builder. I show you how to do this a little later in this chapter.

Some actions require you to provide additional information in order for Access 2007 to carry out the action. These are called arguments. Other actions give you an option to include an argument or don't require an action at all.

If you want to display a message on the screen using the MsgBox action, Access 2007 needs to know the title of the message box, the message, the type of message box, and the tone to sound when the message box is displayed. You must provide this information in the Macro Builder after selecting the action.

There are two kinds of macros:

■ Standalone macro is a collection of one or more related actions stored under a single macro name.

■ Macro group is a collection of related macros stored under a single macro name and run in sequence.

Setting conditions

Access 2007 executes actions sequentially within a macro. It starts with the first action and continues until the last action is performed; afterward the macro ends.

However, you can set a condition that must be met in order to run an action. A *condition* states criteria in the form of a logical expression. The result of a logical expression is either true or false. If the logical expression is true, then Access 2007 runs the action, otherwise the action is skipped.

The expression can result in true/false, yes/no, zero or non-zero. A 0 is considered false and therefore the action is skipped.

You can have the same condition affect more than one action. That is, tell Access 2007 to run a sequence of actions if the condition is true.

If the condition is true in the first action of the sequence, then Access 2007 runs the entire sequence of actions, otherwise the sequence is skipped. I show you how this is done later in this chapter.

Embedding a macro

A macro becomes part of the form, report, or control when assigned to its event. This is referred to as embedding the macro. The macro is automatically copied when you copy its corresponding form, report, or control.

This assures you that the macro is always available when your Access 2007 database application runs. You don't have to copy macro files separately from your database files.

Creating a macro

Enough about talking about macros, you can now create one. Macros are created by using the Macro Builder. The Macro Builder is a tool that is part of Access 2007.

Here's how to start the Macro Builder:

1. Click Macro (see Figure 18.1) in the Other group on the Create tab. This displays three options.

2. Click Macro. Access 2007 opens the Macro Builder.

   The Macro Builder (see Figure 18.2) has several rows each representing an action and three columns. These are:

   ▪ **Action.** This is a combo box that contains all actions that Access 2007 can perform.

   ▪ **Arguments.** This is where you enter information Access 2007 needs to perform the action. Arguments are required, optional, or not required, depending on the nature of the action.

   ▪ **Comment.** This is where you enter reminders about the action. Access 2007 ignores comments when running the action.

Figure 18.1. Click Macro to start the Macro Builder.

Inside Scoop

A description of the action and explanation of arguments are displayed when you select an action.

Figure 18.2. Use the Macro Builder to create a macro.

Making a standalone macro

A standalone macro is a simple macro to build since it isn't in a macro group. You can focus on actions within the macro without being concerned by macros running before and after it in a macro group.

Before creating any macro decide what action Access 2007 should perform when the macro runs. Scroll down the action combo box in the Macro Builder to get an idea of the kinds of actions you can choose from.

Let's simply have Access 2007 display a message on the screen using the MsgBox action. The message appears in a message box. The MsgBox action has the following four arguments:

- **Message.** This is the text of the message you want displayed on the screen. You can display up to 255 characters. Alternatively, you can use an expression. Access 2007 then evaluates the expression and displays the result as the text of the message.

- **Beep.** This tells Access 2007 whether or not to sound a beep when the message is displayed. Enter Yes, and the beep sounds, otherwise Access 2007 doesn't make a sound when the message box is displayed.

Inside Scoop

The message can be visually divided into three sections. The first block of text appears in the first section, and then insert the @ symbol preceding text you want displayed in the next section.

■ **Type.** Access 2007 can display a built-in icon in the message box that gives a clue to the nature of the message. Your choices are None (no icon), Critical, Warning! Or Information. Pick the one that is appropriate for your application.

■ **Title.** This is text that is displayed in the title bar of the message box.

Here's how to create a standalone macro.

1. Click the first column in the first row. Access 2007 highlights the cell.

2. Click the down arrow. Access 2007 displays a list of actions.

3. Click MsgBox. Access 2007 displays the MsgBox arguments in the Action Arguments section at the bottom of the Macro Builder (see Figure 18.3).

Figure 18.3. Select an action and enter arguments for the action.

4. Type **Hello world** in the Message argument.

5. Type **Yes** in the Beep argument.

6. Type **None** in the Type argument.

7. Type **My First Macro** in the Title argument.

8. Right-click the Macro1 tab. This displays a menu.

9. Click Save. The Save As dialog box is displayed.

10. Type **My First Macro** as the name of the macro.

11. Click OK. Access 2007 saves the macro and places it in the Unassigned Objects section of the navigation pane.

12. Click Run in the Tools group on the Design tab. Access 2007 runs the macro (see Figure 18.4).

Figure 18.4. Here's the macro you created.

Making a macro group

A macro group is a macro that contains two or more macros. You create a macro group practically the same way as you build a standalone macro except that you specify each macro name in the Macro Name column on the Macro Builder. You'll probably notice that there isn't a Macro Name column displayed in the Macro Builder. You have to insert this column by clicking Macro Names in the Show/Hide group on the Design tab of the Ribbon.

Macros begin with a value in the Macro Name column. The first action of the macro is on the same row as the macro name. Additional actions for the same macro appear in subsequent rows. These rows don't have a macro name. The absence of a macro name tells Access 2007 that the action is part of the previous macro.

Access 2007 knows when a macro ends when Access 2007 when the macro name changes.

Here's how to create a macro group:

1. Open the Macro Builder. (I showed you how this is done previously in this chapter.)

2. Click Macro Names in the Show/Hide group of the Design tab of the Ribbon. This inserts the Macro Name column into the grid.

3. Click the first row in the Macro Name column.

4. Type the name of the macro. I typed Macro1.

5. Click the first row in the Action Column.

6. Select MsgBox action to display a message box on the screen.

7. Type values for the Message and Title arguments at the bottom of the grid. I entered *Macro 1* as the title and *Hello world* as the message.

8. Click the second row in the Macro Name column.

9. Type the name of the macro. I typed Macro2.

10. Click the second row in the Action Column.

11. Select MsgBox action to display a message box on the screen.

12. Type values for the Message and Title arguments at the bottom of the grid. I entered *Macro 2* as the title and *Goodbye world* as the message.

13. Right-click the Macro1 tab. This displays a menu.

14. Click Save. The Save As dialog box is displayed.

15. Type **My First Macro Group** as the name of the macro.

16. Click OK. Access 2007 saves the macro and places it in the Unassigned Objects section of the navigation pane.

17. Click Run in the Tools group on the Design tab on the Ribbon. Access 2007 runs the macro.

Running a macro

The moment of truth comes once you build your macro. Will Access 2007 do what you *tell* it to do when the macro runs? The answer is always yes.

However, the question you want answered is, will Access 2007 do what you *want* it to do when the macro runs? The answer is maybe and maybe not.

Access 2007 always follows directions that you write as actions in a macro, but you may or may not have written the correct directions to achieve your objective.

The only way to determine this is to run your macro. If Access 2007 achieves your objective, then your macro is ready to go to work for you. And if the results are unexpected, then you go to work debugging your macro, trying to discover incorrect actions. I'll give you tips on debugging later in this chapter.

For now, let's run your macro. There are a number of ways to do this.

1. Click Run in the Tools group on the Design tab on the Ribbon. Use this when you're in the Design View building or modifying the macro.

2. Double-click the name of the macro in the navigator pane.

3. Right-click the macro name in the navigator pane and click Run on the pop-up menu.

4. Assign the macro name to an event. Access 2007 runs the macro when the event occurs.

5. Run a macro from another macro. I show you how this is done in the next section.

A macro can be run from another macro. If the macro is a standalone macro, then simply reference the name of the macro. If the macro is part of a macro group then reference the macro as *MacroGroupName.MacroName*. Replace *MacroGroupName* with the name of your macro group and replace *MacroName* with the name of your macro that is defined within the macro group.

An action is used in a standalone macro to run another macro. The first action displays a message on the screen. The next action runs a macro. A third action displays another message once the macro finishes running.

The next example creates a macro that runs two other macros. The first macro that it'll run is the *My First Macro* that you created previously in this chapter. You'll need to create the second macro the same way as you created the first macro. I set the Title argument to *My Second Macro* and the Message argument to *Goodbye world* and saved the macro *as My Second Macro*.

Here's how to run a macro from a macro.

1. Open the Macro Builder.

2. Click the first row in the Action column and select RunMacro.

3. Type **My First Macro** as the Macro Name argument. Leave the other arguments empty.

4. Click the second row in the Action column and select RunMacro.

5. Type **My Second Macro** as the Macro Name argument. Also leave the other arguments empty.

6. Right-click the tab.

7. Click Save from the pop-up menu. Doing this displays the Save As dialog box.

8. Type the name of the macro. I call it My Macro Running Macros (see Figure 18.5).

9. Right-click the tag.

10. Click Close from the pop-up menu.

11. Click Run in the Tools group on the Design tab on the Ribbon to run the macro.

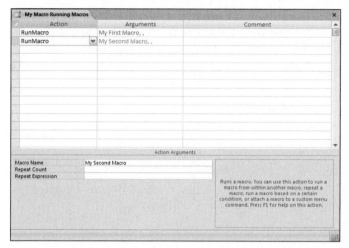

Figure 18.5. A macro can run other macros by using the RunMacro action.

Running a macro in an event

No doubt you've been more than a little curious about the Event tab on the Property Sheet. The Event tab lists events that might occur when using a form, report, or control.

When Access 2007 detects an event, it first looks to see if you have special instructions you want followed to respond to the event. If you have, then Access 2007 follows those instructions. If not, then Access 2007 uses its default response. Sometimes Access 2007 follows your instructions and then uses its default response depending on the event that occurs.

As you probably surmise, your instructions are actions in a macro that you assigned to the event in the Event tab of the Property Sheet.

Hack

Instructions are also written as a Visual Basic subroutine, which is then assigned to an event. A subroutine is a small program written in the Visual Basic programming language that gives you greater control over Access 2007 than you have with a macro.

Choosing an event

There are so many events to choose from. Where do you begin? Understand that you don't have to assign a macro to every event. In fact, you'll probably write instructions for a handful depending on your application. And many applications don't require you to respond to any event.

Your choice of event depends on what you want to do. Suppose that you want to validate data entered into a Text Box control. One way to do this is to assign a macro to the After Update event. Access 2007 then runs your macro each time the user finishes making changes to the value of the Text Box control.

Names of events contain words that give you a clue to the nature of the event. Most events become self-explanatory if you know the clue words that are commonly used in event names. Here they are:

- **On.** When the action occurs, such as On Exit.
- **Before.** Before the default action occurs, such as Before Update, which is before Access 2007 updates the information.
- **After.** After the default action occurs such as After Update.
- **Got Focus.** When the form, report or control is selected.
- **Lost Focus.** When a previously selected form, report, or control is no longer selected.
- **Down.** The mouse button or keyboard key is pressed.
- **Up.** The previously pressed mouse button or keyboard key is released.
- **Mouse Move.** The mouse cursor is moved.
- **Keypress.** A keyboard key is pressed and released.
- **On Click.** The mouse button is pressed and released.
- **On Not in List.** An item is entered into a Combo Box control that is not on the Combo Box control's list.

Assigning a macro to an event

You can create a Button control on a form and use it to display My First Macro, which you created previously in this chapter. Access 2007 runs the macro each time the button is clicked.

Here's how to do assign a macro to an event:

1. Click Form Design in the Forms group on the Create tab on the Ribbon. This opens the Form Design tool. You learned about forms in Chapter 12.

2. Click the Button control in the Controls group on the Design tab on the Ribbon.

3. Click the form. Access 2007 automatically starts the Command Button wizard.

4. Click Finish. I'll show you how to directly set the Button properties without using the Command Button wizard.

5. Click Property Sheet. This displays the properties for the Button control.

6. Click the Format tab.

7. Highlight the name of the picture in the Picture property and press Delete. This removes the picture from the Button control.

8. Click the Caption property and type **Welcome**. Welcome is displayed on the button.

9. Click the Event tab.

10. Click the On Click event. Access 2007 displays a combo box containing available macros.

11. Select *My First Macro*. Access 2007 displays the *My First Macro* as the value for the On Click event property (see Figure 18.6).

12. Click View in the Views group on the Design tab on the Ribbon. Access 2007 displays the form.

13. Click the Welcome button and Access 2007 runs *My First Macro*.

Inside Scoop

Clicking the ... button in the On Click event property when the On Click event is selected displays the Macro Builder, enabling you to create a new macro that is automatically associated with this On Click event.

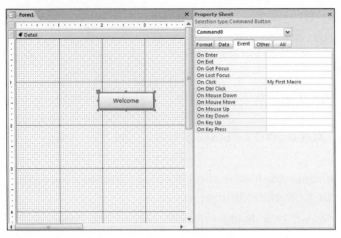

Figure 18.6. Assign the macro to the On Click event.

Setting a condition for an action

There are times when you want Access 2007 to skip an action in a macro because the action doesn't apply to the current circumstance.

For example, you might want to display a message on the screen if the person using your Access 2007 application doesn't enter the correct information. However, you'll want Access 2007 to skip this action if the correct information is entered.

You tell Access 2007 when to execute an action by setting a condition for the action. A condition is stated as a logical expression that is placed in the Conditions column of the action in the Macro Builder. The logical expression must evaluate to either a true or false. If the expression is true, then the action is performed; otherwise Access 2007 skips the action and moves on to the next action in the macro.

Inside Scoop

Click Conditions in the Show/Hide group on the Design tab if you don't see the Conditions column in the Macro Builder.

Creating a condition for an action

Before creating a condition that decides if the macro should run, modify the form you created in the previous section that contains the Welcome button.

Here's what you need to do:

1. Click the Text Box control in the Controls group on the Design tab.

2. Click the form. Access 2007 displays a Label control and a Text Box control.

3. Click the Label control and change the text to **Enter your user ID:**.

Now create the condition for the macro.

1. Right-click My First Macro on the navigation pane. This displays a pop-up menu.

2. Click Design View. This opens the macro in the Macro Builder.

3. Click Conditions in the Show/Hide group on the Design tab on the Ribbon. This inserts a Condition column in the grid.

4. Right-click the first row under the Condition column. This displays a pop-up menu.

5. Click Build. This opens the Expression Builder (see Chapter 9).

6. Click Forms, Loaded Forms, Form1 or the name of your form in the first column. This shows the list of controls on the form that contains the Welcome button.

7. Double-click the Text Box control in the second column. Access 2007 displays reference to this Text Box control in the expression at the top of the Expression Builder.

8. Click the = button in the row of buttons. This inserts an equal operator in the expression.

9. Type **"Bob"** in the expression (see Figure 18.7).

10. Click OK. Access 2007 places the expression in the first row in the Condition.

11. Right-click the tab and click Save to save the macro.

12. Click the Form1 tab or open the form.

Inside Scoop

You can tell Access 2007 to apply the same condition to subsequent actions by entering the condition for the first action and then placing the ellipsis (...) in the condition column of the subsequent actions.

13. Click View in the Views group on the Design tab on the Ribbon. This displays the form.

14. Type **Bob** in the text box and click Welcome. Access 2007 runs the macro.

15. Type **Mary** in the text box and click Welcome. Access 2007 doesn't run the macro because the condition to run the macro hasn't been met.

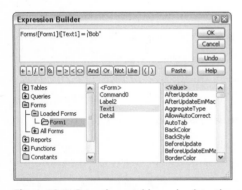

Figure 18.7. Enter the matching value into the expression.

Making decisions within a macro

You tell Access 2007 to perform one action if a condition exists or another action if a different condition exists. Let's say that you want to display a welcome message if the user ID is Bob and an Invalid User ID message if the user ID isn't Bob.

In the real world user IDs are validated by comparing them to valid user IDs in a database. In this example I simply validate the user ID using two conditions in the macro.

Display My First Macro in the Macro Builder by right-clicking the macro name to display a pop-up menu and clicking Design View. The first action is fine because the condition displays the welcome message if the user ID is Bob.

Insert a second action by following these steps:

1. Right-click the first row under the Condition column. This displays a pop-up menu.

2. Click Build. This opens the Expression Builder.

3. Click Forms, Loaded Forms, Form1 in the first column. This shows the list of controls on the form that contains the Welcome button.

4. Double-click Text in the second column. Access 2007 displays reference to this Text Box control in the expression at the top of the Expression Builder.

5. Click the <> button in the row of buttons. This action inserts the not equal operator in the expression.

6. Type **"Bob"** in the expression.

7. Click OK. Access 2007 places the expression in the second row in the Condition.

8. Right-click the tab and click Save to save the macro.

9. Click the Form1 tab or open the form.

10. Click View in the Views group on the Design tab on the Ribbon. This displays the form.

11. Type **Bob** in the text box and click Welcome. Access 2007 runs the hello greeting.

12. Type **Mary** in the text box and click Welcome. Access 2007 displays the Invalid User ID message.

Debugging a macro

You know about bugs, the kind that cause your computer program to misbehave, because all of us have encountered a computer bug at some point. You'll experience bugs with macros that you write and it's your responsibility to find and remove them.

There are two kinds of bugs:

- **Syntactical bugs.** You used the wrong words in your macro.

- **Logical bugs.** You used the correct words but didn't give proper directions. This is similar to giving incorrect driving directions to your house.

A Syntax bug, commonly referred to as a *syntax error,* usually causes Access 2007 to display a warning message either as you're writing the macro or the first time that the macro runs.

Logical bugs, known as *logical errors,* are harder to discover because no warning messages are displayed. Your macro runs uninterrupted, but the results are not what you had in mind.

For example, a warning icon is displayed in a message box when you didn't want an icon displayed. You simply gave Access 2007 the wrong instruction.

Debugging is the process of uncovering and removing a bug. Nearly all the time you'll be debugging errors in logic rather than syntax errors because Access 2007 automatically identifies syntax errors for you.

Debugging your macro requires you to carefully examine the result of each action to determine if the action achieves the desired result. If it doesn't, then a bug exists.

Finding the bug can be time-consuming and frustrating. Fixing the bug is faster than finding it because you know how to fix your error.

It's like the time my friend got lost coming to my house. He drove around for an hour before giving me a call. We then played 20 questions trying to learn his location. Once I pointed him in the right direction, it took seconds for me to give him clearer directions to my house.

Using debugging tools

Access 2007 gives you two great tools to use to find bugs in your macro:

- **Single Step.** You can execute the macro one action at a time by using the Single Step option in the Tools group on the Design tab.

- **SingleStep action.** This is an action that is inserted into a macro that tells Access 2007 to enter the single-step mode. Actions prior to the SingleStep action are performed in sequence without interruption. Actions after the SingleSetp action are performed, and then Access 2007 waits until you press Step before performing the next action.

Inside Scoop

If your macro refers to a form or other Access 2007 object, you may have to open that object before running the macro; otherwise Access 2007 displays an message saying it can't find the object.

Using the Single Step tools

Step through the *My First Macro* macro by following these steps:

1. Open My First Macro in the Macro Builder. (I showed you how to do this previously in this chapter.)

2. Click Single Step in the Tools group on the Design tab on the Ribbon.

3. Right-click the tab and click Save to save the macro.

4. Double-click the name of the form used in the previous section. You need to open the form reference in the macro, otherwise Access 2007 will complain. Access 2007 places the form in Form View.

5. Double-click the name *My First Macro* on the navigation pane. Access 2007 runs the Macro in Single Step mode and displays a description of the current action on the screen (see Figure 18.8).

6. Click Step to move to the next action in the macro.

7. Click Stop All Macros to stop the macro.

8. Click Continue to exit the Single Step mode and return to the application.

Figure 18.8. Click Step to move to the next action.

Using the SingleStep action

Another way to run a macro in SingleStep mode for debugging purposes is to insert the SingleStep action into the macro where you want to step through the macro.

Here's how to do this.

1. Display My First Macro in the Macro Builder, which you learned to do previously in this chapter.

Inside Scoop

When you select SingleStep, Access 2007 automatically inserts a breakpoint after each action. A breakpoint tells Access 2007 to pause after an action and wait until Enter is pressed.

2. Select the first row by clicking the selector box that appears to the left of the first column.

3. Click Insert Row in the Rows group on the Design tab. Access 2007 inserts a new row about the selected row.

4. Select SingleStep as the action for the Action column (see Figure 18.9).

5. Right-click the tab and click Save to save the macro.

6. Open the form that is associated with macro.

7. Double-click My First Macro on the navigation pane. Access 2007 runs the macro in Single Step mode.

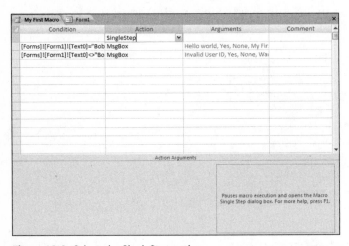

Figure 18.9. Select the SingleStep action.

Modifying a macro

Changing actions, arguments, and/or conditions in a macro is a straightforward process. First open the macro in the Macro Builder by right-clicking the name of the macro in the navigation pane and then clicking Design View. Once opened, here's how to modify the macro.

Inside Scoop

Always retest the macro after changing it to be sure that the macro performs as expected. If the macro isn't performing properly, then reverse the changes.

Insert an action:

1. Click the action above the row where you want the new action inserted into the macro.
2. Click Insert Rows in the Rows group on the Design tab. This inserts a new row below the row you selected.
3. Enter an action, argument, and condition as required by your application.

Delete an action:

1. Click the action that you want deleted.
2. Click Delete Rows in the Rows group on the Design tab. Access 2007 removes the action and moves up actions below it.

Reorder an action:

1. Drag the row selector, located left of the action name, to the new position in the macro.
2. Drop the row selector. Access 2007 automatically moves down the action and drops the action into its new position.

Just the facts

- A macro is a set of instructions that tells Access 2007 to do something.
- A macro can be run manually by clicking Run in the Tools group on the Design tab or when an event occurs.
- An instruction is called an action.
- A macro is built by assembling one or more actions from an action combo box in the Macro Builder.
- Some actions require you to provide additional information (called arguments) in order for Access 2007 to carry out the action.

- A standalone macro is a collection of one or more related actions stored under a single macro name.

- A macro group is a collection of related macros stored under a single macro name and run in sequence.

GET THE SCOOP ON...
Interacting with the database ▪ Working with the
OpenTable action ▪ Running a query ▪ Outputting data ▪
Selecting an object ▪ Finding data

Using Macro Actions

After reading the last chapter you're probably thinking of routine tasks that you want to automate using a macro. At least that's how I felt after learning to write a macro.

Coming up with tasks to automate is easy. Writing the macro that automates those tasks requires that you learn about various actions available in Access 2007.

Learning these actions is similar to learning a language. You want to learn actions that you'll use every day and leave learning the other actions to sometime in the future when you start building advanced macros.

That's how I approached writing this chapter. I get you up to speed by showing you the most commonly used actions — and a few that might get you a wow from anyone using your Access 2007 application. You can learn about the less frequently used actions by clicking the Help icon in Access 2007.

Interacting with the database

One of the most frequent requests I receive is to automate a process that interacts with a database. Some are simple requests, such as opening a table when the user clicks a button. Other requests are more complicated, such as finding a particular record in a table or in a query result.

413

Chapter 19

Bright Idea

Drag and drop a table from the Navigation pane to the macro action column to automatically create an OpenTable action in Datasheet view.

However, Access 2007 has an action suited for practically every inter-action your macro needs to make with a database. Here are the database actions that I use frequently.

Working with the OpenTable action

As the name implies, the OpenTable action tells Access 2007 to open a table in any view, such as Datasheet view, Design view, or Print Preview. The OpenTable action has three arguments. These are:

- **Table name.** This required argument is the name of the table. A list of available tables is listed in the Table Name argument combo box.

- **View.** This argument determines the view Access 2007 uses when opening the table. Your choices are Datasheet (default), Design, Print Preview, PivotTable, or PivotChart, which appear in a combo box when you click the argument column.

- **Data mode.** If you select Datasheet as the value of the View argu-ment, you'll need to select a data mode. Add, Edit (default), or Read Only are your choices. Add lets you insert new records but not edited records. Edit lets you insert a new record and edit. Read Only lets you see but not touch the data.

Running a query

Run a query from within a macro by using the OpenQuery action. The query must be part of the database. You can't use this action to run a query that is connected to another database such as Microsoft SQL Server.

You need to supply nearly the same three arguments as is required by the OpenTable action except instead of the Table Name argument you'll need to supply the Query Name.

Outputting data

I find the OutputTo action very useful. You use it to output an Access 2007 database object, such as a table, query, form, report, module, or

Inside Scoop

Use the SetWarnings action to prevent system messages from displaying while your macro runs.

data access page (Web page generated by Access 2007), to Excel, HTML, Rich Text Format, or plain text files.

You'll need to provide Acceess 2007 with seven arguments. These are:

- **Object type.** Table (default), Query, Form, Report, Module, Server View, Stored Procedures or function. This is a required argument.

- **Object name.** The name of the object that you are going to output.

- **Output format.** Select Excel 12, Excel 12 Xml, Excel 5-7, Excel 97-2003, HTML, Rich Text Format, Text File. The numbers represent versions of Excel. You can let the person who runs the macro decide the output format by leaving this argument blank. Access 2007 then prompts the person to enter the format when the macro is running.

- **Output file.** This is the name of the output file. Leave this blank and Access 2007 prompts the person running the macro to enter the output file name.

- **Auto start.** Set this argument to yes and Access 2007 automatically runs and loads the output file in its application. If it is an Excel file, Access 2007 outputs the file and opens the file in Excel.

- **Template file.** This is the name of the file you want to use as a template for an HTML output file. You probably want to always define a template if your output is HTML; otherwise templates are not very useful.

- **Encoding.** This argument tells Access the character encoding format to use. Your choices are MS-DOS, Unicode, or Unicode (UTF-8). I leave this blank and let Access 2007 decide the form. It uses Windows default encoding for text files and the default system encoding for HTML files.

Selecting an object

You need to select a table, query, form, or other database object. This is similar to clicking it. When you do, Access 2007 gives this object focus

Inside Scoop

Access 2007 automatically changes the object's Visible property to Yes if the object is initially hidden.

and then uses it for subsequent instructions, such as finding data until another object is selected.

Use the SelectObject action to select a database object. The SelectObject action has three arguments. These are:

- **Object type.** Your choices are Table, Query, Form, Report, Macro, Module, Data Access Pages, Server View, Diagram, Stored Procedure, or Function. This is a required argument.

- **Object name.** This is the name of the object that you want selected. You can leave this blank if you set the In Navigation Pane argument to Yes.

- **In Navigation pane.** If set to Yes, then the macro uses the object that is selected in the navigation pane. If set to No (default), then you must provide the name of the object in the Object Name argument.

Finding data

You've probably used Find on the Home tab to locate information in the currently selected object. The FindRecord action has the same effect except within a macro. The FindRecord action finds the first instance of the information that meets your search criteria.

The FindRecord action has seven arguments. These are:

- **Find what.** This is the search criteria. This can be text, a number, date or an expression and wildcards (See Chapter 8). This argument is required.

- **Match.** Here's where you tell Access 2007 where to look for the Find What argument within the field. Your choices are Any Part of Field, Whole Field (default), or Start of Field.

- **Match case.** Choose Yes to match the uppercase and lowercase of the Find What argument, otherwise pick No (default).

- **Search.** This tells Access 2007 the direction to search based on the current record. Your choices are Up, Down, or All (default).

- **Search as formatted.** Choose Yes to have Access 2007 match the format of the Find What argument, otherwise select No (default).

- **Only current field.** Choose Yes (default) if you want the search limited to the current field in each record, which is a fast search, otherwise choose No. This tells Access 2007 to search every field in each record.

- **Find first.** Choose Yes to have Access 2007 begin searching with the first record (default); otherwise choose No and the search begins at the current record.

Finding the next record

The FindNext action is used to locate the next record that matches the search criteria specified in the FindRecord action. Think of this as repeating the FindRecord action once Access 2007 finds the first record that matches the search criteria. This is the same as clicking Find Next in the Find and Replace dialog box.

The FindNext action doesn't have any arguments.

Making a record the current record

The GoToRecord action is used to make a specific record the current record. This is like clicking Go To on the Home tab of the Ribbon. The GoToRecord action has four arguments. These are:

- **Object type.** This is the type of object that you are using. Choices are Table, Query, Form, Server View, Stored Procedure, or Function. You can leave this blank and Access 2007 uses the object that is currently selected when the macro runs.

- **Object name.** This is the name of the object you selected. Leave this blank if you leave the Object Type blank. Access 2007 determines the name of the currently selected object.

- **Record.** This is where you determine which record becomes the current record. Your choices are Previous, Next (default), First, Last, Go To, or New.

- **Offset.** This is an integer or an expression that results in an integer. The integer represents one of two values depending on the Record argument. If the Record argument is Go To, then Access 2007 treats the Offset argument as a record number. Suppose the Offset

Inside Scoop

The Offset argument is ignored if the Record argument is the First, Last, or New.

argument is 10. Access 2007 makes record number 10 the current record. If the Record argument isn't Go To, then Access 2007 adds or subtracts the Offset arugment to the record number of the current record to decide the next current record. If the Record argument is Next, then Access 2007 adds the Offset argument to the current record number. If the Record argument is Previous, then Access 2007 subtracts the Offset argument from the current record number. Let's say the Record argument is Next and the Offset argument is 10. The number of the current record is 20. Access 2007 makes record number 30 the current record.

Using a query or a filter

As I mention in Chapter 8, you can select a subset of information contained in a table by using a query. You can also do the same by applying a filter or using a WHERE clause in an SQL statement.

The ApplyFilter action is used to apply a query, filter, or an SQL WHERE clause to a table from within a macro. The ApplyFilter has two arguments. These are:

- **Filter name.** This argument is the name of the query or filter.
- **Where condition.** This argument is a SQL WHERE clause or expression that specifies criteria for the data subset. Leave this blank if you entered a value for the Filter Name argument. If a value is entered for both arguments, then Access 2007 applies the value of the Filter Name argument to create the data subset and then applies the value of the Where Condition argument to the data subset to create a final data subset.

Removing filters

Return to the full data set by using the ShowAllRecords action to remove a filter that has been applied to the table. The ShowAllRecords action doesn't have any arguments.

Interacting with forms, reports, and controls

Perform behind-the-scenes magic by writing a macro that interacts with forms, reports, and controls and create an intelligent interface for your application.

In this section, I show you how to open a form, access a control on a form or report, move to a particular page, and print a report from within a macro.

Opening a form

You open a form in Form View, Design View, Print Preview, or Datasheet View by using the OpenForm action. Furthermore, you can determine access rights to data on the form. You determine if a person can add data, edit data, or simply view data without the capability of changing it.

OpenForm is the same as double-clicking the form name on the navigation pane or right-clicking the form on the navigation pane and then selecting View.

The OpenForm action has six arguments. These are:

■ **Form name.** This argument is the name of the form and is required.

■ **View.** This argument determines the form's view. Choices are Form (default), Design, Print Preview, Datasheet, PivotTable, or PivotChart.

■ **Filter name.** This argument is the name of the query or filter used to generate data for the form. The query must include all fields on the form.

■ **Where condition.** This argument is an SQL WHERE clause or expression used by Access 2007 to select records that can be displayed in the form. This SQL WHERE clause is applied to the subset of data returned by the query or filter if one is specified in the Filter Name argument.

■ **Data mode.** This argument determines access rights to the data shown in the form. Choices are Add, Edit (default), or Read Only. Add lets the person insert data but not edit data. Edit enables the person to add and edit data on the form.

■ **Window mode.** This argument tells Access 2007 the type of window to use to display the form. Choices are Normal (default), Hidden, Icon (minimize), or Dialog box.

Watch Out!

Only enter the name of the control or field such as Customer First Name. Don't enter the full qualified identifier, which is Forms!Customers![Customer First Name].

Selecting a control

The GoToControl action is used to select a control or field in the active form or datasheet. First open the form using the Open Form action and then use the GoToControl action to give a focus to a specific control on the form. At this point, your macro can interact with the control.

The GoToControl action has one argument: Control Name.

Selecting a page

Select a page of a form by using the GoToPage action once the form is selected by using the OpenForm action. The GoToPage action has three arguments. These are:

- **Page number.** This is the number of the page that you want to become the active page. Leave this blank if you want to use the Right and Down arguments to display part of the current page.

- **Right.** This is an integer representing the horizontal position on the current page measured from the left edge of the window that contains the page. This is required if you set a value for the Down argument.

- **Down.** This is an integer representing the vertical position on the current page measured from the top edge of the window. This integer is required if you set a value for the Right argument.

Displaying and printing a report

The OpenReport action is used to open a report in either the Design View or Print Preview. It is also used to send the report to the printer.

Inside Scoop

Measurements are in inches or centimeters, depending on Windows' regional settings.

OpenReport has a handy feature that lets you restrict the reports that are printed in the report.

There are five arguments for the OpenReport action. These are:

- **Report name.** This argument is the name of the report and is required.

- **View.** This argument specifies the view used to open the report. Choices are Print (print the report immediately) (default), Design, or Print Preview in the View box.

- **Filter name.** This argument is the name of the query or filter used to restrict records that can be printed in the report.

- **Where condition.** This argument is an SQL WHERE clause used to return a subset of the data for the report.

- **Window mode.** This argument tells Access 2007 the window to use when displaying the report. Choices are Normal (default), Hidden, Icon, or Dialog in the Window Mode box.

Interacting with windows

Make windows large, minimize them, and move them around the desktop all from behind the scenes using a macro. This is more than a little Access 2007 hocus-pocus — show off your Access 2007 skills.

Having control over the size and position of windows on the desktop lets you make those fine adjustments to your application that enhances the way someone uses it.

The following sections detail the actions that I find useful when interacting with the windows.

Maximizing, minimizing, and restoring a window

The Maximize and Minimize actions are used to simulate clicking the Maximize and Minimize buttons in the right corner of a window. The Maximize action enlarges the active window so that it fills the Access window. The Minimize action shrinks the window to the the Title bar on the Access 2007 window.

Use the Restore action to return a window to its previous size. If the window is maximized, the Restore action minimizes the window. If the window is minimized, then the Restore action maximizes the window.

Moving a window

The MoveSize action is used to relocate or resize the window that is currently active in your Access 2007 application. Position and size are measured in either inches or centimeters, depending on the regional settings in Microsoft Windows on the computer that runs your Access 2007 application.

The MoveSize action is similar to clicking Move or Size on the Microsoft Windows Control menu. The MoveSize action has four arguments. These are:

- **Right.** This argument is an integer representing the new horizontal position for the window's upper-left corner. This is measured from the left edge of the window that contains the Access 2007 window that you are moving.

- **Down.** This argument is an integer representing the new vertical position for the window's upper-left corner. This is measured from the top edge of the window that contains the Access 2007 window that you are moving.

- **Width.** This argument is an integer representing the window's new width when resizing the window.

- **Height.** This argument is an integer representing the window's new height when resizing the window.

Importing and exporting

I'm always being asked to automate the importing and exporting of information from and to Access 2007.

Sometimes I create a button on a form called Convert To Excel and then assign a macro to its Click event (see Chapter 18). In that macro, I use the TransferSpreadsheet action, which I show you how to use later in this chapter. The person using my Access 2007 application simply clicks the button, and my macro does all the work to export the table to an Excel spreadsheet.

Other times, I use the TransferSpreadsheet action as the last action in a multiaction macro that processes information because my users prefer to work with information in Excel.

There are other formats that you can import from and export to. Access 2007 has an action suited to automate each one.

Transferring text

The TransferText action is used to import or export text. You can import information contained in a text file into Access 2007 or you can take data from Access 2007 and export it to a text file.

The TransferText action has seven arguments. These are:

- **Transfer type.** This argument specifies the type of transfer. Choices are Import Delimited, Import Fixed Width, Import HTML, Export Delimited, Export Fixed Width, Export HTML, Export Word for Windows, Merge, Link Delimited, Link Fixed Width, or Link HTML.

- **Specification name.** This argument tells Access 2007 where to find specifications for importing, exporting, or linking a file. Access uses predetermined specifications for many file formats; therefore you can leave this argument blank.

- **Table name.** This argument is the name of the Access 2007 table that is used for importing data, exporting data, or linking text to data. Access creates a new table containing the imported data unless you selected Import Delimited, Import Fixed Width, or Import HTML in the Transfer Type argument, which causes Access 2007 to append the data to the table.

- **File name.** This argument is the name of the text field that either contains the data being imported into Access 2007 or is the file receiving data being exported from Access 2007 or linked to it. If the name of the text file is the same as an existing text file, then Access 2007 replaces the existing file.

- **Has field names.** Select Yes if the first row in the text file contains field names. Select No (default), and Access 2007 assumes the first row contains data.

Hack

The imported text belongs to Access 2007. Alternatively, you can link to the file. Linking shares the file with other applications, such as Word and Excel.

- **HTML table name.** This argument is the name of the table in an HTML file that you want imported or linked to Access 2007. This argument is used only if the Transfer Type argument is Import HTML or Link HTML; otherwise this argument is ignored by Access 2007. If you leave this blank and the Transfer Type argument is Import HTML or Link HTML, the Access 2007 imports the first table or list in the HTML file.

- **Code page.** This argument is the name of the character set used in the file.

Transferring to a spreadsheet

As I mentioned previously in this section, the TransferSpreadsheet action is used to import or export data between a spreadsheet and Access 2007.

In addition, you can link a spreadsheet to your Access 2007 application. This means the spreadsheet can appear in a form or report while still being used by Excel. Changes made to the spreadsheet using Excel appear immediately on the form or report.

The TransferSpreadsheet action has six arguments. These are:

- **Transfer type.** This argument specifies the type of transfer. Choices are Import, Export, or Link

- **Spreadsheet type.** Choose the type of spreadsheet format. All the popular spreadsheet formats are available.

- **Table name.** This argument is the name of the Access 2007 table that you are using.

- **File name.** This is the name of the spreadsheet file. If the spreadsheet file already exists when exporting from Access 2007, Access 2007 overwrites it with the exported data. A new spreadsheet is created if the spreadsheet file doesn't exist.

- **Has field names.** Select Yes if the first row of the file contains field name. Select No (default) if the first row contains data.

- **Range.** Enter the range of cells or link from the spreadsheet such as A1: C10. Leave this argument blank if you want to import or link to the entire spreadsheet. Leave this argument blank when exporting from Access 2007.

General actions

In this section, I go over some actions that I find useful. They don't fit into a single category, so I'm listing them in a general category. These actions include sounding a beep while your macro runs, changing the mouse pointer to an hourglass, controlling how your macro behaves, and printing a database object.

Try these out and then put them in your macro bag of tricks because you never know when you will encounter a situation when these will come in handy.

Beeping

You've heard your computer beep every now and then. Now you have a chance to beep someone else's computer by using the Beep action. The Beep action simply tells the computer to sound a beep.

Place the Beep action in your macro whenever you want the beep to sound. I do this whenever I want to draw the user's attention to something important that occurs when the macro runs.

The Beep action doesn't have any arguments. Keep in mind the user's local settings may override this, so don't depend on it working. The user might have the sound turned off.

Display the hourglass

No doubt you've seen the hourglass appear as the mouse cursor. It signifies that your computer is busy doing something such as processing information.

You can display the hourglass while your macro is busy doing something by using the Hourglass action. I use this whenever an action takes more than a few seconds to complete. The Hourglass action turns on or turns off the hourglass icon. This affects only the hourglass icon that your macro displays. The hourglass icon used by other applications remains unaffected.

The Hourglass action has one argument:

Hourglass On: Select Yes to display the hourglass icon or No (default) to display the normal mouse pointer.

Stopping a macro

There will be times when you want the macro to stop running before the last action is performed. This happens during debugging when you need to test a group of actions within the macro.

There are several ways to stop a macro. You can use the StopMacro, StopAllMacros, or Quit actions.

The StopMacro action stops the current macro. The StopAllMacros stops all macros currently running. Neither of these have arguments.

The Quit action stops the macro and exits Access 2007. This has one argument:

Options: This tells Access 2007 what to do with unsaved objects. Choices are Prompt, Save All, and Exit. Prompt prompts the person using the macro to decide if the unsaved objects are to be saved. Save All automatically saves these objects, and Exit terminates Access 2007 without saving them.

Cancelling an event

In Chapter 18, I show you how to assign a macro to an event. You might encounter a situation when the event that triggered the macro must be cancelled.

You can cancel the event by using the CancelEvent action in the macro at the point when you want the event cancelled. The CancelEvent action doesn't require any arguments.

Closing an object

The Close action is used to close an object such as a table, query, form, report, and so on. There are three arguments you set for the Close action. These are:

■ **Object type.** This is the type of object you're closing. Choices are Table, Query, Form, Report, Macro, Module, Data Access Page, Server View, Diagram, Stored Procedure, or Function. If you leave this blank, Access 2007 closes the active window.

■ **Object name.** This is the name of the object you're closing. Leave this blank if you leave the Object Type argument blank.

■ **Save.** Select Yes and Access 2007 saves the object before closing it. Select No to have Access 2007 close the object without saving, or select Prompt (default) to prompt the person who is using your application to decide whether or not the object is saved.

Turning off warnings

You probably encounter more than your share of warning messages when running various applications on your computer. A warning message is the way that an application or Windows lets you know that it sees something that isn't quite right. It isn't necessarily wrong, but it might be wrong.

Depending on the situation, you might choose to ignore the warning message because the condition that is being questioned isn't critical to your application.

Warning messages can also appear when running your macro. You can turn off display of warnings messages by using the SetWarning action. The SetWarning action has one argument. This is:

Warnings On: Select Yes to turn on warning messages and No (default) to hide warning messages from the screen.

Hiding the results of the macro

You have a choice of whether or not to display the results of the macro on the screen. Sometimes you'll want to run the macro behind the scenes with nothing appearing on the screen. Other times, you'll want to see the output of the macro. The Echo action lets you specify whether or not the result is displayed on the screen. The Echo action has two arguments. These are:

■ **Echo On.** Select Yes (default) to display the results and No to hide the result from the screen.

■ **Status Bar Text.** This text appears in the status bar when the Echo action turns off the display. I usually enter "Macro Running" as the value of this argument; otherwise nothing on the screen indicates that the macro is running.

Setting the value of a field, control, or property

Here's an action that I couldn't live without. It's called the SetValue action and is used to set the value of a field, control, or property on a form or report. The reason that this is so popular is that I use the SetValue action to streamline data entry.

Let's say the data entry form has two radio buttons: One is called new customer and the other returning customer. A new customer provides more information than a returning customer provides. By clicking new customer, I execute a macro that displays controls on the form to collect the additional information from the new customer. The controls are present all the time. I simply have the macro change the Visible property to Yes, making these controls visible. I do this by using the SetValue action.

The SetValue action can also be used to select or deselect any control based on whatever the person enters into the form.

The SetValue action has two properties. These are:

- **Item.** The name of the field, control, or property whose value is being set. You must use the full syntax, which is Form!formname!controlname.

- **Expression.** This is the value you want to set. You must also use the full syntax such as Form!formname!controlname.value=’10’.

Printing an object

It might come in handy to know how to print a datasheet, report, form, or a data access page, which is a Web page published from Access 2007. You do this by using the PrintOut action. The PrintOut action is similar to clicking Print.

The PrintOut action has six arguments. These are:

- **Print range.** This argument tells Access 2007 the portion of the object to print. Choices are All (default), Selection, or Pages. All tells Access 2007 to print the entire object such as the entire report. Selection causes Access 2007 to print the part of the object that is selected. Pages causes Access 2007 print specific pages.

- **Page from.** This argument is an integer representing the first page that Access 2007 is to print. Access 2007 starts printing at the beginning of this page. This argument is required if the Print Range argument is set to Pages.

- **Page to.** This argument is an integer representing the last page Access 2007 prints. Access 2007 stops printing at the end of this page. This too is required if the Print Range argument is set to Pages.

- **Print quality.** Choices are High, Medium, Low, or Draft. High is the highest quality available from the selected printer and is usually the slowest printing speed. Draft is the lowest quality and usually the fastest speed.

- **Copies.** This integer specifies the number of copies Access 2007 should print. Access 2007 prints at least one copy.

- **Collate copies.** Select Yes (default) to have the object printed as a full set. Select No if you don't want copies collated. It's best to select Yes; otherwise you'll spend time collating by hand.

Transmitting keystrokes

Sometimes all you need is to write a macro that sends the same keystrokes to Access 2007 as if you enter those keys yourself. So if you wanted to print the current report, you'd enter (SHOW KEYS USED TO PRINT) in the macro rather than entering the actions that I showed earlier in this section. Access 2007 reads each keystroke from the macro as if you entered them at the keyboard.

You can send up to 255 characters of keystrokes by using the SendKeys action. The SendKey action has two arguments. These are:

- **Keystrokes.** These are the keystrokes that you want to send to Access 2007 when the macro runs. Enter each key in the Keystroke box in the argument. This argument is required.

- **Wait.** Select Yes if you want Access 2007 to pause until the keystroke is processed before reading the next keystroke. Select No (default) if you want Access 2007 to keep reading the keystroke as other keystrokes are processed. I usually select No unless I notice a delay in processing a keystroke.

E-Mailing an object

Here's another action that I use a lot. It's called SendObject and it builds an e-mail using the default e-mail program on the computer that runs your Access 2007 application. The person using the application can then send the e-mail.

Watch Out!

Don't send confidential information using the SendKey action because a malicious user might intercept the keystroke and compromise the security of your Access 2007 application.

Here are the arguments for the SendObject action:

- **Object type.** This identifies the type of object that is being sent. Choices are table, form, report, module, data access page, server view, stored procedure, or function.

- **Object name.** This is the name of the object that will be attached to the e-mail.

- **Output format.** This is specifies the format of the object that you're sending. Choices are HTML, Microsoft Excel 12 Biff (*.xlsb), Microsoft Excel 12 Xml (*.xlsx), Microsoft Excel 5-7 (*.xls), Microsoft Excel 97-2003 (*.xls), PDF Format (*.pdf), Rich Text Format (*.rtf), Text Files (*.txt), or XPS Format. Access 2007 prompts you to enter a format if you leave this argument blank.

- **To:** This is the e-mail address of the person who is going to receive the e-mail. Use a semicolon (;) to separate multiple e-mail addresses.

- **Cc:** This is the e-mail address of the person who is receiving a copy of the e-mail.

- **Bcc:** This is the e-mail address of the person who is receiving a blind carbon copy of the e-mail.

- **Subject:** This is the subject line of the e-mail.

- **Message text.** This is the text of the e-mail.

- **Edit Message.** Select Yes if the e-mail text message can be edited before it is sent. Select No (default) if it is sent without being changed.

- **Template file.** This is the path and filename of the template file that contains HTML tags if the e-mail is in HTML.

Running an application from within Access 2007

You can run either a Windows or MS-DOS application such as Excel, PowerPoint, and Word from within Access 2007 by using the RunApp action. Access 2007 loads and runs the specified application in the foreground. You can exchange data between Access 2007 and the other application using the Clipboard.

The RunApp action has one argument:

Command Line: This is the path, application name, and command line argument (if any) that are used to start the other application. This is a required argument.

Running VBA code

And now for something completely different. Macros give you a taste of how to automate Access 2007 using a list of instructions. However, developers who build Access 2007 applications write more elaborate instructions for Access 2007 using Visual Basic for Applications (VBA).

VBA is a programming language. With it you can do nearly anything imaginable with Access 2007. You may want to try your hand at VBA once you are finished reading this book. You can run VBA code from a macro by using the RunCode action. The RunCode action has one argument. This is — Function Name: This is the name of the VBA code. VBA code is divided into groups of instructions. Each group is called a function. This is similar to a macro. Each function is assigned a name similar to the name of a macro. This argument is required.

Just the facts

- OpenTable action tells Access 2007 to open a table in any view.

- Run a query from within a macro by using the OpenQuery action.

- OutputTo is used to output an Access 2007 database object.

- Use the SelectObject action to select a database object.

- FindRecord action has the same effect as clicking Find on the Home tab.

- FindNext action is used to locate the next record that matches the search criteria specified in the FindRecord action.

- The GoToRecord action is used to make a specific record the current record.

Database Administration

GET THE SCOOP ON...
Understanding garbage information ▪ Preventing garbage
from entering the database ▪ Locating the source of the
data ▪ Identifying potential sources for errors ▪ Devising
solutions to reduce errors

PART VII

Managing and Maintaining a Database

Chapter 20

Garbage in. . . garbage out is the creed of many database developers who realize that information generated by a database application is taken as gospel by practically everyone who reads it.

Database developers also realize that the accuracy of information stored in a database is only as good as procedures implemented to manage and maintain the information.

A poorly managed and maintained database generates garbage, unreliable information that gives the appearance of respectability but is really junk information.

Database developers cannot prevent garbage information from finding its way into a database, but there are steps that can be taken to minimize it. I show you these steps in this chapter so that you can implement them in your Access 2007 database application.

Understanding garbage information

Most of the garbage entries I've found in databases are simply data-entry errors, old information that hasn't been updated, and errors by the developer when importing or exporting data.

Before writing this chapter, I reviewed how garbage information got into some of my database applications over the years. Here are some of the problems I discovered:

- **Misspelling.** The data-entry person misread a person's handwriting.

- **Inconsistent spelling.** This happens particularly with corporate names where there is a formal name and several informal ways of referring to the company.

- **Transposing numbers.** Reversing numbers in a telephone number.

- **Typographical errors.** Simply pressing the wrong key on the keyboard.

- **Data substitution.** Someone doesn't have the requested information at hand and provides alternative information. I see this happen a lot when the database application requests the direct line to a contact in a company and someone enters the company's general telephone number.

- **Choosing an inappropriate option.** Someone checks an option that is inconsistent with other options selected on a form.

- **Old data.** Even an Access 2007 database can crash or become corrupted, making it impossible to access information in the database. Nearly every organization backs up the database regularly. The backup database is used if the current database is unavailable. However, the backup database doesn't have up-to-the-minute information.

Preventing garbage from entering the database

You can't prevent all garbage information from entering a database, but you can take steps to minimize it by reviewing the flow of information within your organization.

Begin your review by identifying the source of information. Think of this as being a detective who follows the paper trail, although instead of paper you'll trace a mixture of paper, electronic data, and plain old data entry into a computerized form.

Locating the source of the data

Your objective is to determine how the original information is collected. Here's what I typically discover when backtracking information for my database applications.

- **Transcribed conversations.** Sales representatives and service representatives make handwritten notes of their conversations with customers that are transcribed to a paper or electronic form.

- **Second-hand information.** An assistant enters information supplied by a sales representative or service representative into the database application.

- **Partial information.** Multiple persons who may not communicate with each other supply portions of information to the database application. The sale representative supplies initial customer and order information. The service representative enters inquires from the customer.

- **Importing information.** A sales representative uses a laptop to gather orders while on the road and then transmits the orders electronically to the database application.

- **Electronic data exchange.** The database is updated with information supplied electronically by a vendor.

- **Paper forms.** Customers provide handwritten information on a printed form that is then entered into the database application.

- **Electronic data entry.** Customers enter information electronically into the database application such as an ATM.

- **Web forms.** Customers use the Web to enter information into a database application such as an online ordering system.

Identifying potential sources for errors

Examine each original data source and determine how inaccurate information can find its way into the database. The best way to do this is to observe the flow of information.

Some of your co-workers may worry that you're a spy for the boss or that you're trying to automate them out of a job. Before those thoughts cross their minds, be upfront and explain that you're trying to make their job easier by changing the system, so they have all the information that they need to enter accurate information into the database application.

In my years of upgrading database applications, I always found that those involved in the information flow are competent. The problem usually lies with the system used to gather the information. By system, I mean both manual and electronic systems.

For example, a customer's order may not fit options available on the electronic order form, which forces the sales representative to select an invalid option simply to have the order processed.

Devising solutions to reduce errors

Don't expect to eliminate garbage from getting into your database; rather aim to reduce the likelihood that errors will occur.

The best practice is to assign ownership of the information to one person and give that person exclusive access to enter and update the information. For example, the sales representative owns information about his customer. Only the sales representative can enter and update information about the customer in the database. If the information is inaccurate, then the sales representative is at fault.

The purpose of assigning ownership is not to place blame when errors occur. Instead it is designed to avoid the information gap. The information gap occurs when different people are responsible for part of a process but no one has overall responsibility for the entire process.

Assigning responsibility to one person doesn't eliminate the information gap but clearly identifies who must assure the accuracy of the information in the database. That person actively collects all the information and enters it into the database.

The next challenge is finding the person to take ownership of the information. I always choose the person who has the highest stake in keeping the information accurate, such as the sales representative for customer information. The organization financially rewards the sales representative, based on his customer's orders. He has a vested interest in assuring that information in the database about his customer is accurate.

Minimizing data-entry errors

You can't make people write more clearly. You can minimize the information that they need to write if you require them to directly input information into an electronic form rather than use a paper form. Eliminating or minimizing the use of a paper form reduces errors caused by transcribing conversations or having to interpret handwriting.

Ideally, the sales representative has the electronic form in front of him while he speaks with the customer. The electronic form is a guide for asking questions to the customer so that no information is overlooked. Answers are immediately entered into the electronic form.

Designing the paper form

The electronic form may not be available when gathering information. In this situation, it is best to create a paper form that is identical to the electronic form.

This serves two purposes. First, you are assured that all the information will be asked and no information will be overlooked. Also, the person transcribing information from the paper form to the electronic form can match field by field when entering information. No guessing is necessary.

Minimizing text information

Garbage information frequently enters the database when information is entered into the electronic form. Therefore, it is best to use check boxes, radio buttons, list boxes, lists, and other controls that give the person the opportunity to choose information rather than type information into a text box.

By reviewing information already entered, you'll be able to make frequently entered information part of a pick list, check box, or radio button.

I frequently use a query associated with a combo box. The query retrieves unique values in a field and displays them on the list of a combo box. The person can either pick an item from the list or enter a new value in the combo box. The new value is then automatically added to the combo box list.

Testing for common sense

Your database application should review data entered on an electronic form to decide if it makes sense and display a warning message asking the person to confirm the entry.

This validation process is unique to each application. I always check to make sure that the values are within an acceptable range. If no one ever ordered more than 10 units, then my database application questions quantities greater than 15 units. I usually give a five-unit buffer before displaying a warning message.

I also determine if selections coincide with other selections. If the total amount for an order is $10 and delivery is $50 because the order is being sent by guaranteed overnight delivery, then I usually ask the person to confirm the method of delivery. It doesn't make sense that the delivery charge is five times the amount of the order; however, a customer might need the product tomorrow so it's not necessarily an error.

Encouraging review of information

I design an in-your-face application whenever critical information is being entered into the database. Immediately after data entry, I display the electronic form on the screen and ask the person to verify the information.

In particular, I use this technique when information is imported into the database. This assures that the person sees information that is imported and can detect any problems when importing the information. If a problem occurs, I provide a button linked to a macro that the person can use to back out the information.

Scheduling backups

Every database must be backed up regularly to minimize the loss of information should the active database become disabled or infected with erroneous information. Developers use the term *infected* to refer to inappropriate data saved to the database. It has nothing to do with a bacterial or virus infection.

The schedule for backing up the database depends on the frequency that the information in the database changes. A database containing information that rarely changes doesn't have to be backed up as often as a database that is always changing, such as data used by a credit card company or retail store.

Inside Scoop

Maintain multiple backups of the database, one for each day for several weeks. This way, you'll be able to restore a database should you discover that you backed up a corrupt database. You can't assume that you'll always discover the corrupt database right away.

The schedule also is influenced by business demands. The database is unavailable while it is being backed up. This isn't a problem for some businesses but others, such as financial firms, can't have the database unavailable during business hours.

Backing up the database

Access 2007 provides an easy way to back up a database by using the Microsoft Office button. Access 2007 renames the backup copy of the database using the database name followed by the date that the database is backed up.

You can overwrite this name. I do whenever I have a database application where I need to have multiple backups during the day. I simply insert the time at the end of the name Access 2007 recommends for the backup.

Here's how you back up a database.

1. Open the database. I'm using the Northwind 2007 database.

2. Click the Office Button. A menu is displayed.

3. Click Backup Database. The Save As dialog box is displayed (see Figure 20.1).

4. Type a name for the backup database in the File name text box.

5. Click Save. Access 2007 creates a backup of the database.

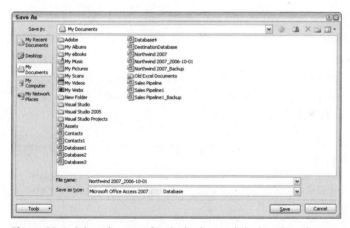

Figure 20.1. Select the name for the backup and the location where you want to store the backup.

Watch Out!

Don't save the backup database to the same disk and computer that has the active database because the backup might be destroyed at the same time as the active database. Instead, save the backup database to a network server or removable medium such as a Flash drive or CD. Do this by selecting the location in the Save As dialog box.

Restoring a backed-up database

Access 2007 makes restoring a backed-up database as easy as creating a backed-up database. You simply open the backed-up database as you open any database.

Here's how to do it:

1. Click the Office Button.

2. Click Open.

3. Double-click the name of the backed-up database.

Compacting the database

Few of us have the patience to wait for anything. And this is true when it comes to waiting for a response from an Access 2007 database application. We want to click a button and have the information instantly appear on the screen.

The response time of your Access 2007 database application is dependent on a number of factors. These include:

▪ **Sharing the database.** Several colleagues will use your Access 2007 databases simultaneously. Although not very common, Access 2007 might temporarily postpone responding to a request if it is busy fulfilling a request from another colleague.

Inside Scoop

The restored database still has the name of the backed-up database. Therefore, make sure to save the backed-up database under the name of the active database before using it.

- **Network traffic.** Databases located on a network server are at the mercy of network traffic. Just like a highway, the network can get bogged down in high-volume traffic during peak periods during the day that delays your Access 2007 database application from receiving a request and returning a response.

- **Database fragmentation.** As records are deleted and new records added to the database, the way Access 2007 organizes data within the database can become inefficient. This inefficiency slows the processing of requests and therefore delays the response.

Increasing performance

You can do little about delays caused by sharing the database or delays caused by network traffic jams. You could have your colleagues open the database in exclusive mode. Everyone except your colleague are locked out of the database until your colleague is finished using the database. However, you'll receive plenty of complaints from the others when they are unable to access the database.

The network administrator can fix network traffic jams by redistributing the network traffic to alleviate the traffic jam. This is like telling someone stuck in traffic to use a different highway. However, you're at the mercy of the network administrator to reconfigure the network.

Defragging your database

You can easily increase the performance by defragmenting the database. This is referred to as compacting the database. To appreciate how compacting works, you need to understand the inner workings of Access 2007.

Each time information is deleted from the database, Access 2007 really doesn't delete the information. It still remains in place except that Access 2007 ignores it, treating the information as if it was removed from the database.

There are two reasons for doing this:

- Access 2007 can retrieve the data when you click Undo. Undo tells Access 2007 not to ignore the information that was recently deleted.

- You can save time because Access 2007 doesn't have to rearrange information in the database to take up the space left vacant by the deleted information.

I like to think of this as my attic where I store my books all neatly organized by topics. Whenever I receive a new book I leaf through it, place it on the dining room table, and within a week my wife dumps the book in the attic.

When I'm looking for information, I head up to the attic and browse. I start at the beginning of the category and then jump over to those books I don't need anymore to find new books in the category located at the end of the row.

Before long, I find myself taking forever trying to find the information I need because I have to jump around the row of books. Of course, I could simply remove the books I don't need and then reorganize the remaining books into categories — but that is time-consuming.

This is what basically happens with your Access 2007 database over time. Performance decreases while Access 2007 jumps over information that is marked for deletion but hasn't been deleted.

Purging the information

Once a year, my wife and I head for the attic to remove my "deleted" books and reorganize the remaining books. Although it takes some arm-twisting to get me started, I can find any information I need within minutes after we're finished reordering the books.

You do the same thing when compacting your database. Out goes information marked for deletion, and the remaining information is reorganized so that Access 2007 can find it in a fraction of a second.

Compacting affects the internal way Access 2007 organizes information and doesn't affect records and fields of your database. However, you won't be able to retrieve information marked for deletion. It's gone forever.

Compacting the database

Compacting your database is simple to do. There are two ways to do this. You can open the database or select the database from the Database to Compact From.

Here's how to compact an open database.

1. Open the database.

2. Click the Office Button. Doing this displays a menu.

3. Move the cursor over Manage. A submenu appears.

4. Click Compact and Repair Database (see Figure 20.2). Access 2007 chugs away a few seconds and compacts the database.

Figure 20.2. Click Compact and Repair Database to compact the database.

Here's how to compact an unopened database:

1. Click the Office Button. Doing this displays a menu.

2. Move the cursor over Manage. A submenu appears.

3. Click Compact and Repair Database. Access 2007 displays the Database to Compact From dialog box.

4. Double-click the name of the database that you want to compact. Access 2007 chugs away a few seconds and compacts the database.

Using database properties

Each database has a set of properties. These properties are similar in concept to properties that you used throughout this book. As you'll recall, a property is a name/value pair where the name is the name of the property, and a value is a value that is associated with the name.

Properties are used for a variety of purposes. Some are used to tell Access 2007 how to use an object such as displaying the value in a Text Box object in bold type. Other properties are used to convey your preference to anyone viewing or accessing the property, such as title of the database.

Properties can be accessed by Access 2007 behind the scenes by using the Properties List, and from within a module using Visual Basic for Applications.

Exploring database properties

An Access 2007 database has a number of properties that are of value to use when managing your database. These properties are displayed in the Properties dialog box.

You'll need to open a database before displaying its properties. After the database is opened, then:

1. Click the Office Button.

2. Click Manage. This opens a submenu.

3. Click Database Properties. This displays the Properties dialog box (see Figure 20.3).

Database properties are organized into five groups each represented by a tab in the Properties dialog box. Access 2007 opens with Summary tab by default or the previously selected tab.

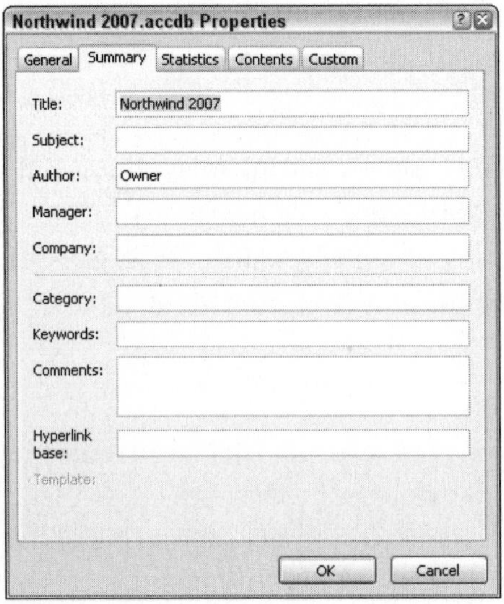

Figure 20.3. The properties dialog box contains properties for your database.

Using the Summary properties

The Summary properties describe the database. Access 2007 assigns default values to two of them. The title is assigned the name that you give to the database. The author is the computer's login ID of the person who created the database, which is probably Owner depending how you set up logins on your computer.

The other properties are optional and self-explanatory. I usually leave these properties blank unless it is useful to the application. For example, I'll enter the name of the company in the Company property if I'm building the application for a client.

Using the General properties

The General tab describes the database. It gives you the name of the database, type, location, and database size. This is where you'll also learn when the database was created, last modified, and last accessed. I find this information handy when comparing two copies of the same database to determine which one is the latest copy.

You'll also find the Attributes property in this tab. This tells you whenever the database is Read Only, Hidden, Archive, or System.

Using the Statistics properties

I use the Statistics tab to learn how the database is used. It contains the date and time when the database was created, modified, and accessed, which is the same information as contained in the General tab.

However, the Statistics tab also tells you when the database was printed, the login ID of the person who last saved the database, the number of the revision, and the time that elapsed editing the database.

Using the Contents tab

The Contents tab lists objects contained in the database. These are table, queries, reports, macros, and modules. You won't be able to change these from the Contents tab. You can do so from within the database.

At first I didn't feel that this tab was useful; however occasionally I use it to glance at the contents of the database without having to screen through the navigation pane in the database.

Using the Custom tab

The Custom tab enables you to create customized properties for the database. A customized property is one that Access 2007 doesn't use, but can be used by modules that read it using Visual Basic for Applications and by others who simply use the Custom tab to view the property.

The Custom has four components. These are:

- **Name.** The name of the property. Access 2007 supplies a list of common customized properties that you can choose from. Alternatively you can simply type the name of the property in the name combo box.

- **Type.** This is a combo box that lists data types for the property. Choose from Text, Date, Number, Yes or no.

- **Value.** Enter the value that you want assigned to the property.

- **Properties.** This list customizes properties.

Creating a customized property

Creating a customized property is straightforward. Here's what you need to do:

1. Type the name of the property in the Name combo box. I typed MyProperty. Add becomes active (see Figure 20.4).

2. Select the type for the property. I picked Yes or no.

3. Select the value. Access 2007 changes the Value to access a value appropriate for the Type. It changed to two radio buttons because I selected Yes or no as the type.

4. Click Add and Access 2007 inserts the property on the customize properties list.

5. Click OK to create the customized property.

Deleting a customized property

It is always best to clean house occasionally and remove customized properties that are no longer useful to the database. You do this by deleting the property in the Custom tab in the database properties dialog box.

Figure 20.4. Enter the name and value of your customized property.

Here's how to remove a customized property:

1. Click the property you want deleted in the Properties list in the Custom tab. Delete is activated.

2. Click Delete. Access 2007 removes the property from the custom property list.

Dealing with a growing database

One of the most challenging tasks of managing an Access 2007 database is maintaining response times as the database grows. Response time is the time Access 2007 uses to process a request.

There are several factors that influence response time, one of which is the size of the database. The database grows each time a record is inserted into a table. It also grows when you add objects to the database, such as forms and reports.

Forms and reports take up the most space in the database. At first this is seems odd, because you would think data takes up the most space. However, forms and reports are comprised of several control objects and each control object has a multitude of properties. All of this takes up space in the database.

Another high consumer of space is Visual Basic for Application code, which is used to create modules. The more lines of code used in the module, the more space is needed in your database.

The least space-consuming objects are links and queries. A link is a reference to graphics, video, audio, and other kinds of files that are not included in the database.

Understanding lightweight and heavyweight objects

Access 2007 developers use the terms *lightweight* and *heavyweight* to refer to the relative amount of space an object uses in the database. A lightweight object uses less space than a heavyweight object.

Reports and forms that use modules containing VBA code are heavyweight objects, even if the module contains one line of code. This is because of the way Access 2007 handles modules.

Likewise, reports and forms that use embedded OLE objects such as Word and Excel files are heavyweights because these files are stored as part of the report or form in the database.

Reports and forms that don't contain VBA code or link to rather than embed OLE objects are lightweight reports and forms and, as a result, take up less room than a heavyweight report or form.

Understanding cleanup

Access 2007 doesn't always clean up after itself, which you learned previously in this chapter. When you delete or modify an object, Access 2007 makes a copy of the object, effectively duplicating the object's space in the database. That space isn't cleaned up until you compact the database, which I showed you how to do in a previous section.

Sometimes I'm shocked at how quickly the database grows while I'm developing an Access 2007 database application. I spend hours making this change and that change, not realizing that Access 2007 duplicates the object each time.

Remember always to compact your database after a long work session. Do this and your database won't be filled with garbage at the end of the day.

Shrinking VBA code

One problem with using VBA code in a module is that the module size can nearly quadruple in size quickly. You can't avoid this simply because it's how Access 2007 handles VBA code.

However, you can reduce its size after you finish writing VBA code. Here's what you need to do:

1. Click Module in the Other group on the Create tab. This displays a menu.

2. Click Module. This opens the VBA editor.

3. Click Debug.

4. Click Compile. This compiles the VBA code into efficient code.

5. Click Save. This saves the compiled VBA code that is contained in modules.

6. Click the Office Button.

7. Click Manage.

8. Click Compact and Repair Database.

Giving your database a thorough cleaning

Call me quirky, but I like to use a not-so-widely known way of giving my database a top-bottom cleaning before I begin prerelease testing of my Access 2007 database.

Here's what I do. I create a new database and the import all objects from my existing database. To do this, follow these steps:

1. Open the new database.

2. Click Access in the Import group on the External Data tab of the Ribbon.

3. Enter the name of the database to import from.

4. Click OK. The Import Objects database is displayed.

5. Click each tab and click Select All.

6. Click OK. Access 2007 then imports all the objects from the database.

7. Click Close once importing is completed.

Repairing a corrupt database

Access 2007 will have no problem storing and retrieving data most times—unless the data is corrupt.

Corrupt data is information that Access 2007 is unable to read correctly. Sometimes when the data becomes corrupt you'll see information containing smiley faces and strange characters dispersed through the text. And other times, you won't see anything except maybe an error message.

From decades of experience with computers and databases, I've learned to focus on fixing the corrupt data problem rather than spending time figuring out why it happens. This saves a lot of frustration.

Fixing the corrupt database problem isn't the same as fixing the data that became corrupted. Corrupt data might prevent Access 2007 from accessing other information in the database. Therefore, removing the corrupted data is the fastest way to resolve the corrupt data problem.

There are several techniques I use for dealing with corrupt data. Usually one of these techniques work and Access 2007 is able to read information stored in the database again.

Here's what I do:

- Run Compact and Repair Database as I showed previously in this chapter. Access 2007 performs a bit of behind-the-scenes magic to fix common problems that are fixable.

- Remove the corrupted record(s). Display the table that contains the corrupted data (see Chapter 5), if possible and then delete the record(s) that contains the corrupted data.

- Export the information into a text file and then view the text file in a text editor, such as Notepad or Wordpad. The corrupted data should pop out because it usually has strange characters. Delete the line that contains the corrupt data. Save the file and then import the file into a new Access 2007 table. Remember to delete the table that contains information that you exported to the text file.

Watch Out!

Avoid this common mistake. Don't overwrite an existing backup when backing up the current database. Keep each backup separate and identify each by the date it was backed up.

Just the facts

- Garbage information is inaccurate information contained in a database.

- You can't prevent all garbage information from entering a database, but you can take steps to minimize it by reviewing the flow of information within your organization.

- Examine each original data source and determine how inaccurate information can find its way into the database.

- Don't expect to eliminate garbage from getting into your database; however there are common practices developers employ to reduce the likelihood that errors occurs.

- Every database must be backed up on a regular basis to minimize the loss of information should the active database become disabled or infected with erroneous information.

- You can easily increase the performance by defragmenting the database.

GET THE SCOOP ON...
Securing your database ▪ Using the Trust Center ▪
Working in disabled mode ▪ Using add-ins ▪ Enabling a
disabled object ▪ Using a database in trusted mode

Securing a Database

I t seems that you can't pick up a newspaper these days without reading about someone hacking into a database — even government databases that you'd think would be as secure as Fort Knox.

The question you're probably asking yourself is how secure is the data in my Access 2007 database application? The answer depends on whether or not you correctly implemented security features that are available in Access 2007.

Nothing guarantees that your database won't be hacked. However, you can place obstacles that a hacker must overcome to gain access to information in your database.

In this chapter, I go over how to use the Access 2007 security features to secure your Access 2007 database application.

Securing your database

Security in the Access 2007 database application is more involved than security in other applications. Simply storing your application on a password-protected computer and backing up files to a CD and then squirreling it somewhere in your office might be adequate protection for your spreadsheets and Word documents, but it isn't for your Access 2007 application.

An Access 2007 application is exposed to security risks that are not found with your Excel and Word files. An Access 2007 application is designed to be stored on a networked computer shared by a multitude of users concurrently. You might have little or no direct control over computers running your application or the network used to access it.

An Access 2007 application consists of tables, forms, reports, queries, macros, modules, and other interrelated objects, rather than a simple file.

Queries, macros, and modules that contain Visual Basic for Application code take an active role manipulating tables and other objects such as modifying information in a table or changing information contained on a report or form.

So the security threat not only comes from persons using your application over the network but also from wayward queries, macros, and modules that can modify objects in your Access 2007 application.

Using the Trust Center

How does your Access 2007 application know who and what objects to trust? It does so by using the Trust Center. The Trust Center is used to identify trusted locations and establish security settings for your Access 2007 application that determine the behavior of the application.

Whenever the database opens, the Trust Center determines if it is safe to open it or if the database should be disabled until someone in authority (such as you) manually enables the database.

If the database is opened from a trusted location, then the person who opens it has the right to run all the application's objects without having to determine security clearance to use each object.

If it is opened from an untrusted location, then the person must manually enable it each time the database is opened.

Applications built using earlier versions of Access can avoid the Trust Center verification if the application package comes with a valid digital signature from a trusted publisher.

Think of a digital signature as a special code. The person who creates the application includes the digital signature when the application is installed on the networked computer. If your computer recognizes the digital signature as authentic, then it is considered trusted and the Trust Center isn't necessary.

Inside Scoop

All users can see the contents of all Access 2007 objects at all times once the database application is opened.

Inside Scoop

User-level security is unavailable in Access 2007, but is available in databases created by previous version of Access. However, user-level security is lost once a database created by a previous version of Access is converted to the Access 2007 format.

Looking inside the Trust Center

The setting of the Trust Center determines security features employed when your Access 2007 database application is opened. You or the system administrator adjust these settings on the computer that runs your application.

When a request is made to open the application, the Trust Center verifies the location that is trying to open it trustworthy. If it isn't, then the Trust Center disables the application and displays a message on the message bar informing of its decision and presenting options to continue.

Depending on security settings, the Trust Center may enable some objects of the application and disable others. For example, the person opening the application might be able to view information in a form but not be able to modify the information.

Working in disabled mode

When the Trust Center disables an Access 2007 application, only objects of the application that are deemed unsafe are disabled so they can't do any harm to the information or other objects in the application.

The following objects are disabled:

- Macros that modify information in the database or the database itself.
- Macros that access resources outside the database application.
- Action queries that add, update, and delete information in the database.
- SQL pass-through queries that send SQL statements to a database server.
- Visual Basic for Application code contained in modules.
- Expressions that modify information.
- ActiveX controls.
- Data Definition Language (DDL) queries used to modify tables and procedures.

Using add-ins

An add-in is functionality provided to Access 2007 by another program. Think of this as installing a GPS system in your car. Your car came with nearly all the features you wanted, but not a GPS system, so you acquired it after buying your car.

The same is true about add-ins with Access 2007. You probably will never need to acquire an add-in, but that option is always available by searching the Internet or Microsoft's Web site.

When an add-in is loaded into your Access 2007 application, the Trust Center reviews it and decides if the add-in is trustworthy. If so, then the add-in is enabled and you can use it. If not, then the add-in is disabled.

Enabling a disabled object

You — not the Trust Center — have the final say in whether or not an object is enabled. The Trust Center displays a message bar telling you that the object is disabled.

Click the button on the message bar to enable the object. Access 2007 then treats the object as if the Trust Center found it trustworthy for the session. Understand that clicking the enable button makes the disabled object enabled for the session. It doesn't change the setting in the Trust Center. The Trust Center will disable the object the next time the application opens, unless you change its settings in the Trust Center.

Using a database in trusted mode

Trusted mode is when the Trust Center has determined that the application is trustworthy based on settings you or the system administrator made to the Trust Center. You make these settings on your computer and the system administrator makes them on computers run at work or in school.

The job of the Trust Center is to protect the desktop computer that runs an application located somewhere on another computer that is connected to the network.

Inside Scoop

The Trust Center also examines wizards that you might add to Access 2007 to determine if they are trustworthy.

The Trust Center determines if an application is trustworthy based on the location of the application. If the location of your Access 2007 application (for example, the computer where it is stored) is considered a trusted location, then your application is considered trustworthy by the Trust Center.

Understanding the concept of a trusted location

The concept of trusted location is probably new to you. Here's the way a colleague explained it to me.

An Access 2007 application is built on a desktop computer. The application is then moved to a server once the application is tested and debugged.

A server is a computer similar to your desktop except it is shared among users. Servers are used for various purposes such as a Web server is used to serve up Web pages, a database server is used to serve up data, and an application server is used to serve up applications.

A server can be located practically anywhere on a network. It can be next to your desk, in the next building, or on the other side of the world. Think of the network as a highway. There's the Internet, which is a network that connects desktop computers and servers throughout the world. There's the Intranet, which a local network that connects desktop computers and servers within an organization.

Think of a server as a location where you can store your Access 2007 application after it is tested and debugged. The desktop that uses your application doesn't know if your application is trustworthy. It could contain a malicious macro or module.

If the Trust Center on the desktop knows your location is trustworthy, then your entire application runs. If it is deemed untrustworthy, then certain objects that I told you about previously in this chapter are disabled. A message is then displayed, prompting the user to enable those objects.

Creating a trusted location

The person using your application needs to set the Trust Center on their computer to recognize the location of your application as a trusted location. You can't do this except on computers that you control.

Here's how to create a trusted location in the Trust Center.

1. Click the Office Button.

2. Click Access Options. Access 2007 displays the Access Options dialog box.

3. Click Trust Center.

4. Click Trust Center Settings.

5. Click Trusted Locations.

6. Click the Add new location button.

7. Access 2007 displays the Microsoft Office Trusted Location dialog box.

8. Enter the trust location in the Path text box (see Figure 21.1).

9. Use the Browse button to navigate to the location if you don't know the path.

10. Click OK to create the new trusted location.

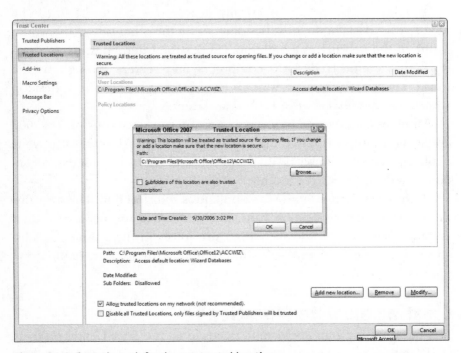

Figure 21.1. Enter the path for the new trusted location.

Placing your application in a trusted location

No doubt you're wondering how to find a trusted location for your Access 2007 application. A location is deemed trustworthy by the desktop that accesses the location and not by the location itself.

Suppose you want to distribute your Access 2007 application to your colleagues by moving it to an application server on your organization's network. Your colleagues then access your application by connecting the application server.

Each colleague adds the application server as trusted location to the Trust Center. When your colleague opens your application, the Trust Center on his computer determines if the location of your application is a trusted location.

Use Windows Explorer to move your Access 2007 application to an application server. There are three ways to do this, depending on the way you connect to the application server:

- Link to the server as a drive and then copy and paste your application to the server.

- Link to the server using an FTP connect and then upload your application to the server.

Packaging and signing an application

The Package-and-Sign is another security feature available in Access 2007. Its concept is simply that you trust applications delivered by a trusted author.

A trusted author is a person or company that you trust to supply safe applications. For example, developers in your IT department are trusted authors. However, my applications are untrustworthy until you decide that I'm a trusted author.

Each person sets his own definition of a trusted author. Once that determination is made, then any application signed by the author is considered a trustworthy application.

The Package-and-Sign feature is used to package your Access 2007 database application into an Access Deployment file. Some developers simply refer to this as the package.

Inside Scoop

An Access Deployment file is faster to transfer over a network than your database application files because it's put into a compressed format.

Access 2007 then digitally signs the package identifying you as the author and signifies that the package hasn't been tampered with. The package is then distributed to the application server or to a person's desktop computer. The digital signature is examined to determine if the package is from a trusted author. If so, then the database application files are extracted from the package.

Creating a signed package

In order to digitally sign a package you need a digital certificate. You can obtain one from a commercial certificate authority (CA) such as VeriSign and GTE. These firms verify that you are reputable before issuing you a digital certificate.

However, don't go through this fuss if you're distributing your Access 2007 database application among friends and colleagues or within your organization. Unless you're selling your application, you can use the SelfCert tool that comes with Microsoft Office Professional 2007 to create a self-signed certificate.

You do this by running the SelfCert.exe from the Program Files\Microsoft Office\Office12 folder on your computer. This displays the Create Digital Certificate dialog box, where you enter a name for your certificate in the Your certificate's name text box. Click OK twice and SelfCert creates your certificate.

After your certificate is created, you're ready to digitally sign the package. Open your database and do the following:

1. Click the Office Button.

2. Click Email.

3. Click Package and Sign. Access 2007 displays the Select Certificate dialog box.

4. Select the digital certificate.

5. Click OK. Access 2007 displays the Create Microsoft Access Signed Package dialog box.

Inside Scoop

If you don't find SelfCert.exe, then you'll need to install it from your Microsoft Office Professional 2007 CDs.

6. Select a location for your digitally signed database package from the Save in list.

7. Enter the name for the digitally signed package in the File name text box.

8. Click Create. Access 2007 creates the .accdc files and places it in the location that you specified in the dialog box.

Using a signed package

After the digitally signed database package is created, you can distribute it to a network server or give it directly to your colleague who'll use it on his desktop computer.

Your Access 2007 application must be extracted from the package before it can be used. This is done by the person who uses your application. Here's how to extract the application from the package.

1. Click the Office Button.

2. Click Open. Microsoft Office displays the Open dialog box.

3. Select Microsoft Office Access Signed Packages (*.accdc) from the File of type list.

4. Select the folder in the Look in list that contains the package (.accdc).

5. Click Open. The Extract Database To dialog is displayed.

6. Select the location in the Save in list where you want to extract the database.

7. Enter the name you want to use for the extraction in the File name text box and click OK.

The previous steps trusted the digital certificate contained in the package. Nearly the same method is used to trust all digital certificates from the same publisher. A publisher is the person or organization who created the application.

Enabling disabled content

You'll probably come across the message saying that content has been disabled because the database application is not from a trusted source. You can enable the content manually; however doing so enables potentially malicious objects (i.e. queries, macros, modules) that might be contained in the Access 2007 application. You probably don't have to worry about this happening if you are using an application built by a colleague or by a developer in your IT department.

Here how to do this:

1. Click Options on the message bar. The Microsoft Office Security Options dialog box is displayed.

2. Select Enable this content.

3. Click OK.

The Microsoft Office Security Options dialog box has the Help protect me from unknown content option. Click this and all potentially dangerous components as defined by the folks at Microsoft are disabled.

Sometimes I get annoyed seeing the enabled option on the message bar each time I open the database application, especially when I only want to work with already-enabled objects of application.

If you feel the same way, then hide the message bar. Here's how to do it:

1. Close the message bar.

2. Click Message Bar in the Show/Hide group on the Database Tools tab.

3. Click Hide. The message bar is hidden the next time you open the application.

Using encryption

You can hinder prying eyes from looking at information in your database by encrypting the database. Encryption scrambles letters and numbers,

Inside Scoop

If the message bar is hidden, click Message bar in the Show/Hide group on the Database Tools tab.

making it unreadable unless a special routine is used to unscramble this information. This is referred to a deciphering.

You can't pick up a newspaper or watch a TV newscast without hearing the term *encryption* being mentioned. Encryption applies an encryption algorithm to scramble information.

An encryption algorithm is simply a defined way of scrambling information. In grammar school you might have created a simple encryption algorithm such as spelling words using the number of the letter of the alphabet such as 10 9 12 for Jim.

It takes seconds for a hacker to identify a simple encryption algorithm and then use it to decipher a message. That's why no one uses the number of the letter of the alphabet to encrypt a message.

Access 2007 uses a strong encryption algorithm that protects your information from most prying eyes. It uses encoding and a database password.

Encrypting your database

Encrypting your database is straightforward. You don't need to know the encryption algorithm. All you do need to know is how to tell Access 2007 that you want your database encrypted.

Here's how to do this:

1. Click the Office Button.

2. Click Open. The Open dialog box is displayed.

3. Select the database that you want to open.

4. Click the arrow on the Open button and select Open Exclusive. No one else can open the database (see Figure 21.2).

5. Click Encrypt with Password in the Database Tools group on the Database Tools tab. The Set Database Password dialog box appears.

6. Enter a password in the Password text box.

Bright Idea

Create a strong password by combining uppercase and lowercase letters with numbers and symbols, such as punctuation. Ideally the password should contain 14 characters.

7. Enter the password again in the Verify text box (see Figure 21.3).

8. Click OK.

Figure 21.2. Click Open Exclusive.

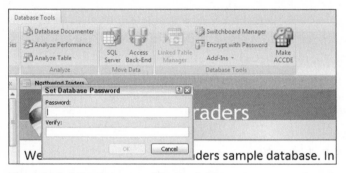

Figure 21.3. Enter the password for the database.

The next time the database is open, Access 2007 displays the Password Required dialog box, prompting you to enter the password. If the password is valid, then Access 2007 deciphers the database before giving you access to it.

Removing a password

Honestly, sometimes I find the password more a hindrance than a help in protecting the database. My Access 2007 database applications are always located on a computer that has its own password protection to prevent unauthorized eyes from seeing the information in the database.

I'm more concerned about forgetting the password and thereby preventing myself and everyone else from accessing the information. If you feel the same way after creating a password for your application, then remove the password.

Watch Out!
The folks at Microsoft cannot retrieve your password. If you forget it you won't be able to gain access to information and objects in the database.

Inside Scoop

Access 2007 developers protect their data and applications. They store tables on a server. I use a Microsoft Window SharePoint service, which I tell you about in Chapter 22. Developers store forms, reports, and other database objects on a networked computer that is accessible to everyone who uses the application.

To do this, follow these steps:

1. Open the database. You'll need to enter your password to gain access to it.

2. Click Decrypt Database in the Database Tools group on the Database Tools tab. The Unset Database Password dialog box is displayed.

3. Enter your password in the Password text box.

4. Click OK. Access 2007 removes the password and returns the database to an unencrypted state.

Just the facts

- The Trust Center is used to identify trusted locations and establish security settings for your Access 2007 application that determine the behavior of the application.

- The Trust Center determines if the database is safe to open or if the database should be disabled until someone in authority (such as you) manually enables the database.

- If the database is opened from a trusted location, then the person who opens it has the right to run all the application's objects without having to determine security clearance to use each object.

- If it is opened from an untrusted location, then the person must manually enable it each time the database is opened.

- A digital signature is a special code. The person who creates the application includes the digital signature when the application is installed on the networked computer.

- Only objects of the application that are deemed unsafe are disabled.

- An add-in is functionality provided to Access 2007 by another program.

- The Trust Center reviews the add-in and decides whether it is trustworthy.

GET THE SCOOP ON...
Looking at SharePoint ▪ Exploring a SharePoint site ▪
Document Libraries and Shared Workspace ▪ Creating a
Document Library ▪ Uploading a document in a
Document Library

Working with SharePoint Sites

I t's nice to share the work and collaborate with a colleague on a project. However, we run the risk of working on the same component simultaneously, which is fraught with all kinds of risks.

Using SharePoint mitigates those risks. Think of it as a librarian in that it keeps track of information. Only one piece of information can be modified at any time. Colleagues can view the information but not change it.

SharePoint can do more than serve as a librarian. It also facilitates sharing your project with colleagues who have access to the SharePoint site, which is a Web site that houses your project.

I tell you more about SharePoint and SharePoint sites and how to use them for your projects in this chapter.

Looking at SharePoint

SharePoint is a way for you and your colleagues to collaborate on a project without leaving your desk. Microsoft calls this Microsoft Windows SharePoint Services (WSS). Some developers simply refer to this as WSS, which is how I refer to it in this chapter.

WSS consists of a SharePoint site and one or more SharePoints. A SharePoint site is a Web site that runs a Microsoft Windows Server and is used as a central storage

469

facility for any documents or information — referred to as SharePoint. You and your colleagues can use it for collaboration — including an Access 2007 database.

The concept of sharing documents over a network isn't new. Developers have being doing this for decades. However, WSS has the flexibility of using a Web server minus the hassles of the Web-publishing process.

A SharePoint site is a Web site. It has a URL that you use to access the SharePoint site using your browser. Some organizations make the SharePoint site available only on the Intranet, so you must log into their Intranet first to access the site. Others make the SharePoint site available from the Internet.

Regardless of where the SharePoint site is hosted, you'll probably be required to log into the SharePoint site using a user ID and password provided by the administrator of the SharePoint site. Your user ID is typically assigned to a user group, and the user group is given rights to documents on the site. However, the SharePoint site can be configured for anonymous access. An anonymous user has basic read-only access to the contents of the site.

A SharePoint site is organized into lists, Document Libraries, picture libraries, discussions, and surveys (see Figure 22.1).

Figure 22.1. Information is organized into lists, Document Libraries, picture libraries, discussions, and surveys.

Bright Idea

If you don't have a SharePoint site available, then look up a SharePoint hosting partner in your favorite search engine. There are a number of vendors that provide SharePoint sites for you to use. I'm using the SharePoint hosting service provided by www. Apptix.com for this book.

- Lists are places to store and present data that can be exported to Access 2007 and other Microsoft Office 2007 products.

- Document libraries contain files that are shared amongst your colleagues. These include your Access 2007 database, Word documents, and Excel spreadsheets.

- Picture libraries are where you store graphic images.

- Discussions are where you and your colleagues can post questions and comments about your project. I find this better than using e-mail because everyone can read each others' comments without having to be bombarded with a series of sometimes disjointed e-mails.

- Surveys are used to poll the feeling of your colleagues on an issue.

Like Web pages, a SharePoint site is customized but all have the same components, one of which is the Quick Launch Bar. The Quick Launch Bar is a menu that gives you fast access to areas of the SharePoint site.

Document Libraries and Shared Workspace

Two features of WSS that I find useful for collaboration are the Document Library and Shared Workspace because they let my colleagues and I share information in real time.

The Document Library is a central repository for files, much like a public library is for books. Practically any type of file can be stored in the document library except file types that the SharePoint site administrator blocks for security reasons. There are about 20 file types that are blocked by default. These can be overridden by using the CharPoint Central Administration tool. You won't find this tool on the SharePoint site. You'll need to connect the server that runs SharePoint and run the CharPoint Administration tool from the server.

A shared workspace is a SharePoint site within the SharePoint site. It becomes your own private area that can be shared with your friends. This is where you and your colleagues can work on a project and then place the finished project in the document library for all to see.

Peeking inside the Document Library

Documents are listed in a datasheet view. Each one is listed by type and name. It lists when the document was last modified and by whom. And it indicates who checked out the document, if it isn't available. When something is checked out, everyone can still view it but they can't make changes or upload a new version. Only the person who checked it out can upload a new version that contains changes.

The menu bar contains tools you need to work with the Document Library. These are:

- **New Document.** This tool lets you create a new document directly within the Document Library rather than uploading a file from your computer. When you select New Document, you are presented with a document template that the SharePoint site administrator determines. Simply enter information and save the new document and it appears in the Document Library list.

- **Upload Document.** This tool displays an HTML page that contains a browse button and a button to upload multiple files from your computer to the Document Library.

- **New Folder.** This tool enables you to organize the Document Library into folders much like you do with your own computer. You can then place documents into their appropriate folders.

- **Filter.** This tool is used to filter the document list so you don't have to scroll to find a document. Each column in the filter is a combo box that contains criteria values. Set the criteria and let the filter find your document.

- **Edit in Datasheet.** This tool lets you edit the entry of the document in the datasheet view if the column can be edited.

Inside Scoop

You can always add more property columns to the Document Library Datasheet view if you want to display additional information about the file. Property columns appear in the Document Information tab of the Shared Workspace task pane.

Hack

You'll need a browser that can use ActiveX controls and has ActiveX control active, otherwise you won't be able to edit the document list in a datasheet. The ActiveX control is installed when you install Microsoft Office.

Creating a Document Library

A Document Library is easy to create and involves clicking a few links on the SharePoint site. You can have a document library created in no time by following these steps.

1. Click Document Libraries on the Quick Launch bar.

2. Click Create Document Library.

3. Click Document Library. The New Document Library screen is displayed (see Figure 22.2). Alternatively, you can click Form Library to create a library of forms.

4. Type the name and description for the Document Library.

5. Click Yes to display the library on the Quick Launch bar. Alternatively, click No if you don't want the Document Library to appear on the Quick Launch Bar.

6. Click Yes if you want the SharePoint site to track versions of documents. Each time a document is edited, the SharePoint site saves it as a new copy of the document rather than overwriting the existing document. Alternatively, click No to have the existing document overwritten each time it saved to the SharePoint site.

7. Click the Document template combo box and select the document template to use for new files created in the document library. This doesn't affect documents that are uploaded to the library. Only documents that are created from within the SharePoint site use the default document template. I leave this as a Microsoft Office Word document.

8. Click Create to create the Document Library.

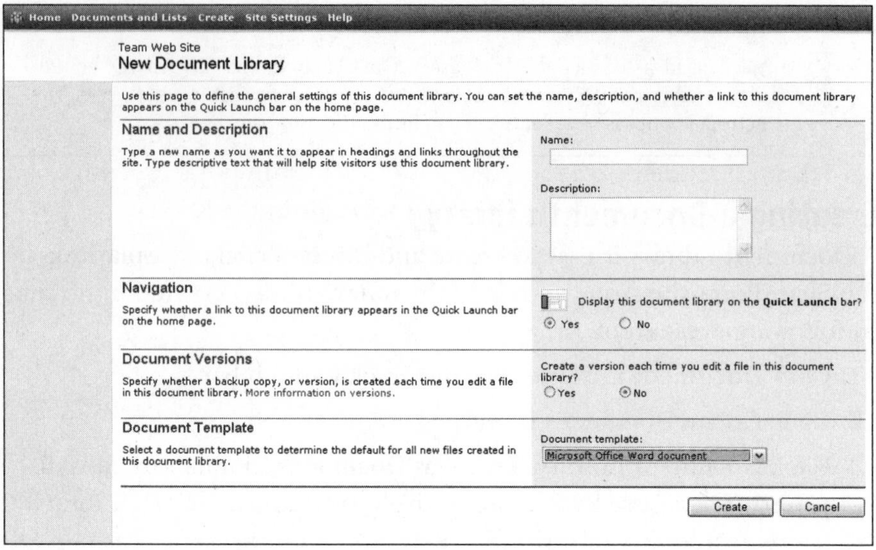

Figure 22.2. Enter the description of the new Document Library.

Uploading a document in a Document Library

Placing a document into a Document Library is fairly straightforward. I'm using the Shared Documents Document Library, but you can use any Document Library that is available on your SharePoint site.

Here's how to upload the document:

1. Click Shared Documents on the Quick Launch Bar to display the library.

2. Click Upload Document on the menu bar. This displays the Shared documents: Upload Document screen.

3. Enter the name of the document. Alternatively, click Browse to find the document on your computer.

4. Click the Overwrite existing file check box. If you don't, then the SharePoint site saves your document as a copy and doesn't replace the existing document with the new document.

5. Click Save and Close. The document is placed in the Document Library.

Checking out a document from a Document Library

Borrowing a document is a simple process. Here's how to check out the document that I placed into the Shared Document Library in the previous section of this chapter. You do this to notify your colleagues that you've updated the document and tell them that they can't change the document until you check the document back into the library.

1. Click Shared Documents on the Quick Launch Bar to display the library.

2. Move the cursor over the name of the document. An arrow appears to its right.

3. Click the arrow. A pop-up menu is displayed.

4. Click Check Out. The SharePoint site places your login name alongside the document in the Checked Out To column.

Returning a document to the Document Library

Checked-out documents must be returned if your colleagues are going to be able to do more than read it. Here's how to check in the document.

1. Click Shared Documents on the Quick Launch Bar to display the library.

2. Move the cursor over the name of the document. An arrow appears to its right.

3. Click the arrow. A pop-up menu is displayed.

4. Click Check In. Doing this displays the Check In screen.

5. Click Check in document.

6. Click OK. Your name is removed from the Checked Out To column. You or your colleagues can check out the document.

Deleting a document from the Document Library

Permanently removing a document from the Document Library is done by using the same pop-up menu used to check in and out the document. Here's how to delete the document:

1. Click Shared Documents on the Quick Launch Bar to display the library.

2. Move the cursor over the name of the document. An arrow appears to its right.

3. Click the arrow. A pop-up menu is displayed.

4. Click Delete. A warning message is displayed asking you to confirm your decision.

5. Click OK. The document is removed.

Creating a shared workspace

You can create your own shared workspace within the SharePoint site. It is like a special place for your team to meet and exchange ideas and documents. It functions just like the SharePoint site except with a different URL.

Here's how to create the shared work. Once created, use the new URL to access it.

1. Click Create on the menu bar. The Team Web Site Create Page is displayed.

2. Click Sites and Workspaces located at the bottom of the page. This displays the New SharePoint Site screen.

3. Type the title and description for the new SharePoint site.

4. Type the Web site address for the new SharePoint site. The address is usually a continuation of your current new SharePoint site. For example, mine is jimkeogh.sharepointsite.com. My new SharePoint site is jimkeogh.sharepointsite.com/teampub where teampub is the name of the new SharePoint site within my hosted SharePoint site.

5. Click Use same permissions as parent site. All the permissions assigned to the login ID for the parent SharePoint site are applied to the new SharePoint site. Alternatively, you can click Use unique permissions, but it's best to keep permissions the same.

6. Select the language for the SharePoint site. I leave this set at English.

7. Click Create to create the new SharePoint site. You're prompted to select a template for the new SharePoint site. Several are listed, but I simply accept the default.

8. Click OK. The new SharePoint site is created.

Inside Scoop

Moving the database and all its objects to the SharePoint site can be time-consuming depending on the size of the database, the number of objects that you're moving, and the data transfer rate of your connection. You can always click Stop to terminate the transfer.

Moving the database to the SharePoint site

Making your Access 2007 database available on a SharePoint site is referred to as publishing. Publishing is moving your database to a Document Library on the SharePoint site.

You do this by using the Move to SharePoint Site wizard located in the SharePoint Lists group on the External Data tab.

The wizard backs up your database on your computer and creates links to the lists from the tables. The wizard makes it easy to locate the data on the SharePoint site when using Access 2007. The wizard represents relationships among the tables as links between the SharePoint lists. Any problems transferring the data are reported in the log table in the Access 2007 database.

Here's how you do this:

1. Click Move to SharePoint in the SharePoint Lists group on the External Data tab. This runs the Move to SharePoint Site wizard.

2. Enter the URL of the SharePoint site.

3. Click Save a copy of my database to the SharePoint site.

4. Click Browse and select the Document Library in which to store the database. Make sure that you are connected to the network. You'll be prompted to log into the SharePoint site.

5. Click the name of the Document Library and click OK.

6. Click Next. Your database is uploaded to the SharePoint site. A warning is displayed if errors occurred when uploading.

7. Click Finish. You'll find the database in the Document Library on the SharePoint site. The Move to SharePoint wizard also creates a link in Access 2007 to the database on SharePoint site.

Inside Scoop

Click the table name in Access 2007's Navigation bar to link to the copy of the database on the SharePoint site.

Troubleshooting transfer problems

The Move to SharePoint Site wizard displays a message indicating if errors were encountered during transmission. You can find details of each error in a table called Move to SharePoint Site Issues in the Navigation pane on Access 2007. Access 2007 creates this table if errors occur.

Common errors occur when data of an unsupported data type is transferred if the information being transferred uses a feature that isn't supported by the SharePoint site. Fields containing the errors are not moved to the SharePoint site.

I found that the SharePoint site doesn't support the following:

- COM Object data type
- Binary data type
- Dates prior to 1900
- New line characters in single line text fields
- Decimal date types (use Number or Double Integer data types instead)
- Replication ID data type (use a single line text data type instead)
- Referential integrity
- Default values that are dynamic (Static default values in text, number, and date data types are accepted.)
- Data validation rules
- Multiple unique indexes fields (Only one unique index field is moved.)
- Relationships with cascading deletes or updates
- Multiple automatic numbering fields (Only one automatic numbering field is accepted.)

Importing from a SharePoint site

As changes are made to the database on the SharePoint site, you'll probably want to import the data to the database on your local computer. You can do this by using SharePoint List in the Import group on the External Data tab.

Follow these steps:

1. Open the database.
2. Click SharePoint List in the Import group on the External Data tab. This runs the Get External Data — SharePoint Site wizard.

3. Enter the URL of the SharePoint site.

4. Click Link to the data source by creating a Linked table.

5. Click Next. Lists on the SharePoint Site are displayed.

6. Click the Lists for tables in the database that you want to import.

7. Click OK.

Exporting to a SharePoint List

Exporting data copies data from your database to the database on the SharePoint Site so you can share the data with your colleagues. You do this by running the SharePoint List Export wizard in the Export group of the External Data.

Follow these steps:

1. Open a database.

2. Open a table.

3. Click SharePoint List in the Export group of the External Data tab. This displays the Export — SharePoint site dialog box.

4. Enter the URL for the SharePoint Site and click OK.

Just the facts

- SharePoint is a way for you and your colleagues to collaborate on a project.
- Microsoft calls SharePoint Microsoft Windows SharePoint Services (WSS).
- WSS consists of a SharePoint site and one or more SharePoints.
- SharePoint site is a Web site that runs Microsoft Windows Server and is used as a central storage facility for any documents or information.
- WSS has the flexibility of using a Web server minus the hassles of the Web-publishing process.
- Use the SharePoint site's URL to access the SharePoint site with your browser.
- A SharePoint site is organized into lists, Document Libraries, picture libraries, discussions, and surveys.

Programming with VBA

GET THE SCOOP ON...
What is a module ■ Types of procedures ■ Subprocedures
■ Function procedures ■ Passing parameters ■ Declaring
parameters ■ Parameter data types ■ Parameter name ■
Calling a sequence of subs and functions

Creating Modules

D arn, that computer is smart. I've said that thousands of times whenever a computer application zips through tasks that take me hours — and sometimes days — to perform.

And then the question — how did it do that?

The answer I learned many years ago. Computers are smart, smart enough to follow instructions written by a programmer who creates the computer application.

The programmer decides what tasks the computer performs, how it performs those tasks, and writes instructions using a programming language to show the computer how to do it.

You may not have thought of yourself as a programmer, but that will change after you read this chapter and the next few chapters. In them I show you how to write your own programs that put Access 2007 through its paces using the Visual Basic for Applications programming language.

What is a module?

You may not be familiar with the term *module,* at least as it relates to Access 2007, yet a module is arguably the most important feature of Access 2007 that enables you to automate your Access 2007 application.

A module is a container that stores small programs called a procedure. When you want Access 2007 to do something, you call the appropriate procedure and Access 2007 follows instructions that are contained in the procedure.

I found this confusing the first time I learned about procedures, but a colleague described it in noncomputer jargon that made things clearer.

I have driving directions to places that I travel infrequently in a notebook that I carry in the glove compartment of my car. One page I titled Uncle Al's mountain hideaway, and it contains step-by-step driving instructions to my uncle's summer house. Another page I have titled John Harm's Theatre in Englewood. That's where my daughter's cheering competition is held each year. On the page are directions to get there.

The notebook is like a module in Access 2007. Each page is a procedure. The title of the page is the name of the procedure and driving instructions are like lines of programming code that instructs Access 2007 to do something.

Whenever we're headed for the yearly cheering competition, my wife tells me to follow the John Harm's Theatre in Englewood instructions. I open the notebook to that page and follow those directions.

Conceptually the same thing happens when you automate your Access 2007 application. You decide what you want Access 2007 to do and then create a procedure to do it. You give the procedure a name and you write step-by-step instructions telling Access 2007 how to do it. You then tell Access 2007 the name of the procedure that you want it to perform.

Let's pause. Chances are pretty good that you are a bit overwhelmed with the prospects of writing a program unless you've written one before. Writing a program isn't difficult. You discover this later in this chapter after I walk you through the process of writing your first program.

Writing a program can be as challenging as solving your favorite jigsaw puzzle where you see the complete picture first and then assemble pieces to get the results.

The picture is what you want Access 2007 to do. Puzzle pieces are words of Visual Basic for Applications (VBA), which is the programming language used to write instructions for Access 2007 to follow. This is like words in English.

You assemble VBA words to form a statement, which is like an English sentence — one step in the driving instructions. I think of this as

Hack

VBA is a version of the well-known Visual Basic programming language that programmers use to develop complex applications. VBA is used to automate Microsoft Office applications such as Word, Excel, PowerPoint, Outlook, and Microsoft Project, in addition to Access.

connecting puzzle pieces together. You continue to form statements until you have all steps that you want Access 2007 to perform.

I show you VBA words and how to piece them together to form a statement in the next chapter.

Types of procedures

There are two types of procedures — sub procedure and function procedure.

Sub procedures

A sub is a procedure (simply referred to as a sub or subroutine) that is usually called from an event. I introduced events to you when you learned how to create macros in Chapter 18. An event is something that occurs while your Access 2007 database application is running such as a value changed in a control on a form or report or when a button control is clicked.

You can link a sub to a particular event. Access 2007 then executes statements with in the sub automatically when the event occurs. Later in this chapter, you'll be writing a sub that tells Access 2007 to beep your computer when a button control is pressed on a form.

A sub cannot be used in an expression because a sub doesn't return a value after Access 2007 finishes executing the sub's instructions. If you want to use a sub in an expression, then you need to rewrite the sub as a function, which is easy to do (as you learn in the next chapter).

Function procedure

A function procedure (known as a function) does practically the same thing as a sub. That is, it contains a set of instructions that Access 2007 executes when the procedure is called. They differ in that a function returns a value and a sub doesn't return a value.

No doubt this concept sounds confusing if you've never programmed before. The best way I know to explain this is using money. Let's say that we want Access 2007 to give everyone a $100 raise. We write a procedure called NewSalary that adds the $100 to the existing salary and returns the amount of the new salary.

Because the NewSalary procedure returns the new salary, we need to write a function rather than a sub because a function is capable of returning a value and a sub can't return a value.

I show you how to write a function and sub in the next chapter. For now, let's assume that we've written the NewSalary function. We call the NewSalary function in an expression. You remember expressions from your school days and from Chapter 9, where I showed you how to use the Expression Builder.

Here's the expression:

```
Salary = NewSalary
```

Access 2007 recognizes NewSalary as the name of a function and then follows instruction contained in the NewSalary function. The return value, which is the new salary, is then assigned the Salary. Think of Salary as a box inside your computer where the new salary is stored. You learn in the next chapter that this is called a variable.

Passing parameters

Sometimes a procedure needs information to complete its task and that information isn't available when you create the instruction. You need to pass this information to the procedure when the procedure is called.

This is the case with the NewSalary function, which adds $100 to the current salary to arrive at the new salary. The current salary is known when the NewSalary function is called — not when you write the NewSalary function.

Missing information is provided to a procedure when the procedure is called. The missing information is referred to as a parameter, and providing the missing information when the procedure is called is known as passing a parameter.

Both a sub and function can have no parameters, one parameter, or multiple parameters, depending on the needs of the procedure.

Declaring parameters

Access 2007 must be told that a procedure has a parameter when you write the procedure. This is called declaring a parameter. (I show you how to declare a parameter later in this chapter when you create the SoundBeep sub.) For now, simply understand that you must specify a data type and name when declaring a parameter.

Parameter data type

What is data type? You're probably doing a little head-scratching. The simplest way to understand data type is to imagine that your computer has blocks of memory — call them boxes. My computer buddies hate when I use the term boxes, but it is the best way to explain it.

Access 2007 needs to know the kind of information you want stored in those boxes. Is it a date? Is it a number? Maybe text?

You tell Access 2007 the kind of information you want to store in those boxes by specifying the data type of the parameter. VBA has several words, and each describes a different data type. (I discuss these in the next chapter.) For now, understand that you'll simply need to match the parameter to the right VBA word to use to declare the data type of the parameter.

Parameter name

The parameter name is a name that you give to the parameter. I like to think of it as the label for boxes in memory that you reserved when declaring the parameter's data type. You use the parameter's name in statements within the procedure to refer to the missing data.

For example, you could declare a parameter named CurrentSalary for the NewSalary function. Within the NewSalary function you can write the expression:

```
CurrentSalary + 100
```

Supplying missing data

Missing data is supplied between parentheses when the procedure is called, such as NewSalary(1000). Access 2007 places the missing data into the boxes reserved when you declare the data type for the parameter. Access 2007 replaces the name of the parameter in statements within the procedure with the missing data and then executes the statement.

In the NewSalary function, Access 2007 replaces CurrentSalary with 1000 as:

```
1000 + 100
```

- ▪ If the procedure doesn't have a parameter, then the parentheses are empty, such as Name().

- ▪ If the procedure has multiple parameters, then each parameter is separated by a comma, such as Name(para1, para2).

Calling a sequence of subs and functions

Instructions in a sub or a function can call another sub or a function. This may sound strange. Why would you ever need to call other subs and functions?

Having each procedure do one thing very well is best. You can then link each one by calling them in sequence to have Access 2007 do multiple things.

For example, say you want Access 2007 to create a new salary by increasing the old salary by $100 and then beep your computer when finished.

Create a function called NewSalary, which I told you about previously in this chapter. Create a sub called SoundBeep that simply beeps your computer. First, NewSalary is called and then the NewSalary function calls SoundBeep.

Anytime you want to sound the beep in your Access 2007 database application, you simply call the SoundBeep sub.

Categories of modules

Remember that a module is a container of procedures. There are two categories of modules. These are:

- ▪ **Standard modules.** A standard module is a module that contains procedures that are not associated with events. I like calling them independent procedures because procedures in a standard module can be called from anywhere within the Access 2007 database application.

- ▪ **Form/Report modules.** A form/report module is a module that contains procedures that are associated with events of a form/report. I call these dependent procedures because they can only be called by its corresponding event within the form/report. This is referenced to as code behind form (CBF) and code behind report (CBR).

Using standard modules

Professional Access 2007 developers organize related procedures into a group and then create a standard module for that group. For example, all procedures that manipulate salaries could be stored in a standard module called Salary Procedures.

Procedures in any standard module — regardless of its name — can be called by procedures in other standard modules and procedures in Form/Report modules.

Using Form/Report modules

A form/report module is created for you whenever you create a form or report and becomes an integral component of the form/report just as if it is a control. Whenever you copy the form/report, the form/report module and its procedures is automatically copied with it.

Although you could place procedures not related to the form/report in the module, it is best to only place related procedures in there.

Creating a module and procedures

Now that you understand how modules and procedures are used to automate your Access 2007 database application, you're probably anxious to try your hand at writing them.

Let's get started by creating a standard module and then create the SoundBeep sub that causes your computer to beep whenever the sub is called from within your Access 2007 database application.

First create a standard module:

1. Click the arrow at the bottom of Macro in the Others group on the Create tab. Doing this displays a menu.

2. Click Module. Access 2007 opens the new module called Module1 in the VBA Editor code window (see Figure 23.1). Access 2007 inserts one statement in the new module. This is the Option Compare

Inside Scoop

Each module is divided into two sections: the Declaration Section and the Procedure section. The Declaration Section contains statements that define options and variables used by all procedures within the module. The Procedure section contains definitions of procedures.

Database statement. There are other options also. This statement tells Access 2007 how you want to compare different types of data.

Code window   VBA editor

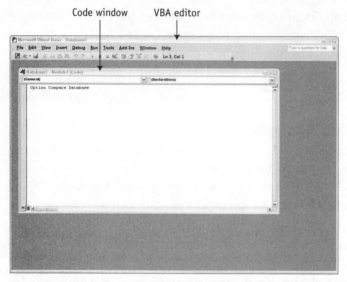

Figure 23.1. The Code window in the VBA editor is where you declare procedures.

Next, create a sub procedure. Call it SoundBeep. It won't have a parameter. Here's what you need to do:

1. Move the cursor to the line following the Option Compare Database statement and click the left mouse button.

2. Type **Sub SoundBeep** and press Enter. Access 2007 automatically inserts the parentheses, and empty line and End Sub on the fourth line.

3. Type **Beep** on the empty line between Sub and End Sub (see Figure 23.2).

Figure 23.2. Enter the procedure on the second line of the module.

Inside Scoop
Press F5 to test the procedures in the Code window.

Testing your procedure

I'm sure that you want to know if your procedure works. This is an easy and quick way to determine because you can test it within the Code window of the Visual Basic Editor. Here's how you do it:

1. Click Run on the menu. Access 2007 displays a submenu.

2. Click Run Sub. The Macro dialog box opens.

3. Click Run. Access 2007 executes the procedures just as if it were called from part of the your Access 2007 database application.

Compiling procedures

After you're satisfied that your procedure works the way you intend it to work, you should compile it. Compiling is the process of transforming your procedure into a format that a computer understands.

During the compiling process, Access 2007 checks your procedure for code errors. This is called syntax checking. I like to think of this as a spell-checker for VBA. It makes sure that Access 2007 understands everything in your procedure.

Access 2007 displays an error message box indicating the type of error if an error is detected during compiling. Sometimes I find the description of the error too technical for me to understand, so I simply review each statement in the procedures looking for typos or other typical errors. I'll explain the common errors in the next chapter.

Here's how to compile your procedure:

1. Click Debug on the menu. This displays a submenu.

2. Click Compile. Doing this is the first item on the submenu and is usually followed by the name of the current database.

If compiling is successful, the Compile submenu item is grayed, indicating that all procedures in the module are compiled. Compile becomes active again after you change any of the procedures in the module.

If compiling is unsuccessful, then an error message box is displayed. Click OK and then carefully review statements in your procedure.

Changing the name of the module

Access 2007 automatically names a new module Module followed by the number of the module based on the last module it named. You probably want to change its name to something more meaningful that represents the type of procedures that you'll store in the module.

To change the module name:

1. Click View on the menu. Doing this displays a submenu.

2. Click Properties Window to display the Properties Window.

3. Highlight the name of the module and enter a new name.

Saving the module

The last step is to save the module. You do this the same way as you save any file in Windows. Here's how:

1. Click File on the menu. This displays a submenu.

2. Click Save. This displays the Save dialog box that lists all the modules that are opened.

3. Click yes to save the module. Access 2007 displays the Save As dialog box. If you changed the name as I showed you in the previous section, then the new name appears in the Save As dialog box. Otherwise enter an appropriate name for the module.

4. Click OK to save the module.

Opening a saved module

The module name appears in the Unrelated Objects section of the database's Navigation pane. Double-click the module's name to open it in the VBA Editor.

Creating procedures in a form/report

You'll experience the real power of procedures when you write one that reacts to an event associated with a form or report. I like to call this a little behind-the-scenes magic because you can have Access 2007 do practically anything out of sight of the user of your application by writing a procedure.

Rather than telling you about it, I'll let you experience this magic yourself by writing a procedure that is linked to an event on a form. You start off with the basics and then progress into more complex routines in the next chapter.

Create a simple form

First, you need a form that has at least one control in order to demonstrate how to create a procedure for an event. No doubt you're an expert at creating a form since you already read Chapter 12.

This is a bare-bones form that I'm using for this example contains one button control. The objective is to call the SoundBeep sub every time the button control is clicked.

Here's how I created this simple form — just in case you need your memory jogged (I discuss this in Chapter 12).

1. Open a database. Use the same database that you open when creating the module previously in this chapter.
2. Click Form Design in the Forms group on the Create tab. Doing this opens a blank form in the Form Designer.
3. Click the Button in the Controls group in the Design tab on the Ribbon.
4. Click the blank form. Access 2007 starts the Command Button wizard.
5. Click Finish. This step closes the Command Button wizard and places the Button control onto the form.
6. Click the Button control on the form. Access 2007 highlights it.

Creating and linking a procedure to the control

Now that the form is created, you can focus on creating the procedure that will execute when the button is clicked. You can use these same steps to create and link procedures to any event.

Follow these steps:

1. Click the Property Sheet in the Tools group on the Design tab to display the Property Sheet (see Figure 23.3).

2. Click the Event tab on the Property Sheet.

3. Click the ellipsis button (the button with the three dots next to the On Click line). Access 2007 displays the Choose Builder dialog box.

4. Double-click Code Builder. Access 2007 opens the Code window for the form and creates a sub procedure called Command0_Click. Command0 is the default name for the button control on the form. The Command0_Click procedure is automatically called when the On Click event occurs, which is when someone clicks the button.

5. Type **SoundBeep** on the first line of the Command0_Click sub procedure (see Figure 23.4). This calls the SoundBeep procedure that you created previously in this chapter.

6. Select Run from the menu and then RunSub/UserForm from the submenu. This displays the Macros dialog box.

7. Click Run to test the procedure. You should hear your computer beep. This means that Access 2007 executed the Command0_Click procedure, which called the SoundBeep procedure that caused your computer to beep. If you didn't hear the beep then maybe you created the SoundBeep procedure in a different database.

8. Click the red X in the upper-right corner to close the VBA Editor and return to the Form Designer.

9. Click View in the Views group on the Design tab. Doing this displays a list of views.

Figure 23.3. Click to open the Properties Window.

10. Click Form View.

11. Click the button on the form. Access 2007 executes the Command0_Click sub procedure, which in turn calls the SoundBeep sub procedure that causes your computer to beep.

Figure 23.4. Call the SoundBeep procedure that you previously created.

Modifying an existing event procedure

Once the procedure is created and linked to an event, you can easily modify the procedure by redisplaying the procedure in the VBA Editor. Here's how you do this:

1. Click View in the Views group on the Design tab on the Ribbon. This displays the form in the Form Designer.

2. Click the button control to highlight it.

3. Click Property Sheet in the Tools group on the Design tab on the Ribbon to display the Property Sheet for the button.

4. Click the Event tab.

5. Click the On Click event.

6. Click the ellipsis button for the On Click event. Access 2007 displays the Command0_Click sub procedure in the VBA Editor, where you can modify the procedure.

Deleting a procedure

Deleting a procedure is a straightforward process. Display the procedure as I showed you in the previous section. Instead of editing the procedure, highlight the entire procedure and press the Delete key on your keyboard.

Return to the form in the Form View and click the button. You'll notice that Access 2007 no longer beeps your computer.

Comparing macros to procedures

Back in Chapter 18, you learned a quick-and-easy way to automate your Access 2007 database application by creating a macro. A macro, you recall, is a sequence of predefined actions. Each action tells Access 2007 to do something.

A procedure also tells Access 2007 to do something; however you define what Access 2007 does by using VBA statements rather than being dependent on the relative limited set of actions available to a macro.

When I first learned to program Access 2007, I was under the impression that learning macros was the first step in learning to write procedures — and that I'd never create a macro once I mastered VBA.

That's not always the case. Some developers learn to write macros before moving on to writing procedures using VBA. Yet other developers learn VBA and never learn to write a macro.

To set the record straight, procedures don't replace macros. There are situations when a macro is the best choice — and sometimes the only choice — to automate Access 2007. This is the situation when assigning a global key assignment. It simply can't be done in VBA.

Here's a list of the rules I follow when deciding how to automate Access 2007.

I create a macro when:

■ The task is simple to perform.

■ There is an action or sequence of actions available to perform the task.

■ I want to automate running a form or report.

■ Interacting with multiple records, such as updating or deleting records.

I create a procedure when:

■ There isn't an action defined to perform the task.

■ I want to use one record at a time.

■ I want to build the task into the form or report.

■ I want to manipulate objects on a form or report within a task such as setting values for check box objects.

Inside Scoop

Some actions require arguments while other actions use optional arguments. An optional argument enables you to overwrite the default value used by the action to perform the task.

Replicating a macro in a procedure

One thing I discovered that might help you is that many actions available in a macro can by run from within a procedures by using the DoCmd object in a VBA statement.

As you find out in Chapter 24, an object is a component of your Access 2007 database such as a form, report, and controls on them. Each object has name and properties associated with it. I introduced you to properties in Chapter 12 when you learned how to create forms.

You refer to a property of an object in a procedure by specifying the object name, a dot, and the property name such as:

```
ObjectName.PropertyName
```

The DoCmd is the name of the object. The action name is the name of the property. Suppose that you want to call the Close action. You'd write:

```
DoCmd.Close
```

Remember that some actions require additional information in order to perform its task and you provide it when you call the action. This is called passing an argument to the action.

You can pass an argument to an action from within your procedure by writing:

```
DoCmd.GoToRecord , , Record
```

Actions that can't be called from a procedure

Not all actions can be called from within a procedure using the DoCmd object. Here's the ones you can't call.

- AddMenu
- MsgBox
- RunApp
- RunCode
- SendKeys

Inside Scoop

VBA has an alternative way to replicate actions that can't be called using the DoCmd by using VBS, which I show you in the next chapter.

- SetValue
- StopAllMacros
- StopMacros

Converting a macro to VBA

All the hard work spent writing macros for your Access 2007 database application isn't wasted because you can have Access 2007 convert a macro to a module very easily. I'll show you how this is done.

I'm going to convert My Second Macro that we created in Chapter 12 for the Northwind Traders database. Figure 23.5 shows this macro. Re-create it if you can't find it in your database, or use another macro.

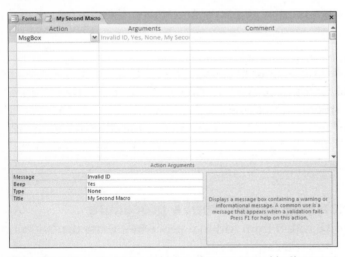

Figure 23.5. Open the My Second Macro that you created in Chapter 12.

Now let's covert the macro to a module:

1. Click the Office Button in the upper-left corner. The Office menu is displayed.

2. Click Save As. The Save As dialog box displays (see Figure 23.6).

Figure 23.6. Change the As value from Macro to Module.

3. Click the As combo box and select Module.

4. Change the name to My Second Macro Module or whatever name you wish to use.

5. Click OK. Access 2007 displays a dialog box (see Figure 23.7) asking if you want to add error handing and include macro comments. Both are checked by default.

6. Click Convert. Access 2007 converts the macro, opens the VBA Editor, and displays a message box telling you when it finishes.

7. Click OK.

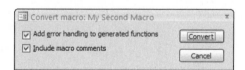

Figure 23.7. Accept the default selection.

You won't see the converted macro in the VBA Editor. All you see is the module listed. In order to see the converted macro you need to display the Project Explorer. Here's how to do it:

1. Click View on the menu to display the submenu.

2. Click Project Explorer to display the Project Explorer in the upper-left pane of the window.

Inside Scoop

You can press Ctrl+R to display the Project Explorer.

3. Double-click Converted Macro to see the procedure that Access 2007 created for you (see Figure 23.8). No doubt you'll have trouble reading this. You'll find this less challenging to read after you learn VBA in the next chapter.

Figure 23.8. Here's the converted macro that Access 2007 created for you.

4. Double-click other elements that were created by Access 2007 to see all the coding that Access 2007 wrote for you.

Just the facts

- A module is a container that stores small programs, called procedures.
- A procedure is a small program that contains instructions for Access 2007.
- Visual Basic for Applications (VBA) is a programming language used to write instructions for Access 2007 and other Microsoft Office products.
- There are two types of procedures. These are sub procedures and function procedures.
- A sub procedure doesn't return a value.
- A function procedure returns a value.
- A parameter is information a procedure needs that is supplied at the time the procedure is called.
- Passing a parameter is the term that describes providing information to a procedure when the procedure is called.

GET THE SCOOP ON...

Planning ▪ Using pseudo code ▪ Using literals, constants, and variables ▪ Using an array ▪ Using Private and Public ▪ Expressions and Statements

Writing VBA Code

Chapter 24

Show me the meat! I'd be saying this about now if I were reading this book because you are probably like me and want to begin writing heavy-duty VBA code that gives you behind-the-scenes control of how Access 2007 performs tasks.

Well, this is the chapter you've been waiting for. I start with elementary concepts that form the foundation for more involved aspects of the language that you discover later in this chapter as well as in the next two chapters.

By the end of this chapter, you'll know how to create a procedure that is found in most Access 2007 database applications. This procedure is called from a form; reads information from a form, performs calculations, and displays the results on the form.

So roll up your sleeves and get comfortable — it's time to write code.

Before writing your first instruction

Access 2007 is ready to do practically anything you can imagine as long as you give it instructions written in a language Access 2007 understands, which is Visual Basic for Applications (VBA). And before you can write those instructions, you'll need to learn the words and syntax that make up the VBA programming language.

Don't be too concerned. VBA is easier to learn than Spanish, French, or other languages you might have attempted in school. This is because VBA uses a mixture of English words and abbreviations mixed with a few rules you must follow when writing instructions. I show you these nuances in this chapter as well as the next two chapters.

However, before learning VBA it is important that you have a good understanding of how developers automate Access 2007 using VBA.

Making a plan

Step one in automation is to decide what you want Access 2007 to do. Some developers call this a task. Sounds obvious, but it is more involved than you imagine because you have to break down tasks into specific steps and then determine the sequence in which those steps are performed.

Let's say you want Access 2007 to calculate the sales tax and display the sales tax and the total amount in a text box on a form. A straightforward process. . . or is it?

Here are the steps needed to perform this task:

1. Read the value of the price text box control on the sales order form.

2. Is the value a valid number?

3. If no, then display a message saying the price hasn't been entered and then wait for the OK on the message box to be clicked before closing the message box and ending the task.

4. If yes, then read the value of the Postal Code text box.

5. Is there a value?

   If not, the display another message saying that the user needs to enter the Postal Code. Wait for the OK on the message box to be clicked and then close the message box and end the task.

   If yes, then look up the Postal Code in the sales tax table.

6. If the Postal Code isn't found, then display a message box saying that the Postal Code is maybe invalid and that the sales tax could not be calculated. Wait for the OK on the message box to be clicked and then close the message box and end the task.

   If the Postal Code is found, then read the sales tax field.

7. Is the value of the sales tax field greater than zero?

   If not, then enter 0 in the sales tax text box on the form.

If yes, then multiply the value of the sales tax field by the value of the price text box. Round the result to two decimal places. Enter the result in the sales tax text box on the form.

8. Add the value in the price text box to the value in the sales tax text box. Enter the sum in the total price text box on the form.

Using pseudo code

At first glance you might think this is overkill — but it isn't. You must detail every step you want Access 2007 to perform, so you can translate those steps into VBA statements.

Access 2007 developers lay out their plan for each procedure using pseudo code. Pseudo code is mostly English with a smidgen of VBA thrown into the mix. I like to think of pseudo code as an outline for a procedure similar to an outline you might have written for a report. However, the outline is structured similar to a VBA procedure where related statements are indented.

Here is the previous task rewritten in pseudo code. You probably don't have any problem reading the pseudo code because it is written in English. You'll notice that If...Else...End If statements are used. This is VBA, which you can learn about later in this chapter.

For now simply understand that if the If statement is true, then Access 2007 follows instructions under it. If it isn't true, then Access 2007 skips those instructions and follows instructions under the Else statement. But you probably figured that out yourself.

Indenting If...Else...End If statements and instructions makes it easier for you to read.

```
Read Price text box control on the sales order form
If the price is not greater than 0 then
    Display message box "No price is entered."
 End Procedure
Else
 Read valPostal Code text box
 If valPostal Code is empty then
    Display message box "No postal code entered."
    End Procedure
 Else
```

Inside Scoop

You don't have to write a task in pseudo code before writing instructions in VBA. Access 2007 developers usually write pseudo code for complex tasks because doing so helps to flush out the logic of a task and reduces the chance than the procedure will have a bug.

```
    Get Sales Tax field from Sales Tax table where
Postal Code field = valPostal Code
    If Not Found then
        Display message box "Postal Code not found.
Unable to calculate sales tax."
        End Procedure
    Else
        Read fldSales Tax field
        If fldSales Tax = 0 then
            Enter 0 in Sales Tax text box
        Else
            Sales Tax text box = fldSales tax * price
text box
        End If
        Total Price text box = Price text box + Sales
Tax text box
    End If
  End If
```

Using literals, constants, and variables

After you have outlined in pseudo code what you want Access 2007 to do, you then focus on translating pseudo code into VBA statements. I think of this like translating British English into American English because many of the words are the same. However, before you begin translation you'll need to learn VBA programming language.

Take a look at the data — numbers and text written directly into a procedure. These are referred to as a *literal*. There are three ways to write a literal depending on the type of value.

- String literal is text written within quotations, such as "Bob."

- Numeric literal is a number written without quotations and without commas, such as 100234.40.

- Date literal is a date and written within the pound symbol (#), such as #1/ 1/2009#

- Time literal is a time value and is also written within the pound symbol, such as #12:45:23#.

Working with constants

Use some values often when writing procedures. Rather than write them as literal values, you can use a symbol to represent the value in your procedure.

The symbol is called a constant and is already defined for you in VBA. A constant is a symbol whose value doesn't change while Access 2007 runs your procedure. I'll show you how to use constants in your procedures later in this chapter when you learn about If...Else...End If statements.

Constants that you'll use the most are:

- Yes

- No

- True

- False

- Null

Null is used to represent no value similar to leaving a field in a table empty.

Working with variables

Many procedures you write use values that change frequently, making it impractical to write literals in the procedure. There simply wouldn't be enough room, even if you had time to enter them into your code.

Imagine calculating sales tax for many sales orders. You would have to type all that information into the procedure to have Access 2007 determine the sales tax to place on the order. Obviously this is nonsense.

Instead of using literals, a temporary storage space inside your computer called a variable is used to hold a value while Access 2007 performs the calculation. After the calculation is completed, the value is replaced with the next value, and the calculation is repeated.

You briefly learned about variables in Chapter 23. A variable is like a box. The box is designed to store a specific kind of literal. Some boxes can hold a string (text). Others can hold numbers and still others can hold dates and times. The box has a label that uniquely identifies that box from other boxes.

Hack

You can use a variable without declaring it by specifying the name of a variable in an expression. Access 2007 guesses at the variable's data type and then automatically creates the variable for you. This is frowned upon by Access 2007 developers because Access 2007 might use a less-efficient data type and you could change the data type midway through the procedure, making your code very hard to maintain and hard to read.

Declaring a variable

Before you can place a literal into a box (variable), you must tell Access 2007 to create the box. This process is called declaring a variable. You do this by writing a Dim statement. A Dim statement requires that you specify a variable name (like the label on the box). You should also specify a data type for the variable. A data type tells Access 2007 the kind of data that you store in the variable. If you omit the data type, then Access 2007 uses the variant data type. A variable that is a variant data type can hold any kind of data, however, this can be inefficient and increase time spent performing calculations.

Here's the Dim statement. SalesTax is the variable name, and Currency is its data type. Table 24.1 contains data types and the kind of data that can be stored in the variable.

```
Dim SalesTax As Currency
```

Data type can be intimidating. I frequently use String, Integer, Currency, and Date, which includes time. The others I rarely use. If I know that I want to use the variable to store a value from a field of a table, I define the variable as the same data type as the data type of the field. However, this can be tricky, because fields have different data types than variables. Table 24.2 shows my choice when these data types don't match.

Table 24.1. Available data types

Data Type	Kind of data that can be stored in the variable
Boolean	True False, Yes No
Byte	0 to 255
Currency	-922,337,203,685,477.5808 to 922,337,203,685,477.5806

Data Type	Kind of data that can be stored in the variable
Decimal	+/-79,228,162,514,264,337,593,543,950,333 with no decimal point +/-7.9228162514264337593543950335 with 28 places to the right of the decimal; smallest nonzero number I + 0.0000000000000000000000000001
Date	01 Jan 100 to 31 Dec 9999
Double	-1.79769313486231E308 to -4.94065645841247E-324 for negative values and 4.94065645841246544E-324 through 1.79769313486231570E308 for positive values
Integer	-32,768 to 32,767
Long	-2,147,483,648 to 2,147,483,647
Object	Reference to any object
Single	Negative values: -3.402823E38 to -1.401298E-45 positive values: 1.401298E-45 to 3.402823E38
String (variable-length)	0 to 2,000,000,000
String (fixed-length)	1 to 65,400
Variant (with numbers)	Any numeric value up to the maximum value of the double data type
Variant (with characters)	0 to 2,000,000,000

Table 24.2. Matching field data types with variable data types

Variable Data Type	Field Data Type
Boolean	Yes/No
Byte	Number Byte
Currency	Currency
Date	Date/Time
Double	Number Double
Integer	Number Integer
Long	AutoNumber, Number Long Integer

continued

Table 24.2. *continued*	
Variable Data Type	**Field Data Type**
Single	Number Single
String	Text, Memo, OLE object, Hyperlink

Naming a variable

You can name a variable anything — well, almost anything. VBA has some restrictions, and you probably want to adhere to naming conventions that Access 2007 developers have adopted over the years.

Let's first review the restrictions known as naming rules. Access 2007 won't create or use a variable that violates these rules.

Names:

- Must begin with an alphabetical character.

- Cannot contain a period in the name.

- Cannot be the same as a reserve word. A reserve word is a word that is part of VBA vocabulary, such as Dim.

- Must be less than 256 characters.

- Must be unique. You cannot have two variables with the same name in the same procedure or module. More on this later in this chapter.

- Must not be case sensitive. Uppercase and lowercase letters are treated the same. That is, PRICE, Price, and price are considered the same name.

A naming convention is different than naming rules because no one — including Access 2007 users — enforces a naming convention. Consider this an honor system among Access 2007 developers.

Here are the naming conventions that you should consider using.

- Capitalize the first letter of compound names used as a variable name such as SalesTax.

- Variables used as a counter in a loop should be lowercase. I show you this later in this chapter when you learn about loops.

- The first letter(s) of a variable name should be a prefix for the variable's data type, such as strProductName, where the ProductName variable is a String data type. Table 24.3 contains prefixes that I use.

Table 24.3. Data type prefixes for variable names	
Data Type	**Prefix**
Boolean	b
Byte	bt
Currency	cur
Date	dt
Double	dbl
Integer	i
Long	l
Single	s
String	str
Variant	v

Using the scope of the variable

The scope of a variable determines what part of your Access 2007 database application can use the variable. Think of your Access 2007 database application as divided into containers — procedures and modules.

A variable declared within a procedure is known only to that procedure. The scope of that variable is said to be within the procedure. Statements within the procedure can use the variable. Statements outside the procedure cannot use the variable.

A variable declared with a module is known to all procedures contained within that module. The scope of that variable is said to be within the module. Statements within any procedure defined in that module can use the variable. Statements outside the module cannot use the variable.

Let's say you create two procedures — New Order and Sales Tax Calculation. You declare the curPrice variable in the New Order procedure. The statement to calculate the sales tax is in the Sales Tax Calculation procedure.

There's a problem. The curPrice variable isn't known to the Sales Tax Calculation module because the curPrice variable is out of scope and cannot be used by the Sales Tax Calculation.

One way to fix this problem is to declare the curPrice variable in the module — outside the definition of any procedure. The curPrice variable is then available to the New Order, and the Sales Tax Calculation procedures are defined in that module.

Using an array

Variables can be cumbersome to use when you want to store a set of similar information such as a list of product names. You don't want to create a variable for each product name because it's challenging to devise a unique name for each variable and awkward to use them.

A better approach is to declare an array. An array has one or more elements. Each element is like a variable in that it is used to store data.

The power of using an array comes with how the array and its elements are identified. The array is given a name much like the name of a variable. You pick the name. Elements are automatically assigned a number. The first element is 1, the second element is 2, and so on.

You reference an array element by using the array name and number of the element. The number appears within parentheses. Here's how the first element is referenced:

```
MyArray (1)
```

You can have Access 2007 manipulate elements of an array by writing one statement within a loop. I show you how to do this later in this chapter when you learn how to create a loop in a procedure.

Declaring an array

There are two types of an array that you can declare. These are a fixed-size array and a dynamic array. A *fixed size* array is declared when you know the number of elements for the array when you write your procedure. A dynamic array is declared when the number of elements won't be known until the procedure is called.

Declare a fixed-size array similar to how a variable is declared except you specify the number of elements you need within parentheses.

Here's how to declare an array of Integers that has 10 elements. Elements have the same data type as the array.

```
Dim iMyArray (10) As Integer
```

A dynamic array is declared nearly the same way except that you don't include a number within the parentheses. The number of array elements will be determined when you resize the array later in your application

Inside Scoop

The dots (...) in examples of code mean that any number of other statements can be inserted in the code at this point. Typically you won't change the dimension of a dynamic array immediately after you declare it.

when you know the number of elements that you need. Here's how to declare a dynamic array of integers:

```
Dim iMyArray () As Integer
```

Resizing a dynamic array

The ReDim statement is used to resize a dynamic array. This statement requires that you specify the upper bound for the array. The upper bound is the total number of elements you need. You can also specify the lower bound, which is a reference to the first element of the array, but this is optional.

By default, the first element of the array is referenced using 1. Some developers override the default value with 0, which means the first element is referenced with 0 instead of 1.

Try resizing the dynamic array to have 100 elements. Here's what you need to write:

```
Dim iMyArray () As Integer
. . .
ReDim iMyArray (0 TO 99)
```

Expect to lose any value assigned to elements when you redimension the dynamic array. However, you can avoid this problem by using the Preserve keyword as illustrated in this next example. The Preserve keyword tells Access 2007 to retain values assigned to elements of the array.

```
Dim iMyArray () As Integer
. . .
ReDim Preserve iMyArray (0 TO 99)
```

Storing different data types in the same array

One way to store different data types in the elements of the same array is to declare the array as a Variant data type. Access 2007 performs behind-the-scenes maneuvers to assure that each value is handled properly. Here's how to declare an array as a Variant data type. You can also

Watch Out!

The Preserve keyword slows processing. If you reduce the number of elements, values assigned to those elements are not Preserved.

declare a fixed-size array as a Variant by specifying the number of elements in the parenthesis.

```
Dim vMyArray () As Variant
```

Using an array element

Reference an array element by using the array name and the element's number. The element's number is called an index. You use an element the same way as a variable is used.

Here's how to assign a value to the third element of the iMyArray (assuming you're using the default behavior to start the index numbers at 1):

```
iMyArray(3) = 42
```

You reference the value assigned to an element the same way as you reference a value assigned to a variable. Let's assign the value stored in the third element of the iMyArray to the variable iMyVariable.

```
iMyVariable = iMyArray(3)
```

Assigning an array to another array

Here's a simple way to assign all the elements of an array to another array. Before doing this, make sure that the array receiving the element is declared dynamically and both arrays are the same data type. Then write the following. Notice that you only need to assign the array name to the other array. Access 2007 knows that you want to assign all the values assigned to elements of iYourArray to elements of iMyArray.

```
Dim iMyArray () As Integer
Dim iYourArray (10) As Integer
...
iMyArray = iYourArray
```

Hack

Any array can be assigned to an array declared as a Variant data type.

Initializing array elements

Initializing is the task of assigning a value to an empty array element. There are a number of ways to do this, one of them is when you declare the array by using the Array() function.

First, declare a variable and then use the Array() function to transform it into an array. Place initial values for each element within the parentheses of the Array() function, each separated with a comma. Access 2007 creates an element for each value and assigns the value to the element. The number of values that you specify in the parentheses determines the dimension of the array.

Here's how to create an array of four elements and assign each element an initial value.

```
Dim iMyArray As Variant
iMyArray = Array (43, 75, 65, 87)
```

Using Private and Public

Variables that are declared within a module are called private variables. I like to think of this module as being for the private use of statements within the procedure defined in the module.

You can make a private variable available to procedures in all modules by declaring the variable public by using the Public keyword. By declaring it public, you are telling Access 2007 that any part of your Access 2007 database application can use the variable.

However, you get an error message if you attempt to declare a variable declared within a procedure as a public variable. Public variables are declared at the module level. (See Figure 24.1).

Here's how you declare a variable public:

```
Public SalesTax As Currency
```

Inside Scoop

The Private keyword can be used to declare a variable private, but I don't recall ever having to use it because all variables are private by default.

Figure 24.1. Declare public variables at the module level.

Hidden problems with public variables

One of the major drawbacks of using public variables is that it reduces the flexibility you have for naming variables. The name of a variable must be unique within the scope of the variable, otherwise the variable can be accessed by any part of your application.

Here are tips for naming variables.

- The name of a variable declared private in a module must be unique to the module and all procedures defined in the module.

- The name of a variable declared public in a module must be unique to your entire Access 2007 database application.

Handling the public variables

Plan your variables carefully. If a variable is only going to be used by statements within one procedure, then declare the variable within that procedure. If a variable is going to be used by multiple procedures, then define all those procedures in the same module and then declare the variable private to the module.

Declaring a variable public should be the exception and not the rule.

Expressions and statements

An instruction is called a statement. Think of a statement as a sentence in English. A statement is composed of one or multiple expressions similar to a sentence.

Chances are good that you already know a lot about an expression because you learned how to create them in grammar school when you were taught addition, subtraction, multiplication, and division. That is, 1 + 1 is an expression.

Looking inside an expression

An expression is made up of two parts. These are an operator and an operand. An operator is a symbol such as the plus sign that tells Access 2007 the operation that you want to perform. An operand is something Access 2007 uses to perform the operation.

In the expression 1 + 1, the addition operator (+) tells Access 2007 you want it to perform addition. Both 1s are operands that Access 2007 uses in the addition operation.

Using operators

Some operators, such as those used in arithmetic, are old hat to you. However, there are many more operators that are available than those used for arithmetic.

There are five classifications of operators. These are arithmetic, comparison, logical, concatenation, and special operators. I've listed them in Table 24.4. Recall that I explained these in Chapter 9 when you learned how to write expressions in a query. You use those same techniques to write expressions in a statement.

Table 24.4. Operators understood by Access 2007

Operator	Description
Arithmetic operators for calculating a value	
+	Sum two values. Example, Value1 + Value2
-	Find the difference between two values. Example, Value1 - Value2

continued

Table 24.4. *continued*

Operator	Description
Arithmetic operators for calculating a value	
*	Multiply two values. Example, Value1 * Value2
/	Divide the first number by the second number. Example, Value1 / Value2
\	First, round both values and then divide the first value by the second value. Finally, truncate the result to an integer. Example: Value1 \ Value2
Mod	First, divide the first value by the second value and then return only the remainder. Example, value1 Mod Value2
^	Raise a value to the power of an exponent. Example: Value1 ^ Exponent
Comparison operators for comparing two values	
<	Determine if the first value is less than the second value. Example, Value1 < Value2
<=	Determine if the first value is less than or equal to the second value. Example, Value1 <= Value2
>	Determine if the first value is greater than the second value. Example, Value1 > Value2
>=	Determine if the first value is greater than or equal to the second value. Example, Value1 >= Value2
=	Determine if the first value is equal to the second value. Example, Value1 = Value2
<>	Determine if the first value is not equal to the second value. Example, Value1 <> Value2
Logical operators combining two values to determine if they are true or false	
And	True when Expression1 and Expresssion2 are true. Example, Expression1 And Expression2
Or	True when either Expression1 or Expression2 is true. Example, Expression1 Or Expression2

Operator	Description
Eqv	True when both Expression1 and Expression2 are true or both Expression1 and Expression2 are false. Example, Expression1 Eqiv Expression2
Not	True when Expression1 is not true. Example, Not Expression1
Xor	True when either Expression1 is true, or Expression2 is true, but not both. Example, Expression1 Xor Expression2
Concatenation operators combining two text values	
&	Combines two strings to form one string. Example, String1 & String2
+	Combines two strings to form one string. It also propagates null values. Example, String1 & String2
Special operators	
Is Null or Is Not Null	Determines whether a value is Null or Not Null. Example, Value1 Is Null
Like "pattern"	Matches string values by using wildcard operators ? and *. Example, Value1 Like # and []
Between val1 and val2	Determines whether a numeric or date value falls within a range. Example, Between Value1 and Value2
In(string1,string2...)	Determines whether a string value is contained within a set of string values. Example, In(String1, String2)

Using operands

You probably figured that a literal is used as an operand in an expression. However, you can also use the name of a variable as an operand, too. Remember that a variable name is like a label on the box where the box is the variable that contains a literal.

When you write an expression such as

```
curPrice * curSalesTax
```

Access 2007 replaces the name curPrice with the value that is in the curPrice "box." An Access 2007 developer calls this using the value assigned to the curPrice variable. Access 2007 does the same with the curSalesTax variable.

Using properties of an object

An operand can be an identifier of an object. This probably sounds a bit technical, but you already know what I talking about. Back in Chapter 12 you learned about forms, and in Chapter 15 you learned about reports.

A form and a report are objects that contain other objects called controls, such as a text box, check box, and so forth. Each object has a list of properties that describe the object.

You'll remember that controls have a property called Value that represents the value of the control such as the text in a text box and whether or not a check box is checked.

You can use properties of objects as an operand in an expression by using its identifier. This can seem a little complicated because you must explicitly tell Access 2007 the object value you want to use.

Suppose that you want to use the value of the curPrice text box on the frmMyForm. You need to tell Access 2007 that you want to use:

- A form

- The frmMyForm, which is the identifier (name) of the form.

- The tPrice, which is the identifier of the control on frmMyForm. Access 2007 assumes you want to use the value of the control when you specify the name of the control and not the name of a property.

You tell Access 2007 this by following these rules:

1. Begin by specifying the type of object, such as Form or Report.

2. Specify the identifier of the object, such as frmMyForm. This is the actual form you want to use. Place this within square brackets.

3. Separate the type of object from the object identifier with an exclamation operator such as Form![frmMyForm].

4. Specify the identifier of other objects contained within the object such as the name of a control such as sPrice. This too must be within square brackets.

5. Separate object identifiers with an exclamation operator, such as Form![frmMyForm]![sPrice]

Here's the complete operand.

```
Form![frmMyForm]![sPrice]
```

Bright Idea

The Me special keyword is used to refer to the currently opened object. Assume that frmMyForm is already opened when the procedure runs. You can refer to the sPrice text box by writing Me![sPrice].Value.

Using field values of a table

You can use a value of a field as an operand; however, the best way to do this is using the Structured Query Language (SQL) to create a query that is embedded into a statement within your procedure.

With SQL you can create a query that returns values from fields in one or from multiple tables and can manipulate data stored in fields of a table. I'll show you how to use SQL within a procedure in Chapter 26.

Creating an expression

Now that you know the parts of an expression, let's create a simple one:

1 + 1

Don't yell! Yes, I realize you didn't need to read this chapter to learn to write that kind of expression. However, I wanted to start with something you know and then show you a few complex expressions used in real-life programming.

An expression can contain multiple operations to form a complex expression such as:

5 + 2 * 10

What is the result of these operations? Is it 70 or 25?

The answer depends on the order in which these operations are performed. It is 70 if addition is performed before multiplication, otherwise the answer is 25 if multiplication is performed first.

It is important that you understand the order of operations so that you're sure that Access 2007 performs that calculation that you expect it to perform. The order of operations is called operator precedence. Table 24.5 contains the operator precedence that Access 2007 follows when calculating a complex expression.

Looking at this table you'll see that multiplication is performed before addition, so the result of 5 + 2 * 10 is 25.

Inside Scoop

To avoid confusion, place the operations that you want Access 2007 to perform first within parenthesis.

Table 24.5. Operator precedence

Order of Operations

Exponentiation

Negation

Multiplication or division (left to right)

Integer division

Modulo

Addition and/or subtraction (left to right)

String concatenation

Equal

Not equal

Less than

Greater than

Less than or equal to

Greater than or equal to

Like

Not

And

Or

Xor

Eqv

Imp

Creating statements

Access 2007 executes statements in the order in which they appear in a procedure. It simply starts with the first statement and then continues with the second and so on until it reaches the last statement in the procedure. You decide the order of statements based on the pseudo code that you created for the procedure.

If you place statements out of order, Access 2007 tries to execute them anyway. Sometimes this can lead to syntax or logical errors.

A syntax error occurs when Access 2007 doesn't understand what the statement means, such as asking Access 2007 to use a value of a text box that isn't on the form that you specified in the statement.

A logical error is when you tell Access 2007 to do something at the wrong time. This can happen if you place the statement to display the total price of a purchase before the statement that calculates the sales tax. The total price should include the sales tax.

Using statements to declare a variable

Probably the first statement that you'll write declares one or more variables. Here's the statement to declare one variable:

```
Dim curPrice As Currency
```

You can declare two or more variables of the same data type in the same statement by separating the name of the variables with a comma such as:

```
Dim curPrice, curTotalPrice As Currency
```

You need to write additional statements if you want to declare variables of different data types. Here's how to do it:

```
Dim curPrice, curTotalPrice As Currency
Dim strFirstName, strLastName As String
```

Assigning values

Assigning a value is the process of copying a value to a variable or object such as a control or field. The value can be a literal or a value contained in a variable, control, or field.

For example, say that you want to assign 1000 to the curPrice variable. You'd write this like this. (Notice that there isn't a comma separating hundreds from thousands in the 1000.)

```
Dim curPrice As Currency
curPrice = 1000
```

Now let's calculate the sales tax at 5 percent and assign the total amount to the curTotalPrice variable. Here are the statements to do this:

```
Dim curPrice, curSalesTax, curTotalPrice As Currency
curPrice = 1000
curSalesTax = curPrice * 0.05
curTotalPrice = curPrice + curSalesTax
```

Working with values on a form

Statements read values from controls on a form or report and assign values to them. You can rewrite these statements to use controls rather than variables.

In the next example, I created a form that has three labels and three text box controls. I called the text box controls tPrice, tSalesTax, and tTotalPrice. I also placed a button on the form and called it Calculate. The button is linked to the procedure that contains statements that perform the calculation and displays the result in the appropriate text box.

Here's a refresher on how to create this form:

1. Click Form Design in the Forms group on the Create tab on the Ribbon. This displays an empty form in the Form Designer.

2. Click the Text Box control in the Controls group on the Design tab on the Ribbon.

3. Click the form. Access 2007 displays a Text Box control and a Label control.

4. Place two more Text Box controls on the form.

5. Click the Button control in the Controls group on the Design tab on the Ribbon.

6. Click the form. Access 2007 displays the Command Button wizard.

7. Click Finish. Access 2007 displays the button on the form.

8. Double-click the first label and type **Price:**

9. Double-click the second label and type **Sales Tax:**

10. Double-click the third label and type **Total Price:**

11. Double-click the button and type **Calculate:**

12. Click the first text box.

13. Click Property Sheet in the Tools group on the Design tab on the Ribbon. Access 2007 displays the Property Sheet for the text box.

14. Click the Other tab.

15. Change the Name property to tPrice.

16. Follow the same steps and name the second text box tSalesTax and the third text box tTotalPrice.

17. Drag controls into position on the form (see Figure 24.2).

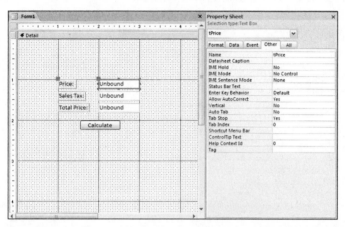

Figure 24.2. Position controls by dragging them into position on the form.

Creating the procedure

Now you can create a procedure that calculates the sales tax for the price entered into the form and then calculate the total price for the sale. I showed you how to create a procedure in the last chapter, however, here's a refresher.

1. Click the Calculate button. This displays the Calculate button's Property Sheet.

2. Click the Event tab on the Property Sheet. This step displays events for the Calculate button.

3. Click the ellipse button alongside the On Click property. Access 2007 displays the Choose Builder dialog box.

4. Double-click Code Builder. Access 2007 displays a module and a sub procedure in the VBA Editor.

5. Enter statements shown in Figure 24.3.

6. Click the Microsoft Access 2007 icon on the task bar to return to the form.

7. Click View in the Views group on the Design tab on the Ribbon. Access 2007 displays the form.

8. Enter **1000** in the price Text Box control (see Figure 24.4).

9. Click the Calculation button. Access 2007 calculates and displays the sales tax on $1,000 and adds the sales tax to the price to arrive at the total price, which is then displayed on the form.

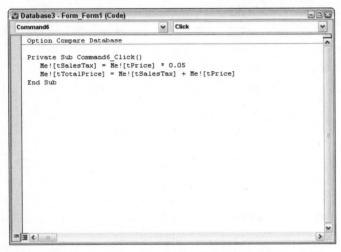

Figure 24.3. These statements calculate the sales tax and display the results on the form.

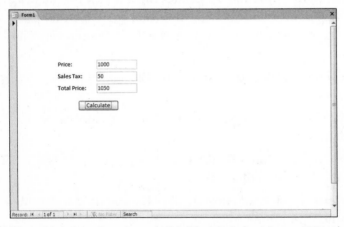

Figure 24.4. Enter the price and click Calculate to have Access 2007 calculate the sales tax.

Watch Out!

Brackets around identifiers are optional if the identifier consists of one word. If the identifier consists of two or more words separated by a space then you must use brackets as in the case of [Default Value].

Notice that I used the special keyword Me in place of the name of the form. I do this because this procedure is embedded with the form. That is, the form must be open to run this procedure.

Also notice that I use the name of the control whenever I want to reference the value of the control. I don't have to specify a property name because Access 2007 assumes that I want to use the value of the control otherwise I would have specified a property name.

Before clicking the Calculation button I enter the price in the tPrice text box. The first statement reads this price, multiplies it by the decimal equivalent of a 5 percent sales tax, and assigns the sales tax to the tSalesTax text box. This causes the sales tax to appear on the form in this text box.

The last statement sums the value of the tPrice text box and the value of the tSalesTax text box and assigns it to the tTotalPrice text box.

Changing the value of a property

You can change a property of a form, report, or control by assigning a different value to a property than the property's current value. To do this, you specify the name of the value in the statement and assign it an appropriate value. I normally look at the values allowed on the property list to determine which value I can assign to the property.

Probably the property that is changed the most is the Enabled property. The value of the Enabled property determines if a control is disabled (grayed preventing the user from changing its value) or enabled (not grayed, allowing the user to change its value).

Here's how to disable the Enabled property. Change the value to Yes to enable the control. This same technique can be used to change any property although the value assigned to it might be different than the value assigned to the Enabled property.

```
Me!rNewCustomer.Enabled = No
```

Letting Access 2007 make decisions

You want Access 2007 to make decisions by applying criteria conditions that exist when your procedure runs. That is, you'll tell Access 2007 the criteria for running a set of instructions. Access 2007 determines when the criteria is met and then executes your instructions; otherwise those instructions are never executed.

Access 2007 developers call this conditional processing. There are two kinds of statements you use to have Access 2007 made a decision. These are the If...Then...End If statement and the Select Case statement.

Using the If...Then...End If statement

You saw the If...Then...End If statement used in pseudo code at the beginning of this chapter. Now we'll see how to use it within your procedure.

This statement simply tells Access 2007 If this condition exists Then follow these instructions. End If signs the end of the If...Then...End If statement.

The condition is a logical expression. A logical expression results in either a true or false. Access 2007 evaluates the expression and decides if the expression is true or false. If the expression is true, then Access 2007 executes the instructions; otherwise, those instructions are ignored.

Here's how to write an If...Then...End If statement. In this example, Access 2007 is told to determine if the value of the tPrice text box on the current form is greater than 0 and is a number. I called the IsNumeric() built-in function. A built-in function is a function that Microsoft created for you to perform routine tasks. I show you other built-in functions in the next chapter. The IsNumeric() function examines the value in the tPrice field and decides if it is a number. If it is, then the IsNumeric() function returns a true; otherwise a false is returned. The And operator joins together both expressions to form a compound logical expression.

Only if the value of tPrice is greater than 0 and is a number will Access 2007 calculate the sales tax. Otherwise the sales tax isn't calculated and Access 2007 continues to execute any statement that follows the End If statement. There are none in this example, but you'll probably have additional statements in your procedures.

```
If IsNumeric(Me![tPrice])Me![tPrice] > 0 Then
    Me![tSalesTax] = Me![tPrice] * 0.05
    Me![tTotalPrice] = Me![tSalesTax] + Me![tPrice]
End If
```

Using the Else statement

A variation of the If...Then...End If statement is the If...Then...Else ...End If statement. This statement provides Access 2007 with two sets of instructions. One set executes if the logical expression is true and the other set executes if the logical expression is false.

You can modify the previous example using the Else statement (see Figure 24.5). The Else statement contains the instruction to display a message box on the screen telling the user why the sales tax cannot be calculated.

The message box is displayed by calling the MsgBox() function, which you learn more about in the next chapter. The MsgBox() function has five parameters, each separated by a comma. Only the first parameter is required. The rest are optional. These are:

- Message (No price entered.)

- Style of button that appears in the message box (vbOKOnly).

- Title (Error)

- Help link that connects to text in the Help file related to the error (none is used in this example).

- Context is used to display text that helps the user understand the error (1).

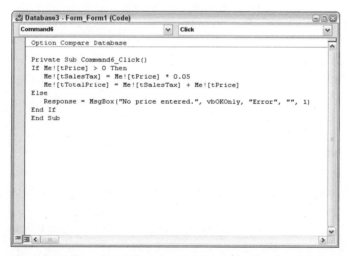

Figure 24.5. The value of the price must be greater than 0, otherwise an error message is displayed.

Nesting If...Then...End If statements

Another variation of the If...Then...End If statement is to place one If...Then...End If statement within another If...Then...End If statement. This is referred to as *nesting*. Nesting is used to have Access 2007 make another decision if the first decision is true.

I'll modify the previous example to illustrate how to nest the If...Then...End If statement. Sometimes it is a good idea to have Access 2007 determine if a value entered into a form is reasonable.

Is it reasonable to assume that a $10,000 value in the price text box is correct or an error?

If the most expensive product you sell has a price of $1,000, then it makes sense to suspect that a price over $1,000 is an error. You can tell Access 2007 to determine if the price is greater than $1,000. If so, then display an error message on the screen rather than calculating the sales tax. You do this by using a nested If...Then...Else...End If statement.

Here's how to write it:

```
If Me![tPrice] > 0 Then
    If Me![tPrice] > 1000 Then
        Response = MsgBox("Incorrect price.", vbOKOnly,
    "Error", "", 1)
    Else
        Me![tSalesTax] = Me![tPrice] * 0.05
        Me![tTotalPrice] = Me![tSalesTax] + Me![tPrice]
    End If
Else
    Response = MsgBox("No price entered.", vbOKOnly,
    "Error", "", 1)
End If
```

Using multiple conditions

You can have Access 2007 make two or more decisions in the same logical expression by creating a compound logical expression. A compound logical expression is one that contains two or more logical expressions.

This sounds confusing I admit, but it is easier to understand when you see it used in an example. I'll rewrite the previous example and have Access 2007 make both decisions in the first If...Then...Else...End If statement.

To do this, place the both logical expressions at the beginning of the If...Then...Else...End If statement. The And operator is used to join the logical expressions.

Both logical expressions must be true for the compound logical expression to be true. If one of those expressions is false, then the compound expression is false.

In doing this, I also rewrote the message in the message box to explain the reasons that Access 2007 did not calculate the sales tax.

```
If Me![tPrice] > 0 And Me![tPrice] < 1000 Then
    Me![tSalesTax] = Me![tPrice] * 0.05
    Me![tTotalPrice] = Me![tSalesTax] + Me![tPrice]
Else
    Response = MsgBox("No price or an incorrect price
    entered.", vbOKOnly, "Error", "", 1)
End If
```

Using the Select Case statement

Take it from my years of experience developing Access applications: Too many If...Then...Else...End If statements become unmanageable to write — although Access 2007 doesn't have any problem reading it.

The Select Case statement is a better alternative in these situations. The Select Case statement is used to test a condition against many possible values without having to write a Select Case statement for each value.

The Select Case statement has three parts. These are:

- **Select Case <test expression>.** This contains the value matched to each Case <expression>.

- **Case <expression>.** This contains the value matched to the Select Case <test expression>. Below the Case statement are instructions that execute if the Case <expression> matches the Select Case <test expression>.

- **End Select.** This terminates the Select Case statement.

There can be as many Case <expression> statements as you require for your application. You place instructions below the Case <expression> statement that you want Access 2007 to follow if its expression matches the test expression.

Access 2007 compares the test expression to the first Case <expression>. If the expressions don't match, then Access 2007 compares the test expression to the second Case <expression>. The sequence continues until either there is a match or the End Select statement is reached.

After there is a match, Access 2007 follows instructions that are beneath the matching Case <expression> statement. After the last instruction is executed, Access 2007 skips the remaining Case <expression> statement and executes the statement that follows the End Select statement.

Here's how to use the Select Case statement. In this example, I'm telling Access 2007 to find the Case that matches NJ. Once found, Access 2007 assigns the appropriate sales tax percent to the lSalesTaxPercent variable, which can then be used to calculate the sales tax.

```
Dim lSalesTaxPercent As Long
Select Case "NJ"
   Case "NY"
      lSalesTaxPercent = 0.04
   Case "NJ"
      lSalesTaxPercent = 0.07
   Case "CA"
      lSalesTaxPercent = 0.0725
End Select
```

A variation of the Select Case statement is the Select Case...Case...Case Else...End Select statement. This statement gives Access 2007 a default set of instructions to follow if none of the Case <expression> statements match the test expression.

You can modify the previous example by entering 0 as the default sales tax if the state abbreviation in the text expression isn't found in the Select Case statement.

```
Select Case "NJ"
   Case "NY"
      lSalesTaxPercent = 0.04
   Case "NJ"
      lSalesTaxPercent = 0.07
   Case "CA"
      lSalesTaxPercent = 0.0725
   Case Else
      lSalesTaxPercent = 0
End Select
```

Inside Scoop

If two or more Case <expression> statements are the same and match the test expression, then Access 2007 executes instructions under the first Case <expression> that matches the test expression. Instructions under the other matching Case <expression> are skipped.

Repeating statements without a lot of code

Expect to write statements that must be repeated many times — but don't expect to duplicate those statements. Instead, you can have Access 2007 repeat instructions by using a loop.

As the name implies, a loop is a statement that tells Access 2007 to continually execute the set of instructions placed inside the loop. The number of times the set of instructions executes depends on the condition you specify in the loop.

You can have Access 2007 execute the loop.

■ While a condition is true.

■ Until a condition is true.

■ A specific number of times.

■ Until you tell it to stop.

The number of times that Access 2007 loops the loop depends on the requirement of your Access 2007 database application and the type of loop that you use in the procedure.

There are two categories of loops, each having several variations. These are:

■ Do...Loop

■ For...Next Loop

Using the Do...Loop

The Do...Loop is used when you want a set of instructions to continue to execute either while a condition is true or until a condition is true. The condition is expressed as a logical expression that Access 2007 evaluates each revolution of the loop.

There are four variations of the Do...Loop. These are:

■ **Do While...Loop.** Executes a set of instructions while the condition is true.

- **Do...Loop While.** Executes the set of instructions at least once regardless if the condition is true or not. The condition must be true for Access 2007 to execute the set of instruction subsequent times.
- **Do Until...Loop.** Executes a set of instructions until the condition is true.
- **Do...Loop Until.** Executes the set of instructions at least once regardless if the condition is true or not. Continues to execute the set of instructions subsequent times until the condition is true.

Let's take a simple example to show how each variation of the Do...Loop works. We'll have Access 2007 count.

Using the Do While...Loop

Here's the Do While...Loop. I've declared a variable called counter and initialized it to 0. The Do While...Loop tells Access 2007 to determine if the value of the counter variable is less than 10. If so, then Access 2007 is to execute the statement within the Do While...Loop, which increments the value of the counter and assigns the new value to the counter variable. If I initialized the counter with the value 10, then the statement within the loop wouldn't execute because the logical expression (counter < 10) is false. Statements within the Do While...Loop execute only if the logical expression is true.

```
Dim counter As Integer
counter = 0
Do While counter < 10
    counter = counter + 1

Loop
```

Using the Do...Loop While loop

You can modify the previous example and use a Do...Loop While loop instead of the Do While...Loop. The concept is basically the same except that Access 2007 evaluates the logical expression after executing the statement inside the loop. This means that the statement executes at least once all the time.

```
Dim counter As Integer
counter = 0
```

```
Do
    counter = counter + 1
Loop While counter < 10
```

Using the Do Until...Loop

The Do Until...Loop is very similar to the Do While...Loop with one important exception. The logical expression must be false, otherwise the statement within the loop isn't executed. In the Do While...Loop the logical must be true for the statement to execute.

In the example, I modify the original Do While...Loop example to illustrate how the Do Until...Loop works. I've initialized the counter variable to 10 and changed the logical expression to counter = 0. Because the counter variable equals 10, the logical expression is false and Access 2007 executes the statement within the loop. This statement subtracts 1 from the value of the counter variable and assigns the new value to the counter variable. When the value of the counter variable is 0, the logical statement is true and Access 2007 stops executing the loop.

```
Dim counter As Integer
counter = 10
Do Until counter = 0
    counter = counter - 1
Loop
```

Using the Do...Loop Until loop

You can also turn around the previous example and have Access 2007 evaluate the logical expression after executing the statement inside the loop one time. I use a Do...Loop Until loop to do this.

Regardless of the value I use to initialize the counter variable, Access 2007 always executes the statement that subtracts one from counter variable. After doing so, however, Access 2007 evaluates the logical expression and only if the value of the counter variable doesn't equal 0 will Access 2007 execute that statement again.

```
Dim counter As Integer
counter = 10
Do
    counter = counter - 1
Loop Until counter = 0
```

Using the Exit Do statement

Sometimes you come across a situation where you want Access 2007 to continue to execute statements until a condition exists; however, the condition is easier to evaluate using statements within the loop than it is with a logical expression either at the beginning or end of the loop.

You can end the loop at any time by using the Exit Do statement within the loop. Think of the Exit Do statement as a stop button that tells Access 2007 to immediately end the loop.

Typically, the Exit Do statement is used in conjunction with an If...Then...Else...End If statement. The logical expression in the If...Then...Else...End If statement determines when Access 2007 executes the Exit Do statement.

Here's a modification of the counting example using the Exit Do statement. Access 2007 always enters the loop. If the value of the counter variable is 10 or less, then Access 2007 increments the value of the counter variable and assigns the new value to the counter variable. However, if the value of the counter variable is greater than 10, then Access 2007 executes the Exit Do statement that tells Access 2007 to terminate the loop.

```
Dim counter As Integer
counter = 0
Do
    If counter > 10
        Exit Do
    Else
        counter = counter + 1
    End If
Loop
```

Using the For...Next statement

The For...Next statement is used when you want Access 2007 to execute a set of statements a specific number of times that you specify at the beginning of the For...Next statement.

There are many situations where a For...Next statement comes in handy. One of them is to initialize elements of an array. The next example shows how this is done. In it, I initialize each element with the value 1. After the array is declared, Access 2007 executes the For...Next loop. First, Access 2007 declares the counter variable, since I didn't previously declare it. I could have, but I usually don't because it'll only be used by the For...Next statement. Access 2007 initializes the counter variable with the value 1 and then increments the counter variable each time it loops through statements contained within the For...Next statement. It stops looping when the counter variable's value is 3.

```
Dim iMyArray (3) As Integer
For counter = 1 To 3
   iMyArray(counter) = 1
Next
```

By default, Access 2007 increments the counter variable by one, however you can specify the increment value by using the Step keyword. The Step keyword requires an integer, which is the increment value.

For example, say that you want Access 2007 to increment the counter variable by 2 instead of 1. This means that Access 2007 adds 2 to the value of the counter variable each time it loops through statements within the For...Next statement.

You can see how this works in the next example where I tell Access 2007 to display a message box that shows the value of the counter variable.

```
For counter = 1 To 6 Step 2
   Response = MsgBox(counter, vbOKOnly, "Value of the
   counter Variable", "", 1)
Next
```

The For...Next statement contains many more statements than ones I showed in previous examples, depending on the nature of the application. It may contain If...Then...End If statements and other loops.

Inside Scoop

You can use any name for the counter variable. You decide the starting value and the ending value for the For...Next statement based on the number of times you need statements executed.

You may have a need to break out of the For...Next statement before the ending value is assigned to the counter variable. You can do this by inserting the Exit For statement whenever you want to break out of the loop. Access 2007 immediately exits the loop and executes the statement that follows the Next.

Let's modify the previous example to show you how this works. I'll stop it when the counter variable value is 3.

```
For counter = 1 To 6 Step 2
    Response = MsgBox(counter, vbOKOnly, "Value of the
    counter Variable", "", 1)
    If counter = 3 Then
        Exit For
    End If
Next
```

Passing parameters to a procedure

In the last chapter, I introduced you to procedures and showed you how to create them. You may not have all the information the procedure needs when you write it. This additional information is passed to the procedure as an argument when the procedure is called.

You must declare the argument when you write the procedure in order to pass the procedure information when the procedure runs. You declare the argument the same way as you declare a variable, except that the declaration appears in the procedure's parentheses.

Declaring an argument

Suppose that you want a procedure to display a message box that personally greets the user. You don't know the user's name when you write the procedure, so you need to declare an argument and pass the procedure the user's name when the procedure is called.

Here's how you do this. Notice that you don't use the Dim keyword to declare the argument.

```
Sub Welcome (sUserName As String)
...
End Sub
```

Using an argument

After the argument is declared, you use the name of the argument within the procedure whenever you want to refer to the value passed to the procedure.

I'll use sUserName in the message box greeting. Notice that the concatenation operator (&) is used to join the value of the argument to the welcome message.

```
Sub Welcome (sUserName As String)
    Response = MsgBox("Welcome, " & sUserName, vbOKOnly,
    "Greetings", "", 1)
End Sub
```

Passing a value to a procedure

The value is passed to the procedure by placing the value between the procedure's parentheses. Access 2007 replaces the name of the argument in the procedure definition with the value and then executes statements within the procedure.

Here's how to call the Welcome procedure.

```
Welcome ("Mary")
```

Working with multiple arguments

A procedure can use multiple arguments by separating each with a comma. First you need to declare the arguments in the procedure definition such as:

```
Sub Welcome (sUserFirstName As String, sUserLastName As
String)
    Response = MsgBox("Welcome, " & sUserFirstName & " "
    & sUserLastName, vbOKOnly, "Greetings", "", 1)
End Sub
```

Watch Out!

Values must appear in the same order when calling a procedure as its corresponding argument in the procedure definition, otherwise results might be unpredictable.

Here's how to call this procedure:

```
Welcome ("Mary", "Smith")
```

Returning a value from a function procedure

Recall that a function procedure is different than a sub procedure in that it returns a value; otherwise both are defined the same way. The data type of the return value must be specified following the function's argument list, but outside of the parentheses. The value returned by the function must be assigned to the function's name.

I'll redefine the Welcome Sub procedure as a function procedure to illustrate how the return value is declared and assigned.

Here's the function definition. The return value is an Integer, so I specify the data type at the top of the function definition immediately following the parenthesis.

The return value is 0, indicating that the procedure ended without error and is assigned to the name of the function. The value returned by your function depends on the nature of the function. For example, a function that calculates sales tax probably returns the sales tax as the return value.

```
Function Welcome (sUserName As String) As Integer
    Response = MsgBox("Welcome, " & sUserName, vbOKOnly,
    "Greetings", "", 1)
    Welcome = 0
End Function
```

The same technique used to call a sub procedure is used to call a function procedure, with one exception. The function call must be used in an expression that uses a value that is returned by the function.

Inside Scoop

Declaring the data type of the return value is optional. Access 2007 returns any value that is assigned to the name of the function.

Here's how to call the Welcome function. The value Mary is a parameter passed to the function. The return value is assigned to the ReturnValue variable in this example.

```
ReturnValue = Welcome ("Mary")
```

As you find out in the next chapter, the return value from a function can be assigned to a variable or directly used in another calculation. Use the name of the function and its parameters in place of the return value in an expression.

Suppose that you want to add the sales tax to the price to arrive at the total price and the CalculateSalesTax () function calculates and returns the sales tax. Here's how to call it in an expression. Notice that the value returned by the CalculateSalesTax() function is immediately used to calculate the total price.

```
curTotalPrice = curPrice * CalculateSalesTax (curPrice)
```

Just the facts

- Step one in automation is to decide what you want Access 2007 to do.
- Lay out what you want Access 2007 to do using pseudo code.
- Pseudo code is mostly English with a smidgen of VBA thrown into the mix. Translate Pseudo code into VBA code.
- A literal is a value.
- A constant is a symbol whose value doesn't change while Access 2007 runs your procedure.
- A variable is a temporary storage space inside your computer where literals are stored.
- Declare a variable using the Dim statement.
- The data type of a variable is specified when the variable is declared, however, this is optional.

- Variable names must conform to VBA naming conventions.
- The scope of a variable determines what part of your Access 2007 database application can use the variable.
- An array is a set of variables called elements that have the same name.
- A fixed-size array is an array whose dimensions are set when the array is declared.

GET THE SCOOP ON...
Identifying built-in functions for your procedure ▪
Categories of built-in functions ▪ Manipulating strings ▪
Finding a series of character in a string ▪ Copying char-
acters from a string ▪ Trimming spaces ▪ Changing the
case of a string

Using Built-In Functions

C ontrary to popular belief the best way to get something done is to have someone else do it. Don't be
misled. I'm not lazy. It's simply that over the years I've
learned there are certain things an expert can perform
more efficiently than me — and probably you, unless
you're an expert.

This is particularly true when it comes to programming.
An expert and sometimes a team of experts can tackle a
task that overwhelms the average Access 2007 developer.

Fortunately for you and me, these teams have built
some of the most commonly used programming tasks and
shared them with us in the form of built-in functions.

All we need to do is know which functions to call, pass
them information they need to do the task, and then
receive and process the value that the functions return. All
the grunt work performing the task is done for us.

There are hundreds of built-in functions — much too
many to cover in a book. In this chapter, I show you the
ones I use all the time.

Working with built-in functions

Microsoft saved you years of work developing your own
functions (see Chapter 23) by giving you hundreds of built-
in functions that perform common and some less-common
tasks that you'll encounter when developing your Access
2007 database application.

With a built-in function, you only need to know how to call the function and how to store the value returned by the function. You don't have to be concerned about how the function works.

In order to call a function, you need to know the name of the function and its parameter list. A parameter list is information that the function uses to perform the task. This is like the parameter list you use for your own functions (see Chapter 24).

Some parameters are required. Access 2007 complains if you don't specify them when calling the function. Other parameters are optional. Access 2007 uses its default value if an optional parameter isn't specified.

Built-in functions are used the same way as you use your own functions (see Chapters 23 and 24). The only difference is that someone else wrote statements the function uses to perform its tasks.

Identifying built-in functions for your procedure

With hundreds of built-in functions to choose from, you're probably wondering how to learn about them. Unfortunately, there isn't room in this book to discuss each, however I've narrowed the list of built-in functions to those that I use the most. I'll show you how to use them in this chapter.

You can find a complete list of built-in functions by clicking Access 2007 Help, which is the question mark icon in the upper-right corner of the screen. Alternatively, you can visit www.microsoft.com and search for VBA functions.

Although there are hundreds of different built-in functions, each is used similarly. That is, there are required and optional parameters passed to the function when you call it and there is a value that the function returns, which you'll use in other statements in your procedures.

Once you learn how to use the built-in functions in this chapter, you should be comfortable trying your hand at using other built-in functions that you'll find in Access 2007 Help and at Microsoft's Web site.

Inside Scoop

A pop-up help automatically appears (see Figure 25.1) when you enter a function name into the Visual Basic Editor showing you the required and optional parameters for the function.

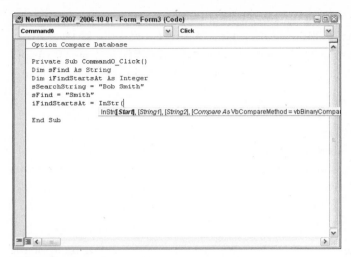

Figure 25.1. A description of the function appears when you begin typing the function in the Visual Basic Editor.

Categories of built-in functions

Built-in functions are grouped into categories. In this chapter, you'll learn how to use built-in functions that manipulate strings, numbers, dates, and times, and others that convert one data type to another data type and let you interact with records.

Manipulating strings

String functions are arguably the most useful built-in functions in VBA because you can use them to take apart text contained in a string, combine strings, and overall poke around the string.

Here are the most commonly used string functions that I use to manipulate text in my Access 2007 database applications.

Finding a series of characters in a string

Occasionally, I'm presented with a string that has a person's first name and last name and I need to know the character position where the last name begins so that I can use the Mid() built-in function to copy the last name to another string.

The way to do this is to use the InStr() function. The InStr() function requires two parameters. The first parameter is the string that will be searched. The second parameter is the string that I'm searching for.

Suppose I'm looking for the starting character position of the name "Smith" in the string "Bob Smith." Here's how I'd call the InStr() function. The return value is an integer that represents the character position of the first character that I'm searching for. A 0 is returned if the string isn't found.

```
Dim sSearchString As String
Dim sFind As String
Dim iFindStartsAt As Integer
sSearchString = "Bob Smith"
sFind = "Smith"
iFindStartsAt = InStr(sSearchString, sFind)
```

The InStr() function returns the character position of the first occurrence of the string. You may encounter instances when the string appears more than once. You can have the InStr() function return the position of the next occurrence by specifying a starting position.

A starting position is an integer that tells the InStr() function the character position where to begin searching. You must pass three parameters to the InStr() function if you are specifying a starting position. The first parameter is the integer representing the starting character position. The second parameter is the string that is being searched, and the third parameter is the string that you are searching for.

You can rewrite the previous example and search for the second occurrence of "Smith." The letter S of the first Smith is at character position 5. Therefore, a second occurrence, if one exists, has to be beyond character position 5, so I tell the InStr() function to start searching at character position 6.

```
Dim sSearchString As String
Dim sFind As String
Dim iFindStartsAt As Integer
sSearchString = "Bob Smith Mary Smith"
sFind = "Smith"
iFindStartsAt = InStr(6,sSearchString, sFind)
```

Inside Scoop

The previous code returns 16 because the first number of the index is 1. In some programming languages the indexes always begin with 0.

Copying characters from a string

Now that you know how to use the InStr() function to locate the starting character position of a string within another string, let's use it to solve a real-world problem.

The part of the string that I'm searching for is called a substring. It is a common practice to copy a substring into its own string. To do that, I'll need to use several string functions. These are:

▪ InStr() function that returns the starting position of a substring.

▪ Len() function that returns the number of characters in the substring.

▪ Mid() function that returns the substring.

You already know how to use the InStr() function. Now we'll take a look at the Len() function and the Mid() function.

The Len() function requires one parameter, which is the string. It returns an integer that represents the length of the string. You'll need to pass this information to the Mid() function.

The Mid() function is the workhorse that copies the substring from the string, which you'll usually assign to a string variable. The Mid() function requires three parameters. The first parameter is the string that is being searched. The second parameter is the character position within that string to be copied. The third parameter is the number of characters to copy.

Use these three functions to copy the substring "Mary Smith" from a string. After declaring variables, I find the starting position of "Mary Smith" in the string by calling the InStr() function and then I call the Len() function to determine the length of this name. I could count the characters, but I always let the Len() function do it for me. Then I use the return value from both functions as parameters to the Mid() function. Mid() function returns the name, which is then assigned to a string variable.

```
Dim sSearchString As String
Dim sFind As String
Dim sSubString As String
Dim iFindStartsAt As Integer
Dim iLengthSubString As Integer
sSearchString = "Bob Smith Mary Smith Roger Smith"
```

```
sFind = "Mary Smith"
iFindStartsAt = InStr(sSearchString, sFind)
iLengthSubString = Len(sFind)
sSubString =
Mid(sSearchString,iFindStartsAt,iLengthSubString)
```

Some of my colleagues look at this code and scream because it can easily be reduced to two statements. I purposely use multiple statements so you can easily follow along.

After you understand how this works, you can rewrite the code in six statements. I prefer using six statements rather than one statement because the value of the search string and the substring might change when I run my procedure, and therefore I'll be using variables to store this data.

Notice that I call the InStr() and Len() functions as parameters to the Mid() function. Access 2007 executes the InStr() and the Len() functions first, replacing the function with its return value. It then executes the Mid() function.

```
Dim sSearchString As String
Dim sFind As String
Dim sSubString As String
sSearchString = "Bob Smith Mary Smith Roger Smith"
sFind = "Mary Smith"
sSubString = Mid(sSearchString,
InStr(sSearchString,sFind),Len(sFind))
```

And so to quiet my colleagues, here's how to write this in two statements. You'll notice that I simply used the literal strings as parameters to these functions.

```
Dim sSubString As String
sSubString = Mid("Bob Smith Mary Smith Roger Smith",
InStr("Bob Smith Mary Smith Roger Smith", "Mary
Smith"), Len("Mary Smith"))
```

Watch Out!

If you leave out the length parameter in the Mid() function, the Mid() function returns all characters to the end of the string.

Watch Out!

Always assign the result of the Trim() function to a variable. A common mistake is to write Trim(sMyString). The Trim() function returns the trimmed string but it isn't assigned to a variable. Therefore, the trimmed string is lost.

Sometimes the substring you want copied starts with the first character in the string or ends with the last character of the string. There are two built-in functions specifically designed for these situations. They are the Left() function and the Right() function.

The Left() function copies the substring beginning with the first character of the string. It requires two parameters. The first parameter is the string and the second parameter is the number of characters to copy.

The Right() function copies the substring endings with the last character of the string. It also requires two parameters. The first parameter is the string, and the second parameter is the number of character to copy.

Return to the string in the previous example and copy the "Bob Smith" and "Roger Smith." I'll use the Left() function to copy "Bob Smith" because the name is at the beginning of the string. The Right() function is used to copy "Roger Smith" because it is at the end of the string. Notice that I call the Len() function to determine the number of characters to copy rather than counting characters myself.

```
Dim sSubString1 As String
Dim sSubString2 As String
sSubString1 = Left("Bob Smith Mary Smith Roger Smith",
Len("Bob Smith"))
sSubString2 = Right("Bob Smith Mary Smith Roger Smith",
Len("Roger Smith"))
```

Trimming spaces

One of the frustrating experiences you'll have while manipulating strings is to eliminate leading and trailing spaces. These are spaces that come before and after characters in a string or substring.

This might be confusing to understand because we normally ignore spaces; however Access 2007 doesn't. So in some situations we need to strip away the unnecessary spaces.

Here's a string " Bob Smith ". There are three spaces — a leading space, a trailing space, and a space separating the names. We only need the space between the names. Other spaces need to be trimmed.

The following functions trim spaces. These are:

- LTrim() — trims leading spaces.
- RTim() — trims trailing spaces.
- Trim() — trims leading and trailing spaces.

All three functions require one parameter, which is the string that contains spaces. And each returns the string minus the leading and trailing spaces.

Here's how to use these functions.

```
Dim sTrimmedString As String
sTrimmedString = LTrim(" Bob Smith ")
sTrimmedString = RTrim(" Bob Smith ")
sTrimmedString = Trim(" Bob Smith ")
```

Changing the case of a string

If you need to change a string to all uppercase or all lowercase, you'll find the UCase() and LCase() functions handy. I rarely need to do this, but a discussion about string manipulation wouldn't be complete without these functions. One very common use is to convert the string to uppercase, and then do a database query comparing the value in the database that is also changed to uppercase using an SQL function. The result is performing an insensitive search of the database.

Both functions require one parameter, which is the string whose case is being changed. And both return the changed string. Here's how to call these functions.

```
Dim sCaseChangedString As String
sCaseChangedString = UCase("Bob Smith")
sCaseChangedString = LCase("Bob Smith")
```

Inserting spaces the easy way

You might come across a circumstance where you need to insert many spaces into a string. The easiest way to do this is to call the Space() function. The Space() function returns the number of spaces that you pass it in its parameter. This is useful for clearing out or initializing strings. If you know that a field is 30 characters, you can initialize the string to Space(30) or use the Space() function to replace the current value with 30 spaces.

If you want to join two strings together but separate them with 10 spaces, you do this by calling the Space() function. The Space() function is passed the literal 10, indicating I want returned 10 spaces. The return value is concatenated to the value of sString1. Notice that I use the string concatenation operator (ampersand &) to do this. The value of sString 2 is concatenated to the 10th space returned by the Space() function. And the completed string is assigned to sString3.

```
Dim sString1 As String
Dim sString2 As String
Dim sString3 As String
sString1 = "Customer Name:  "
sString2 = "Bob Smith"
sString3 = sString1 & Space(10) & sString2
```

Formatting a string

The Format() function is a powerful tool used to impose a formation on a string such as those used with a year, date, time, Social Security number, and telephone number.

You define the format as a pattern using special format characters that take the place of characters in the string. You then apply the format characters to the string.

The Format() function applies the pattern to the string and returns the formatted string. Table 25.1 contains format characters that you can use to create the format pattern.

Table 25.1. Format characters

Format Character	Description
@	Any number
d	A day 1 through 30
dd	A day 1 through 30

continued

Table 25.1 *continued*

Format Character	Description
ww	A week 1 through 52
mmmm	Full name of month
y	A year from 1 through 355
yyyy	A year from 100 through 9666

The Format() function requires two parameters. The first parameter is the string that is being formatted. The second parameter is a string that contains the format pattern.

Let's say you want to format a Social Security number. The Social Security number format is three digits, a hyphen, two digits, a hyphen, followed by four digits.

Here's how to create this pattern and pass it to the Format() function.

```
Dim sFormattedString As String
sFormattedString = Format("555555555","@@@-@@-@@@@")
```

The Format() function can also be used to change the format of a date. Suppose the date is 1/1/2008 and you want it to be formatted as January 1, 2008. Here's how to do it.

```
Dim sFormattedString As String
sFormattedString = Format(#1/1/2008#,"mmmm d, yyyy")
```

Working with numbers

There are many built-in functions available to help you with math, statistics, and finance. Most of these are beyond the scope of this book because they apply to engineering and business.

However, there are three of these that I find handy to use when writing my procedures. These are:

- **Round().** Rounds a value to a specific decimal place.

- **Abs().** Returns the absolute value, which is a positive representation of the number.

- **Rnd().** Generates a random number.

Rounding a number

Here's a situation that drove my crazy until a colleague told me about the Round() function. I write a statement that has Access 2007 perform division. The result is a number with a trail of digits following the decimal. All I wanted was two decimal places.

The solution is to use the Round() built-in function. This function rounds up or rounds down a value based on the number of decimal places specified in its parameter. Values greater than or equal to 5 are rounded up. Values less than 5 are rounded down.

The Round() function requires two parameters. The first parameter is the number that is being rounded. The second parameter is the number of decimal places that must be in the results.

Typically, the first parameter is an expression rather than a value. This is where I place the division operation. Access 2007 evaluates the expression first and then passes the outcome of the expression to the Round() function.

Here's how this works. This example calculates the average size per unit rounded to two decimal places. Division occurs in the expression passed as the first parameter to the Round() function. This expression resolves to 17.66666. Actually the trail of 6s goes on forever. The Round() function is being told to round this value to 17.67, which is then returned by the Round() function and assigned to the dAvgSizePerUnit variable.

```
Dim dTotalSize As Double
Dim iNumberOfUnits As Integer
Dim dAvgSizePerUnit As Double
dTotalSize = 53
iNumberOfUnits = 3
dAvgSizePerUnit = Round(dTotalSize/iNumberOfUnits,2)
```

Removing the sign from a number

A few years ago I was asked to write a report that analyzed discrepancies between actual expenses and the forecast. The business unit cared only if actual expenses were within plus or minus 10 percent of the forecast. It wasn't concerned about whether the actual expense was higher (plus) or lower (minus) than the forecast.

In order to calculate the discrepancy, I had to tell Access 2007 to:

- Subtract the expense from the forecast.
- Ignore the sign.
- Calculate the percentage difference rounding it to a whole number.

Here's the code that does this. Notice how I pass the calculation and call to the Abs() function as the first parameter to the Round() function. Doing this eliminates the need to write each step as its own statement in the procedure.

```
Dim curExpense As Currency
Dim curForecast As Currency
Dim iPercentage As Integer
curExpenses = 6466
curForecast = 6300
iPercentage = Round((Abs(curForecast -
curExpense)/curForecast) * 100,0)
```

Generating a random number

I included how to generate a random number in this section because at some point you may want to try your hand at writing a game (not the kind you run on your PlayStation). The game I had in mind is simple and asks your friends to guess the number that Access 2007 displays on a form. The person who is the closest wins. It's not very exciting, but it does show off your programming skills to your friends.

The Rnd() function is at the heart of the game because it returns a random number each time it is called. The Rnd() function returns a value less than 1 and greater or equal to 0, however I usually set a range of integers such as picking a number from 1 to 10.

Here's how I do it. First, I create a form that contains four Text Box controls. Two are used for contestants to guess the number that Access 2007 will pick. The third is used to display the winner. The fourth is used to display the number picked by Access 2007. You'll also need a Button control to start the game.

Building the game form

Here's how I build the form:

1. Click Form Design in the Forms group on the Create tab on the Ribbon. This displays an empty form in the Form Designer.

2. Click the Text Box control in the Controls group on the Design tab on the Ribbon.

3. Click the form. Access 2007 displays a Text Box control and a Label control.

4. Place three more Text Box controls on the form.

5. Click the Button control in the Controls group on the Design tab on the Ribbon.

6. Click the form. Access 2007 displays the Command Button wizard.

7. Click Finish. Access 2007 displays the button on the form.

8. Double-click the first label and type **Contestant 1:**.

9. Double-click the second label and type **Contestant 2:**.

10. Double-click the third label and type **Winner is:**.

11. Double-click the Fourth label and type **Correct Number is:**.

12. Double-click the button and type **Play:**.

13. Click the first Text Box.

14. Click Property Sheet in the Tools group on the Design tab. Access 2007 displays the Property Sheet for the text box.

15. Click the Other tab.

16. Change the Name property to tContestant1.

17. Follow the same steps and name the second text box tContestant2, the third Text Box control tResult and the fourth text box tPickNum.

18. Drag controls into position on the form (see Figure 25.2).

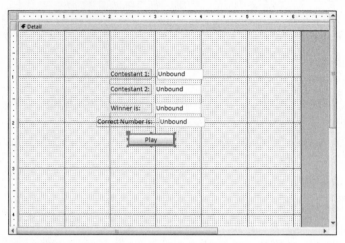

Figure 25.2. Position controls by dragging them into position on the form.

Writing the procedure

Here's the procedure that executes when the player clicks the button. After declaring variables, I call the Randomize statement. This makes sure you get a different sequence of numbers each time you play the game. If you don't call this statement, then you get the same sequence of numbers.

Next, I tell Access to generate the random number by calling the Rnd() function. This statement can be confusing to read. Rnd is the function call but I don't have to use the parentheses because I'm not passing a parameter. The random number is multiplied by the highest value in the range that I picked for the game, which is from 1 to 10. I then add 1 to this value and pass the result to the Int() function. The Int() function returns the integer of the value that is passed to the Int() function — the whole number and truncates the decimal value. This is a value from 1 to 10.

Next, I read the appropriate text box values guessed by the contestants. These values are subtracted from the number that Access 2007 picked and the results are compared to each other. The If...Then...End If statement determines the contestant with the value closest to the number picked by Access 2007 and designates that contestant the winner by placing the result in the Text Box control on the form. To verify that the results are correct, I also have Access 2007 display the number it generated.

```
Dim iGuess1 As Integer
Dim iGuess2 As Integer
Dim iNumPicked As Integer
Randomize
iNumPicked = Int((10 * Rnd) + 1)
iGuess1 = Me![tContestant1]
iGuess2 = Me![tContestant2]
If (iNumPicked - iGuess1) < (iNumPicked - iGuess2) Then
   Me![tResult] = "The winner is Contestant 1"
Else
   Me![tResult] = "The winner is Contestant 2"
End If
Me![tPickedNum] = iNumPicked
```

Here's how to create a procedure:

1. Click the Play button. This displays the Play button's Property Sheet.

2. Click the Event tab on the Property Sheet. This displays events for the Play button.

3. Click the Ellipsis button alongside the On Click property. Access 2007 displays the Code Builder dialog box.

4. Double-click Code Builder. Access 2007 displays a module and a sub procedure in the VBA Editor.

5. Enter statements that I previously described in this section (see Figure 25.3).

Figure 25.3. These statements calculate the sales tax and display the results on the form.

Playing the game

Here's how to play the game:

1. Click the Microsoft Access 2007 icon on the task bar to return to the form.

2. Click View in the Views group on the Design tab on the Ribbon. Access 2007 displays the form.

3. Enter a guess in the Contestant 1 Text Box control (see Figure 25.4).

4. Enter a guess in the Contestant 2 Text Box control.

5. Click the Play button. Access 2007 picks a random number and then determines who won. The winner and the correct number are displayed on the form.

Figure 25.4. Enter the price and click Calculate to have Access 2007 calculate the sales tax.

Using dates and times

I've always found working with dates and times challenging since I find myself having to pick apart elements of a date and perform date calculations.

Access 2007 provides a good number of built-in functions that make working with dates and time a breeze. Let's begin with the Now() function. The Now() function returns a Date object containing the current date and time in the default format, which on most computers is mm/dd/yy hh:mm:ss AM or PM based on the computer's system date. This is usually too much information for my procedure, so I use the Date() and Time() functions to return either the current date or the current time depending on which one I need.

The date can be divided into its components by calling the Month(), Day(), and Year() functions. Each function requires one parameter, which is the date, and it returns and integer that corresponds to the component of the date.

Let's say you want to extract the month of the current date. Here's what you'd write in your procedure:

```
Dim iCurrentMonth As Integer
iCurrentMonth = Month(Date())
```

Access 2007 also offers the Weekday() function. This function returns an integer that represents the day of the week where Sunday is 1 and Saturday is 7. It too requires that you pass the date as a parameter.

Here's a challenge. What is the date 35 days from today? It is easy to calculate if you use the DateAdd() function. The DateAdd() function adds the number of days or other time intervals to the current date and returns the new date.

The DateAdd() function requires three parameters. The first parameter is the symbol specifying the time interval. The second parameter is an integer representing the time interval. The third parameter is the date.

The time interval can be days, weeks, months, quarters, or years. Table 25.2 shows the symbols for each. In this example, I'm using days so I call the function by writing:

```
Dim sNewDate As String
sNewDate = DateAdd("d", 35, Date())
```

Table 25.2. Symbols for time intervals

Symbol	Time Interval
d	Days
ww	Weeks
m	Months
q	Quarters
y	Years

If you want to know the time interval between dates, then use the DateDiff() function. This function subtracts dates and returns the time interval that you specify.

You need to pass the DateDiff() function three parameters. The first parameter is the time interval symbol, which is the same as is used with the DateAdd() function. The second and third parameters are dates. This function returns the number of days, weeks, months, quarters, or years between the date in the second parameter and the date in the third parameter.

Here's how you write it:

```
Dim iDaysDiff As Integer
iDaysDiff = DateDiff("d", Date(), #01/05/07#)
```

Converting from one data type to another

You may recall from the previous chapter that you should tell Access 2007 the kind of information that you plan to store in a variable by specifying a data type when you declare the variable.

Also in the last chapter I showed you how to use the assignment operator (equal sign) to copy a value to a variable. The variable must be a data type that is compatible to receive the value. That is, a string can be copied to a String variable; a number can be copied to a number variable and so on.

From time to time, you'll find yourself needing to copy a variable that is incompatible with the variable such as copying a number to a string variable or a string to a numeric variable.

This isn't a problem because Access 2007 has several built-in functions that convert a value to the appropriate data type before copying it to a variable. These are referred to as conversion functions.

Converting a string to a number

A string is a series of characters, numbers, and symbols such as punctuation that are enclosed with quotations. Access 2007 doesn't treat numbers in a string as numbers. Instead, it treats them the same as characters and symbols. You can't use a number contained in a string in a numeric calculation because only numeric values can be used in a calculation.

However, you can use the Val() function to convert the number to a numeric value and then use it in a calculation. The Val() function requires one parameter. This is a string that contains the number. The Val() function converts the first number portion of the string to a numeric value and returns the numeric value.

This may sound confusing until you consider that a string can contain both characters and a number. The number will be converted to a numeric value as long as the number precedes characters and punctuation in the string.

Here's how this is done. Notice that the number is in the first three positions in the string. The Val() function stops reading the string when it encounters the first non-number. It converts the number to a numeric value, which in this example is 100 and returns where the value is assigned to a numeric variable.

```
Dim sSampleString As String
Dim iSampleNum As Integer
sSampleString = "100 is the price of the unit."
iSampleNum = Val(sSampleString)
```

Converting a number to a string

Converting a number to a string is just as easy as converting a string to a number except you use one of two built-in functions — Str() and CStr(). Both work basically the same way.

Each requires that you pass the numeric value as a parameter. Each function returns the numeric value as a number contained in a string just as if you placed quotations around the numeric value.

The Str() function inserts a leading space in the string before the first digit in the number. The space is used for the sign. No sign appears if the number is positive, and a negative sign appears in the space if a negative numeric value is converted to the string.

Here's how to write this.

```
Dim sSampleString As String
Dim iSampleNum As Integer
iSampleNum = 100
sSampleString = Str(iSampleNum)
```

Converting dates

The last conversion functions I want to show you are those used to convert dates to and from a string.

The CStr() function you learned in the previous section is also used to convert a date to a string. It requires you to pass a date as its only parameter.

Use the CDate() function to reverse this process by converting a string to a date. The CDate() function requires that you pass it a valid date format as a string.

Here's how to use these functions. First CStr() converts 01/01/2008 to "January 1, 2008" and then CDate() converts "January 1, 2008" to #01/01/2008#

```
Dim dtMyDate As Date
Dim sMyString As String
dtMyDate = #01/01/2008#
sMyString = CStr(dtMyDate)
sMyString = "January 1, 2008"
dtMyDate = CDate(sMyString)
```

Working with records

After reading the previous chapter and this one, you're probably wondering when I'm going to get to describing how to interact with information stored in a database.

Most interactions between your procedures and data in tables of your database are handled by embedded SQL statements, which you'll learn about in the next chapter.

However, there will be occasions when you want to write some quick code to access data stored in one or more tables within the database. In those situations, I use a domain built-in function. Domain built-in functions are a group of functions used to interact with records contained in tables, a query dynaset (see Chapter 8), or used in an SQL statement.

I find these quick and easy to use without having to write SQL statements. I'll show several of these functions that I use most frequently when developing an Access 2007 database application.

Looking up data

I'll start with what I consider the most useful, which is the DLookup() function. The DLookup() function returns a value of a field in a table based on search criteria.

The DLookup() function requires three parameters. The first parameter is the name of the field whose value is being returned. The second parameter is the name of the table. The third parameter is the search criteria.

When DLookup() is called, it looks for a record that contains the search criteria in the specified table. When a search criterion is found, the value of the field specified in the first parameter is returned by the function.

So that you can see how this is done, I use the Products table in the Northwind 2007 database. First, I create a new form. The form contains a Text Box control for the search value and a Text Box control for displaying the results of the search. It also has a Button control used to begin the search.

Here's how to build the form:

1. Click Form Design in the Forms group on the Create tab on the Ribbon. This displays an empty form in the Form Designer.

2. Click the Text Box control in the Controls group on the Design tab on the Ribbon.

3. Click the form. Access 2007 displays a Text Box control and a Label control.

4. Place another Text Box control on the form.

5. Click the Button control in the Controls group on the Design tab on the Ribbon.

6. Click the form. Access 2007 displays the Command Button wizard.

7. Click Finish. Access 2007 displays the button on the form.

8. Double-click the first label and type Search **Criteria:.**

9. Double-click the second label and type **Results:.**

10. Double click the button and type **Search.**

11. Click the first text box.

12. Click Property Sheet in the Tools group on the Design tab. Access 2007 displays the Property Sheet for the text box.

13. Click the Other tab.

14. Change the Name property to tSearchCriteria.

15. Follow the same steps and name the second Text Box tSearchResult.

16. Drag controls into position on the form (see Figure 25.5).

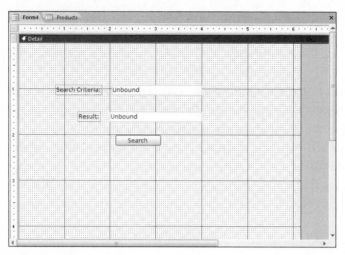

Figure 25.5. Position controls by dragging them into position on the form.

Creating the procedure

Let's create a procedure for the Button control's On Click event. You probably recognize some parts of this procedure and other parts are new to you.

You probably recognize that Me![tSearchResult] and Me![tSearchCriteria] are references to Text Box control on the form. You'll remember that Me refers to the currently opened form.

Square brackets are also use around field names. There are two field names in this statement. These are [List Price] and [Product Name]. The second parameter tells the DLookup() function where to find these fields.

The search criteria parameter tells the function to search the [Product Name] looking for the value that is entered into the Me![tSearchCritera] Text Box control. If found, the value of the [List Price] for that record is returned and assigned to the Me![tSearchResult] Text Box control.

```
Me![tSearchResult] = DLookup("[List Price]",
"Products", "[Product Name] = '" &
Me![tSearchCritera]&"'")
```

Here's how to create the procedure:

1. Click the Search button. This displays the Search button's Property Sheet.

Inside Scoop

The DLookup() function requires that the matching value in the search criteria be enclosed within single quotations. Because we're referring to the name of a Text Box control instead of inserting a value, we need to use the string concatenation operator (&) to place signal quotations around the value in the Text Box control.

2. Click the Event tab on the Property Sheet. This displays events for the Search button.

3. Click the Ellipsis button alongside the On Click property. Access 2007 displays the Choose Builder dialog box.

4. Double-click Code Builder. Access 2007 displays a module and a sub procedure in the VBA Editor.

5. Enter statements that I described previously in this section (see Figure 25.6).

Figure 25.6. These statements calculate the sales tax and display the results on the form.

Displaying the search result

After you've written the procedure, place the form in Form View and enter the search criteria. I'm searching for Northwind Traders Walnuts. Make sure that you use a value that you know is in the field.

1. Click the Microsoft Access 2007 icon on the task bar to return to the form.

2. Click View in the Views group on the Design tab. Access 2007 displays the form.

Here's how to conduct a search:

1. Enter **Northwind Traders Walnuts** in the Search Criteria text box control (see Figure 25.7).

2. Click the Search button. Access 2007 searches the Product Name field for the search value and then displays the value of the 23.25 field when the criteria is found.

Figure 25.7. Enter the price and click Calculate to have Access 2007 calculate the sales tax.

Counting records

Another common chore I've encountered is to count the number of records in a table from within a procedure. Sometimes I need to count all the records and other times only records that meet my criteria.

In both situations, I use the DCount() function. The DCount() function has three parameters. The first parameter is the field being counted. Typically I'll use the key (see Chapter 4) for this parameter. The second parameter is the name of the table. The third parameter is the selection criteria, which is optional.

To count all records in the table, I simply use the first two parameters as shown in this statement. The first parameter is the field ID, which is the key that is automatically generated by Access 2007. This is contained in Table1. The count is returned and displayed in the tOutPut Text Box control on the current form.

```
Me![tOutPut] = DCount("[ID]", "Table1")
```

To count records that meet a specified criteria, I supply all three parameters to the DCount() function. This is illustrated in the next statement that has the DCount() function count the number of records that have 'Company A' as the value in the Company field.

```
Me![OutPut] = DCount("[ID]", "Table1", "[Company] =
'Company A'")
```

Tallying records

There are also built-in functions that can add or average values of a field and also determine it minimum and maximum values. These are:

DSum(): Returns the sum of values in a field.

DAvg(): Returns the average of values in a field.

DMin(): Returns the minimum value in a field.

DMax(): Returns the maximum value in a field.

These functions use the same parameters as the DCount() function. If the third parameter is excluded, then the function's return value represents all records in the table; otherwise, the return value represents records that meet the selection criteria.

Here's how to write these functions:

```
Me![OutPut] = DSum("[Field1]", "Table1")
Me![OutPut] = DSum("[Field1]", "Table1","[Company] =
'Company A'")
Me![OutPut] = DAvg("[Field1]", "Table1")
Avg for value in other field
Me![OutPut] = DAvg("[Field1]", "Table1","[Company] =
'Company A'")
Me![OutPut] = DMax("[Field1]", "Table1")
Me![OutPut] = DMax("[Field1]", "Table1", "[Company] =
'Company A'")
Me![OutPut] = DMin("[Field1]", "Table1")
Me![OutPut] = DMin("[Field1]", "Table1", "[Company] =
'Company A'")
```

Using built-in functions for programming

There are two other built-in functions that I find handy to use. I group these into the programming category because they are useful for a variety of programming situations.

These functions are:

- **IFF():** This is similar to an If...Then...Else...End If statement.
- **IsNull():** Determines if a variable, field, or control is empty of any value.

Using the IFF() function

Some developers call this the inline If statement because it is an If...Then...Else...End If statement in one line of code. The IFF() function has three parameters.

The first parameter is a logical expression just like the logical expression used in an If...Then...Else...End If statement. The second parameter is a statement executed if the logical expression is true. The third parameter is also a statement except this executes if the logical expression is false.

Only one statement can execute if the logical statement is true and one if the logical statement is false. You'll need to use an If...Then...Else...End If statement if you need to execute additional statements.

Here's how to write the IFF() function. In this example, 10% is displayed in the tDiscount Text Box control on the current form is the value in the tTotalPrice Text Box control is greater than 100, otherwise zero is entered.

```
IFF(Me![tTotalPrice] >100, Me![tDiscount] = '10%',
Me![tDiscount] = '0')
```

Using the IsNull() function

Null is a constant (see Chapter 24) that means empty of a value. For example, a Text Box control that has nothing in it is said to have a Null value.

It is important to examine a control, examine a variable, and examine a field to determine if it is Null before using it in a calculation or statement, otherwise Access 2007 might become confused and display an error while your application is running (runtime error), or simply produce unexpected results.

This is where the IsNull() function comes in handy. You can use it to determine if a variable, control, or field is Null. This function requires one parameter, which is the name of the variable, control, or field. The function returns a true if it is Null or a false if it isn't Null.

Typically this function is called as the logical expression in an If...Then...End If statement. Here's how you write it.

```
If IsNull(Me![tPrice]) Then
     Response = MsgBox("No price entered.", vbOKOnly,
  "Error", "", 1)
Else
     Me![tSalesTax] = Me![tPrice] * 0.05
     Me![tTotalPrice] = Me![tSalesTax] + Me![tPrice]
End If
```

Just the facts

- A built-in function is a function already built for you.
- String built-in functions are used to manipulate text data.
- InStr() is used to locate a substring in a string.
- Len() function that returns the number of characters in the substring.
- Mid() function returns the substring of a string.
- Left() function copies the substring beginning with the first character of the string. It requires two parameters.
- Right() function copies the substring endings with the last character of the string.
- LTrim() trims leading spaces.
- RTim() trims trailing spaces.
- Trim() trims leading and trailing spaces.
- UCase() changes characters in a string to uppercase.
- LCase() changes characters in a string to lowercase.
- Space() returns a specified number of spaces.
- Format() is used to format a string.
- Round() rounds a value to a specific decimal place.
- Abs() returns the absolute value, which is a number without a plus or minus sign.

Using SQL in a Procedure

Chapter 26

You may lack power to change the world or even get yourself a raise in pay, but you can acquire the power to master data in an Access 2007 database from within a procedure by using SQL.

SQL is one of those computer terms you read about on the Web and might have heard mentioned by your colleagues, but you may not have had the opportunity to dabble in it.

That's about to change because in this chapter I show you how to retrieve data from a database so that it can be used within your procedures. I also cover how to insert new records into a database, update existing ones, and even remove records, all from within your procedure.

This power comes from learning SQL and in this chapter I show you everything you need to know about SQL and how to put it to work for you today.

Understanding SQL

Structure Query Language (SQL) has become the de facto language for interacting with relational database management software, such as Access 2007.

You don't have to learn SQL. In fact, many of my colleagues who use Access 2007 have never written a single line of SQL in their careers because they create queries using the Query Builder (see Chapter 9) to select information from a database.

Access 2007 generates SQL statements for queries created using the Query Builder. You can see these statements by changing to the SQL View when you build your query.

So if everything I just told you is true, then why would I write a chapter showing how to write SQL statements? The reason is that sometimes you might want to embed SQL statements into a procedure. Embedding simply means that SQL statements are written as a string in a procedure and executed when your procedure is written.

Some Access 2007 developers find writing SQL as part of a procedure more convenient than writing a query using the Query Builder. Others prefer the Query Builder method. You'll have the background to make your choice after reading this chapter.

Creating a model procedure

Before getting into the nuts and bolts of SQL, let's take a moment and learn the VBA statements needed to embed and execute an SQL statement. Afterward, you can insert your own SQL statements and execute them.

I group SQL statements into two categories: those used to retrieve data and those used to modify data, tables, and other features of the database. I do so because the VBA statements used to execute them are slightly different for each category.

Retrieving data from a database

Retrieving data from a database is a three-step process.

1. SQL statements make the request to Access 2007.

2. Access 2007 returns the data in a recordset. Think of a recordset as a temporary table that contains only the information that you requested.

3. VBA statements do something with the information from the recordset based on the nature of your procedure.

Using the model procedure

Here is the model procedure to use when retrieving data from a database. Simply replace the SQL query in this model with your SQL query and modify the statement that accesses data from the recordset as

Bright Idea

If a field name has a space such as List Price, then place the field in within square brackets.

required by your procedure. This retrieves one row from the recordset. Later in the "Working with a recordset" section of this chapter, I show you how to move to other rows in the recordset.

```
Dim dbs As DAO.Database
Dim rst As Recordset
Set dbs = CurrentDb
Set rst = dbs.OpenRecordset("SELECT [List Price] FROM
Products WHERE Category = 'Beverages'")
If rst.EOF Then
    Response = MsgBox("No records found.", vbOKOnly,
    "Search Result", "", 1)
Else
    Me![tResult] = rst![List Price]
End If
rst.Close
```

The first two statements declare variables. The first is used to contain references to the database and the other to the recordset.

The next statement assigns references to the current database to the dbs variable. Access 2007 knows the name and location of the current database because it is opened when the procedure runs. The last statement calls the OpenRecordset() method and passes it to the SQL query. An SQL query is a query that consists of SQL statements. This is where you insert your own SQL query.

The OpenRecordset() method returns a reference to the recordset that contains the requested information. This reference is assigned to the rst variable, where other functions are called to access this information.

Here's what the SQL query is asking.

- The SELECT [List Price] statement requests that the value of the [List Price]field be returned from the database.

- The FROM Products statement tells Access 2007 that the [List Price] field is in the Products table. Access 2007 already knows to look in the current database for the Products table because the reference to the current database is assigned to the dbs variable.

■ The WHERE Category = 'Beverages' clause contains the selection criteria. It tells Access 2007 to return the value in the [List Price] field only if the value of the Category field is equal to Beverages.

The SQL query must be contained with double quotations because it is a string within the procedure.

After the OpenRecordset() method executes the SQL query, it returns a recordset. I like to think of a recordset as a spreadsheet that contains columns of records that match the search criteria. Column names in the recordset are identical to the column names in the SELECT statement.

You can't assume that any records were returned by the OpenRecordset() because maybe no record matched the search criteria. Before attempting to access data from a recordset, you should make sure data was returned. You do that by checking the value of the recordset's EOF property. EOF stands for end of file. You do this by referencing the recordset variable name, the dot operator followed by EOF as illustrated in the same code. I always place this as the logical expression for an If...Then...Else...End If statement.

If EOF is true, then no records were returned and I usually display a message box to that effect.

If EOF is false, then at least one record was returned and I then proceed to access the returned data.

Accessing data is done by referencing the name of the recordset variable followed by an exclamation and the field name in brackets such as rst![FieldName].

The last statement closes the recordset.

Working with a recordset

The OpenRecord() method is just one of several methods that are part of a recordset. Other methods are used to interact with the recordset. I find these very handy when I have to access several records contained in the recordset.

Here are the methods that you'll probably use frequently after retrieving information from a database. Each one is called by specifying the variable name of the recordset, followed by the dot operator and the name of the method. I'll use rst as the name of the recordset variable here to help you understand how to call the method.

- **rst.MoveNext.** Moves to the next record in the recordset.
- **rst.MovePrevious.** Moves to the previous record in the recordset.
- **rst.MoveFirst.** Moves to the first record in the recordset.
- **rst.MoveLast.** Moves to the last record in the recordset.
- **rst.Close.** Closes the recordset.
- **rst.BOF.** True if you are at the beginning of the recordset (beginning of file).
- **rst.EOF.** True if you are at the end of the recordset (end of file).
- **rst.RecordCount.** Returns the number of records that has been accessed by the recordset. Call the rst.MoveLast method before calling the rst.RecordCount method if you want the total number of records in the recordset.
- **rst.FindFirst.** "FieldName = "search value"": Locates the first occurrence of the search value in the field of the recordset. This is used with the rst.NoMatch method.
- **rst.NoMatch.** True if the previous FindFirst doesn't locate the search value.

Modifying records

An SQL query can be used to modify values of fields and records or modify the properties of fields, records, tables, and the database. You'll probably only need to modify values of fields and records using an SQL query such as updating a value or deleting a value in a field or deleting an entire record. I show you how to do this later in this chapter.

Here's the model procedure to use when modifying records in a table. A message box displays the RecordsAffected property, which is the number of records that were affected by the SQL query. Simply replace the SQL query in this example with your SQL query.

```
Dim dbs As DAO.Database
    Dim SQL As String
    Set dbs = CurrentDb
```

```
    SQL = "UPDATE Account SET Balance = 14000 WHERE
CustomerNumber = '1234'"
    dbs.Execute SQL
    Response = MsgBox(dbs.RecordsAffected, vbOKOnly,
    "Number of Records Affected", "", 1)
dbs.Close
```

Notice that this model is a little different from the previous model discussed in the last section of this chapter. The objective of this model is to modify records in a table and not to retrieve information from the database. Therefore, we don't need to call recordset methods.

The first two statements declare variables. The first declares a variable for the database object, and the second declares a string variable.

The first Set statement assigns reference to the current database to the database variable. I then assign the SQL query to the string variable. This SQL query changes the value of the Balance field in the Account table for customer 1234. You learn more about the UPDATE statement later in this chapter.

The Execute method of the database object is then called to execute the SQL query. The Close method is then called to close the database.

Selecting data from a table

I've found SQL to be a friendly language to use because the SQL statement resembles English sentences. This is clearly illustrated in statements used to retrieve information from a database.

In English, we write a sentence to ask someone to get something for us. The first part of the sentence usually tells what we want and the second part tells where to find it.

In SQL, we write two parts of the statement that tell Access 2007 the same things. The first statement is called the SELECT statement and it tells Access 2007 the field names whose values we want for our procedure. Commas are used to separate each field name. The second statement is called the FROM statement. This tells Access 2007 the table name(s) that contain these fields. Each table name is also separated by a comma.

Say that you want names of customers that are contained in the CustomerFirstName and CustomerLastName fields of the Customers table. Here's the SQL statement you need to write.

Inside Scoop

SQL isn't case sensitive. Some developers capitalize keywords in an SQL statement while other developers capitalize the first character of the keyword. The important thing is to be consistent in whatever style you select.

```
SELECT CustomerFirstName, CustomerLastName
FROM Customers
```

Selecting from multiple tables

Access 2007 is smart, but it isn't a mindreader. Access 2007 can find the fields requested if field names are unique to tables specified in the FROM statement. If field names are duplicated in those tables, then you'll need to explicitly tell Access 2007 the table name associated with the field.

Suppose that you want to retrieve customer names and outstanding balance. Customer names are in the Customers table and the outstanding balance is in the Accounts table. Here's how you write this statement.

```
SELECT CustomerFirstName, CustomerLastName, Balance
FROM Customers,Accounts
```

Access 2007 can easily find these fields because each field name is unique to the Customers and Accounts tables. You encounter field names that are duplicated in tables specified in the FROM statement. For example, you'll probably want to retrieve the CustomerNumber field, which is likely a common field used to join (see Chapter 3) together multiple tables. This is illustrated in the next example where the CustomerNumber field appears in both the Customers table and the Accounts table. Access 2007 needs to know which CustomerNumber field you want.

```
SELECT CustomerNumber, CustomerFirstName,
CustomerLastName, Balance
FROM Customers,Accounts
```

You explicitly tell Access 2007 the field you want to use by prefacing the field name with the table name, separating them with the dot operator. Here's how you tell Access 2007 that you want to retrieve the CustomerNumber field from the Customers table.

```
SELECT Customers.CustomerNumber, CustomerFirstName,
CustomerLastName, Balance
FROM Customers,Accounts
```

Using an alias

SQL statements can become complex, which you'll see by the time you finish reading this chapter. Prefacing each field with the table name can be cumbersome for you or your colleagues to read, although Access 2007 won't have a problem doing so.

You can shorten the SELECT statement by using the alias of table names. This is done by first defining the alias in the FROM statement and then using it in the SELECT statement and other statements in the query.

Define the abbreviation by specifying it following the table name in the FROM statement. The table name and the abbreviation must be separated with a space.

This is illustrated in the next example where I defined the letter c as the alias for the Customers table and then used the alias in place of the table name in the SELECT statement.

```
SELECT c.CustomerNumber, CustomerFirstName,
CustomerLastName, Balance
FROM Customers c,Accounts
```

Retrieving specific records

Rarely will you want to retrieve all records from a table. More likely you want to retrieve a set of records that meets certain criteria. You do this by using a WHERE clause in the SQL query.

Think of this as saying, "Here's what I want (SELECT); here's where to find it (FROM); and I only want those that have these features (WHERE)."

The WHERE clause requires that you provide a logical expression Access 2007 uses to determine whether or not a record should be returned to your procedure. You'll recall from Chapter 9 that a logical expression results in either a true or false. Fields that you request are returned only if the logical expression is true.

Let's say that you want to retrieve the customer number, customer name, and balance for customer number 1234. Here's how you write the SQL query.

```
SELECT CustomerNumber, CustomerFirstName,
CustomerLastName
FROM Customers
WHERE CustomerNumber = '1234'
```

Selecting all fields

Although there'll be few times when you want all *records* in a table, you probably want to retrieve all *fields* of a table. Fortunately, you don't have to write all field names into the SELECT statement. Instead, simply use the wildcard character (*) in place of the names.

Here's how to retrieve all the fields from the Customers table.

```
SELECT *
FROM Customers
WHERE CustomerNumber = '1234'
```

Specifying multiple conditions

Rarely am I asked to write an SQL query that has one criteria. Usually there are at least two and sometimes three logical expressions that I need to combine into one.

You'll probably have a similar experience. The solution is to create subexpressions and then concatenate them into a complex logical expression using an SQL concatenation clause.

These are:

- **AND.** Both subexpressions must be true for the complex expression to be true.

- **OR.** Either subexpression must be true for the complex expression to be true.

- **NOT.** Both subexpressions must be false for the complex expression to be true. NOT can also be used in a single expression.

These clauses are used in the WHERE clause of the SQL query. In the next example, I'm asking Access 2007 to return customer numbers for customers whose balance is greater than $5,000 and less than $10,000.

```
SELECT CustomerNumber
FROM Accounts
WHERE Balance > 5000 AND Balance < 10000
```

The NOT clause reverses the logic of the expression and therefore is placed at the beginning of the expression. Here's an SQL query that returns all records except those for customer 1234.

```
SELECT Balance
FROM Accounts
WHERE NOT CustomerNumber = '1234'
```

Selecting a range of values

The BETWEEN operator is used to define a range of values as the selection criteria. Records that match the first value, the last value of the definition, and all those in between are returned by Access 2007.

Say that I want to return customer numbers of customers who have a balance between $5,000 and $10,000. Here's the SQL query that I'd write.

```
SELECT CustomerNumber
FROM Accounts
WHERE Balance Between 5000 And 10000
```

Matching partial values

An SQL query is like playing horseshoes because you achieve your objective simply by coming close. This is because you can use the LIKE operator to have Access 2007 return values that are close to the value you are looking for. This is similar to typing Smi and all the Smiths are returned, along with the Smites and other names beginning with Smi.

The LIKE operator accepts wildcard characters for the portion of the search criteria you're unsure of. Wildcards are placed within the search criteria.

Here are the wildcard characters:

- **Underscore (_).** A single character wildcard character such as Sm_th.
- **Percent (%).** Multicharacter wildcard character used to match any number of characters such as Smi%.

The LIKE operator is used in place of the equivalent (equal) sign as illustrated in this next example. Here I'm asking Access 2007 to return all customer numbers of customers whose last name begins with Smi.

```
SELECT CustomerNumber
FROM Customers
WHERE CustomerLastName LIKE 'Smi%'
```

Finding blank fields

This next SQL operator is worth its weight in gold. I can't remember the number of times when I'm asked to find missing data, such as orders without order dates or my favorite, customers' missing telephone numbers.

The IS NULL operator is practically all you need to find missing data because it asks Access 2007 to determine if a field is empty. That's what NULL means.

I use the IS NULL operator in the search criteria to find empty data. Here's how I locate missing telephone numbers.

```
SELECT CustomerNumber
FROM Customers
WHERE CustomerOfficePhone IS NULL
```

Getting rid of duplicates

Anyone who writes SQL queries normally experiences this frustration at some point in their career. Your search criteria return many duplicate records unexpectedly.

This happens when I search for customers who ordered a particular product. I expect to have one order per customer. What I normally get are multiple orders for the same product placed by the same customer, which makes sense.

Duplicate records can be removed from the recordset returned by Access 2007 by using the DISTINCT modifier in the SELECT statement. Here's the SQL query I used to eliminate duplicate customer numbers from being returned by Access 2007.

```
SELECT DISTINCT CustomerNumber
FROM Orders
WHERE ProductID = '1234'
```

Selecting several values the easy way

Here's a method of simplifying the WHERE clause when you want Access 2007 to use multiple search values. Instead of creating a complex logical expression, use the IN modifier and give Access 2007 the values you want to match.

The IN modifier is used with multiple values, each of which is searched for by Access 2007. Access 2007 tries to match each one and returns records that match.

Revisit the previous example and use the IN modifier to search for three product IDs.

```
SELECT DISTINCT CustomerNumber
FROM Orders
WHERE ProductID IN ('1234', '6578', '9087')
```

You can reverse this logic and have Access 2007 return records that don't match values in the IN modifier list. This is accomplished by using the NOT IN modifier in place of the IN modifier.

I tell Access 2007 to return records containing products other than these three products by writing:

```
SELECT DISTINCT CustomerNumber
FROM Orders
WHERE ProductID NOT IN ('1234', '6578', '9087')
```

Joining tables

The key design element of an Access 2007 database is to remove redundant data and place the remaining data into tables and then use key values to relate records of different tables together (see Chapter 9). Linking tables is called *joining*.

You can join tables in an SQL query so that you can return data from the joined tables. Joining is a two-step process. First, identify the tables in the FROM statement. Then create an expression in the WHERE clause that creates the join.

 Watch Out!

Place single quotations around text values. Quotations are not used for numeric values.

Inside Scoop

Joining too many tables in an SQL query can slow performance.

Say that you want to retrieve a customer's name, telephone number, and account balance. The customer name and telephone number are in the Customers table, and the balance is in the Accounts table.

You need to tell Access 2007 which fields to use to join the tables. Remember from Chapter 9 that joins are made using a field of each table that contains the same value. Sometimes they also have the same field name, but Access 2007 uses values, not field names, to join the tables.

If both tables use the same field name, then you must explicitly identify each field using the table name or the table alias, which I showed you previously in this chapter.

Here's how to create the join in the WHERE clause. After this is made, you can use field names from either table in the SELECT statement as if they were part of the same table. However, you must explicitly identify each field if the field name is duplicated in the other table.

```
SELECT CustomerFirstName, CustomerLastName, Balance
FROM Customers, Accounts
WHERE Customers.CustomerNumber =
Accounts.CustomerNumber
```

You can select records by transforming the join expression into a complex logical expression by using the AND clause, which you learned how to do previously in the chapter.

Calculating data in an SQL query

There are situations when you want to calculate records in a table rather than retrieving its data. SQL has several built-in functions you can use for this purpose. These functions return the result of the calculation.

Typically an SQL function is used in the SELECT statement. The name of the field being calculated is passed to the SQL function.

Here are commonly used SQL calculation functions.

▪ **SUM(FieldName).** Tallies values in the field.

▪ **AVG(FieldName).** Averages values in the field.

- **MIN(FieldName).** Determines the minimum value in the field.

- **MAX(FieldName).** Determines the maximum value in the field.

- **COUNT(FieldName).** Determines the number of records in the field.

Here's how to use an SQL calculation function in an SQL query. In this example, I'm counting the number of distinct (no duplicates) customers who ordered product 1234. It's common in some situations to remove duplicates before performing the calculation.

```
SELECT DISTINCT COUNT(CustomerNumber)
FROM Orders
WHERE ProductID = '1234'
```

Grouping and ordering data

I always massage raw data retrieved from a database and place it in some kind of order so that it is easy to read and understand. There are two ways to massage raw data. These are by grouping data and by ordering data.

Grouping places rows with similar values in the same group. For example, it makes sense to group orders by customer.

Ordering places rows in sort order based on a value in one or more fields. I usually group orders by customer, and then within the group I sort orders by date.

Using the GROUP BY clause

The GROUP BY clause is used to specify groupings for records retrieved from a database. The GROUP BY clause requires that you specify the field name used to group records.

In this next example, I'm retrieving information about orders from the Orders table and grouping them by customer number. This places all orders for the same customer under the customer's order number.

```
SELECT CustomerNumber, OrderDate, TotalPrice, Count()
As "Total Customers"
FROM Orders
Group BY CustomerNumber
```

You can create a subgroup within a group by specifying the field name for the subgroup. Let's say that you want to group orders by customer and within customer by sales representative.

Here's how to write this SQL query. First, Access 2007 groups orders by customer number and then within each customer number orders are further grouped by sales representative.

```
SELECT CustomerNumber, SalesRep, OrderDate, TotalPrice,
Count() As "Total Customers By Sales Rep"
FROM Orders
Group BY CustomerNumber, SalesRep
```

Limiting records within a group

Records within a group can be limited based on a logical expression by using the HAVING clause. The HAVING clause does basically the same thing as the WHERE clause in that both tell Access 2007 to include only records that pass the logical expression text.

The logical Expression in the HAVING clause:

■ Must results in a true or false value.

■ Must appear in every field named in the logical expression.

■ Can include SQL calculation functions.

Here's how to use the HAVING clause. In this example, only customers who have total orders worth more than $500 are returned.

```
SELECT CustomerNumber, SalesRep, OrderDate, TotalPrice
Count() As "Total Price Greater than 500"
FROM Orders
GROUP BY CustomerNumber, SalesRep HAVING
SUM(TotalPrice) > 500
```

Using the ORDER BY clause

The ORDER BY clause is used to sort records retrieved from a database and is written similar to how you write the GROUP BY clause in that you specify the name of the field to use for the sort.

In the following example, I'm sorting customer orders by customer number.

```
SELECT CustomerNumber, OrderDate, TotalPrice, Count()
As "Total Orders "
FROM Orders
ORDER BY CustomerNumber
```

You can create an order within an order. These refer to major and minor sort keys. The major sort keys are the first fields specified in the ORDER BY clause and minor sort keys are subsequent fields.

Now modify the previous example. Sort the order by customer number and then by order date. I do this by specifying the CustomerNumber field as the major sort key and the OrderDate field as the minor sort key. These are separated by a comma.

```
SELECT CustomerNumber, OrderDate, TotalPrice, Count()
As "Total Orders by Date "
FROM Orders
ORDER BY CustomerNumber, OrderDate
```

I can combine ORDER BY with GROUP BY to have Access 2007 group records and then sort records within the group. This is illustrated in the next example, where I've inserted the GROUP BY clause to group records by customer number.

```
SELECT CustomerNumber, SalesRep, OrderDate, TotalPrice,
Count() As "Total Orders Greater than 500"
FROM Orders
ORDER BY CustomerNumber, OrderDate
GROUP BY CustomerNumber, SalesRep HAVING
SUM(TotalPrice) > 500
```

In addition to choosing the field to order, you can also decide the direction of the sort by using the ASC or DESC modifier. The ASC modifier, which is the default setting, tells Access2007 to sort in ascending order. The DESC modifier causes a descending sort.

Here's how to change the default sort to descending.

```
SELECT CustomerNumber, SalesRep, OrderDate, TotalPrice,
Count() As "Total Orders"
FROM Orders
ORDER BY CustomerNumber, OrderDate DESC
GROUP BY CustomerNumber, SalesRep HAVING
SUM(TotalPrice) > 500
```

Inside Scoop

Use the model procedure discussed in the "Modifying records" section of this chapter for SQL queries that insert, update, and delete records.

Inserting a record into a table

A new record can be inserted into a table from your procedure by using the INSERT INTO statement. The INSERT INTO statement requires that you provide the name of the table that is receiving the record and the values to be inserted. Values are specified using the VALUES clause.

Values are inserted into the new record in the order that the values appear in the SQL query. That is, the first value is placed into the first field, the second value into the second field, and so on.

This technique exposes you to a potential problem. A colleague might have restructured the table without you knowing it — or you simply forgot what the table structure looks like. The table structure is the order in which fields appear in the table.

I avoid this problem by specifying field names whenever I insert a record into a table using an SQL query. In this way, Access 2007 and I both know which fields get what values.

In the following example I'm inserting a new record into the Customers table. The first set of parentheses contains field names. The second set contains values. Each value is placed into its corresponding field. That is, 1234 is placed in the CustomerNumber field of the new record; Tom is placed into the CustomerFirstName field, and so on.

```
DIM SQL as String
SQL = "INSERT INTO Customers (CustomerNumber,
CustomerFirstName, CustomerLastName, DateAcquired)
VALUES ('1234', 'Tom', 'Jones', '10/18/2008')"
```

Watch Out!

Be sure to include all required fields; otherwise Access 2007 will reject the record and display an error message. Likewise, make sure that data matches the data type of the field.

Updating records in a table

Updating a record is the process of changing the current value of a field(s). This is achieved by using the UPDATE statement and the SET clause.

There are three steps to updating a record. These are:

- Specify the table name in the UPDATE statement.
- Specify the field and new value in the SET statement.
- Identify the record being changed using a logical expression in the WHERE clause.

You can change the balance of customer 1234 in the Accounts table. Here's the SQL query that I need to write.

```
DIM SQL as String
SQL = "UPDATE Accounts SET Balance = 15000 WHERE
CustomerNumber = '1234'
```

You can update multiple rows by using the IN clause in the WHERE statement. The IN clause specifies multiple values to match. In the next example, I'm changing the sales representative for three customers identified by customer numbers in the IN clause.

```
DIM SQL as String
SQL = "UPDATE Accounts SET SalesRep = '45' WHERE
CustomerNumber IN ('1234', '6557', '9867')"
```

Another very common technique is to update a value of a field if the field is empty. This is done by using the IS NULL clause in the WHERE clause.

You can assign sales rep 36 to all customers who have not been assigned a sales rep. Here's how to do this:

```
DIM SQL as String
SQL = "UPDATE Accounts SET SalesRep = '36' WHERE
SalesRep IS NULL"
```

And then sometimes you'll want to update a field for every record in the table. Here, I'm changing the regional office number to 90 for every customer.

```
DIM SQL as String
SQL = "UPDATE Accounts SET RegionalOffice = '90'"
```

Updating multiple fields

Multiple fields can be updated simultaneously by specifying more than one field in the SET clause. In the next example, I'm changing the sales rep and regional office for customer 1234. You can update as many fields as needed by simply separating each with a comma in the SET clause.

```
DIM SQL as String
SQL = "UPDATE Accounts SET SalesRep = '36',
RegionalOffice = '90' WHERE CustomerNumber = '1234'"
```

Updating using calculations

The new value of a field can be the result of a calculation. You do this by placing the expression as the value of the field. Let's say you want to give all employees a $500 raise in pay. Here's how to do it. The $500 is added the current value of the Salary field, and the sum replaces the current salary.

```
DIM SQL as String
SQL = "UPDATE Employees SET Salary = Salary + 500"
```

Deleting a record from a table

The DELETE FROM statement is used to delete a record from a table. This statement requires that you specify the table name and you should identify the record using a logical expression within the WHERE clause; otherwise all records in the table are deleted.

You can delete orders where the value of the TotalPrice field is less than a dollar because these are obvious erroneous orders. Here's how to do this:

```
DIM SQL as String
SQL = "DELETE FROM Orders WHERE TotalPrice < 1"
```

Watch Out!
Be sure that other tables are not negatively affected by deleting a record.

Just the facts

- Structure Query Language (SQL) has become the de facto language for interacting with relational database-management software such as Access 2007.

- OpenRecord() method is used to retrieve a recordset from a database using an SQL query.

- MoveNext: Moves to the next record in the recordset.

- MovePrevious: Moves to the previous record in the recordset.

- MoveFirst: Moves to the first record in the recordset.

- MoveLast: Moves to the last record in the recordset.

- Close: Closes the recordset.

- BOF: True if you are at the beginning of the recordset (beginning of file).

- EOF: True if you are at the end of the recordset (end of file).

Appendixes

PART IX

Glossary

Access 2007 A Database Management System (DBMS) that manages information.

action query Used to perform an action such as appending, updating, and deleting records.

ActiveX control A control that you can build, or usually you acquire it from a third party other than Microsoft. It usually is a feature that isn't available in Access 2007.

add-in Functionality provided to Access 2007 by another program.

ad hoc query A query used to generate a last-minute request for information

Append action query Copies records from one or more tables into another table.

ApplyFilter action Used to apply a query, filter, or an SQL WHERE clause to a table from within a macro.

arguments Additional information provided to a macro for it to carry out the desired action.

attachment data type Used to store images, audio, video, and binary files generated by other Office programs (i.e. Word, Excel, and PowerPoint). Use this instead of the OLE Object data type. The Attachment data type can hold 700 Kbytes if the file is not compressed and 2 gigabytes for a compressed file.

auto generated A primary key that is automatically generated by Access 2007.

AutoNumber data type   Used to have Access 2007 generate a value each time a record is inserted into the table. The value can be incremented sequentially, incremented by a value of your choosing, or a random number. Use the AutoNumber data type to have Access 2007 automatically create a Primary Key.

avg built-in function   Calculates the average value in the field.

backspace   Delete the character to the left of the insertion point.

beep action   Tells the computer to sound a beep.

binary object   A spreadsheet, presentation, or similar object created by other Windows applications.

blank Form   An empty form.

Boolean value   A value that can be either true or false, on or off, yes or no, 1 or 0. Use this for storing decisions.

bound   A link between a control and a field in a table.

Bound Object Frame Control   Similar to the Unbound Object Frame control, except it displays OLE objects and embedded pictures that are associated with a field in the database.

bug   An error in an application, macro, or module.

built-in function   Performs a calculation without you having to create an expression.

byte   Number between 0 to 255.

calculated control   An unbound control that displays the result of calculating an expression such as the total number of orders that a customer placed.

calculated data   Data derived from other data such as the purchase price of an item on an invoice.

calculated query field   An empty field on the query grid that contains a mathematical expression describing the calculation.

CancelEvent action   Place in the macro at the point when you want the event cancelled.

caption Text that is displayed whenever its corresponding field is displayed.

Cartesian join Selects records from both tables.

cascading update When Access 2007 finds all tables where the primary key value is used as a foreign key and changes them when the primary key changes.

check box control Used for data display and data input. It limits data input to one of two values — on/off.

close action Used to close an object such as a table, query, form, and report.

columnar form Shows one record at a time as used most commonly for data-entry forms, dialog boxes, message boxes, and for navigating through your database application. Sometimes a columnar form is referred to as a full screen form.

columnar report A report is also known as a form report and is used to display one record on a page and resembles a data-entry form.

combo box control Similar in appearance and function to a Text Box except the user has a choice of entering a value into the Combo Box or selecting a value from a pop-up list.

command button control A push button that causes Access 2007 to perform an action.

complex query A query that has multiple query criteria.

Compound Primary Key A primary key that contains values of two or more fields.

Concatenation operator An ampersand (&) tells Access 2007 to place the beginning of one text at the end of another text.

control An element on a form such as a label, a text box, and a check box.

Controls wizard A wizard used to create controls for a form or report.

Count built-in function   Counts the number of records in the field.

Crosstab   A specialized Total Query in the form of a spreadsheet where some fields of a table are column headings and other fields are row headings. Cells contain summary of the fields.

Crosstab query   A query that displays its result in a cross-tabular form.

Crosstab wizard   A wizard used to create a crosstab.

Currency   Data type for any monetary value. Use this for prices, salaries, and similar data.

data   A fact that on its own has no meaning.

Data definition query   Used to modify the database definition.

data entry   The process of entering data into one or more tables of the database.

data size   The amount of space occupied by data.

Data type   A characteristic of data that tells what data values can be stored in a field.

data validation   The process of assuring that only correct data enters the database.

database   Composed of tables, queries, reports, forms, and other objects used to enter, display, and manipulate data.

Database application   A computer program used to make requests to the DBMS.

Database Management System (DBMS)   Computer software that manages data.

database name   The name of a database.

datasheet   Used to interact with data the way you expect to when using a spreadsheet.

datasheet form   A permanent datasheet that displays multiple records in a spreadsheet-like format.

datasheet tab   Contains features for interacting with a datasheet.

Datasheet view   Resembles a spreadsheet because records and fields appear as rows and columns.

Date/Time data type   Used for dates.

DBMS   See Database Management System.

debugging   The process of removing errors from an application, macro, or module.

decimal   A number between -1028 to +1038. By default 18 decimal places can be displayed but you can change this to 28 decimal places.

deciphering   The unscrambling of an encrypted file.

decomposing   The process of transforming information in an entity into data for the Access 2007 database.

default value   The value Access 2007 assigns to a field in the absence of a value.

delete action query   Removes records from a table.

delimited text file   A text file where each line:a record, fields are separated by a comma, text appears in quotations.

Design view   Shows each field and its description, but no data.

destination table   Where records are appended to.

Details section   The body of the form.

Double   A number between -1.787×10^{308} to $+1.797 \times 10^{308}$. Up to 15 significant digits.

Dynaset   Contains records returned by a query.

embedded macro   A macro that is part of a form, report, or contol that executes when a specified event occurs.

encryption   Scrambles letters and numbers, making it unreadable unless a special routine is used to unscramble this information. This is referred to as deciphering.

end   Move the insertion point to the end of the field in a single line field or end of the line in a multiline field.

entity   A component of a system such as an order and customer.

Equi-join   (also known as an inner join)Selects records from both tables that have the same value in the field used to join the tables. Records that don't match are not selected. This is the default join.

Esc twice   Undo changes in the current field or current record if both have changed.

event   Something that happens when someone uses the form.

exporting   Copy data and objects from an Access 2007 database.

Expression Builder   A tool used to create an expression interactively.

field name   The name of a field.

field property   Information that defines a field.

field size   The amount of space reserved in a field for data.

filter   Changes the selection of data that appears in a Datasheet, Form, Report, or Layout view based on your filter criteria, but leaves other data intact and out of sight.

Filter By Form   Filters records by values entered into a form.

filter criteria   Consist of one or more values that Access 2007 compares to one or multiple fields in the underlying table.

FindNext action   Used to locate the next record that matches the search criteria specified in the FindRecord action.

FindRecord action   Finds the first instance of the information that meets your search criteria.

First built-in function   Returns the first value in the field.

First normal form   Requires that a single value is at the intersection of every record and field.

fixed width text file   A text file where each line is a record and each field is a specific number of characters.

foreign key   A primary key of another table used to relate two tables.

form   Used to display and interact with data in a free-form display.

Form designer   A tool that lets you build a form from scratch.

form footer   Displayed at the bottom for each page when viewed and at the bottom of the form when the form is printed.

form header   Displayed at the top of each page when viewed and at the top page when the form is printed.

Form wizard   A wizard used to create a form.

GoToControl action   Used to select a control or field in the active form or datasheet.

GoToPage action   Used to select a page on a form once the form is selected.

GoToRecord action   Used to make a specific record the current record. This is like clicking Go To on the Home ribbon.

Graphs form   Displays information as a bar chart, pie chart, line graph, or other kind of graphic format.

GroupBy built-in function   Groups records using the field you specify and then totals values.

home   Moves the insertion point to the beginning of the field in a single line field or to the beginning of the line in a multiline field.

Home tab   Contains tools used to enter and modify data.

Hourglass action   Displays the hourglass icon as the cursor.

Hyperlink data type   Used to store hyperlinks to Web pages using the Uniform Resource Locator (URL) or files using the Universal Naming Convention (UNC).

image control   Efficiently displays a bitmap picture.

importing   Bringing data and objects into an Access 2007 database.

index   Like a book index where key values are associated with the location of the key value in the database.

information   A collection of data that has meaning.

inline if statement   Used to set criteria for Access 2007 to make a decision. It is written as If(condition, expression1, expression2). Expression1 is calculated only if the condition is true; otherwise expression2 is calculated.

Input Mask wizard   Used to define a pattern or values entered into a field.

integer   A number between -32,768 to +32,767.

key   A value on which a table is indexed.

Label control   Displays text.

Last built-in function   Returns the last value in the field.

Left Outer Join   Where all rows from the left table and matching rows in the right table are selected.

line control   Places a single line on the form.

list box control   Displays a list of items. One or multiple values can be selected for data input.

logical bug   An error in the logical execution of instructions.

long integer   A number between -2,147,483,648 to +2,147,483,647.

lookup column   A field that contains a list of valid values that the user can select when entering data into the field.

Lookup wizard   Enables the user to pick a value from a list of valid values shown in a combo box.

macro   A set of instructions that tells Access 2007 to do something.

Macro Builder   A tool used to create macros.

Macro group   A collection of related macros stored under a single macro name and run in sequence.

mailing labels   A report uses information in the database to create mailing labels. It offers a wide variety of label styles from Avery labels and other vendors. Select the style and Access 2007 makes sure addresses are printed properly on each label. This is very similar to printing labels in Microsoft Word.

Mail-merge report   A report that combines information from a database with a block of text and is used to personalize form letters.

Main/Subforms form   Consists of two forms that have a parent/child relationship.

Make Table action   Query transforms a dynaset into a new table and adds it to the database.

many-to-many relationship   When many records in a table can be related to many records in another table.

mask   Formatting applied during data entry and data display.

Max built-in function   Returns the maximum value in the field.

maximize action   Simulate clicking the maximize button in a window.

Memo data type   Similar to the text data type except a memo field can store up to 1 gigabyte of characters and Rich-Text formatting. 65,535 characters can be displayed at one time.

metadata   Information that describes data, such as a field name.

Min built-in function   Returns the minimum value in the field.

minimize action   Simulate clicking the minimize button in a window.

modal dialog   Blocks interaction with the rest of the application until the person responds to the modal dialog box.

MoveSize action   Used to relocate or resize the window that is currently active in your Access 2007 application.

New Field tool   Used to insert a new field into a table.

normalization   The process of eliminating redundancy in a database.

null   Means nothing, having no value.

Number data type   Holds integers or fractional values used in calculations.

object   A component of a system.

ODBC   Open Database Connectivity standard that makes it possible to access any data from any application.

OLE Object Data Type   Used to store large binary objects up to 1 gigabyte in size.

one-to-many relationship   When a record in a table can be related to many records in another table.

one-to-one relationship   When one record in a table can be related to only one record in another table.

OpenForm action   This action opens a form in Form View, Design View, Print Preview, or Datasheet View.

OpenReport action   This action opens a report in either Design View or Print Preview. It is also used to send the report to the printer.

OpenTable action   This action tells Access 2007 to open a table in any view such as Datasheet View, Design View, or Print Preview.

operator precedence   States the order in which Access 2007 performs operations in an expression.

option button control   A radio button that is used for data display and data input. It limits data input to one of two values. These are on/off. An Option Button is usually grouped with other Option Buttons in an Option Group. Only one Option Button within the group can be on. Access 2007 automatically turns off other Option Buttons in the group.

Option Group control   Visually organizes controls into a group on the form.

Outer join   Selects all the records of one table and records from the second table that has the same value in the field used to join these tables.

OutputTo action   Used to output an Access 2007 database object, i.e. table, query, form, report, module, or data access page (Web page generated by Access 2007), to Excel, HTML, Rich Text Format, or plain text files.

page footer   Displayed before the form footer only when the form is printed.

page header   Displayed after the form header only when the form is printed.

Parameter query   A query that uses user-supplied data when the query runs as criteria for the query.

Pass through query   A query that is passed from Access 2007 application to a database on a database server.

PivotChart   Displays data in a graph.

Pivot Table   Displays data in a cross-tabulation view.

primary key   A unique value that identifies each record in a table.

procedure   How to do something with an entity, such as how to place an order.

query   A request for data stored in the database or for data that can be calculated using information stored in the database.

Query By Example   Known as the query grid and is where queries are built.

Query Design tool   A tool in the Other group on the Create ribbon and is used to create a query.

Query expression   Specifies the rules for including a record in a dynaset.

Query join   A query that joins two or more tables using a common value and then retrieves records that meet the query criteria.

Query properties   Settings that affect how the query runs.

Query wizard   A wizard used to create a query.

Querying a query   The technique of querying the dynaset returned by another query.

Quit action   Stops the macro and exits Access 2007.

ready-to-use filters   Built-in filters.

record   Contains related data such as a customer's name and address.

rectangle control   Places a rectangle on the form.

relating tables   Links together records in two tables using a value common to both tables.

Replication ID   A number randomly generated by Access 2007 used as a globally unique identifier (GUID).

report   Used to display information on paper.

Report wizard   A wizard use to create a report.

required field   A field that must have a value for each record.

Right Outer Join   Where matching rows from the left table and all rows in the right table are selected.

saved query   A query that is saved and can be executed often without having to write the query.

Second normal form   States that each nonkey field be fully dependent on the entire primary key.

Select query   A query that selects records from one or more tables.

selection tool   Used to filter records.

SelectObject action   Selects a database object.

Show Data Picker   The property for data fields that causes a calendar to appear during data entry so the user can pick a date rather than enter the date manually into the data field.

ShowAllRecords action   Removes a filter that has been applied to the table.

single   A number between -3.4×10^{38} to $+3.4 \times 10^{38}$. Seven significant digits.

Smart tag   A task that is automatically performed when a value is entered into a field.

Snapshot report   A version of an Access report that can be read using the Snapshot Viewer, which can be downloaded at no cost from www.microsoft.com.

Source table   Contains records to append.

Split Form   Splits a form into two sections. The top section contains multiple records and the bottom section contains single records.

standalone macro   A collection of one or more related actions stored under a single macro name.

StDev built-in function   Calculates the standard deviation of values in the field.

StopAllMacros action   Stops all macros currently running. Neither of these have arguments.

StopMacro action   Stops the current macro.

Structured Query Language (SQL)   A language used to write a query that Access 2007 understands.

Subform/Subreport control   Creates a subform within the current form or a subreport within the current report.

subreport   A type of columnar report. Think of this as a report within another report. You can use it to have customer contact information appearing at the top of the report and rows of orders in a subreport at the bottom of the report.

Sum built-in function   Calculates the sum of values in the field.

syntactical bug   an error resulting from the use of a word not understood by Access 2007.

system   A way of doing something.

tab control   Displays multiple pages of a form as tabs of a file folder.

Tab index   A control property that determines the order in which controls receive focus when the tab key is pressed.

Tab stop   A control property that tells Access 2007 to give the control focus when the tab key is pressed.

table   A collection of records.

tabular form   Combines features of columnar and datasheet forms.

tabular report   A report is sometimes called a groups/totals report. It presents information in rows and columns and is used to group by one or more fields and summarize information for numeric fields in each group. You can also create page totals and grand totals.

text alignment   Determines how Access 2007 displays text.

text box control   Used to input free-form data.

Text data type   Used to store text, punctuation, and numbers that are not used in calculations. A limit of 256 characters can be stored in a field designated a text data type.

Text qualifier character   A character in a delimited text file used to distinguish between text and nontext data.

Third normal form   Requires that each nonkey field be independent of each other and dependent only on the primary key. This means that fields that are not part of the primary key must have a relationship with all fields that comprise the primary key.

toggle button control   A two state button used for data display and data input. Limits data input to one of two values - on/off.

Toggle Filter tool   Applies and removes a filter.

Total query   A calculation query that summarizes records in one or more tables such as calculating the sum of values in a field or determining the number of records in a table.

TransferSpreadsheet action   Used to import or export data between a spreadsheet and Access 2007.

TransferText action   Used to import or export text.

Trust Center   Used to identify trusted locations and establish security settings for your Access 2007 application that determine the behavior of the application.

trusted mode   When the Trust Center has determined that the application is trustworthy based on settings you or the system administers made to the Trust Center.

unbound   A control without a link to a field in a table.

Unbound Object Frame control   Displays an OLE object or embedded picture that is not associated with a field in the database. Use this for graphs, video, pictures, and sound files.

Union query   Query that combines records from multiple tables.

Unique field   A field whose value must be different than values of other fields in the table.

Update action query   Changes values of existing records in one or more tables.

user interface   The way someone interacts with a computer program.

validation rules   Rules Access 2007 applies to new data to determine if the data is valid.

Var built-in function   Calculates of variance (the square of the StDev) in the field.

virtual record number   A number assigned to a record that is displayed in a form and can be different from the record's real record number in the table.

wildcard character   A character used to represent unknown characters in an expression.

Using Standard Naming Conventions

More than one developer usually works on an Access 2007 database application over the course of the application's lifetime. Therefore, it is important that you make it easy for another developer to read and understand components of your Access 2007 application.

Professional Access 2007 developers use standard naming conventions for names of tables, forms, reports, and other objects used in an Access 2007 database application to help other developers find their way around the application.

If you're building an Access 2007 application for your own use or for use by others in your work group, then adhering to standards might not be worth the effort because you'll be the only developer maintaining your application.

However, if you're building an Access 2007 application that will be used by your organization for years to come, then consider naming components using naming conventions that professional developers use to name components of their Access 2007 applications.

A naming convention is a standard prefix for the name of the component. The prefix describes the type of component while the rest of the name uniquely identifies the component.

Here are naming conventions that are standard for Access 2007.

Object Names

Prefix	Object	Example
cls	Class Module	clsInstall
frm	Form	frmOrder
fsub	Subform	fsubAddress
mcr	Macro	mcrAutoexec
mod	Module	modSalesTax
qry	Query	qryFindCustomer
rpt	Report	rptCustomerSales
rsub	Subreport	rsubSalesRep
tbl	Table	tblCustomers

Table Field Names

Prefix	Object
bin	Number (binary)
bin	Yes/No (Boolean)
byt	Number (byte)
chr	Text (character)
cur	Currency
dbl	Number (double)
dtm	Date/Time
hlk	Hyperlink
idn	Autonumber (random)
idr	Autonumber (replication ID)
ids	Autonumber (sequence)
int	Number (integer)

Prefix	Object
lngz	Number (long)
mem	Memo
ole	OLE object
sng	Number (single)

Form and Report Controls

Prefix	Object
brk	Page break
cbo	Combo Box
chk	Check Box
cht	Chart (graph)
cmd	Command Button
det	Detail (section)
fft	Form footer section
fhd	Form header section
frb	Bound Object frame
fru	Unbound object frame
gft[n]	Footer (group section)
ghd[n]	Header (group section)
grp	Option group
hlk	Hyperlink
img	Image
lbl	Label
lin	Line
lst	List Box

continued

Form and Report Controls *continued*

Prefix	Object
ocx	ActiveX Custom Control
opt	Option Button
pft	Page footer (section)
pge	Page (tab)
phd	Page header (section)
rft	Report footer (section)
rhd	Report header (section)
sec	Section
shp	Rectangle
sub	Subform/subreport
tab	Tab control
tgl	Toggle button
txt	Text box

Visual Basic Data Variable Names

Prefix	Object
bln	Boolean
byte	Byte
ccc	Conditional Complicating Constant
cur	Currency
dbl	Double
dtm	Date
err	Error
int	Integer
lng	Long

Prefix	Object
obj	Object
sng	Single
str	String
typ	User Defined Type
var	Variant

Access Database Limitations

Access 2007 may seem to have unlimited capacity once you begin building complex Access 2007 database applications; however, there are limitations to what Access 2007 can do for you.

The following tables show those limitations. Be sure to review these limitations before building your next big application, otherwise you might discover once you are depending on the application that the application exceeded the capabilities of Access 2007.

Databases	
Item	**Limitation**
Characters in object name	64
Concurrent User (number)	255
File Size	2 GB including space required by the system. However, size is limited only by available disk space if tables are attached in multiple files.
Modules	1,000 (number)
Objects in database (number)	32,768
Password (characters)	14
User Name (characters)	20

Tables

Item	Limitation
Characters in a field property	255
Characters in a record	4,000 excluding memo and OLE object fields and Unicode Compression property set to Yes.
Characters in a table description	255
Characters in a text field	255
Characters in a validation message	255
Characters in a validation rule	2,048
Characters in field name	64
Characters in memo field	65,535 entered from the keyboard. 1 GB entered from within the program.
Characters in a table name	64
Fields in an index (number)	255
Fields in a record (number)	255
Indexes in a table (number)	32
OLE Object field	1 GB
Opened tables (number)	2,048
Table size	2 GB including space required by the system.

Queries

Item	Limitation
AND in a Where or Having clause (number)	99
Characters in a cell of the design grid	1,024
Characters in an SQL statement	64,000
Dynaset size	1 GB

Item	Limitation
Enforced relationships	32 for each table
Fields in a recordset	255
Level of nesting in a query	50
Sort limit	255 characters
Sorted fields in a query	10
Tables in a query (number)	32

Forms and Reports

Item	Limitation
Characters in a label	2,048
Characters in a text box	65,535
Controls or sections	754
Headers and footers (number)	1
Height of all sections	200 inches
Levels of nesting	7
Printed pages in a report	65,536
Section height	22 inches
Width	22 inches

Macros

Item	Limitation
Actions in a macro	999
Characters in a comment	255
Characters in a condition	255
Characters in an action argument	255

Symbols

"" (empty string), 238
(pound) signs, 135
wildcard character, 100, 129
wildcard operator, 219
% (percent) with LIKE, 578
% wildcard character, 129
& (concatenation operator), 236, 563
* (asterisk) wildcard character, 100, 577
* (asterisk) wildcard operator, 218, 219
[] (brackets), 128, 232, 525, 562
^ wildcard character, 129
_ (underscore) with LIKE, 578
_ wildcard character, 129
< (less-than) operator, 99
<> (not equal) operator, 99
= (equal operator), 405
! wildcard character, 100, 129
? wildcard character, 100, 129
? wildcard operator, 219

A

Abs() function, 550, 552
.accdc files, 463
Access 2007
    automating using VBA, 502–504
    basic concepts, 31–33
    environment, 5–9
    getting started with, 9–10
    making decisions, 526–531
    starting, 3–5
Access Deployment file, 462
Access options, 8
access rights for a user ID, 48

action combo box, 395, 396
action queries, 243–253
Action query type, 197
actions
    assigning to a Command Button control, 334
    creating conditions for, 405–406
    deleting from macros, 411
    described, 413
    inserting into macros, 411
    by macros, 394
    not callable from within a procedure, 497–498
    reordering in macros, 411
    setting conditions for, 404–407
active filter, 139
ActiveX control, 320, 321, 335–336
ad hoc query, 196
Add Existing Fields tool, 88
add-ins, 458
Advanced Filter/Sort option, 147–149
alias for table names, 576
aligning controls, 302
alignment of text, 68
Alignment tab, 389
All Dates In Period filter, 140–141
All Tables pane, 169
Allow AutoCorrect property, 310
Allow Zero Length, 68
Alt key, viewing shortcut keys, 14
Alternate Fill/Back Color tool, 117

C

calculated data, 45, 62

calculated fields, 259

calculated information on reports, 341

calculated query field, 231–232

calculating controls, 276

calculation queries, 231–241

calculations

> building into reports, 349, 350
>
> changing in PivotCharts, 267
>
> on a form versus a report, 340
>
> performing with text, 236
>
> updating using, 587
>
> using, 309–310

calendar, picking a date from, 112

Can Grow property, 360

Can Grow Textbox property, 369

Can Shrink property, 360

Can Shrink Textbox property, 369

CancelEvent action, 426

caption for each data element, 67

Caption property, 354

Cartesian join, 228

Cascade Update Related Fields check box, 125, 126

cascading updates, 124–126

Case <expression> statements, 529, 530

Case <test expression>, 529

CBF (code behind form), 488

CBR (code behind report), 488

Cc: argument, 430

CDate() function, 560

cells, copying from Excel, 163

CGI program, 46

characters

> adjusting using properties, 276
>
> copying from a string, 545–547

CharPoint Administration tool, 471

Chart wizard, 386–388

charts

> building, 386–388
>
> choosing, 381–385
>
> converting to images, 389
>
> creating, 385–390
>
> editing, 388
>
> labeling, 382–383
>
> modifying, 389–390

Check Box control

> creating, 330
>
> described, 296, 297, 298, 320, 321, 328
>
> events for, 323

Choose Builder dialog box, 494

cleaning databases, 451

cleanup, 450

Clip setting, 373

Clipboard, 118

Clipboard tool, 118–120

Close action, 426

Close method, 574

code behind form (CBF), 488

code behind report (CBR), 488

Code Builder. *See* Visual Basic Code Builder

Code page argument, 424

Code window, testing procedures, 491

Collate copies argument, 429

color tool for lines, 283

colors, 116–117

column headings, 260

columnar form, 272

columnar report, 341

columns

> in datasheets, 113–114
>
> defining a primary key, 38
>
> in tables, 34

combo box, 333–334

Combo Box control

> described, 296, 297, 298, 320, 321
>
> using, 332–334

comma delimited file, 176

Command Button control, 296, 297, 320, 321

Command Button wizard, 334–335

Command0_Click procedure, 494

Command0_Click sub procedure, 495

commands

> adding to the Quick Access toolbar, 7, 8
>
> choosing on the Ribbon, 5

comments in Macro Builder, 395

commercial certificate authority (CA), 462

Common Button control, 334–335

Common Expressions folders, 238

common sense, 439–440